THE MYTH OF AMERICAN DIPLOMACY

THE MYTH OF
AMERICAN
DIPLOMACY

National Identity and

U.S. Foreign Policy

Walter L. Hixson

YALE UNIVERSITY PRESS   NEW HAVEN & LONDON

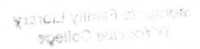

Designed by James J. Johnson and set in Minion Roman by The Composing Room of Michigan, Inc.
Printed in the United States of America by Sheridan Books, Inc., Ann Arbor, Michigan.

Library of Congress Cataloging-in-Publication Data

Hixson, Walter L.

The myth of American diplomacy ; national identity and U.S. foreign policy / Walter L. Hixson.

p.   cm.

Includes bibliographical references and index.

ISBN 0-300-11912-7 (alk. paper)

1. United States—Foreign relations.   2. Nationalism—United States—History.   3. National
characteristics, American.   4. United States—Foreign relations—Historiography.   5. United
States—Foreign relations—Philosophy.   6. United States—Military policy.   7. Militarism—
United States—History.   I. Title.

E183.7.H595   2008

327.73—dc22   2007031173

A catalogue record for this book is available from the British Library.

The paper in this book meets the guidelines for permanence and durability of the
Committee on Production Guidelines for Book Longevity of the Council on
Library Resources.

10   9   8   7   6   5   4   3   2   1

That is the true myth of America. She starts old, old, wrinkled and

writhing in an old skin. And there is a gradual sloughing off of the old skin,

towards a new youth. It is the myth of America.

—D. H. LAWRENCE

Contents

Acknowledgments

In the years this study has been percolating I have accumulated debts to family, friends, colleagues, and other scholars. To my family, especially Kandy, Ashley, and Keith, but also Bill, Allie, Bud, Emma, Catalina, Maiza, Nathan, Jon, Chloe, Norma, Traci, Mike, Sue, Tom, Tommy, Nick, Alex, Milo, and Zippy, thanks for being there. To my friends, especially those I have not kept up with, forgive me.

Writing history is a notoriously solitary endeavor, but writing history well requires collaboration. Several scholars critiqued this study and, while they bear no responsibility for its mistakes, lapses, and misjudgments, they did make it better. My greatest debt by far is to my doctoral student David Zietsma. David decided to migrate south from Canada and study the United States from within, and I am incredibly fortunate that he decided to do so with me. While I introduced David to cultural theory and foreign relations, he soon became the master rather than the pupil. This manuscript benefited enormously from his insight and unsparing criticism, which flowed from our shared ability to transcend the hierarchies of our positions.

Michael S. Sherry read an absurdly long and convoluted version of this book and gave the best advice: cut it by a third. I almost got there, Michael, but in any case your criticism was invaluable. Bruce Cumings, Michael H. Hunt, Akira Iriye, Scott Laderman, Kathryn Statler, and William W. Walker III read and critiqued various chapters. Akira Iriye, Andrew Johnston, and another (anonymous) scholar read the manuscript at a stage when it left much to be desired. I thank them for their considerable and thankfully complementary insights, suggestions, and the recommendation to publish. At Yale University Press, Lara Heimert at the beginning and then Chris Rogers, Laura Davulis, and Lawrence Kenney nurtured the project and showed good judgment in several suggestions.

Over the years I have accumulated debts to many colleagues. Shelley Baranowski was especially helpful in reading the full manuscript and making invaluable suggestions. T. J. Boisseau introduced me to what proved to be essential theoretical texts and insights. Michael Carley, Ted Easterling, Lesley Gordon, Peter Guiler, Janet Klein, Christine Lober, Elizabeth Mancke, Jerry Mushkat, and Martha Santos read and critiqued chapters, while Constance Bouchard and Stephen Harp supported me as department chairs. Kym Rohrbach and Wade Wilcox offered no end of good-humored assistance. Krista Tortura was a big help with the illustrations. Jamie Newhall kept the computers working. Barbara Clements, David Kyvig, and Christine Worobec offered unfailing support over the years. The University of Akron granted me a research leave to finish the manuscript. At nearby Kent State University, Mary Ann Heiss and Ken Bindas helped me along the way. Down I-71 in Columbus, Michael Hogan, Peter Hahn, and now Robert McMahon heard me out. During my ten months as a Fulbright Lecturer at Kazan State University (Russia), in the midst of Soviet disintegration in 1990–91, Leonid Sidorov and his family as well as many other Russian and Tatar friends taught me a lot about the world. Many years ago at Northwestern University, Sherry, Henry Binford, Carolyn Dean, Laura Hein, David Joravsky, Robert Wiebe, and a host of graduate students enhanced my work. At the University of Colorado, I was fortunate to work under Robert D. Schulzinger, who provided direction and allowed me more free rein than he probably thought advisable. Bethann Berliner, Mark Colvin, Barbara Engel, Robert Ferry, Ralph Mann, Suzanne Neushatz, John Pauly, Robert Pois, and Sherry Smith enhanced my graduate experience in Boulder. Prior to that, the History Department at Western Kentucky University got me started.

In the foreign relations field, Robert Buzzanco, Frank Costigliola, Lloyd Gardner, Petra Goedde, George Herring, Michael Hogan, Richard Immerman, Fred Logevall, Michael Krenn, Chester Pach, Jason Parker, Thomas Paterson, Emily Rosenberg, Jeremi Suri, and Randall Woods encouraged my work, though they may not agree with it.

Several institutions and organizations enabled me to present papers on the themes of this book. They include the Society for Historians of American Foreign Relations, Historians Against the War, Appalachian State University, the

College of Wooster, Oberlin College, Ohio State University, Michigan State University, West Virginia University, the University of San Diego, and the University of Houston, where toils my close and supportive friend Philip A. Howard.

Finally, it would be a grievous omission to fail to thank hundreds of students over the years. My relations with graduate students at various institutions have been especially rewarding, and I thank all of them. Countless undergraduates patiently heard me over the years and then offered their frequently insightful perspectives on U.S. foreign policy, for which I am deeply grateful.

Introduction

The Myth of America

Before signing with the New York Mets for the 2006 season, Carlos Delgado consented to the baseball club's request that he join his teammates on the field during the seventh-inning stretch for the playing of "God Bless America." A native of Puerto Rico, a neocolonial U.S. "commonwealth," Delgado had aroused the wrath of major league baseball and its fans by taking a principled stand against participating in the patriotic ritual, instituted in the wake of the attacks of September 11, 2001, on New York's World Trade Center and the Pentagon. "The reason why I didn't stand was because I didn't like the way they tied 'God Bless America' and 9–11 to the war in Iraq, in baseball," Delgado explained. But, he added, "the Mets have a policy that everybody should stand for 'God Bless America' and I will be there."[1]

Delgado's acquiescence resolved what seems a minor incident, yet it underscores a major aspect of U.S. cultural identity: the powerful sway of patriotic nationalism, especially in wartime. Clearly the slugging outfielder posed no threat to "homeland security," yet just as clearly his defiance challenged hegemonic conceptions of national identity.

The Delgado vignette illuminates the subject of this book: the cultural production of national identity and its relation to U.S. foreign policy. I argue that national identity is both culturally constructed and hegemonic. I argue, moreover, that national identity drives U.S. foreign policy and reinforces domestic hierarchies. Foreign policy flows from cultural hegemony affirming "America" as a manly, racially superior, and providentially destined "beacon of liberty," a country which possesses a special right to exert power in the world. Hegemonic national identity drives a continuous militant foreign policy, including the regular resort to war.

Having internalized this Myth of America, a majority, or at least a critical mass, of Americans have granted spontaneous consent to foreign policy militancy over the sweep of U.S. history. While specific foreign policies often provoke criticism, to be sure, national identity contains such criticism within secure cultural boundaries. Only by gaining a better understanding of the cultural construction of foreign policy and national identity can we hope to forge a new hegemony, a more equitable society, and a commitment to cooperative internationalism.

To the extent that it attracts attention, *The Myth of American Diplomacy* will be branded as radical or revisionist, as it destabilizes broadly shared conceptions of national identity and foreign policy. While historians routinely incorporate revisionism as part of the process of reconstructing the past, revisionist history nonetheless is widely perceived as subverting objective truth in order to promote a political agenda. On any given day, myriad references to revisionist history—in mundane discussions, political debates, and even sports reports—reflect this popular interpretation of the term *revisionist,* a discourse that marginalizes efforts to challenge patriotic narratives.

The last sustained public challenge to the patriotic foreign policy consensus emerged as a result of the Vietnam War during the 1960s and early 1970s. Even then, however, most public opposition arose as the war dragged on inconclusively for years and claimed growing numbers of U.S. casualties, not because the citizenry had called into question its patriotic identity. Public opinion polls revealed that the antiwar movement always remained more unpopular than the war itself. After the war ended most of the critical "lessons" of Vietnam quickly came under siege; hence the disastrous intervention did not produce a sustained reexamination of national foreign policy.

The failed Indochina intervention did, however, create sufficient cultural space for revisionist historians to make an impact by advancing the Open Door thesis. Revisionist historians subverted national mythology by arguing that foreign policy reflected elite capitalist self-interest rather than the high moral purpose of defending what is called the free world. Not surprisingly, especially with the nation still engaged in the long Cold War struggle against Communism, revisionists came under often vicious attack. Dismissing all nuance, critics focused on the neo-Marxist aspects of the revisionist critique: that the Open Door amounted to little more than Leninist orthodoxy of predatory capitalism. Nationalist historians checked footnotes, wrote intemperate rejoinders, and tried to recast the dissenting analysis through neo-orthodoxies such as a "post-revisionist consensus."[2]

The Open Door revisionists' most significant contribution was reconnecting foreign policy with domestic culture. To the extent that their accounts became essentialist—implying that the Open Door paradigm offered *the* explanation for U.S. foreign policy—they overstated their case. Economic decisions and causation emerge within a broad cultural frame; thus capitalist expansion was part of a larger modernist project. Moreover, the revisionist paradigm did little to analyze the public consent behind national foreign policy.

This last point raises a central, though often overlooked, conceptual problem inherent in the very concept of foreign policy. Paradoxically, the more that thinking about foreign policy centers on U.S. actions and policies *abroad,* the less we understand critically important motivations and compulsions that shape external relations from *within.* As the scholars Amy Kaplan and Donald Pease have noted, "The study of American culture has traditionally been cut off from the study of foreign relations."[3]

The *glasnost* fostered by the revisionists revitalized diplomatic history and paved the way for a wide range of approaches to foreign policy studies. Some new paradigms, such as corporatism and world systems theory, built on the foundations provided by Charles A. Beard, William A. Williams, Immanuel Wallerstein, and others. The end of the Cold War fostered a new international history in the 1990s, which exploited new archives and placed U.S. foreign policy in much sharper comparative dimension with other nations. While productive of new knowledge, this trend tends to deflect attention away from analysis of foreign policy rooted in domestic cultural identity.[4]

The Cultural Turn

In recent years the so-called cultural turn focused attention on cross-disciplinary learning and critical theory. The cultural turn recasts traditional diplomatic history, which focused overwhelmingly on U.S. actions and interactions with other countries while devoting less attention to the narratives that produce consent behind foreign policy.[5] Similarly, on the cutting edge of political science scholarship is a "growing body of work by international relations scholars that has broken with the model of the state as a unitary rational actor to ask when and how domestic factors account for the choices states make in foreign policy."[6]

For well more than a generation now many historians have taken the lead of anthropologists in probing for structures of meaning, or ways of life, that distinguish a given culture. Indeed, while anthropologists once "owned" culture, today the study of history "has become increasingly anthropological." If Clifford Geertz could better understand Balinese villagers by studying the significance of their cockfighting and other rituals, we might do the same for the United States by analyzing the structuring power of rituals, symbols, and mythology. Understanding culture "as a medium in which power is both constituted and resisted," scholars in many fields "are beginning to work out an exciting body of thought."[7]

Despite the growing prominence of the cultural turn, many historians express suspicion and often contempt for cultural studies. "The cultural turn came late to diplomatic history" and has proven "strangely controversial," Andrew Johnston notes. In January 2007 one diplomatic historian described the cultural turn as a "huge detour" that lacks relevance and, he supposes, distances us from "such profound political and moral questions as war and peace." In 2002 the president of the guild of foreign policy historians warned that the history of the Vietnam War was "too important" to be "abandon[ed] to the cultural historians, the cultural studies specialists, and the political polemicists."[8] This sort of gatekeeping flows from methodological conservatism inherent in the empiricist tradition.

Traditional diplomatic historians express suspicions of cultural approaches as a result of their preoccupation with archival sources and conventional methodology. Despite adopting a theoretical approach in which history is to be found, not made, the discipline nonetheless has always been politicized by ostensibly objective historians. Objectivity is a mythical quest, a "noble dream," as history cannot possibly be rendered in a fashion that allows the facts to speak for themselves. For example, I can, and do, take the facts of Harry Truman's presidency and call into question crucial decisions in which he took the nation in directions (into northern Korea, for example) that it ought not to have gone. David McCullough takes the same facts and constructs a portrait of an authentic national hero. The difference is not in the facts; what really matters is the interpretation.[9]

If achieving security implies defense of core values, protecting "our way of life," then culture becomes foundational. While diplomatic historians do a splendid job of mining the available archives, a focus on documents alone crowds out critical thinking and leaves diplomacy disconnected from the domestic culture from which it springs. A culturally driven foreign policy fosters "a relatively coherent, emotionally charged, and conceptually interlocking set of ideas," Michael Hunt explains.[10] Heritage, tradition, faith in progress, and the cultural construction of race, religion, and gender establish boundaries within which national foreign policy must operate. As such boundaries are inherently subjective and difficult, if not impossible, to quantify, the cultural turn presents an insoluble dilemma to the empiricist.

Taking the cultural turn destabilizes realist interpretations of national security policy. While realists claim they approach the world empirically, as opposed to those who posit a normative frame of idealism, realism is a *theory* of world politics and as such is ineluctably rooted in discourse. The national interest—like the nation itself—is culturally constructed rather than real. This is not to deny that perceptions of national interests, state-to-state relations, and balance-of-power considerations influence international relations. However, in order to understand why states behave the way they do in world affairs, culture and national identity must be analyzed.

Cultural analysis illuminates the remarkable continuity of U.S. foreign policy flowing from a distinctive national identity. Despite breathtaking socioeconomic and technological change—from royal charters to multinational corporations, from powder muskets to bunker-busting nuclear warheads—foreign policy has proven remarkably continuous. This seemingly ahistorical argument for continuity flows from a powerful identity of imperial nationalism. In the U.S. historiographic tradition, as Kaplan observes, most historians make the mistake "of viewing empire as a twentieth-century aberration, rather than as part of an expansionist continuum."[11] Diplomatic history has long been plagued by relative neglect of pre–World War II and especially pre-twentieth-century studies.[12]

Analyzing the cultural construction of national identity and foreign policy over the broad sweep of history, the project I have undertaken requires innovative methodologies, including theorization. *The Myth of American Diplomacy* thus departs from traditional diplomatic history through its embrace of the linguistic turn, deconstruction, psychoanalytical theory, and postmodernism. The analysis flows from the theoretical foundation, which I outline in appendixes A–D, which the reader may wish to consult before reading the text.

As foreign policy constitutes the relations between and among states, perceptions of the other play a critical role. Identity can be constituted only in relation to difference. No subject exists without an other. For example, man cannot exist absent the otherness of woman. Black people cannot exist apart from conceptions of whiteness, and so on. Such identities have no a priori existence but rather are culturally constructed. Establishing identity entails "a constructed form of closure" achieved by linking one subject with its other(s). The other provides the mechanism by which subjects assume their existence. "Identities can function as points of identification and attachment only *because* of their capacity to exclude," Stuart Hall explains. "Identification is, then, a process of articulation, a suturing [to an other], an over-determination"[13] (see appendix D).

Modernity and Nationalism

Only by locating the analysis within modernity can we fully grasp the continuity of U.S. foreign policy.[14] Euro-American history emerged within the broader frame of modernity, which defined itself in contrast with others, perceived as primitive or backward. Modernity may be defined as a worldview emanating from Enlightenment rationalism in the sixteenth, seventeenth, and eighteenth centuries and exported globally from Europe through imperial expansion. Through Enlightenment principles white male elites understood and shaped their world within a universe they perceived as being ordered. Religious cosmologies remained deeply embedded in culture, to be sure, yet increasingly in the Age of Reason empowered European men sought to direct the forces of history rather than live in the shadow of an omnipotent God. At the same time, Europeans achieved a global reach, as revolutionary advances in shipbuilding and navigation enabled them to fan out across the seas to Africa, the Americas, and Asia.[15] An Atlantic world community linked four continents, as Europeans set out to discover, map, classify, and conquer the natural world.

Gradually weakened by these forces of modernity, the structured order of the ancien régime, anchored by centralized church authority, monarchy, and aristocracy, imploded in a process that culminated in the U.S., French, and Latin American revolutions. Modernity required masses of people to define a new identity, to relocate themselves in a world in which conditions had undergone profound change. At this point, *culture* began to replace the *structure* of the ancien régime in establishing a foundation for the new modern world. Culture comprised the realm in which shared values and political meanings were digested, contested, constructed, and affirmed.[16]

Modernity comprised a rational and reasoned worldview that Europeans came to view as the only legitimate path to progress. Modern international relations (foreign policy) evolved as technology enabled Westerners to transport their culture and way of life, which they equated with progress, under God, onto foreign shores. The transmission of this Eurocentric worldview represented "nothing but the most original and powerful ethnocentrism in the process of imposing itself upon the world," the French theorist Jacques Derrida observed. "Metaphysics—the white mythology which reassembles and reflects the culture of the West: the white man takes his own mythology, Indo-European mythology, his own *logos,* that is, the *mythos* of his reason, for the universal form."[17]

Colonialism and imperialism thus flowed from the aggressive expansion of a western European worldview that apotheosized its way of life as ordered, reasoned, and providentially sanctioned. By implication, those peoples of the world who lived under divergent worldviews were viewed as unreasoned, unenlightened, and unchosen and thus subject to various forms of control and domination. When this effort at domination provoked resistance, modernists "externalized and projected" the violent disorder onto "the non-Western other, thus helping to stimulate the desire to penetrate, police and control, while at the same time validating a narcissistic Western identity."[18]

Once located within the long sweep of modernity, the focus narrows on the unique subjectivities of the U.S. national community. International relations "are built around the premises of nationalism." A nation constitutes a named community within a unified territory, with a history and culture, collective memories, a sense of ancestry, customs, sacred texts, language, religion, economy, mass education, and legal structure.[19] As a critical building block of the modern world, the nation constituted a "new totality of power." With the rise of modernity, "the spiritual identity of the nation rather than the divine body of the king now posed the territory and population as an ideal abstraction."[20]

Scholars analyze nations as products of the "invention of tradition" and as "imagined communities." Nationalism evolved in an effort to unite common territories and pull together ethnic, regional, linguistic, and otherwise segmented communities. If nations are invisible, intangible, and fundamentally imagined, they therefore must be represented symbolically and in a manner reflecting the distinctiveness of a particular culture. Understanding the behavior of a state requires analysis extending beyond merely invoking the named community, as if what it represents reflects an ontological status, a universally accepted state of being. Thus one cannot fully grasp the foreign policy of the United States without examining the nation's identity.[21]

The United States became, in many respects, the epitome of modernity. The existence of the North American "frontier," what Frederick Jackson Turner famously defined as the "meeting point between savagery and civilization," provided a vast staging ground for the expansion of modernity and the erasure of non-Western cultures. Massive violence and virulent racial formation and subjugation permeated this entire process. At the same time, the settlement process provided unprecedented freedom of opportunity to "self-made" Western white males. The frontier liberated men from state authority and powerfully influenced the American Revolution, which produced the first sweeping antimonarchical and anticolonial upheaval.

As they "settled" a putatively virgin land, the early Euro-American communities and then the United States had to be more fully imagined, had to do more to invent their traditions than most. Louis Hartz long ago argued that "American exceptionalism" stemmed from the absence of the structure of the ancien régime—the centuries of European religious, monarchical, and aristocratic order.[22] U.S. nationalism assumed overdetermined characteristics that created community bonds in the absence of those traditions undergirding the modern European nations. "If all states are 'imagined communities,' devoid of ontological being apart from the many practices that constitute their reality," David Campbell notes, "then [the United States] is the imagined community par excellence."[23] "America" became particularly dependent on representation to produce consent behind national identity. [24]

I argue that foreign policy plays a profoundly significant role in the process of creating, affirming, and disciplining conceptions of national identity. As Campbell puts it, U.S. foreign policy is "global in scope yet national in legitimation." Only by analyzing the mutually reinforcing relationship between the domestic and the foreign, under the canopy of national identity, can we glean a clearer understanding of the functioning of power both at home and abroad.

History is a critical yet contentious subject because nations require a "usable past" to promote patriotic consensus and build a common national identity. Societies "reconstruct their pasts rather than faithfully record them," Michael Kammen explains, as the "needs of contemporary culture" require "manipulating the past in order to mold the present." The usable past typically promotes a triumphal narrative that elides (suppresses or glosses over) aspects of national identity, especially violence and aggression, which reflect negatively on the society.[25]

History thus emerges as indispensable to the functionality of any modern nation. Promoting an "immemorial past," one that unites masses of people behind sacred traditions and memories, serves to fix core aspects of national identity within the collective imagined community. "Identities and memories are not things we think *about*," John Gillis astutely observes, "but things we think *with*."[26] Memories, traditions, structures of meaning, cultural experiences, the forces that shape national identity, are historical in nature. These experiences and perceptions form a culturally determined, sacred past, one that legitimizes certain outlooks and actions, both at home and abroad, and delegitimates alternative conceptions. History thus emerges as a critical battleground for understanding and shaping national identity and foreign policy.

The centrality of the usable past in establishing and defending an imagined national identity manifests itself dramatically in heritage struggles. "In celebrating symbols of their histories, societies in fact worship themselves," David Lowenthal explains. "National identity requires both having a heritage and thinking it unique. It is heritage that *differentiates* us; we treasure most what sets us apart." When national identity appears threatened, its defenders turn to heritage over history and invoke "a founding myth meant to exclude others."[27]

The Myth of America and Cultural Hegemony

I argue in this book that U.S. foreign policy, bolstered by a usable past, encompasses a vast realm of representation and linguistic discourse that has served to create, affirm, and maintain cultural hegemony (see appendixes A and B). Masses of citizens consciously and unconsciously consent to Myth of America identity as they repeatedly engage in such rituals as pledging allegiance to the flag, singing the national anthem and "God Bless America," and celebrating Memorial Day, Independence Day, and Thanksgiving. Pervasive nationalist discourse and representation effectively contain counterhegemonic challenges and marginalize purportedly subversive critics through a cultural process that is ongoing (organic) and integral to national identity.

Patriotic representation and marginalization of dissent ensure maintenance of a hegemonic usable past rooted in national mythology. Mythology supplies a narrative linking past and present. Myths are "stories, drawn from history, that have acquired through usage over many generations a symbolizing function that is central to the cultural functioning of the society that produces them," Richard Slotkin explains. To Alan Dawley, "Myths are stories with high moral purpose pointing to some transcendent destiny." As the public internalizes national mythology, conveyed through representation, culturally constructed narratives assume an aura of truth.[28]

Once naturalized and embedded within culture over many generations, national mythology provides a metanarrative—an explanation of the past, present, and future trajectory of a people and a nation. Myth produces a usable past while at the same time empowering certain groups within society at the expense of others. This relationship between myth and power explains why a mythical past must be policed and reaffirmed through the exercise of cultural hegemony.

While scholars in various disciplines analyze mythology, my own efforts to link myth, national identity, and foreign policy appropriate a trope popularized by Sacvan Bercovitch. A Canadian scholar of American studies, Bercovitch identified a "myth of America" rooted in Puritan Massachusetts and providing "an astonishing cultural hegemony" that prevailed across the sweep of U.S. history. The Puritan jeremiad, a ritualized denunciation of sin with an attendant call for redemption, forged a mythical community, promoted middle-class consensus, and offered a metanarrative of progress and future glory for an increasingly polyglot, sectarian, and otherwise disunited people: "The ritual of the jeremiad bespeaks an ideological consensus . . . unmatched in any other modern culture."[29]

In the context of foreign policy, the Myth of America frames a culturally constructed consensus on world affairs. While elites may conduct diplomacy, consensus remains crucial to understanding how and why foreign policy, including the resort to war on a regular basis, plays out. The Myth of America creates a structure of consent that enables the hegemony of a militant foreign policy. Broad internalization of such discursive regimes as taming the frontier, advancing civilization, leading the free world, or ridding the world of terror creates spontaneous consent, the prerequisite for hegemony, thus enabling imperial conduct abroad while reinforcing domestic hierarchies.

Hegemony has no a priori or permanent existence and hence must continually be affirmed through the production of culture within an organic society. As the purpose of hegemony is to affix meanings in order to establish and affirm relationships of power, resistance inevitably emerges. "Hegemony is about gaining permission to rule," Johnston explains, "and always entails resistance and counter-hegemonies."[30] In order to sanctify hegemonic national identity, it proved essential to police dissent and to elide inequalities, exploitation, domination, and exclusion. Bercovitch argued that the Myth of America functioned by "imposing metaphor" upon the society, which served to "compartmentalize dissent so as to absorb it, incrementally, into a dominant liberal discourse." A free people might dissent but only within bounds contained by national identity and thus not threatening to cultural hegemony.[31]

External aggression reinforces domestic cultural hegemony by uniting the imagined national community in campaigns against a continuous succession of external enemy-others. These foreign campaigns serve to undermine domestic reform movements, marginalizing progressives and peace internationalists who might threaten the cultural hegemony of the Myth of America. The more the nation focused its attention and resources on external enemies, the less cultural space remained for domestic reform initiatives on health, education, and public welfare.

Foreign aggression tightens the bonds of national unity by sidelining or purging counterhegemonic forces, often depicted as subversive. "More than most societies," M. J. Heale notes, "Americans have been defined by shared values rather than by ancient institutions, and have thus always been sensitive to the prospect of ideological subversion." As John Bodnar points out, "The fundamental appeal to loyalty is usually made as part of an effort either to defend the political community against external threats or to purify it of unwanted elements within the community."[32]

Discourses of race, gender, class, and religion sanction external violence against foreign enemy-others while at the same time reinforcing domestic cultural hegemony. "Racial modernity"—the production and classification of racial hierarchies under modernity—established otherness as a crucial component of national identity. "The concepts of nation, people, and race are never very far apart," Michael Hardt and Antonio Negri point out.[33] Hence Euro-Americans and subsequently Americans equated the violent subjugation and conquest of allegedly inferior races with progress and the advancement of civilization. The national narrative thus became a story of the triumph of advanced civilizations over primitive and savage peoples.

Just as racial alterity often manifested itself in terms of the superiority of whiteness, gendered discourse emphasized the virtues and primacy of masculinity. Gendered analysis problematizes the cultural production of knowledge prescribing various traits and roles associated with men and women. Gen-

der thus plays a critical role in the formation of identity. "Nations have historically amounted to sanctioned institutionalization of gendered difference,"
Anne McClintock points out. Nationalism typically flows from "masculinized
memory, masculinized humiliation and masculinized hope," Cynthia Enloe
argues. Gender analysis denaturalizes the male-female binary—what Joan W.
Scott describes as "the entirely social creation of ideas about appropriate roles
for women and men."[34]

I analyze gendered perceptions, like racial perceptions, as critical components of national identity. Gendered discourse powerfully influenced foreign
policy, for example, through conceptions of honor, get tough policies, manly
intervention, upholding credibility, drawing lines in the sand, and vowing to
never cut and run. As Lynda Boose observes, "Ambiguities and doubts belong to
the feminine." Throughout history, psychologists argue, "maleness is by far the
biggest risk factor for violence." The creation and maintenance of "a hegemonic
militarized masculinity" strongly influences U.S. culture and diplomacy, Christina Jarvis argues. It would be impossible, Susan Jeffords adds, to understand
"war and its place in American culture without an understanding of its gendered relations."[35]

By their cultural production of otherness and hierarchy, racial and gendered perceptions underscore the critical linkages between foreign policy and
domestic life. Ethnic cleansing of Indians and the enslavement of Africans fueled capitalism and freedom for white men. Likewise, exaltation of masculinity,
the strenuous life, and "Be all you can be" brought young men into the military
while at the same time empowering masculine virtues in invidious contrast
with soft and sentimental characteristics ascribed to women. Foreign policy reinforced heterosexuality as well by linking campaigns against homosexuals,
dubbed lavender boys, with anti-Communist containment or through the ongoing purges of gays and lesbians from the military.[36]

Under U.S. national identity, foreign policy militancy and domestic cultural hegemony thus proved mutually reinforcing. The primacy of foreign policy, national security, and homeland security emphasized the traditional role of
males as protectors of vulnerable women and children. The masculine virtues
of assertiveness, preparedness, militancy, and technological know-how enabled
the nation to emerge as the world's dominant nuclear power and arms merchant. Advocacy of peaceful and cooperative internationalism could be feminized as the purview of squaw men, pantywaists, and wimps.

Analysis of religion, like race and gender, "historicizes a connection between domestic culture and foreign policy," as Seth Jacobs observes. Like the myth of a classless society, Myth of America identity fosters the illusion that in the United States freedom from religion prevails alongside freedom of religion. Religious faith permeates U.S. history and culture and carries profound domestic and foreign policy implications. As David Zietsma points out, "The function of religious discourse as an organizing symbolic structure embedded in the very constitution of national identity remains obscure."[37]

Religious millennialism fused with an overdetermined U.S. nationalism to inculcate a powerful crusading spirit within Myth of America identity. Euro-American and U.S. religious expression, highly emotional and anxiety ridden, produced a fervency of faith manifested in a continuous series of so-called great awakenings. National destiny, under God, "has been such a powerful myth for the nation that it has decisively shaped our foreign relations as well as our own internal developments," Conrad Cherry argues. Transcendent religious destiny fueled foreign policy universalism. Israel's exodus became New England's "errand into the wilderness," which became the U.S. mission to the world. An overwhelming majority of Americans embraced such a fervent faith in God and country that the two became virtually synonymous, as reflected in the nation's currency, the Pledge of Allegiance, and continuous assaults on secular humanism. Culturally driven by what Max Weber called the "Protestant work ethic and the spirit of capitalism," the United States produced wealth and abundance, though unevenly shared, sufficient to affirm its assumed identity as "God's new Israel."[38]

Manifest Destiny, as myriad scholars have explicated, thus applies to far more than the Mexican War as a trope sanctifying the nation's mission of boundless expansion. Religious faith profoundly influenced foreign policy, and especially war, as the United States confronted a procession of "heathen" enemies, "godless Communists," and "evildoers" in a continuous history of violent conflict. The frontier encounter unleashed "violence unparalleled (proportionately) by even the Spanish conquistadores," Bercovitch avers, "and sustained into the twentieth century by a rhetoric of holy war against everything un-American."[39] Much of the public viewed these apocalyptic struggles as divinely sanctioned reflections of national destiny. Victory in war, even the ultimate resolution of a bitter Civil War, affirmed the guiding hand of Providence. A critical mass of citizenry thus "continually reaffirmed . . . the conviction that America is a nation called to special destiny by God."[40]

Choosing War

Violence against external enemies, from Indian savages to modern-day terrorists, emerges as integral not merely to foreign policy but to national identity. The simple yet chilling implication of this conceptualization is that it places war at the center of U.S. identity. I argue that the United States *chooses* to go to war, seizing opportunities to engage in militarism throughout its history. Thus to a far greater extent than popularly acknowledged, even in academic circles, the United States emerges as a warfare state, a nation with a propensity for initiating and institutionalizing warfare.

War—like nothing else—forges emotional bonds of unity, loyalty, and patriotism that powerfully reaffirm Myth of America identity. War spurred nation building and brought cathartic relief in the contexts of taming the frontier, Manifest Destiny, overseas imperialism, world war, the Cold War, and wars on terror. Although not all wars were popular, particularly when they became prolonged and inconclusive, they nearly always served to reaffirm national identity and cultural hegemony and to promote campaigns of countersubversion. "War," Hardt and Negri point out, "always requires strict hierarchy and obedience and thus the partial or total suspension of democratic participation and exchange."[41] By affirming the Myth of America, the wars, even unpopular wars, paved the way for the next wave of pathological violence.

Regenerative war intensified the bonds between the people and the abstraction of the nation. The promise of the nation, as the "beacon of liberty" for all mankind, inspired massive external violence. War and the memory of war, as underscored by the *Enola Gay* incident in 1995,[42] became a sacred part of national tradition and the usable past. War became associated with heroism and consensus as the nation came together like a "band of brothers" in the life-and-death struggles with evil enemy-others. By making the ultimate sacrifice, the nation's war dead sanctified the Myth of America. They gave their lives that we might live, and such sacrifice could only be honored, not called into question.

While most Americans honored their obligation to support the troops, antiwar protesters subverted national identity. Advocates of peaceful internationalism thus find themselves policed, stigmatized as unpatriotic, and often incarcerated in a continuous series of countersubversive campaigns. War thus repeatedly functioned to reinforce cultural hegemony, diverting resources and attention away from peace internationalism and domestic inequalities, which might otherwise empower reform. Over the course of U.S. history, a succession of wars gradually erected a heavily militarized warfare and national security state.

Psychic Crisis

Choosing war in affirmation of national identity betrays profound psychic anxieties inherent in the human condition. Richard Hofstadter drew on elementary psychology—"Men often respond to frustration with acts of aggression"—in advancing the interpretation that "aggressive irrationality" flowed from a "psychic crisis" in the United States.[43] Yet the psychic crisis was more than a historian projecting into the past. Although I employ Hofstadter's trope of psychic crisis in the context of U.S. history, psychoanalytic theory suggests that psychic crisis inheres in identity and thus is central to the human condition in all societies (see appendix D).

I explore here the interconnections between psychic crisis, aggression, national identity, and foreign policy. Trauma, anxiety, and fear of the unknown inhered in the frontier encounter with the indigenous first enemy-other, producing an especially violent form of identification. In the continuous history that followed, going to war with external enemies invariably offered short-term cathartic relief from psychic crisis. To the considerable extent that U.S. external aggression responds to unacknowledged internal anxieties, the nation's violence is pathological.

Much of the theoretical work discussed in this introductory chapter, work that illuminates the relationship between representation and power within cultural studies, can be subsumed under the term *postmodern* (see appendix C). A representation of the art of history, *The Myth of American Diplomacy* proceeds on the basis of understanding that we offer our own texts "not as new truths and authoritative works" but rather "as further moves in continuing conversations."[44] That said, this is a work of scholarship, not pure invention, and it draws heavily on the work of scholars of history and other disciplines.

While an author can usually count on critical reviewers to point out weaknesses in his or her work, no one should grasp those potential weaknesses more fully than the author. I recognize, for example, that I employ the Myth of America as an essentialist trope in order to frame my argument about U.S. identity and foreign policy. I make no apology for this usage, as a thesis almost by definition tends toward the reductive. The Myth of America thus reflects my best effort to navigate, as Hall puts it, "the Scylla of a reductionism which must deny almost everything in order to explain something, and the Charybdis of a pluralism which is so mesmerized by 'everything' that it cannot explain any-thing."[45]

Finally, while I fully support analysis of U.S. foreign policy in comparative dimension, I make only limited attempts to pursue that goal here. The analysis focuses on U.S. national identity and the pathological foreign policy it nur-tures. While this analysis undoubtedly leaves me vulnerable to being consigned to the "blame-America-first crowd," I am, of course, aware that other nations have distorted their pasts and engaged in patterns of violent aggression, and also that to some extent such aggression may be hardwired into the human species.[46] For decades, masses of people in Germany blamed World War II and the Holocaust on the Nazi elite, yet clearly many average German citizens facil-itated the genocide. Japanese textbooks elide brutal aggression in Asia, which they refer to as merely an "advance," out of a determination to eschew a "masochistic perception of history."[47] The People's Republic of China contin-ues to struggle mightily with the tumultuous Maoist legacy. The Soviet Union collapsed in part because it could not overcome the legacies of its murderous Stalinist past. The French, still struggling with a lost *grandeur,* have not fully confronted the violence they orchestrated in Algeria, Indochina, and elsewhere. Many Britons lionize the imperial Victorian era even as they have long over-looked, to cite one example, a genocidal campaign that killed perhaps hundreds of thousands of Kenyan Kikuyu people (the so-called Mau Mau) during the in-nocuously labeled European "scramble for Africa."[48] Turks have long denied their responsibility for the Armenian genocide. Israel today evades its ongoing aggression and dispossession of Palestinians. Sadly, the above is only a partial list. In any case, I do not consider the United States uniquely evil, though I do consider its national identity unique and its foreign policy a critically impor-tant subject worthy of independent investigation.

CHAPTER 1

Birth of a Nation

A benign narrative of discovery and settlement established a frame conducive to the construction of Euro-American and U.S. identity in the New World. Within this frame, Europeans landed on virgin shores and proceeded to conquer the wilderness as part of the advance of civilization under the biblical God. Early modern European expansion brought immediate economic benefits, notably land, gold, sugar, slaves, and other valuable commodities, thus cementing imperial expansion as a sine qua non of the modern world.

In the tenth century Norsemen (Vikings) had landed in North America, but conquest began some five hundred years later with the arrival of Christopher Columbus and the Spanish *conquistadores.* Hernán Cortés, Francisco Pizarro, and Hernando de Soto instituted slavery, harvested the riches of gold and silver, and conducted depredations against the indigenous peoples of the Americas. Although the Protestant English denounced the Spanish cruelties, they promptly dispatched a coterie of pirates, adventurers, and colonization schemers of their own in a quest to catch up with the Iberians in the race to conquer the New World.

This New World was an ancient one, having been "discovered" in a previous millennium, when the actual first settlers had made their way across a Bering Strait land bridge. People had inhabited, cultivated, and "changed the land" for centuries.[1] Before Columbus's arrival, the Western Hemisphere, as Charles Mann notes, was "a thriving, stunningly diverse place, a tumult of languages, trade, and culture, a region where millions of people loved and hated and worshipped as people do everywhere." Indian civilizations thrived from the West Coast to midcontinent—site of the massive Mississippian culture at Caho-kia—to the Mound Builders centered in today's southern Ohio, up and down the East Coast, and throughout today's Canada to the north and Central and South America to the south. In comparison with the Europeans suddenly in their midst, Indians were generally taller, cleaner, and in some ways more ad-vanced, as in their comfortable moccasin footwear and fine birch-bark canoes but especially in their gardens, maize fields, and ability to feed themselves. The Europeans, however, brought fascinating things previously unseen by Indians, such as colored glass, steel knives, and guns.

The Europeans ultimately denied Indians legitimacy as fellow human be-ings. Europeans' discourse represented Indians as savages in the path of discov-ery, settlement, and progress, under God. "So thorough was the erasure," Mann notes, "that within a few generations neither conqueror nor conquered knew that this world had existed."[2]

The Christian Europeans arrogated to themselves a culturally constructed higher morality than that which they ascribed to the aborigines. The con-querors embraced the concept of *vacuum domicilium,* vacant or virgin lands across the sea that God had set aside for them to exploit and colonize. The Eu-ropeans found sanction for violent ethnic cleansing in the Old Testament (Deuteronomy 7: 1–6): "When the Lord your God brings into the land which you are entering to take possession of it, and clears away many nations before you . . . the Lord your God gives them over to you, and you defeat them; then you must utterly destroy them; you shall make no covenant with them and show them no mercy."

While Columbus and his successors justified violence and plunder in the name of God, it was the diseases the Europeans brought that devastated Indian civilization. Throughout the Americas, smallpox, typhus, influenza, bubonic plague, and other pathogens spawned shattering epidemics that reduced the Indian population of perhaps 2 million before modern European contact to 250,000 by 1750, by which time 1.25 million Europeans and Africans inhabited the land.[3] Thus, while Indians died by the multitudes, the European population soared and profited through the acquisition of land, wealth, and opportunity.

From the outset, then, the Euro-Americans linked their advancement, sanctioned under the biblical injunction to go forth to claim new lands for Christendom, with the destruction of heathen and savage peoples standing in the way of the Pilgrims' progress. While Indian societies were being "destroyed by [pathogens] their opponents could not control and did not even know they had," Europeans such as William Bradford of Plymouth Plantation naturally perceived "the hand of God" in this chain of events. Clearly, the Lord, in order to "make room for us," had brought on the deaths of "great multitudes of the natives."[4]

As Euro-American settlement evolved, this cultural process of categorizing inferior enemy-others manifested itself in references to aborigines, savages, heathens, dark, evil, and uncivilized native peoples. With the enemy so defined, and with the discourse of the Christian mission on American shores fully articulated, conquest of the savage enemy assumed the mantle of just war. Despite the perpetual conflict between Protestants and Catholics throughout the early modern era, both embraced conquest of Indians and European conquest of the Americas.

Although they considered the Spanish papists less civilized than themselves, the English Protestants actually displayed the least interest in humanitarian and missionary activity among indigenous peoples. Beginning in the sixteenth century the French, for their part, proved far more willing to live among, and even marry into, Indian cultures in the North America interior. Thus it was the New English, and ultimately the American settlers—living apart from and typically encountering mainly to destroy—who proved to be the rightful heirs of England's Irish conquest and the militancy of the *conquistadores*. "Extermination, rather than colonization or enslavement, was the early English response to otherness," David Campbell observes.[5]

As the Virginia colony of Jamestown strengthened its numbers, settlers advanced the campaign of conquest into the interior, showing their contempt for the aborigines by killing, dismembering, and burning homes and crops, along the lines of the sixteenth-century conquest of Ireland. On March 22, 1622, the Indian sachem (political-military leader) Opechancanough launched a murderous assault on the growing English community, killing in a single day some 340 settlers, more than a quarter of the Virginia population. Captain John Smith saw opportunity in the massacre, however, declaring, "We have just cause to destroy them by all means possible." After several months of warfare, the Virginians summoned the Indians, ostensibly for peace talks, at which time they offered them a toast of poisoned alcohol running through some 250 natives with swords. The Virginia governor, Francis Wyatt, succinctly put the war of extermination into its broader context, explaining the necessity of the "expulsion of the savages to gain the free range of the country for increase of cattle, swine, etc. It is infinitely *better to have no heathen among us,* who at best were but as thorns in our sides, than to be at peace and league with them" (emphasis added).[6]

The comforting intercultural love story of Pocahontas elides a history of ethnic cleansing and underscores the critical cultural work performed by a mythic usable past. Daniel Richter argues that the significance of Mataoka, nicknamed Pocahontas, in her willingness to embrace the Europeans (literally, as she married one of them, John Rolfe, in 1614), "conveys lessons about a road not taken, about an intercultural cooperation that should have been, about a Native American who not only welcomed colonizers with open arms but so thoroughly assimilated in their ways that she changed her name and her religion in order to become one of them."[7] Indians thus generally proved far more willing than the Euro-Americans to strive for cultural coexistence.

Events followed a similar pattern in the Pequot War (1636–37) in New England, as marauding settlers drove the Pequot out of the fertile Connecticut valley. In doing so they slaughtered as many as seven hundred Indians, mostly women, children, and old men along the Mystic River. The New English exploited long-standing rivalries among the indigenous tribes, who viewed themselves as independent peoples rather than adopting a collective identity as Indians. The Narragansett and the Mohegans joined with the settlers against the Pequot enemy, though Indians typically did not massacre one another. Stung by criticism over the ungodly violence, the Puritans belatedly launched "praying towns" to convert Indians to Christianity and compel their adoption of European cultural mores. The religious communities appealed to few, as most tribes disdained enforced cultural conformity of short hair, European dress, and particularly the divergent Western gendered ways in which men were expected to do farming and gardening, viewed as women's work in most Indian cultures, while the women were taught how to maintain a home like an English "goodwife." "Because the English could not conceive of permitting the Indians to remain independent and culturally autonomous peoples," Alan Taylor notes, "they had to convert or die."[8]

The "foreign policy" of destroying savage enemy-others flowed from a Puritan identity of manly frontier conquest and an uncompromising religiosity. Forging a powerful link between material well-being and personal salvation, the Puritans laid the foundation for an acquisitive Christian culture on North American shores. Anxious, sanctimonious, and self-absorbed, the Puritans focused relentlessly on their perceived mission from God to redeem Christianity from the hopeless corruption of the Anglican Church and English society. Like the Old Testament Jews fleeing Egypt for the Promised Land, the Puritans would build a new commonwealth in Massachusetts as a model for all peoples of the world. They intended to carry out "the glorious work of God, so often foretold in scripture which . . . shall renew mankind," John Winthrop explained. "And there are many things that make it probable that this work will begin in America."[9] Never doubting their cultural superiority, the Puritans embraced a Manichean worldview that perceived human existence as a deadly struggle between divine goodness and satanic evil.

Like the legend of Pocahontas, the Thanksgiving holiday elides ethnic cleansing with a romanticized rendering of peaceful cooperation in the New England settlement process. The Plymouth colonists and the Wampanoag did indeed achieve a tenuous level of mutual understanding, marked by the celebrated feast of 1622. The Algonquians played a pivotal role in trade between interior tribes and the colonists. Metacom, a sachem now thought to be a grandson of the Wampanoag leader Massasoit, had grown up benefiting from the economic and cultural interaction of the burgeoning Atlantic trading network. Metacom became a prominent figure in Boston, began to wear European-style clothing, took the name Philip, and prospered under the integrated economic system.

As the Puritans strove to redeem the "howling wilderness" from the "atheistical" and "diabolical" savages, a brief but vicious race war erupted in 1675–76. The New English named the conflict King Philip's War, thus placing the onus on the Indian leader. In proportion to population this war inflicted a higher rate of casualties than any other in all of Euro-American history, as some one thousand whites and three times as many Indians perished. The Algonquian peoples had never experienced a war of extermination, yet they fought to the finish in an ultimately futile effort to preserve their lands, cultures, and ways of life. In an offensive launched by Metacom against more than fifty communities, the Indians lashed out at English property by burning houses, killing the livestock that had trampled their crops and gardens, destroying towns, and leaving their English victims scalped and stripped naked—deliberately depriving them not only of their property but also the civilized cloth on their backs and sometimes of their body parts as well. The English, oblivious to the calculated symbolism of the Algonquian violence, attributed these monstrous cruelties to the subhuman characteristics of swamp-dwelling savages. Yet, like their countrymen who had fought and conquered the Irish "barbarians," the English responded in kind by slaughtering, torturing, dismembering, and enslaving their own victims.

The war ground to an end when King Philip was shot and killed near Mount Hope. The English quartered his body and hung the pieces from four trees while staking his severed head on a pole, where it remained for decades as a ghastly relic of the fate that awaited Indians who opposed the righteous might of the New English.[10]

Euro-American identity ultimately precluded coexistence with Indians. Relations with the Algonquians deteriorated as the New Englanders seized more and more land for themselves, replaced wampum with silver for currency, tried to enforce Christianity, and generally rejected opportunities for coexistence. The ongoing assault against Indian autonomy underlay the all-out attack by Metacom and his followers against the New English invaders. However, given "Philip's" demonstrated willingness to adopt some English ways and to coexist with the European settlers, it would be wrong, Richter argues, to assert that he unleashed the attack against the English for their mere presence: "It would be far more accurate to say he rebelled on behalf of *cooperation*—on behalf of the system of relatively equal intercultural relations under which he and his people had previously prospered, but that the mid-seventeenth-century English were determined to destroy."[11]

The label *King Philip's War* thus framed the conflict as an Indian uprising when it was the Europeans who had rejected the path of mutual coexistence. Despite their victory, however, the bloodletting left the Puritans of Massachusetts badly shaken. Puritan elders, famous for their jeremiads, or political sermons, on the urgent necessity to root out evil and reform society, offered troubled reflections on the war's meaning. The violence had been horrific, and the destruction required decades of rebuilding. God must have been displeased to visit such carnage upon them. The war nearly had been lost, and in the end they prevailed only as a result of Metacom's failure to build alliances—indeed, he had fought simultaneously against rival Indians, including the powerful Mohawks, and had been correspondingly weakened. "As to Victoryes obtained," concluded Increase Mather, "we have no cause to glory in anything we have done."

In part the gloominess stemmed from a realization that while the war of conquest had been won, the moral purity to which the New Englanders aspired had been badly compromised in the process. The Puritans had shown that they were every bit as vicious, if not more so, than the savage enemy-other. It occurred to the more thoughtful Puritans that violent conquest characterized their identity in the New World. In 1692, Cotton Mather, son of Increase, reflected ironically on the savagery shown by the Puritans themselves: "We have [become] shamefully Indianized in all those abominable things. Our Indian wars are not yet over."[12] The Mathers thus anticipated that Metacom's failed resistance was neither the first nor the last violent chapter in the struggle for a continent.

A foreign policy of expropriation and extermination of enemy-others flowed from an emergent American identity. Employing tropes of rebellion and treason, the New English frequently *chose* wars that embroiled their entire society in bitter struggle. Existential anxiety, living amid savages in the howling wilderness, with the Devil lurking in the forests, created a pervasive sense of psychic crisis that frequently played out in violence and hysteria. The series of major, bloody Indian wars took a toll on the Puritans and may well offer the best explanation, as Mary Beth Norton has argued, for the hysteria over witchcraft in Salem and other towns.[13]

The early Americans internalized massive violence, which endured in subsequent centuries as a critically important component of national identity. "Extravagant violence," often directed against noncombatants, established the Americans' "first way of war both temporally and in terms of preference," the U.S. Air Force military historian John Grenier argues. "Americans created a military tradition that accepted, legitimized, and encouraged attacks upon and the destruction of noncombatants, villages, and agricultural resources," launching "shockingly violent campaigns to achieve their goals of conquest," Grenier explains. The Indian wars ingrained within the Americans a tendency to conduct "unrestrained" warfare to achieve the "complete destruction of the enemy."[14]

Blaming all the violence on the Europeans, however, risks association with the noble savage stereotype—an image of peaceable Indians living in an Edenic state of nature until corrupted by the invading Europeans. A history of intertribal conflict, tribes' willingness to ally with the Europeans against other Indians and whites, and various cultural practices within Indian communities all belie the stereotype. Indians "often were stupid and as vicious as Europeans," Francis Jennings points out, as "they belonged to the same human species."[15] More subtly, however, Richter argues that while Indians were fully capable of irrationality, cruelty, and various human frailties, "the essence of eastern north American spirituality was respectful reciprocity in a complicated world of human and other-than-human persons." Without romanticizing the indigenous peoples, scholars note that a commonality among Indians encouraged them to view the European interlopers as fellow humans, or brethren, with whom they should seek cooperation, or at least coexistence.[16]

While Euro-American conquest pushed Indians further into the "frontier," the Indians who survived the epidemics and the violence remained a powerful force well into the eighteenth century. In 1677, under an accommodation known as the Covenant Chain, New York represented other colonies in conducting trade and diplomacy with the Iroquois Confederation, which possessed the power to compel cooperation from other Indians. As a result of the burgeoning Atlantic trading network, which profited everyone (except slaves, animals, and the environment), Indians could sell or barter animal pelts and other products while accessing clothing, firearms, alcohol, and a variety of European goods. Thus, although the European quest to tame the wilderness brought dramatic changes, such as depleted hunting grounds and an unrelenting assault on their culture, Indians also displayed a remarkable ability to adapt. Myriad Indians who attempted accommodation or acculturation with Euro-American society adapted well, engaging in effective trade and intercultural relations, but unknown thousands succumbed to alcoholism, disease, disillusionment, and depression over the assault on their way of life.

By the eighteenth century, and especially after the Tuscarora and Yamasee wars of 1711–16 in Carolina, Indians generally understood that armed resistance to whites ultimately would prove suicidal. At the same time, more and more began to identify themselves not merely as members of their own tribe but as "red" Indians who possessed a collective spirituality inimical to the ethnocentric violence at the core of Euro-American expansionism. A grudging coexistence thus prevailed, with Indians engaging in trade and also able to maintain a tenuous equilibrium by exploiting imperial rivalries between Britain, France, Spain, and other countries. A complex economic, cultural, and diplomatic interaction linking the Covenant Chain, Indian leaders, royal officials, missionaries, traders, military officers, interpreters, buyers, and sellers created enough mutual self-interest to perpetuate the uneasy balance until the decisive wars of the second half of the eighteenth century.

Racialized and gendered captivity narratives, which featured tropes of marauding savages and female innocence, reinforced a manly white cultural hegemony in North America. Beginning in 1682 with the harrowing story of Mary

Rowlandson, the captivity narrative emerged as a staple of frontier mythology. These narratives typically involved women or missionary victims being rescued from Indians by heroic male conquerors of the savage wilderness. "Captivity narratives instantly turned the invader into the invaded and created the foundation for any act of retribution that might follow," Tom Engelhardt observes.[17]

Captivity narratives illuminate a cultural process in which the demonization of one subordinate group simultaneously reinforces power over yet another group. Treacherous savages took the hostages, but the vulnerable women also required men to save them. "The rescue of the helpless female hostage," Michael Paul Rogin explains, "established sexual as well as racial difference— against the threats of racial uprising, female independence, and the feminization of helpless white men."[18] Gender relationships varied between regions, yet everywhere cultural hegemony empowered patriarchal dominance, as ordained by God. Women accessed power in other ways, to be sure, as no hegemony is totalizing, but overall women inherited the English tradition of "civil death," leaving them bereft of political and economic rights. "Not only were seventeenth-century Anglo-American wives subordinated to husbands," Norton points out, "their independent identities were literally erased from society's consciousness."[19]

The banishment of Anne Hutchinson in Puritan Massachusetts in 1637 underscores gender hegemony in British America. Most New English women knew better than to affront the male elite and would have suffered far greater consequences than Hutchinson, who was exceptionally bold, capable, and well stationed in her community. A prominent and respected midwife, the mother of eleven children herself, Hutchinson challenged Puritan doctrine by embracing individual salvation, which prompted the Massachusetts authorities to banish her on the justification that "you have stept out of your place, you have rather bine a Husband than a Wife and a preacher than a Hearer; and a magistrate than a subject."[20]

"Blacke Gold"

Euro-American identity reinforced hegemony over Indians, women, and also over slaves. The traffic in human beings, the largest forced migration in history, prevailed from the late fifteenth to the early nineteenth century. Slavery was "an intrinsic and indispensable part of New World settlement," David Brion Davis

1. *Rescue* (1853) by Horatio Greenough. This sculpture in marble represents the triumph of civilization over savagery on the American frontier. The towering frontiersman easily subdues the weaker, tomahawk-wielding Indian. The woman and child, passive and defenseless, serve to justify the regenerative violence implicit in *Rescue*. The sculpture, completed in 1853, reposed on the east facade of the U.S. Capitol until its removal in 1958. Photo courtesy of Architect of the Capitol.

emphasizes, "not an accident or a marginal shortcoming of the American experience." By the twenty-first century, U.S. academics had begun to acknowledge that slavery constituted a "crime against humanity."[21]

Like Indian conquest and the marginalization of women, slavery flowed from the cultural process of asserting alterity, or otherness, between people. Racial classification, which became deeply embedded in Euro-American and U.S. identity, served to fix group identities and exalt whiteness in concert with the subjugation of other races. The culturally constructed alterity drawn between black and white, as between red and white, facilitated both seizure of Indian lands and expropriation of slave labor.

Slavery also derived sanction from biblical discourse and parallels drawn with animal species. The Bible associated darkness with evil. European discourse subsequently classified Africans as black, an exaggeration of West African skin color. The un-Christian "blacke heathens," with their "disfigured" facial features and "horrid curles" of hair, thus became an immediate source of enemy-othering and dehumanization. *Oxford English Dictionary* definitions of *black* included "deeply stained with dirt; soiled, dirty . . . having dark or deadly purposes, malignant; sinister, foul, iniquitous, horrible, wicked." The English sometimes referred to African slaves as black Moors, a pejorative reference to nonwhite Muslim enemy-others. Abetted by African middlemen who captured and sold the slaves, slave traders took their human cargo to the shore in coffles before subjecting them to the horrific and often fatal middle passage to the North American colonies.[22]

North American slavery began in the Creole communities of coastal West Africa, spread to the sugar-producing Caribbean, and then extended to the rice swamps and cotton fields of southern North America. Euro-American relations with slaves and others of African descent varied widely among regions and over centuries of time, thus reflecting far more complexity than the simplistic black-white binary stereotype of cotton picking on the plantation. Slave communities existed, as did something very different—communities with slaves. In the former, slaves worked harder and longer, received less food and worse housing, had their African names changed, and might be subjected to dismemberment for attempted escape. In other communities, slaves had more power to negotiate their status, such as less time spent working and more cultivating their own gardens. Moreover, in myriad communities free blacks coexisted with European settlers, including white indentured servants, and freely engaged in trade, owned property, and formed their own communities. Among those of African descent, wide variations prevailed, some maintaining their African dialects and cultural practices whereas others possessed no knowledge of such language, customs, and conventions, which they sometimes mocked.[23]

As the modern Atlantic world evolved, linking Europe with Africa, the Caribbean, and the two American continents, a flourishing commerce ignited greater demand for slaves. English sea power and mercantilism enabled the Crown to solidify control of the North American seaboard between French Acadia and Spanish Florida. Profits from the thriving Atlantic trade in slaves, sugar, rice, timber, cotton, tobacco, meat, fish, grain, furs, indigo, rum, molasses, and much else fueled the burgeoning British Empire.

Thus early modern America thrived as a result of the massive surplus value of uncompensated slave labor. The impact of slavery radiated far beyond the southern colonies. By the mid–eighteenth century more than 70 percent of slaves entered North America on Rhode Island slave ships, making Newport's shipping industry dependent on the trade.[24] John Brown, the eponymous benefactor of Brown University, was a leading slave trafficker, as was the Duke of York, New York's royal founder and the eventual King James II. Slavery persisted in the North even beyond the Revolution of 1776, as Yankee traders recognized their own dependence on the institution as an indispensable part of the Atlantic-world trading network. Without slave labor to produce agricultural export of southern commodities, northerners would not have enjoyed the array of goods and commercial partnerships, ranging from London to the West Indies and across the plantation south, which fueled their own economies and lifestyles.

Euro-Americans thus constructed an identity in the context of accessing land and wealth through violent subjugation of darker-skinned people. Indian conquest provided productive land, at no cost, while slavery produced free labor, often "from sun to sun," as the engine of the flourishing Atlantic-world trading network. All colonies, including Quaker Pennsylvania, engaged in dispossession of Indian lands as an essential element of the trading system, and all colonies profited directly or indirectly from slavery.

Nevertheless, Indian and African resistance, inherent in hegemonic relationships, embedded anxiety and a perpetual sense of psychic crisis within colonial Americans. Racial alterity and categorization fostered constant vigilance against the dangers of rebellion posed by Indians and slaves. As slavery grew in importance with the expansion of the Atlantic-world system, a palpable sense of the dangers from within prevailed in plantation societies. The forced slave migration had been so vast and profitable that Africans outnumbered Euro-Americans throughout the West Indies and in parts of the South. Slave revolts, such as the Stono River uprising in Carolina in 1739, produced deep-seated fears, if not outright phobia. Euro-Americans projected their own violence onto slaves, depicting the "black demons" as inclined toward torture and mutilation and inherently rapacious of female innocence.

Even as colonial society affirmed gender and racial hierarchy, ethnic, class, and religious conflict brought challenges to elite white male hegemony. "Complex systems of inequality divided people throughout the Atlantic world," Ronald Schultz notes, "and placed them in hierarchical relations of wealth, power, and social prestige."[25] Bitter land disputes and internecine class and ethnic conflict among Euro-Americans prompted a series of late seventeenth-century uprisings that underscored the fractious character of the British American colonies. The Dutch in New York, Germans and Quakers in Pennsylvania, recalcitrant Puritans in New England, and backcountry rebels and "regulators" in the Chesapeake and Carolina attested to the often-violent disunity inherent among Euro-Americans in the heterogeneous settlements of British North America. Rapid and diverse immigration partly explained the disorder. Whereas the English dominated immigration before 1680, Scottish, Scots-Irish, Germans, French Huguenots (Protestants), Swiss, and some Jews began to flood in thereafter.

Collectively, however, the Euro-Americans gradually found that race provided the best means to manage their own considerable ethnic and class differences. Erupting in 1676, Nathaniel Bacon's rebellion against Crown authority revealed the dangers and ultimate futility of attempts to deprive disempowered Euro-American white males of the lands they desired for upward mobility. As Governor Alexander Spotswood of Virginia later explained, the rebellion had been "occasioned purely by the governor and council refusing to let the people go out against the Indians who at that time annoyed the frontiers." Accordingly, "a governor of Virginia has to steer between Scylla and Charybdis, either an Indian or a civil war."[26]

Spotswood neatly illuminated the crucial linkage between foreign war and domestic consensus that inheres in Myth of America identity. The Virginia uprising, along with the subsequent Leisler's Rebellion in New York and outbreaks in other colonies as well, reflected seething class, ethnic, and religious tensions throughout British North America. Whereas landholding helped maintain aristocracy in Europe, the existence of "free" land in North America destabilized class relations. Social stratification, ensconced as the most fundamental characteristic of English society, could be challenged within the fluid frontier environment. As they pursued upward mobility, white men no longer readily accepted John Winthrop's dictum, "In all times some must be rich and some poore, some highe and eminent in power and dignitie, others meane and in subjeccion."[27]

Through an emphasis on racial rather than class differences, the cultural construction of whiteness obscured disparities of wealth and thus helped contain antagonism within the Euro-American communities. The demand for available land for a growing, restive, and potentially violent male frontier population came at the expense of Indians, who continued to lose ground, and blacks, who became the slaves on new plantations. The ever-present threats of Indian attack or slave revolt reinforced psychic anxieties as well as the hegemony of white males as the protectors of female innocence.

In the wake of the Virginia rebellion, European indentured servitude declined sharply as planters imported masses of slaves, most now directly from Africa. For many planters operating within the burgeoning Atlantic trading network, slavery produced vast wealth, thus providing ample incentive to overlook the inhumanity of enslavement, including the breaking up of families, rape, whipping, "gelding," "full power to dismember," and other tortures. African Americans resisted, as the tortures demonstrate, and adjusted, but the essence of slavery was hegemony backed by systematic violence.

Enlightened Modernity

While rapid change, anxiety, and violence roiled the colonies, dramatic developments in European culture and politics undermined Crown authority. The Glorious Revolution of 1688, in which Parliament ousted the Catholic King (and New York slave trader) James II for the dual Protestant sovereigns William and Mary, ended British mercantile rule over the Bay Colony. Efforts to rein in the ever-recalcitrant Puritans and Yankees henceforth would prove futile. Colonial governors could no longer command absolute authority, as they grudgingly gave ground to local lower houses of assembly, such as the Massachusetts General Court and the Virginia House of Burgesses. As this change unfolded, a Crown imperial policy of "salutary neglect" allowed the North American colonies largely to go their own way so long as the English-dominated Atlantic trade network continued to flourish. However, "despite the remarkable

success of Britain's eighteenth-century empire," as Jon Butler points out, "feelings of unease typified almost everyone's thoughts about the imperial transatlantic relationship between 1680 and 1760."[28]

Despite the emphasis on naturalizing the rights of man, Enlightenment
thought accelerated the cultural construction of racial identities. While "an almost pervasive culture of racially configured othering and infantilization" of
Indians and blacks already prevailed, notes David Theo Goldberg, the Enlightenment naturalized these prejudices as such foundational theorists as Jean-
Jacques Rousseau viewed Indians, Africans, and non-Europeans as savages who
were incapable of accessing the "rights of man."[29] Under enlightened modernity, women, Indians, blacks, Hispanics, Muslims, Asians, and other nonwhites,
incapable of self-mastery, rationality, and fulfillment of God's destiny, were
subject to categorization and exclusion. Increasingly "the racially inferior
[were] seen as surplus value, both as usable labor and discardable detritus,"
Goldberg observes. Moreover, "patterns of accumulation and denial firmly established between 1680 and 1770 as slaveholding expanded in America," Butler
notes, "long outlasted slavery as one of America's most enduring patterns."[30]

Armed with confidence, free land, slave labor, and a liberating knowledge of
the physical world, Europeans fired the engines of modernity. Enlightenment
rationalism, conjoined with technological achievements in shipbuilding, navigation, cartography, and printing, ushered in a dynamic era of early modern
capitalism. Burgeoning world trade, unprecedented mobility, and the power of
the printed word fueled the rise of an increasingly cosmopolitan world system
of buying, selling, cultural exchange, and diffusion of science and Enlightenment thought.

Enlightened modernity promoted a deep-seated metanarrative emphasizing the advance of civilization through the application of scientific rationalism
to the global environment. The new rationalism sanctioned the exploiting of
the human environment, primarily Indians and slaves, as well as the physical
environment for the spread of modernity. The only rights of man available to
Indians and African American slaves was to abandon their land or culture or
both in acquiescence to the authority of modernist hegemony. This hegemony
underscores the power inherent in knowledge, representation, and culture in
addition to the more familiar realms of economics and military might. "In
shaping the 'New World' according to the demands of the new sciences of geography, botany, and anthropology," Donald E. Pease explains, "imperialism un-

derstood itself primarily as a cultural project involved in naming, classifying, textualizing, appropriating, exterminating, demarcating, and governing a new regime."[31]

The Enlightenment rationalist worldview spread throughout the colonies by virtue of the printing press. British America sported its own colleges and co-terie of Enlightenment rationalists, as personified in the astonishing native ge-nius of Benjamin Franklin. The Philadelphian exalted scientific rationalism as well as prosperity, hard work, and thrift ("A penny saved is a penny earned"), thus going a long way toward defining a distinctly American style of individu-alistic capitalism.

Enlightenment rationalism had a paradoxical impact on North American religious convictions. Revelations of an ordered and scientifically explicable universe prompted Deists to perceive God as the Creator but "man" in control of his own destiny on Earth. Deism, however, was the rarefied worldview of en-lightened intellectuals. For the most part, Enlightenment rationalism spurred a turn to a fiery Protestant revivalism that engulfed British America.

The Great Awakening embedded a revivalist paradigm that would remain continuous in U.S. identity, one that would emerge with particular force in times of psychic crisis. With its uniquely American character and rejection of both established church and state authority, the First Great Awakening fore-shadowed the coming colonial rebellion against English political as well as reli-gious power. The New Light ministers, most notably George Whitefield, the fiery English Calvinist orator who crossed the Atlantic fifteen times between 1740 and 1770 and preached before audiences of as many as five thousand, chal-lenged the authority of the Anglican Church throughout the colonies, as the Puritans had been doing since their arrival.

The Great Awakening underscored the psychic energies rumbling beneath the surface of the rapidly changing continent. Even the more restrained Prince-ton man Jonathan Edwards, "the greatest American-born theologian of the eighteenth (or any) century," feared the erosion of faith amid the thriving com-merce and frontier mobility of British America. Edwards warned of the suf-fering that would accrue to "sinners in the hands of an angry God," yet he preached that America had been chosen as the land in which individual salva-tion would pave "the way for the future" and usher in the "glorious times" of the millennial second coming of Christ. "He inherited the concept of a new chosen people," Sacvan Bercovitch explains, "and enlarged its constituency from saintly New England theocrats to newborn American saints."[32]

In its zealotry, intolerance, and contempt for central authority,—its volatile brew of modernist individualism and reactionary fire and brimstone—the Great Awakening embodied critical aspects of American identity. The Awakening reaffirmed the Puritan mission of carrying out the Protestant Reformation on uncorrupted American shores. The rapid influx of new immigrants—the colonial population increased *twentyfold* over the eighteenth century—gave rise to such denominations as Presbyterians, Methodists, Baptists, and Congregationalists, producing a uniquely American religious identity. Even though many Christians called for saving Indians and the Awakening swept through African American communities, the new religiosity did more to reaffirm than unsettle racial formation demarcating the children of God from the devil's minions. Similarly, religious revivalist Protestantism reinforced the biblical patriarchy inherent in the narrative of woman's creation from Adam's rib. At the same time, however, women played an active role in churches and comprised a majority of the total membership, although they rarely served as officeholders or ministers.

Despite the growing religious diversity, Protestantism remained a source of unity within the British Empire in opposition to the enemy-other embodied in the Catholic imperial rivals Spain and France. Though not quite stripped of their humanity like Indians, Africans, and Islamic Moors, the Catholic powers were nonetheless profoundly detested. England fought four wars with France from 1689 to 1763 before at last prevailing in a decisive victory of sweeping international consequence. The ultimate victory of British American arms in the Great War for Empire (1754–63) ended a round of conflict that had erupted in the trans-Appalachian west with a clash over the French outpost Fort Duquesne. The sweeping military victory in North America, the West Indies, West Africa, and Europe proved ephemeral, however, as spiraling indebtedness left Britain weak and ultimately unable to thwart the colonial rebellion. The Great War for Empire thus illustrates that even in military triumph, victory often proves illusory.

Despite the humiliating defeat suffered by the French and the exhaustion of British resources, the Indians lost the most. Britain's triumph in the French and Indian War removed the French from the western frontier and left Indians to confront a now-undivided tide of avaricious Euro-American expansion. Indian interests received predictably little attention during the Paris treaty-making process that brought the conflict to an end in 1763. Left to face the British Americans alone and bereft of their ability to practice diplomacy by forging alliances with the French, thereby playing off the European powers against one another, a pan-Indian coalition now mobilized for war. Under the leadership of the Ottawa sachem Pontiach, the Delaware, Seneca, and several other tribes assaulted British forts and settlements from the trans-Appalachian frontier to the Great Lakes.[33]

Superior British American arms repulsed the pan-Indian attack after a series of bloody confrontations, dismissively referred to in historical discourse as Pontiach's rebellion. This trope represents the conflict as a rebel uprising against legitimate Euro-American authority, as opposed to an Indian struggle for homeland security and preservation of cultural identity. Both the war and the discourse of war deepened already embedded racialized perceptions of Indian savagery. The exterminationist mentality gained momentum as many Indians, concluding that diplomacy with Euro-Americans was useless, embarked on a series of brutal assaults against settlers. British commanders such as Jeffrey Amherst, infamous for attempting to spread smallpox by means of an infected blanket, urged "every other Method that can Serve to Extirpate this Execrable Race."[34]

Bitter violence raged across the frontier, including in Quaker Pennsylvania, where the Paxton boys defied legal authority by butchering several Indians, including 14 hauled out of jail and massacred in Conestoga. Only royal military authority and outrage expressed by Franklin, among other prominent Pennsylvanians, prevented a mob from killing 140 additional Indians in Philadelphia.

Exhausted from the latest round of war on numerous fronts, the British resolved to take action to curb conflict with the frontier tribes. Having long since forgotten the lessons of Bacon's Rebellion, the Crown issued the Proclamation Line of 1763, which proscribed colonial expansion west of the Alleghenies in order to focus imperial resources on recovery and liquidation of the unprecedented £130 million of debt.

The Proclamation Line outraged colonials as an assault on the right of a superior race to civilize the frontier through ethnic cleansing and expropriation of free land in the name of God and progress. After drawing the line against expansion, the Crown minister's Grenville laws, including new but reasonable taxes on the British Americans, undermined the profits of various traders and prominent smugglers such as John Hancock. By 1774, the year the Quebec Act codified postwar boundaries not only by reaffirming the line across the Appalachians, but also by sanctioning permanent French possessions to the North, an all-out struggle for independence emerged.

America Imagined

Well before anticolonial sentiment coalesced, the nascent imagined community had begun to manifest itself culturally, in language, dress, custom, housing, material culture, economy, religion, clubs, associations, fraternal organizations, and other aspects of an increasingly distinct identity. National identity remained inchoate, ambiguous, and contested. As an organic process, nation building required nurture and maturation, as opposed to a sudden, fully formed arrival into the world.

Modern nationalism evolved as the Reformation brought an end to Roman Catholic religious hegemony and the Glorious Revolution dealt a staggering blow to monarchy. The decline in Latin and the swift rise of vernacular languages across Europe further eroded centralized church and royal authority. Developments in shipbuilding, navigation, and cartography fueled global capitalism and the birth of the modern world. By the eighteenth century the explosive impact of print capitalism enabled millions of people to access the geographical, scientific, economic, and political impact of modernity. Undermined by the spread of knowledge and the challenges to traditional authority that it brought, the ancien régime could not long endure.

The Revolution of 1776 was the first *nationalist* revolt, and thus its significance transcended the fates of the United States and the British Empire. Nationalism, an organizing force that would dominate world politics into the twenty-first century, thus received powerful impetus from the birth of the United States. Benedict Anderson argues that the modern nation arose first, not in Europe, as many believe, but in the "Creole states" of the Americas. The thirteen British colonies nurtured nationalism more swiftly and efficiently than Latin America because of their significantly smaller geographic size and the relative speed of communication within increasingly linked seaboard cities from Boston to New York, Philadelphia, and Charleston. As they consumed information and absorbed Reformation and Enlightenment modernist thought, Americans—75 percent of them literate and overwhelmingly English-speaking—forged a common identity. The significance of the printed word was such that tens of thousands of people who did not know and would never meet one another could come to have a common identity and a mutual understanding of the concept of what it meant to be an American.[35]

The colonial rebellion was the first revolution under modernity, yet at the same it was a revolution within modernity. While the fight for independence was often bitter, as in any war, the Revolution might best be understood, Kevin Phillips argues, as one of a series of "cousins' wars" among fellow white English-speaking peoples. Many prominent Englishmen, including some leading militarists, sympathized with the rebels, just as many Americans, perhaps even a majority, remained loyal to the Crown.[36]

The Americans did not rebel against the prevailing social order or challenge domestic cultural hegemony based on race, class, and gender. Domestic hierarchy, social status, and economic and cultural ties with European states endured. The Revolution of 1776 was an anticolonial rebellion against being governed from afar. To a considerable extent it was a revolution that opposed being governed at all. Indeed, intense hostility to "big government" became an enduring component of U.S. national identity from the outset.

Despite the natural affinity among cousins, modern nation building required "the emphasizing of differences between one national community and another, and the effacing of differences within."[37] As nations are not real but rather are imagined, discourse and representation comprise their essence. By the mid-1770s, revolutionary discourse, sanctified by war, sharply advanced the organic process of nation building. The architects of the colonial rebellion combined Enlightenment thought, the pursuit of their natural rights in an ordered political universe, with the English Whig tradition that rejected absolute Crown authority. The Revolution drew upon a usable past, as pamphleteers compared their own cause with the English Civil War and the Glorious Revolution.

Nationalism typically evolves from a homogeneous *ethnie,* a preexisting ethnic core identified and articulated by secularizing intellectuals. The Founding Fathers played this role through nation building and cultural hegemony. By 1776 tens of thousands of Americans consented to a new collective identity that fueled the rebellion. "The public is, as it were, one great family," *Boston Magazine* averred in an essay on patriotism. "We are all children of one common mother, our country, she gave us all our birth, nursed our tender years, and supports our manhood."[38]

Christian millennialism permeated revolutionary discourse, suggesting that not everyone saw the British as cousins. Ruth Bloch found it "striking how quickly American colonists in the forefront of the rebellion saw their struggle with Britain in terms of a conflict between the forces of righteousness and those of the devil." While "America was intended to usher in the Kingdom of God," the "diabolical" and "infernal" British sought to stand in the path of that divine mission. A "large reservoir of American millennial hopes and apocalyptic fears spilled into print on the eve of the Revolution."[39]

The American Revolution was thus not merely a political but also a spiritual phenomenon, a sacred event ordained by God for the redemption of all of mankind. Even Franklin, the leading scientific rationalist, declared, "Our cause is the cause of all mankind, and we are fighting for their liberty in defending our own. It is a glorious task assigned us by Providence." A decade before the outbreak of fighting at Lexington and Concord, John Adams observed, "I always consider the settlement of America with reverence and wonder, as the opening of a grand scheme and design of Providence for the illumination and emancipation of the slavish part of mankind all over the earth."[40]

Victory in the anticolonial struggle powerfully fueled the Myth of America as a discourse of global redemption. "The eighteenth-century emancipation of the United States," as Andrew Johnston explains, "provided the moral and cultural model by which subsequent U.S. foreign policy equated American liberty with the teleology of history itself, squaring its nationalism with internationalism."[41] Modern nationalism required a symbolic and unifying usable past in order to promote the sense of collective identity so essential to nation building. Hence the Revolution could not be explained in the mundane terms of British imperial overstretch and diplomatic bungling or as a sideshow in a larger, ongoing global struggle for empire.[42] The patriotic narrative emanating from the Revolutionary War vindicated the virtues of divinely sanctioned republicanism and free market capitalism, ushering in a glorious new era not merely for the United States but for "all mankind."

God's New Israel had become God's new republic; his destiny was America's destiny. "In American political theory, sovereignty rests, of course, with the people," Robert Bellah observes, "but implicitly, and often explicitly, the ultimate sovereignty has been attributed to God." Thus above the pyramid on the great seal of the United States are the words, in Latin, "God has favored our undertaking." George Washington established a pattern that would be repeated throughout U.S. history by offering in the first inaugural address "fervent supplications" to the "Almighty Being," as it appeared that "every step by which we have advanced to the character of an independent nation seems to have been distinguished by some token of providential agency." From the outset, then, religion permeated "the whole fabric of American life, including the political sphere."[43]

Virtue, republicanism, and classical economics melded seamlessly, under

God, within the new imagined community. The faith in free trade reflected the influence of classical economic theory, as set forth in Adam Smith's *The Wealth of Nations* (1776). Appearing revolutionary in the context of British mercantilism, Smith and other classical theorists argued that the free market would bring natural order and harmony. In essence, the free market would do for economics what republicanism would do for politics in the new Age of Reason. The "invisible hand" of the self-regulating marketplace would function without government oversight, now viewed as an impediment, just as monarchy and aristocracy inhibited the evolution of the natural rights of man. Moreover, productive capacities unleashed by the free market would spur international trade, empowering individual men, producing the necessities to pursue life, liberty, and happiness, and eliminating the need for state rivalries and war. "The secular concept of progress fused with old millennial hopes" to spur forward the ebullient new republic.[44]

The Revolution: Discourse and Identity

Natural rights philosophy forged consent behind the idea that governments that governed least, governed best. Faith in virtue, the free market, and opposition to the established church, standing armies, and central government authority all led logically to the loose grouping of states embodied in the Articles of Confederation, enacted by Congress in 1777. While the aversion to centralized government would endure, to be sure, the founding patriarchs, in essence an early "national gentry,"[45] concluded after only a decade that the decentralized government they had put in place could safeguard neither the nation's economy nor its security.

The pure republican vision of a naturally ordered universe thus revealed its starkly utopian character within a decade of independence. The nation languished in a debilitating indebtedness, precipitating uprisings like Shays's Rebellion (1786) in Massachusetts. The founding patriarchs soon concluded that in the absence of a stronger central government, the *universal* triumph of republicanism, under God, would be imperiled. Myth of America identity thus undergirded the drive for a new framework of government.

Foreign policy provided compelling arguments for creating the new federal Constitution and also ensured that the document itself would facilitate an imperial vision. The United States confronted a sneering disrespect for its nationalism, as Britain occupied forts along the northern border while the Spanish held Florida and the critical port of New Orleans. Some settlers in the South and West plotted a closer association with Great Britain or Spain for protection against Indians, who continued to resist white landed expansion. The United States lacked a navy, possessed a small ground force, and could barely pay its diplomats abroad or maintain their missions.[46]

The monarchical tradition had more of a hold on the Framers than they cared to admit, as they created a powerful chief executive, thus ensconcing the imperial presidency under a new commander in chief. The Framers created a bicameral legislature and a federal high court, but only belatedly incorporated a Bill of Rights putatively safeguarding the individual liberty of all white men.

The Constitution reflected the increasingly entrenched cultural hegemony of Myth of America identity. The discursive reference to "We the people" elided hierarchies of race, class, and gender. The Revolution promoted an enduring national discourse of individual freedom, but words could not transform the racial violence embedded within Euro-American identity under modernity. Natural rights philosophy aside, all men were not, of course, created equal—sharp racial, class, and gender distinctions prevailed.

The renewed sanctioning of Indian conquest and slavery underscored that racialized violence remained at the core of Myth of America identity. For Indians, the Revolution furthered the ominous work of the Great War for Empire. Led during the Revolutionary War by George Washington, whom Indians dubbed the "Town Destroyer," the United States sundered the Iroquoia–New York Covenant Chain, which had maintained mutually beneficial trade and diplomacy for most of the eighteenth century. After the war, the new republic "systematically set about dispossessing even the loyal Indians of their territory through a policy of threats, deception and guile."[47]

The Revolution thus perpetuated a continuous foreign policy that rejected coexistence in deference to relentless dispossession and annihilation of people singled out in the Declaration of Independence as "merciless Indian savages." Even Thomas Paine, among the most radical republicans, linked the nation's destiny with control of "unoccupied land"; hence he excoriated the Crown for its "barbarous and hellish power, which hath stirred up the Indians and Negroes to destroy us."[48] Thomas Jefferson wrote virtually the same words in the Declaration, charging the king with unleashing on "the inhabitants of *our* frontiers the merciless Indian savages, whose known rule of warfare is an undistinguished destruction of all ages, sexes, and conditions" (emphasis added). While

Jefferson sometimes referred to Indians as "My Son," or "Children," the pater-nalist discourse masked an "ominous will to exterminate," a vision of Indians "extirpated from the earth."[49]

Identity driven racial violence manifested itself most notoriously in the sanction the U.S. revolutionaries provided for the continuance of slavery. The nation's usable past has long depicted the Framers as well intentioned on the matter yet unable to put their egalitarian principles into effect on behalf of the slaves. While the founding patriarchs engaged in protracted debate over the new Constitution, a "great silence" hung over the issue of slavery. The "depth and apparent intractability of the problem" meant that it could not be prof-itably discussed. The founding patriarchs summarily dismissed a Quaker peti-tion against slavery. In a sense the gag rule, a term normally associated with southern efforts to table antislavery petitions in the antebellum period, actually prevailed from the outset.[50]

While the Framers remained silent about slavery, thus ensuring its perpet-uation, the British high court condemned human bondage as odious and phased it out of the British Empire. The United States, by contrast, incorpo-rated slavery into federal law by agreeing to count "other persons" as three-fifths of a person in apportioning congressional representation based on popu-lation. As slaves represented one-sixth of the U.S. population in 1790, this action alone gave the southern states a vested interest in maintaining slavery for as long as possible. Moreover, each slaveholding state received two senators, providing even more disproportionate political power to the less populated re-gion.

The "dirty compromise" culminating in a "proslavery Constitution" may have been necessary to form the Union; however, it also reflected the new na-tion's hegemonic racialized identity. Even the constitutional provision guaran-teeing continuance of the international slave trade for twenty more years did not require its elimination in 1808, though it did come to pass. Moreover, the fugitive slave clause of the Constitution explicitly sided with slaveholders' rights to retain their property and paved the way for an even more definitive Fugitive Slave Law of 1793. The Northwest Ordinance of 1787, which opened a vast new territory north of the Ohio River to settlement while supposedly ex-cluding slavery, offered no prohibitions against the capture of fugitive slaves and made no statement with respect to the status of children born in the new territories to a slave. As a result of such ambiguities, and the failure to consider a more definitive provision for gradual emancipation, the ordinance actually allowed slavery to remain ensconced, especially in Indiana and Illinois, until the antebellum era.[51]

Virtually without exception the American patriarchs exalted whiteness, a reflection of their collective internalization of racial modernity. Franklin, the "first American," once owned a few slaves and wished to exclude "all Blacks and Tawneys, of increasing the lovely White."[52] The venerable Washington freed his slaves at death, but while he was alive Washington was a typical Virginia planter, not especially cruel but perfectly willing to whip and work his slaves hard, break up their families, and confine them to the barest of living conditions.[53]

That Jefferson did not view himself as a hypocrite underscores how deeply the culture had internalized racial modernity. He often expressed his sincere contempt for slavery even as the stark realities of Monticello—site of the daily grind of buying, selling, whipping, and fornicating of slaves—unfolded under his supervision. When he drafted the Declaration of Independence, Jefferson owned more than 150 slaves, men, women, and children that, with a select few exceptions, the sage of Monticello never set free, even at his death. Jefferson condemned slavery, yet he rejected opportunities to join other Virginians who lobbied for gradual emancipation. Finally, the same man who judged blacks "inferior to the whites in the endowments of body and mind" and even complained of their "disagreeable odour"[54] conducted a longtime intimate relationship with the "mulatto" Sally Hemings, who was his own slave, his deceased wife's illicit half sister, and almost certainly the mother of his children.[55]

Putting slavery at the center of analysis helps unpack the national narrative glorifying the Myth of America and sanctifying U.S. moral leadership of the world. The DNA evidence on the Jefferson-Hemings relationship, confirmed in 1998, spurred a long-deferred historical reassessment of the complexity and significance of slavery in Euro-American history. Thus even Gordon Wood, the leading proponent of the radicalism of the American Revolution, acknowledges the importance of emphasizing that "the new United States was not just a republic, it was a slaveholding republic. . . . Not only does the overwhelming presence of slavery in early America cast a dark shadow over the sunny aspects of the founding but it is also driving a huge rethinking of our history."[56] That the nation yet required a "huge rethinking" of slavery—some five hundred years after its beginning, more than two centuries after its sanction in the Constitution, and a century and a half after the Civil War—underscores the internalization of racial hierarchy within the national consciousness.

The long-deferred and not yet fully achieved reckoning with the national crimes against humanity stems in part from Jefferson's greatest achievement, the Declaration of Independence. Ostensibly written for the "opinions of mankind," the Declaration gradually achieved the status of "American scripture."[57] Jefferson sutured into the fabric of the nation a hegemonic discourse that not only elided slavery and ethnic cleansing of Indians but also anchored "consent of the governed" for at least some twelve score years. The Declaration pronounced the birth of a nation in which "all men are created equal," a nation chosen by "Divine Providence" to act as a beacon of liberty for all peoples of the world. Such a nation could find ultimate justification for almost any act of aggression as long as it furthered the glorious cause of advancing an "empire of liberty."

CHAPTER 2

The White Man's Continent

As offspring of the British Empire and men well schooled in the classics of Greece and Rome, the Founding Fathers viewed themselves as architects of a manly empire. Alexander Hamilton spoke for many when he viewed the United States as "Hercules in the cradle."[1] The allusion to Hercules foreshadowed a day when the new nation was to function not merely as a "city on a hill" but as the splendid, unchained embodiment of aggressive masculine power. George Washington referenced the "rising American empire" while Jefferson provided the most ironic trope, an "empire of liberty."

Despite the reference to Hercules, manliness did not yet depend upon the vast military establishment that would characterize the United States later in its history. Cultivating a relatively small, defense-oriented military reflected the classical republican vision that equated large standing armies with tyranny. Seemingly determined to avoid the corruptive influence of a warfare state, classical republicans offered a haunting, prescient critique of the fate of societies given over to militarism. A large military, Thomas Paine declared, would promote chauvinism and war because the state "will have no excuse for its enormous revenue and taxation, except it can prove that, somewhere or another, it has enemies." Thus war represented "the art of conquering at home," an opportunity for the "predatory classes" to prey on the "productive classes."[2]

Perhaps even more threatening than militarism was radicalism, especially as the French Revolution unfolded. At first, the overthrow of the French monarchy in 1789 provided powerful vindication of the Revolution of 1776 and the nation's "destiny" to spread republicanism. Americans had been grateful for

LIBERTY.
In the form of the Goddess of Youth giving Support to the Bald Eagle.

2. *Liberty* (1796) by Edward Savage. This engraving features a maiden in the form of the goddess Hebe as she nurtures a bald eagle, the symbol of American liberty. With her right foot she suppresses chains, a scepter, a key, and other symbols of tyranny. Boston, the center of the American Revolution, appears at the lower right, beneath a sky illuminated by lightning and in which the American flag also appears. Courtesy of the Library of Congress.

French assistance in the Revolutionary War, as reflected in the wildly enthusiastic crowds that turned out to welcome Gilbert du Motier de Lafayette as he traveled extensively in the United States and "gave his American audiences every reason to celebrate their national history and to believe that their Revolution was equally important to Europeans."[3] However, after 1793, with the execution of Louis XVI followed by the reign of terror, most American elites grew alarmed as the Jacobins took charge in France. The subsequent Quasi War with France over assaults on merchant ships deepened already bitter divisions in U.S. politics while spurring militarization and undermining civil liberties. The nation created a Navy Department, opposed by Jefferson, outfitted new warships, and strengthened the army.

While avoiding all-out war with France, President John Adams launched the first in a continuous series throughout U.S. history of assaults on domestic political opponents amid foreign policy crises. The Alien and Seditions Acts emphasized the trope alien, thus equating criticism of national policy with being un-American. Decrying the "reign of witches," Jefferson rallied his nascent Republicans against the violations of the Bill of Rights inherent in the heavily politicized arrests and deportations. Although he immodestly styled his subsequent election to the presidency as "the Revolution of 1800," it was the Revolution of 1776 that Jefferson treasured above all else; hence he offered an olive branch in an inaugural address: "We are all republicans, we are all federalists."[4]

Jefferson soon applied the salve that would perennially soothe the wounds of contested national identity: aggressive pursuit of the empire of liberty. The serendipitous manner in which the United States took possession of the sprawling Louisiana Territory in 1803 must have appeared as irrefutable confirmation of providential national destiny. With the militarist Napoleon Bonaparte having seized power in Paris, Federalists and Republicans alike now condemned France, which had assumed Louisiana from Spain by treaty and controlled the vital port of New Orleans.

Jefferson feared an inevitable war with dictatorial France, but unlike many of his successors in the executive office he adhered to classical republican wariness of militarism and thus viewed war as a last resort. Napoleon promptly rewarded Jefferson's quest for a diplomatic solution with a stunning offer, immediately accepted, for the sale of the entire 828,000-square-mile Louisiana Territory. The windfall for the United States was internationally sanctioned possession of the heart of a continent, a vast tract of land larger than all of western Europe, at a sale price of three cents an acre, or some fifteen million dollars.[5]

The Louisiana Purchase powerfully affirmed the discursive regime of an empire of liberty, yet the United States did not actually seek to liberate subjugated peoples. As slaves launched a revolt on the French-held Caribbean island of St. Domingue, even the antislavery Hamilton joined Washington, who found it "lamentable to see such a spirit of revolution among the blacks"; and Jefferson, who worried "nothing indicates as yet that *the evil* is at its height" (emphasis added).[6] The United States sided with the French planters against Toussaint-Louverture, and Congress declined to recognize Haitian independence in 1804. The concept of a black republic was a contradiction in terms and moreover incited inveterate fears of slave rebellions within the United States. Thus while the Haitians fought for freedom against the French, the U.S. government mobilized a slave labor force to construct the Capitol building in the new Federal City.

Confrontation with the Barbary pirates also underscored the cultural construction of race and the drive for a manly response to affronts to national honor. The rulers of Algiers, Tunis, Tripoli, and Morocco had long preyed upon foreign shipping in the Mediterranean, including U.S. merchant vessels, by seizing cargo, taking prisoners, and demanding ransoms. In 1785, for example, Algerians captured the Boston schooner *Maria,* inciting an "oppositional rhetoric of liberty and slavery" albeit within the world's largest slaveholding nation. As U.S. seamen languished in North African confinement, righteous indignation fueled the organic process of constructing and affirming national identity. Underscoring the crucial relationship between identity and foreign policy, John Jay observed, "The more we are ill-treated abroad the more we shall unite and consolidate at home."[7]

The North Africans provided an enemy-other that the United States condemned with Orientalist discourse—essentialist depictions of racial and cultural inferiority. Throughout the formative years of U.S. history, Malini J. Schueller argues, discourse "variously embodied as vigorous, active, masculinized, and morally upright Columbia-as-empire, against versions of a decaying, demasculinized, deviant, or spiritual Orient."[8] The North African conflict thus introduced *Turk, Mohammedanism,* and other Orientalist slurs that would prevail in U.S. discourses toward the Arab world and the so-called Middle East for generations.

In 1805 Jefferson decided on a manly assault against the North Africans to demonstrate the United States was not impotently in the grasp of "Quaker principles."[9] A few marines and a large contingent of irregular forces mounted the assault on the shores of Tripoli, culminating with a dramatic draping of the

American flag on the walls of the port city of Derna and eventually giving rise to the martial Marine Corps hymn. The assault attained the release of U.S. captives, though the United States still had to pay a sixty-thousand-dollar ransom. In the "cultural imaginary" this became "a narrative of imperial might" as "the North African War helped glorify the vision of a powerful, imperial nation" that for the "first time spread the American eagle in Africa."[10]

Although Jefferson claimed that the empire of liberty would "conquer without war," the nation's deeply internalized racial classifications meant that just the opposite would occur. Absorption of the vast Louisiana Territory would require conquest *with* war, as the Indians would not give up their lands without resistance. Moreover, the opening up of vast new lands for cultivation would lead to a dramatic expansion of slavery. As the master of the discourse of freedom, yet the architect of campaigns of racial oppression, Jefferson demonstrated yet again that he was, in Bernard Bailyn's felicitous phrase, "a poet of American aspirations and at the same time a cunning manipulator of power."[11]

As white men responded enthusiastically to the call to forge an empire of liberty, they reinforced the nation's militant cultural hegemony. Jeffersonian discourse, conjoined with a foreign policy of Indian dispossession and expansion of slavery, received consent. Backed by a majority of white men, the Virginia Republicans spearheaded a one-party state for the next quarter century. Surprisingly, in view of the ineffectual stewardship of his own plantation, Jefferson proved to be a skilled politician, party builder, and president.

Despite his penchant for romanticizing the yeoman farmer, Jefferson personified the planter class. He and other plantation owners had depleted their own lands raising tobacco, prompting them to move west into the Piedmont, seizing more Indian lands. "We can buy an acre of new land cheaper than we can manure an old one," Jefferson explained. Aided by favorable terms in federal land sales, commerce pervaded with fraud and corruption, speculators and wealthy elites rather than yeoman farmers profited most from Indian dispossession.

Jefferson, who summarily rejected the legitimacy of Indian land claims, often linked "obtaining lands" with "exterminating" the "merciless Indian savages" that he referenced in the Declaration. Alexander McGillvray, the head of the Creek nation, denounced the Louisiana Purchase as an illegitimate transaction in which whites bought and sold land long held by Indians. McGillvray demanded at least a setting aside of Indian homelands, but Jefferson brooked no compromise with "merciless . . . savages," including the articulate McGillvray, who was half "white." Jefferson "would not tolerate proposals to incorporate Indians in their own chosen associations and in their traditional homelands within the United States," Roger Kennedy notes. It was Jefferson, Anthony F. C. Wallace avers, who established "the federal policy of removal—involuntary or voluntary—as the solution for dealing with Indians who rejected 'civilization' or waged war on the United States."[12]

Despite his putative hope that slavery would wither away, Jefferson knew that the cotton gin spurred a cotton boom and that the new territories and states of Kentucky, Tennessee, Mississippi, Alabama, and Missouri would import masses of slave laborers. Moreover, the planter class would dominate the region, buying the best land as they depleted their own, relegating yeomen to marginal land, dispossessing Indians, and enslaving record numbers of African Americans. The empire of liberty thus enhanced the cultural hegemony of the planter class as yeoman farmers gave consent through their internalization of culturally constructed racial formation.

The Patriotic War

Westward expansion powerfully affirmed national perceptions of providential destiny and manly empire, but the European powers remained contemptuous of the new republic. As the Napoleonic wars roiled the waters of the Atlantic, menacing trade and freedom of the seas in the process, neutral rights won little respect from France and even less from Great Britain, which for years had boarded U.S. vessels at will, hanged alleged deserters, and impressed seamen into the British navy. When the British *Leopard* assaulted the *Chesapeake* just twelve miles off the Norfolk coast in 1807, righteous anger erupted.

The ongoing campaign of humiliation directly impinged on manliness and national honor. As patriotic indignation reached feverish levels, Jefferson remained reluctant to choose war and its attendant risks, costs, and accumulation of centralized state power. Desperate for a solution, Jefferson implemented the Embargo (1807), cutting off trade with the European powers, presumably to instruct them on their dependence on the U.S. market, long a republican panacea. The initiative proved disastrous, as the Embargo crippled shipping and commerce, especially in New England, and heightened rather than quelled popular anxiety. In the West, where an influential new constituency arose in the expanding white republic, Henry Clay of Kentucky and other War Hawks decried the "shameful degradation" to which the decadent European powers subjected the new nation.[13] Men who had "tamed the frontier" through violent conquest over Indians and nature would not back down against any external foe.

A pervasive discourse of manliness demanded a violent response against the English bully, known as John Bull. In an era in which men still satisfied affairs of honor through the *code duello,* the nation, too, could maintain its masculine dignity only by responding to the challenge. "Americans of the present day will prove to the enemy and to the World," South Carolina's John C. Calhoun declared, "that we have not only inherited the liberty which our fathers gave us, but also the will and power to maintain it."[14]

Arriving with some reluctance at the same conclusion, James Madison, Jefferson's successor, decided that an address to Congress outlining Great Britain's affronts to neutral rights represented the appropriate protocol to seek a declaration of war. Madison ignited a seventeen-day debate that culminated, despite widespread opposition from the New England Federalists hurt most by the Embargo, in an affirmative vote of 79–49 in the House but only 19–13 in the Senate. Much as Jefferson had feared, the decision for war proved reckless, premature, and very nearly disastrous. Unbeknownst to Washington, London withdrew the orders-in-council that targeted U.S. shipping on the eve of the conflict. As John Quincy Adams later wrote of the war, "Its principal cause and justification was removed at precisely the moment when it occurred."[15]

Although the central government had been strengthened under the Constitution, the nation went to war stunningly ill-prepared: it possessed an inadequate army, appropriated woefully insufficient federal funding, confronted an angry enemy aided by revanchist Indian allies, and faced strident internal opposition from the Federalists. The nation thus went "tail foremost" into a war that quickly became an "exercise in frustration, ineptness, and survival."[16] The United States suffered a series of defeats, including another ill-conceived imperial thrust into Canada, which once again rejected the bayonet-point invitation, as it did during the Revolutionary War, to join the empire of liberty. With Napoleon's abdication in April 1814 and Britain assured of victory in Europe, the United States suffered humiliation that summer when British forces conducted a punitive expedition into Washington, sacked the city, and burned the presidential mansion, forcing James and Dolley Madison to flee into the countryside with a portrait of George Washington and a few other priceless possessions.

Exhausted from the Napoleonic wars and as usual preoccupied with wider domestic and imperial concerns, Britain settled for a peace accord with the

United States. On January 8, 1815, before word of the Peace of Ghent reached U.S. shores, the Tennessee militia leader Andrew Jackson obliterated British invaders in the battle of New Orleans. U.S. forces had rallied to record battlefield successes on Lake Erie, the River Thames, at Plattsburg, and Baltimore, none of which could compare, however, with New Orleans, in which Britain paid for a foolhardy assault against entrenched positions with seven hundred dead and some two thousand additional casualties to twenty-one for the United States. The ringing victory invigorated manly national identity, giving rise to an "era of good feelings" and to the irrepressible political phenomenon of Jackson himself.

Underrated in its significance and innocuously labeled in historical discourse as the War of 1812, the second conflict with Britain is best understood as a patriotic war whose primary significance was an emotional reaffirmation of national identity. Calling the conflict the Second War for Independence offers little clarity insofar as the ultimate existence of the nation had never really been in doubt. The term *Patriotic War* underscores the essence of the conflict, which reflected the *domestic* drives inherent in national identity.

Like many subsequent conflicts fought ostensibly over foreign policy, state violence responded to internal psychic anxieties. The Patriotic War offered relief from a wrenching domestic transition while creating cultural space for the reaffirmation of national identity. The war had been reactionary, in a pure sense of the word, as it served to revive the flagging emotions of Revolutionary era patriotism. The culminating triumph in New Orleans created in Jackson the first national military hero since the venerable Washington. The war powerfully stimulated the imagined community, offering a usable past of a culminating ringing victory that overshadowed the lack of preparedness, myriad defeats, and the war's relative international insignificance as a sideshow to the epic struggle for Europe.

The Patriotic War, in short, offered rebirth, regeneration, and gave rise to good feelings at home. Steven Watt notes that the "wartime fusion of revitalized national strength, liberal individualism, and godly affirmation of the republic surfaced everywhere in peace commemorations by Republican enthusiasts." Francis Scott Key immortalized the nation's destiny to endure, that through the "perilous fight" the Stars and Stripes yet waved "o'er the land of the free and the home of the brave." Editorial writers proudly proclaimed America's arrival "in the first rank of nations" after a "triumph of virtue over vice, of republican men and republican principles over the advocates and doctrines of Tyranny." Commemorations repeatedly invoked discourses of patriotic destiny "under God." "No nation, save Israel of old," exalted one writer, "hath experienced such great salvations" of liberty and national vindication.[17]

Myth of America identity increased the power of the army and the state while marginalizing opponents of militant nationalism. Just as the Revolutionary War targeted loyalists, and the Quasi War the Republicans, the Patriotic War demonized the New England Federalists as virtual traitors in the nation's midst. The dominant patriotic discourse exploited the Hartford Convention (1814) to destroy the Federalists as a force in national politics, entrenching a one-party state in its wake. The Federalist call at Hartford for changes in the "national compact," including reconsideration of the proslavery Constitution, now appeared subversive and un-American. The discursive regime, reinvigorated by foreign war, thus further ensconced and fatally sanctioned the expansion of slavery. The number of slaves doubled between 1800 and 1820 and continued increasing despite the end of the international slave trade in 1808, as the national economy became more rather than less dependent on the plantation system.

The Patriotic War flowed from psychic anxieties associated with the nation's transition from a seaboard republic presided over by a wig-wearing, knee-breeched national gentry to a more sprawling "frontier" nation rising around a dominant ethos of market capitalism and an egalitarian mythology of the common man. The entrepreneurial energy unleashed by the Revolution and fueled by the mass of land seized from Indians brought a sharply rising population, flourishing agriculture, commerce, ambition and opportunity, massive social and geographic mobility, and a culture of acquisitiveness. Such sweeping social change produced disorder and anxiety that coalesced in a cathartic foreign policy context. By focusing energies and emotions on the vanquishing of external foes, the national community could accommodate itself to destabilizing changes associated with rapid cultural transformation while at the same time disparaging as subversive the critics of militant nationalism.

Confirming the fears of classical republicanism, the Patriotic War spawned the U.S. warfare state, giving rise to a nation that would maintain a powerful "defense" establishment and employ state violence to perpetuate its own cultural imaginary. Preparing for war and *choosing* war thus inhered in national identity. The good feelings that arose in the war's aftermath foreshadowed similar anxiety-assuaging responses to the "splendid" imperial burst in 1898, the "good war" in 1945, and victory in the Cold War in 1991.

Another legacy flowing from national identity was the association between foreign war and domestic economic growth, as reflected in the Market Revolution that unfolded in the decade after the conflict. The war spurred nascent industry through government purchasing and investment in manufacturing. After the Napoleonic wars, economic dislocations in Europe brought sharply rising demand for U.S. food and grain. British mills drove a ceaseless demand for cotton, as U.S. farm output soared and new states in the South and Midwest entered the Union. From the Revolution to the end of the Patriotic War, the nation thus transitioned from a localized agrarian republic to a complex economy, with myriad interregional and broadened international connections. Dramatic population growth, stable and supportive government, individual ambition, Protestant anxieties, and a culture of acquisitiveness coalesced in a liberal capitalist society.[18]

The discourse of wartime triumph, combined with the economic boom, reaffirmed the destiny and superiority of the white republic over war-plagued Europe, a continent characterized by "regal turpitude and unmanly subjection." Unlike the European monarchies and class-based social system, liberal capitalism "offered ordinary people an escape from the self-denying virtue of their superiors" thereby fostering support among white men for an ostensibly free republican government.[19] Proud citizens viewed the United States as a land of enterprise, hard work, nascent industry, and opportunity for the common man. "No quality has so marked the character of American social life as individual aspiration," Joyce Appleby notes, "turning the United States into a magnet for immigrants and a wellspring of hope for the adventurous."[20] Hegemonic patriotic discourse silenced oppositional voices. The United States thus well reflected the Gramscian model of "spontaneous consent" on the part of masses of free whites in support of the hegemony of a burgeoning liberal capitalist order.

The persistent myth of the self-regulating market notwithstanding, local, state, and federal governments as well as the courts facilitated the Market Revolution with various forms of assistance and favorable policy decisions. Economic growth, while dynamic, was also uneven, as the "Panic of 1819," in actuality a serious recession, reflected the boom and bust cycle of early U.S. capitalism. The crash revealed the pervasive impact of the Market Revolution, however, as it marked the first truly national economic recession in U.S. history.

The vicissitudes of the market economy did not impede the inexorable expansion of the empire of liberty. John Quincy Adams realized his crowning achievement in the Transcontinental Treaty of 1819, an agreement on the south-western border, from Louisiana to the Pacific Northwest, though not including Texas. At the same time, a series of republican revolutions throughout Latin America powerfully affirmed the nation's identity as the "cradle of liberty" birthing new offspring. For the first but not the last time, the United States deployed in the Monroe Doctrine a discursive regime of decolonization that obscured the nation's identity-driven imperial expansion. Racialized paternalism underlay the claim that the United States alone would shepherd the evolution of republicanism to the south. The Monroe Doctrine was thus not only a forceful assertion of hemispheric separation from Europe; it was also a forceful declaration of hemispheric hegemony already apparent in the appropriation of the term *America* as a signifier of the United States alone. The nation ignored protests of its doctrine emanating from Latin Americans.

Despite the 1819 recession and the gathering storm over slavery manifested in the Missouri Compromise, expansion of the empire of liberty continued to affirm the Myth of America. The Louisiana Purchase and the Transcontinental Treaty opened vast new lands for white Western expansion, while Jackson's heroic victory and the Latin American revolutions affirmed the nation's destiny to lead the world into a new era of global republicanism.

With the passing of the early national gentry, cultural representation of national identity assumed increasing significance. Ballads, broadsides, orations, toasts, celebrations, and the birthdays of the revered fathers became important rituals affirming the imagined community. The "politics of celebration tethered popular sovereignty, resentment against aristocratic privilege, and the idea of American unity to everyday issues and local public life," David Waldstreicher explains. Washington, apotheosized in biography by Mason ("Parson") Weems, joined Benjamin Franklin in achieving the status of virtual saints within the national imaginary. At midcentury George Bancroft set forth a multivolume patriotic history of the nation's destiny, under God, to serve as an exemplar of righteousness and moral progress. Bancroft's narrative elided the expansion of slavery while dismissing Indians as "ignorant of the arts of life" and suffering from "the hereditary idleness of the race."[21]

On the fiftieth anniversary of the Declaration in 1826, the nation celebrated the Jubilee of Independence. Independence Day ensconced as a national holiday since the Patriotic War, assumed an aura of the sacred with the deaths on the same day, July 4, 1826, of John Adams and Jefferson, who had been united as rebels, disunited as bitter political foes, and then reunited in a remarkable late-life correspondence. From this point forward "the Fourth of July and the rituals associated with it had explicitly become central to civil religion in America," Michael Kammen points out.[22] By this time new modes of dress and linkages within the highly mobile society had further eroded the type of formal aristocratic distinctions still prevalent in Europe. The United States also rejected the King's English, as Noah Webster published an *American Dictionary of the English Language* (1828) to underscore the evolution of a distinct usage.

Discourse of the Common (White) Man

The expansion of white male suffrage broadened the base of hegemonic consent within the rapidly expanding nation. The 1819 recession fired the transition, as workers and farmers blamed bankers and big city finance men for the economic pain visited upon them. Such resentments proliferated in 1824, when Jackson, the symbol of the self-made frontier hero, defeated Adams in the popular vote but lost the presidency in the House of Representatives. Adams and Clay had engineered the "corrupt bargain," partly to contain Jackson politically, but also because both supported an ambitious program of federally sponsored internal improvements known as the American System.

As reactionary Jeffersonians—zealous defenders of slavery, states' rights, and limited federal power—the Jacksonians opposed the Hamiltonian system of consolidated federal power. Jackson's landslide victory over Adams in 1828 marked the final passing of the early national gentry and the arrival full-blown of the "age of the common man." Universal white manhood suffrage emerged state by state, enabling more than three times as many white men to vote in 1828 as in 1824. Jackson apotheosized the average white man, who shared the Tennessean's association of Adams and other East Coast elites with a bygone era of powdered wigs and European-style aristocracy.

Jackson embodied the racialized violence at the core of national identity, offering some credence to the timeworn conceptualization of the era as the Age of Jackson. Symbol vastly exceeded substance, as "Old Hickory" rode into the White House on his reputation as a conquering frontier hero and exemplar of patriotic destiny. Born poor in North Carolina in 1767, Jackson moved west, "read law," became a self-made frontier aristocrat in Nashville and eventually the largest slaveholder in Tennessee. In 1788, before he had met and married (in 1791) his wife, Rachel, Jackson took as his first slave a young woman named Nancy, whose duties may well have included sexual satisfaction of a rollicking young master. The survivor of violent encounters, including near-fatal duels, Jackson went on to defeat the British at New Orleans, killed Indians throughout the Southeast, and thus became a legendary national hero. That "a man of violent character and middling capacities" could be so revered was a testament, Alexis de Tocqueville concluded, to "the incredible influence military glory has over a nation's spirit."[23] Jackson's phenomenal appeal enabled him to win the popular vote in three consecutive elections, to anoint his successor in a fourth (Martin Van Buren in 1836), and to live to see a fellow Tennessean, James K. Polk ("Young Hickory"), elected in 1844.

The "era of the self-made *man*" reaffirmed the culturally constructed patriarchy long embedded within national identity. Sons of Liberty had ignited the Revolution of 1776 and Founding Fathers had forged the Constitution. Abigail Adams famously pleaded with her husband to "Remember the ladies" as they framed the new fundamental law of the land, yet women never found a place in the Constitution, either then or since. In the *Federalist Papers* Madison declared that it was "the vigorous and manly spirit" that "actuates the people of America." Jefferson averred that women functioned best as "objects of our pleasure."

The Market Revolution, however, brought destabilizing change and prompted adjustments in hegemonic discourse to preclude women from assuming "unnatural" economic roles. The Market Revolution thus increased opportunities for free white men while powerfully reinforcing a separate sphere for women. Gendered discourses permeated politics, the pulpit, and advice manuals, affirming that men dominated economic life while women possessed moral superiority. Accordingly, with society confronting unprecedented mobility, uncertainty, rampant alcoholism, and other social problems, it was all the more vital that woman assume her "natural" role of regenerating the moral character needed to insulate the home and family from the dangers emanating from the acquisitive market society.[24]

The cult of domesticity soon defined the role of middle-class women for the rest of the century, though they gained agency, to be sure, by carving out autonomous spheres through club, church, reform, and other social and literary activities. Women took a central role in the antebellum northern antislavery movement, often emphasizing slavery's assault on the sanctity of family as reflected in the buying and selling of slaves, keeping of slave mistresses, and rape of slave women. Paradoxically, however, the antislavery defense of the family tended to reinforce separate spheres for men and women by exalting the gen-

dered practices of northern society. In the plantation South, widespread reverence for notions of chivalry naturalized patriarchal dominance, with men serving as knights and protectors of women.[25]

Pervasive cultural representation exalting whiteness reinforced social in-
equality as Indian dispossession and the expansion of slavery reached high tide.
"White identity came to be embraced within the context of anti-Indian violence, capitalist expansion, and nationalism," David R. Roediger explains.[26]
Whiteness, rather than ethnicity, religious affiliation, or trade, became the primary signifier of empowerment. In the early republic, the Shays and Whiskey
Rebellions as well as sharp divisions over the French Revolution and the Jay
Treaty (1794) revealed, like Bacon's and Leisler's rebellions a century before, the
threat of disunity posed by divisions among white men. Anxieties then arose in
the context of the market-driven competition for wages and jobs. Despite the
reassuring discourse of the invisible hand, the market evolved unevenly and
proved susceptible to booms and busts, including another devastating "panic"
of 1837 in the wake of Jackson's Bank War.

Whiteness, implicit in the common man discourse, obscured divisions over
wealth and class by emphasizing the equality among white men based on their
sharing of constructed racial identification. The discourse of whiteness created
the illusion of equality while heading off change that otherwise might have
flowed from a stronger grasp of mounting marketplace disparities. Grounded
in the "ideological fiction of the 'peaceful competitiveness'" Dana D. Nelson
notes, white masculinity contained the "anxious, potentially vicious cultural
and material results" of market capitalism.[27] The persistence of economic inequality, shrouded by a thick cloud of mythic hegemonic discourse, prevails
throughout U.S. history.

The discursive regime of the age of the common man served, paradoxically,
to reinforce cultural hegemony. Culturally ensconced since Franklin produced
Poor Richard's Almanack in colonial Pennsylvania was the mythology that any-
one could get ahead in the fluid society, that hard work and good habits ("early
to bed, early to rise . . . ") could enable any male to become a self-made man.
Americans had thus internalized an understanding, as Appleby put it, "that inequalities were promoted not by capitalist development, but rather by the political privileges of an aristocracy."[28] As the United States had eliminated formal aristocracy in the Revolution of 1776, nationalist discourse offered no
cultural space in which to assert the existence of structural inequalities.

The exaltation of whiteness, the self-made man, and broadened white male political participation thus did not produce economic egalitarianism. By 1860 5 percent of U.S. families owned more than half the nation's wealth. In New York City, while a flood of new immigrants, working poor, beggars, prostitutes, and children called street rats sought to eke out an existence amid the squalor of Five Points and other slums, aristocrats such as Philip Hone meticulously chronicled a daily life of leisure and elite pleasures. The same situation prevailed in other northern cities and certainly in the South, where the planter aristocracy monopolized wealth and political power while retarding regional development that might benefit a majority of the population.

The rich literally got richer during the putative age of the common man, while thousands of farmers and artisans found their way of life undermined by the nascent industrial society. Some adjusted, but countless others became violent and abusive or drank themselves into ruin, as the tensions of the dynamic age converted the United States into a virtual "alcoholic republic."[29] The temperance movement and other antebellum reform initiatives responded to the dislocations brought on by the Market Revolution and rapid social transformation.

As the discourse of the age of the common man sanctified liberal capitalism, it reinforced a culture in which women anchored the domestic sphere while white men sought to possess property and make a profit. Slaves *were* property and a source of profit, while Indians and Mexicans *held* profitable property—from which they were to be removed under the discursive regimes of the empire of liberty and manifest destiny. Thus the dispossession of Indians for new plantations fueled the expansion of slavery, as racial violence begat more racial violence. King Cotton's reach extended far beyond the South, however, as the New England cotton mills (worked initially by "mill girls" ensconced in company towns) had fueled the northern industrial takeoff. The North thus depended on the South to supply cotton and purchase Yankee factory goods.

Even though slavery existed only in the South and abolitionism existed only in the North, the exaltation of whiteness reigned in both regions. In the South, the dominant planter class acquiesced to a measure of cultural but not economic equality among poor whites and yeoman farmers, who supported the maintenance of slave society on the basis of mutual white identity (*herrenvolk* democracy). In the North, manumission had occurred unevenly in the years after the Revolution and had been followed by various efforts to legislate often-stringent economic and social restrictions on African Americans.

Despite some remarkable achievements, including educational and employment opportunities for thousands of African Americans and even legalized interracial marriage in Massachusetts, segregation, police and mob violence, and phobias of racial miscegenation dominated northern society. "On every level, from barrooms to church meeting halls," James B. Stewart found, "the continuing efforts of African-Americans to put themselves forward as equals provoked deepening racial resistance from whites."[30] Such findings affirm the pointed observations of Tocqueville, who concluded that racism was actually strongest in the North, and of the escaped slave Frederick Douglass, who found no free world north of the Mason-Dixon line. Through the pervasive linking of whiteness with the rights of citizenship, Lacy K. Ford observes, "the Jacksonian construction of racial modernity defined not merely the South but the entire American nation-state as a 'white man's country.'"[31]

Throughout the nineteenth century European immigrants flooding into the United States in search of economic opportunity quickly adapted to the cultural construction of racial hierarchies. A Swedish-American maid in Chicago averred that life was better in America, "for here *white* people are free" (emphasis added). The Irish, who poured into Boston and New York in the 1840s to escape the potato famine, had sometimes viewed themselves as a race of people but not as white. However, in the United States they "became white" in order to differentiate themselves from blacks, Indians, and Hispanics and gain higher standing within the heavily racial culture.[32]

On every level, then, from yeoman farmers in the South to Irish laborers in Boston to Swedish maids in Chicago, a shared white racial solidarity anchored a common national identity. While cultural hegemony relegated domestic voices of dissent to the margins, the Frenchman Tocqueville was under no such compulsion to conform. The "tyranny of the majority" reigns as perhaps the most significant of Tocqueville's devastating insights into "democracy in America" gleaned during his extensive stay in the 1830s. Calling attention to the absence of free thought in the "land of the free," Tocqueville observed, "I know of no country in which, speaking generally, there is less independence of mind and true freedom of discussion than in America."

Tocqueville's analysis complements Gramscian "spontaneous consent" anchoring cultural hegemony. Lacking the structures and traditions of the ancien régime, the United States emerged in these formative years as the imagined community par excellence, a nation almost wholly dependent on representation in establishing and constantly affirming an organic identity. "One might suppose that all American minds had been fashioned after the same model, so exactly do they follow along the same paths," Tocqueville wrote. "A strange power" prevailed, a "mighty pressure of the mind of all" that "imposes its ideas and makes them penetrate men's very souls." It was "safe to see that trust in common opinion will become a sort of religion, with the majority as its prophet."

This allusion to "civil religion," a concept that originated with Rousseau, did not obscure for Tocqueville that the United States could hardly be considered a secular state. Indeed, disestablishment and formal separation of church and state actually affirmed religious conviction at the core of Myth of America identity. "By decreasing the apparent power of religion one increased its real strength," Tocqueville perceived. Even though the nation cultivated a wide array of sects and denominations, "Christianity itself is an established and irresistible fact which no one seeks to attack or defend."

After landing in the midst of the Second Great Awakening, Tocqueville observed, "The religious atmosphere of the country was the first thing that struck me." A cultural response to the destabilizing effects of the Market Revolution and its attendant social change, the revival of emotional Protestantism "burned over" New York and rode the Erie Canal into the Midwest. Temperance reformers (typically women), Protestant revivalists, and capitalists often united against alcoholism and "immoral" behavior in the burgeoning western towns and cities that sprang up with the transportation revolution. Together, these groups sought to preserve the social order by containing male drunkenness and vice, thus providing a more stable workforce and greater family stability. Charles Grandison Finney, the leading evangelist of the Second Great Awakening, bridged Jonathan Edwards and twentieth-century revivalists in a continuous U.S. history of culturally rooted Protestant millennialism. "The only difference between Finney's carefully choreographed revivals and those of Baptist preacher Billy Graham in the mid–twentieth century," Richard W. Fox declares, "was Graham's access to radio and television." As the revival spread "like an epidemic," evangelical Christians outnumbered the "rational celebrants of a merely human Jesus by many hundreds to one."[33] At the outset of the Mexican War churches stood in virtually every community of any size, and the number of preachers per capita had increased threefold since the Revolution.

The emotional Second Great Awakening reaffirmed national destiny, under God. As the New Englander Lyman Beecher avowed in 1835, "This nation is, in the Providence of God, destined to lead the way in the moral and political emancipation of the world." The fusion of religious zealotry and patriotic identity produced "a type of millennialism [that] would continue to hold sway over a large part of American religious culture through the crisis of the Civil War and into the late nineteenth century," Ruth Bloch notes.[34]

The pervasive discourse of national destiny, under God, erected an "iron cage" of cultural hegemony from the Patriotic War through the antebellum era. "The inhabitants of the United States have been repeatedly and constantly told that they are the only religious, enlightened, and free people," Tocqueville observed. "They have an immensely high opinion of themselves and are not far from believing that they form a species apart from the rest of the human race." The nation so thoroughly internalized Myth of America identity that "the least reproach offends it, and the slightest sting of truth turns it fierce; and one must praise everything, from the turn of its phrases to its most robust virtues. . . . Hence the majority lives in a state of perpetual self-adoration."

The "Passing" of the Indian

The Jacksonian era project of Indian Removal, culminating two centuries of ethnic cleansing, underscores the indispensable role of enemy-others in affirming national identity. Following the Revolution, the Northwest Ordinance opened millions of acres of Indian land north of the Ohio River, with the subsequent white invasion benignly referenced as settlement. Indians who lived in the region responded with bitter resistance. In 1790, under the chief Little Turtle, the Miami won a major battle, killing some six hundred U.S. troops while losing twenty-one Indian dead and stuffing the dead men's mouths with soil, thus "satisfying in death their lust for Indian land."[35] Backcountry land surveys, squatting, depredations, treaties, removal, and killing of Indians proceeded now with a regenerative vengeance.

The British presence remained a source of hope for indigenous tribes until the Jay Treaty brought withdrawal from the northwestern forts. As the British departed, U.S. General Anthony Wayne defeated the Miami confederation at Fallen Timbers in 1794, compelling the Indians to relinquish 25,000 acres between the Ohio River and Lake Erie in the Greenville Treaty. Not all Indians were helpless victims; some profited from land deals and frontier trade, others acculturated successfully. Nevertheless, the dominant paradigm of conquest through intimidation, violence, fraud, and alcoholism deprived Indians of another 2.5 million acres by 1809.

Deeply angered by the loss of Indian cultural integrity as well as land, the

Shawnee prophet Tenskwatawa and his brother Tecumseh mobilized pan-Indian identity and armed resistance on the eve of the Patriotic War. While preparing for war, the brothers enforced a ban on accommodation or acculturation with whites. Drawing on Jefferson's dehumanizing discourse of "merciless Indian savages," Madison, in his call for war in 1812, cited among his justifications the "warfare just renewed by the savages on one of *our extensive frontiers*—a warfare which is known to spare neither age nor sex and to be distinguished by features peculiarly shocking to humanity" (emphasis added). Destruction of "savage" foes inevitably ensued, particularly as the Indians lost their charismatic leader Tecumseh, who died on the battlefield in 1813.

The series of violent assaults and confiscatory treaties that followed in the wake of the Patriotic War made a mockery of the Ghent Treaty's call for Indian lands to revert back to the prewar status quo. To the south, following Indian attacks and the killing of some four hundred settlers along the Alabama River in 1813, Jackson led combined forces in the slaughter of men, women, and children at Horseshoe Bend. He then compelled the Creeks to sign a treaty ceding some twenty-three million acres as compensation for alleged Indian depredations. Jackson maintained the initiative in 1818 by exceeding his orders and penetrating into Florida, ostensibly to hunt down and punish Seminole marauders. Jackson notoriously hanged two British subjects as instigators during the seizure of St. Augustine. Alone within Monroe's cabinet, Adams defended the action by arguing essentially that taking Florida from Spain and the Indians was far more important than focusing on Jackson's draconian style in conducting the mission. In the wake of the subsequent Transcontinental Treaty, both Britain and Spain abandoned any pretensions of trying to retain Florida in the face of the U.S. continental juggernaut.

Adams's defense of Jackson, whom he loathed, reflected an iron cultural consensus of asserting violent hegemony over the domestic savages. Continuity rather than discontinuity prevailed from the founding patriarchs through the Jacksonian era. In the 1790s Franklin, the venerable first American, alluded to the "design of Providence to extirpate these savages in order to make room for the cultivators of the earth." Washington, an inveterate Indian killer in a series of imperial wars, had advocated removal of the "beasts of prey" unless they surrendered unequivocally. John Adams concurred but preferred the trope "blood Hounds." Jefferson viewed Indians as intellectually and artistically superior to blacks, yet he shuddered at the prospect of coexistence with either. Angered over attempts of the "backward" northwestern tribes to ally with Britain in 1812, the sage of Monticello vowed "we shall be obliged to drive them, with the beasts of the forest into the Stony Mountains." Henry Clay observed in 1825 that "there never was a full-blooded Indian who took to civilization." Calhoun averred that the only solution to the Indian problem—like the "Negro problem"—was that "our views of their interest, and not their own, ought to govern them." In his defense of Jackson, Quincy Adams blamed Spain for allowing "hordes of savages" free rein to carry out "the barbarous and indiscriminate murder of women, infancy, and age."[36]

While he would eventually mount a courageous assault against slavery, Adams's internalization of racialized discourse led him to embrace Indian ethnic cleansing. His sanction of continental aggression—which resulted in the expansion of the slavery he condemned—belies the image of Adams as an isolationist flowing from his famous address of July 4, 1821. Secretary of state at the time, Adams issued a poignant warning against a national foreign policy of seeking out "monsters to destroy." Such a policy, he warned, would divert the nation from its providentially ordained mission to lead through "the benignant sympathy of her example." Continuing to feminize the United States, and thus render it discursively incapable of aggression, Adams warned that were the nation to "involve herself beyond the power of extrication, in all the wars of interest and intrigue," she risked a policy that would "usurp the standards of freedom." If the nation's identity were to "insensibly change from liberty to force . . . she would no longer be the ruler of her spirit. . . . She might become the dictatress of the world."

Adams's warning proved prescient, but his own enemy-othering of the "hordes of savages" prevented him from grasping that the "monster" already lurked within the imagined community and not outside of it.

With the approval of all the nation's leaders, and with the eastern half of the continent now firmly grasped, the full weight of racialized dispossession could be brought down upon the original inhabitants. The Indian Removal Act of 1830, authorizing the government to "transfer any eastern tribe to trans-Mississippi River areas," marked the culmination of the first massive phase of Euro-American continental conquest. Only white men could make proper use of the land to expand the "markett" and advance the "republik," Jackson averred. In presenting the removal plan to Congress, the president declared that the march of progress required "the *extinction* of one generation to make room for another," to replace "a country covered with forests and ranged by a few thousands savages [with] our own extensive Republic, studded with cities, towns, and prosperous farms" (emphasis added).[37]

Jackson dominated the style but not the substance of Indian removal, which reflected hegemonic national identity inherent in the white man's continent. Myth of America discourse invariably converted Indian homeland defense into a vision of bloodthirsty, tomahawk-wielding savages on the warpath. By this time the captivity narrative had become ensconced as a staple in early American literature. The imagery of the sexual vulnerability of nurturing female innocence in the hands of savages inverted conflict with Indians into a struggle for the defense of a white civilization in which women depended upon men for protection and which was thus justifiably patriarchal. Mythic narratives sanctioned racial conquest and exalted the white male frontiersman for his ability to enter the world of the savage, carry out a rescue mission, and return as a heroic figure, unsullied by the encounter with evil.

Paternalist discourse, including the argument that removal would benefit Indians by enabling them to return to their natural state, offered an alternative to the image of the marauding savage. In either case, the discourse facilitated conquest. The Indian removal campaign was so poorly funded, ill-planned, and corrupt that it led not merely to dispossession but to the deaths of between one-quarter and one-third of the affected Indian populace from disease, hardship, and privation. The Cherokee trail of tears marked the most sensational dehumanization, particularly as it targeted one of the five "civilized tribes" which had done more than any other to acculturate and bore no resemblance to the dominant trope of the "merciless Indian savage."[38]

A pervasive cultural hegemony sanctioned Indian removal, as the overwhelming majority of citizens rejected accommodation or coexistence. Only a few voices "opposed the great Jacksonian national embrace of the Paxton Boys' principles," Daniel Richter notes.[39] The minority that advocated acculturation of Indians—mainly Quakers, Protestant missionaries, and various humanitarians—held "primitive" Indian culture in corresponding paternal disdain. These reformers affirmed hegemonic national identity by prevailing on Indians to imitate the white way of life, with men farming and women attending to sewing and weaving in the home. Such ethnocentrism prevented even sympathetic whites from grasping that Indians had been feeding themselves for millennia through their own farming methods and gendered division of labor. Few stopped to recall that Indians had adapted to trade with Europeans, as both producers and consumers, from the earliest days of settlement. Likewise, a lack of respect for Indian spirituality underlay Christianizing efforts. Hundreds did convert, but many more rejected European religion. "You have got our country, but you are not satisfied," one Seneca man bitterly observed. "You also want to force your religion upon us."[40]

As removal capped off ethnic cleansing, cultural representation shifted from marauding savages to mourning and nostalgia for the passing of the noble savage. The United States could remove Indians west of the Mississippi but could not obliterate them from memory and history. Mourning of a bygone era in which the noble savage had lived proudly—"the irreclaimable son of the wilderness," as the romantic historian Francis Parkman put it—materialized in discourse roughly in correspondence with the disappearance of Indians as a military threat. The Pocahontas legend flourished in plays, stories, and on canvas in the early national period. James Fenimore Cooper's popular "Leatherstocking tales," especially *The Last of the Mohicans: A Narrative of 1757* (1826), centered on nostalgia for the inevitable extinction of the noble savage, a process that reassuringly began a generation before 1776. Henry Wadsworth Longfellow's *Hiawatha* also romanticized the bygone era in verse. Painters such as George Caitlan commercialized the noble savage stereotype in nineteenth-century artistic renderings. Indians gradually became perceived culturally not as human beings but as part of nature, like the trees, rivers, and mountains, obstacles in the path of modernist progress. The erasure was so complete that the nationalist historian Arthur M. Schlesinger, Jr., in his monumental *The Age of Jackson,* ignored Indians and Indian removal completely.[41]

No one better symbolized the liminal existence of postremoval Indians than Black Hawk. The Sauk war chief had defied a white edict by crossing the Mississippi to reclaim ancestral lands in Illinois in 1832. Ignoring his white flag of truce, the U.S. army opened fire and took Black Hawk prisoner. The defeated war chief, now in his sixties, was shipped back east for burlesque appearances as a symbol of the once-powerful but now fast-fading Indian. Compelled to adhere to the script, Black Hawk left audiences with the impression of a marauding savage who had come to acknowledge the superiority of civilized white society. Immediately upon liberation from this charade, however, Black Hawk dictated a biography, angrily detailing his capture under a flag of truce and the forcible dispossession of his people.[42]

Anxious Aggression

The passing of the Indians confirmed for many the continental destiny of the superior white race, broadening cultural space for the subsequent invasion of Mexico. The same drives that underlay slavery and Indian conquest fueled the Mexican War, as U.S. history texts benignly reference the 1846 invasion. Not even nationalist historians dispute that the war flowed from aggression that precluded a diplomatic settlement over Texas. The predominantly white lone star republic, which had declared independence in 1836, now sought admission into the Union as a slave state.

Long mythologized by regional lore and national narrative, Texas owed its existence to a half century of brutal racial violence driven by white ethnic cleansing of the Indian and Tejano (Hispanic Texans) enemy-others. The violent hegemony that prevailed in Texas created a militarized culture of war in which the white Texans seized land from the Tejanos as well as the Comanches, Wichitas, Caddos, and other Indians. The Texas Rangers, long depicted as courageous frontier heroes spreading progress, "killed indiscriminately, they robbed, and they raped," as their "goal was to spread terror" and seize land. The Tejanos and the Indians, like Pocahontas and King Philip, strove to accommodate and acculturate in response to the invasion, but the white Texans, driven by "extreme racial hatred and commitment to martial violence [more] than economic needs," Gary C. Anderson argues, responded with unrelenting ethnic cleansing. The Indians ultimately fought back, giving rise to a Texas mythology of brave and innocent settlers fighting off unprovoked raids by merciless savages, but, as in the past, the whites were the aggressors who killed far more than they lost, often indiscriminately.[43]

The militant culture of Texas was not the sole *casus belli* of the Mexican War, as U.S. expropriation by violence of the vast territories of California and the Southwest underscored. Convictions of Anglo-Saxon superiority, providential destiny, and modernist progress underlay westward expansionism as traders, investors, land-hungry settlers, missionaries, miners, farmers, cattle ranchers, and visionaries of an eventual U.S. "empire on the Pacific" flocked to the west and southwest.[44]

Like the Patriotic War, the Mexican invasion offered cathartic relief from the psychic anxieties of the antebellum period. The U.S. population had doubled between 1820 and 1840, by which time more than twelve million of a total population of seventeen million were under age thirty, creating a need to reaffirm the identity of the imagined community as the older generations passed. As the northern antislavery movement gained momentum, fear of violent slave revolts, particularly in the wake of Nat Turner's bloody uprising in 1831, became increasingly acute. Women's activism accelerated in the antebellum reform movement, and many began to link the cultural construction of race in the slaveholding nation to their own gendered marginalization.

Immigrants flowed into the country, heightening nativist anxieties and fueling the drive to reinforce Americanism. After the Revolution, the Alien and Sedition Acts of 1798 brought the first of a continuous series of xenophobic reactions against foreign immigration. The next major wave unfolded in the 1840s in an intensive reaction against the influx of some three million immigrants, predominantly Irish, German, and mostly Catholic. The nativist reaction—defined by John Higham in his classic study as "an intense opposition to an internal minority on the grounds of its foreign (i.e., 'un-American') connections"—underscored the xenophobia inherent in Myth of America identity. "The powerful Know-Nothing movement of the 1850s helped transform xenophobia into an acceptable and powerful form of patriotism, which has survived to this day," Ali Behdad notes.[45]

In national politics, the Whig Party arose to challenge "King Andrew I" and his legacy, seizing the White House in the election of 1840, the first modern U.S. political campaign, replete with mass mailings, parades, stump speaking, and an unprecedented level of participation. The Whigs threatened the Jacksonian Democrats, who no longer had Jackson, and promised to revive the threat of consolidated government through a federally sponsored program of internal improvements.

The "anxious aggrandizement" that provoked the Jacksonians to make war on Mexico stemmed in part from their conviction that westward expansion was the antidote to high tariffs and a Hamiltonian federal system that might undermine state sovereignty—including their "liberty" to hold slaves and displace Indians.[46] Manifest Destiny millennialism and war thus stemmed from the internal drives and domestic anxieties of national identity as opposed to responding to the external environment normally associated with foreign policy. The journalist and imperial expansionist John O'Sullivan popularized the term *Manifest Destiny,* but he hardly invented the concept.

The *revival* of Manifest Destiny discourse in the context of the Mexican invasion reflected congenital aggression and cultural consent for a campaign of state violence against external enemy-others. While proceeding "as offensively to Mexico as possible," Polk recklessly confronted Britain with an exaggerated claim to the Oregon country with a boundary extending well into British Canada at the 54–40 line. In large measure as a result of their shared embrace of "Anglo-Saxon" superiority, the United States found the language of accommodation with the British "cousin," especially after London dispatched warships to the Northwest and beefed up forces in western Canada as well. Though John Bull remained suspect in U.S. eyes, a rapprochement rooted in race, culture, and commerce continued its steady march across the nineteenth century. Under terms of an 1846 treaty with Britain, Oregon, already flooded by waves of determined settlers, became a U.S. territory with a northern border at 49 degrees, well south of "54–40 or fight."

The only diplomacy conducted with the "mongrel" Mexicans, by contrast, was "the diplomacy of annexation."[47] As the United States had no legitimate diplomatic claim to Texas, militant nationalists would seize the territory by aggression. The emotional appeal of Manifest Destiny drowned out the protests of some Whig politicians, who condemned the nation's bellicose mendacity. Whereas Jefferson had sought to avoid war, and Madison had presented more or less the straight story in his 1812 war message to Congress, Polk deliberately misled Congress and the public prior to the declaration of war in May 1846. Young Hickory had sent troops south of the disputed Texas border to the Rio Grande. U.S. warships appeared off the coast of upper California as well. Yet Polk declaimed that despite "all our efforts to avoid it," the war had begun "by act of Mexico" when "American blood had been shed on American soil."

Although Polk affirmed the imperial presidency, the war could not have unfolded without broad-based cultural consent.[48] Thus for the second consecutive generation, the United States *chose* war, not as a last resort, and certainly not for defense, but rather because only regenerative violence would satisfy the psychic drives inherent within Myth of America identity. "The people *must* have something to huzza about," declared the southern diplomat John Slidell. "When we cease to extend, we will cease to be, what we are now, a united and ascendant people," an Indiana congressman declared. As in the so-called Spanish-American War, which began in 1898, ostensibly over Cuba, the battlefront quickly extended far beyond the original focus of Texas, as the United States seized control of California and the Southwest. Senator John A. Dix of New York declared that the seizure of western lands came at "the behest of Providence that idleness, and ignorance, and barbarism, shall give way to industry, and knowledge, and civilization."[49]

The embrace of Manifest Destiny underscores the impact of the Second Great Awakening and the spread of Protestant hegemony. "Strongly anti-Catholic rhetoric," fused with racial contempt for the "vagrant herdsmen shepherd" Mexicans who had no greater claim to hold the land than Indians, led to the conclusion that "God has fought upon our side, to chastise [Mexicans] for their sins." The Texas Rangers ripped crucifixes off Mexican churches and sometimes trampled priests to death with their horses. "The destiny of our nation is to be decided in the West," Lyman Beecher declared. "As trekkers west mastered the territories with rifle, axe, plow, school, church, and railroad," Conrad Cherry observes, "many Americans became doubly convinced of their divine election."[50]

Like Indian removal, Manifest Destiny targeted for dispossession a rival of such putatively inferior racial stock as to have no legitimate claim to land sought by white men for the spread of modernist progress. "Exterminating" Mexico's "weaker blood . . . we regard with as much certainty as we do the final extinction of the Indian races, to which the mass of the Mexican population seem very little superior," the Reverend H. W. Bellows averred in the *Democratic Review* in 1847. Other spokesmen rejected the discourse of ethnic cleansing and adopted "the belief that it was America's duty to redeem the Mexican people" and by doing so to redeem their own nation. Perceiving "God's agency in virtually everything that took place," Americans embraced the war as part of the nation's "great work in reclaiming the world."[51]

Like most U.S. wars, the Mexican invasion excited what Herman Melville described as a "state of delirium" in which "military ardor pervades."[52] Dependent on volunteers, the U.S. invasion force counted only about thirty thousand army regulars out of some ninety thousand combatants. Tennessee, the home state of both Jackson and Polk, became the "volunteer state" as thirty thousand men responded to the state's call for three thousand volunteers. Men from other slaveholding states responded enthusiastically, but the war's initial popularity encompassed all regions. Ohio met its quota within two weeks; New Yorkers rallied to the cause; Lowell, Massachusetts, staged the largest town meeting in history for a prowar rally; and students at Yale passed a prowar resolution. The fighting force transcended ethnicity, as English, Irish, Germans, and Scandinavian immigrants fought together. Ironically, African Americans went to war as slaves and laborers on the U.S. side, whereas Mexico had abolished slavery in 1829.

"Martial manhood" flourished as hegemonic discourse feminized Mexico and represented the war as conquest of the weaker sex, thus reaffirming the cultural construction of manliness on the home front. Notions of honor, chivalry, and a sense of virulent male power, embodied in the most popular song of the day, "Yankee Doodle Dandy," filled the air. Noting that the United States had "penetrated" Mexico, the *Southern Quarterly Review* added that U.S. forces had "punished the insolence of [Mexico's] sons in the sight of her daughters." As marriage was an unequal relationship between a man and a woman, few questioned a man's decision to choose a wife from among the "pretty señoritas" in the occupied territories. It was the destiny of the "lovely specimens of Spanish beauty," known for their "flashing large dark eyes, raven tresses," and "well-developed, magnificent figures," to become the "wives and mothers of a better race." In a graphic allusion to ancient Rome, it was said that Mexico "like the Sabine virgins will learn to love her ravisher."[53]

Rape was among the atrocities in a "hidden dirty war" against the Mexicans. While the usable past teaches schoolchildren to Remember the Alamo as a massacre of martyred national heroes, U.S. forces and volunteers engaged in "an orgy of rape and robbery." Americans engaged in "state-sponsored murder through a loose confederation of communities and irregular companies," Paul Foos points out. The Texas Rangers, today glorified as a major league baseball team, conducted depredations against innocent Mexicans and responded to the death of even one of their own with "often indiscriminate acts of brutality." Only some two thousand of the more than thirteen thousand U.S. dead died in battle, whereas at least fifty thousand Mexicans died in the war. High-ranking officers looked the other way while army regulars engaged in rape, plunder, reprisal killings, and scorched earth policies. The editor of the New Orleans *Picayune,* a supporter of the war, found the U.S. atrocities so egregious "that *negroes* in a state of insurrection would hardly be guilty of" such behavior (emphasis added). Observing his troops "perfectly frantic with the lust of blood and plunder," a U.S. officer—sounding very much like Increase Mather following King Philip's War—mused that the war and occupation had "corrupted our men fearfully."[54]

On September 14, 1847, as the United States pushed into Mexico City after a blood-drenched fight, the call to subdue and incorporate all of Mexico marked the apogee of Manifest Destiny. "Your ancestors, when they landed at Plymouth," responded to Indian resistance by "cheating them out of their land," Sam Houston acknowledged at an "all-Mexico rally. "Now the Mexicans are no better than the Indians, and I see no reason why we should not go in the same course now, and take their land."[55] While some opposed incorporation of Mexican "yellow skins" out of concern for racial purity, Mexican nationalist resistance never abated, hence any attempt at subjugating "all Mexico" would have required a massive, long-term military commitment and a protracted guerrilla war. Growing awareness of the atrocity-filled "dirty war" and mounting Whig opposition in Congress also influenced the decision to come to terms under the Treaty of Guadalupe-Hildalgo in 1848. Under its provisions, the United States withdrew and paid Mexico fifteen million dollars, a small price for the seizure of Texas, California, and the Southwest. Ironically John Quincy Adams, once the ebullient architect of continental destiny, fell dead from a heart attack on the House floor in vehement opposition to the Mexican treaty.

Like nearly all wars in U.S. history, the invasion of Mexico powerfully reaffirmed Myth of America identity. "Every American must feel a glow of enthusiasm in his heart as he thinks of his country's greatness, her might and her power," the *Scientific American* declared. Patriotism was the most "admirable impulse in the human soul," Walt Whitman pronounced, hence no "true American" could fail to express "pride in our victorious armies." As the public celebrated the war in poetry, plays, paintings, books, and song, it became clear that "most people viewed it [as] gloriously triumphant."[56] The war heightened reverence for the flag, increased the prestige of West Point, and produced the first national military hero since Jackson in General Zachary ("Old Rough and Ready,") Taylor, elected president in 1848.

Soldiers and chroniclers of the war drew inspiration from the flag, "the most beautiful of all flags, its colors dyed in the blood of our fore-fathers, and re-dyed in that of their sons." In the midst of brutal fighting in Monterey, a soldier focused his eyes upon the "glorious stars and stripes," whereupon "a thrill of pleasure shot through me and I felt as if I could die."[57]

Identity-driven patriotism, providence, and masculine glory affirmed cultural hegemony while marginalizing opponents of the Mexican War. Despite Polk's mendacity, Congress voted overwhelmingly in favor of the war, 174–14 in the House (all 14 opponents represented antislavery districts) and 40–2 in the Senate. Remembering the demise of the New England Federalists over their opposition to the War of 1812 at the Hartford Convention, potential war critics feared being tarred with subversion. Criticism focused on Polk, not on the war itself, which quickly became sacrosanct. Like twenty-first century Democrats in the context of the Iraq War, one Whig lamely explained, "We support the war though we condemn those who have brought us into it."[58] This pattern of Myth of America cultural hegemony disciplining opposition to violent aggression became a continuous feature of the U.S. warfare state.

Patriotic national identity drowned out discourse from such groups as the American Peace Society, which decried the war as an application of "bloody, vindictive, ferocious patriotism upon the poor, despised Mexicans." Drawing parallels with slavery, William Lloyd Garrison condemned the war "of aggression, of invasion, of conquest, and rapine—marked by ruffianism, perfidy, and every other feature of national depravity"—but antebellum culture had long rejected radical abolitionists, and "the public remained largely indifferent to their arguments." Not even the most eminent intellectuals and opponents of slavery, such as Theodore Parker, could "transcend" their Americanism to mount opposition to the war. As the exemplar of the "superior race, with superior ideas and a better civilization," Parker averred, the United States had a duty to extend the "idea of America" over Mexico. "Peace advocates, Whigs, antislavery reformers, all tempered their stands against the war by seeking some ultimate good in the conflict," Robert Johannsen explains.[59]

Millennial Visions Denied

The republican stirrings in the European Revolutions of 1848, coinciding with victory over Mexico, propelled Americans into a "lather of excitement," as they anticipated a "holy millennium of liberty," Whitman observed. Although the Monroe Doctrine had pronounced nonintervention in European affairs, Young America stood ready to take the credit for every step toward republicanism in Old Europe. In 1851 Americans accorded the visiting Hungarian independence leader Louis Kossuth a wildly enthusiastic reception. Though the Hungarian republican movement had failed, Kossuth nonetheless affirmed beacon of liberty discourse even though, as he pointed out, the United States had taken no steps to help him actually pull off a republican revolution. Perhaps the Hungarian rebel recognized that by heaping adulation on him, the nation affirmed its own identity.[60]

The era of Manifest Destiny and the millennial visions of Young America peaked with the "monomaniacal patriotism" of the filibuster movement.[61] As the deepening sectional crisis put the brakes on state-sponsored aggression, individual crusaders, including O'Sullivan, attempted to manifest their own destinies as extralegal architects of foreign expansion. Filibusterism was so common between the Mexican and Civil Wars as to constitute a "national epidemic." Even before the wave of filibusterism, "examples of Americans mistreating Central American men, with no remorse, fill the accounts of travelers through the region."[62]

Militant national identity and anxieties about manhood permeated the *filibustero* phenomenon. Narciso Lopez, William Walker, and others inevitably failed, and ultimately met their executioner, in attempts to export slaveholding liberty to the supposed backward peoples of Cuba, Baja California, Honduras, and Nicaragua. U.S. diplomats posted in Europe reflected the filibustering spirit by laboring to "detach" Cuba from Spain. However, the antislavery northern press denounced the Ostend Manifesto (1856) as a "buccaneering document." Obsessed with the virility of Young America, O'Sullivan's New York—based *Democratic Review,* however, cheered on the manly conquest of a feminized Cuba, whose "rosy, sugared lips" revealed that "she is of age—take her, Uncle Sam!" The journal also printed a veritable motto of filibusterism: "East by sunrise, West by sunset, North by Arctic expedition, and south *as far as we darn please.*"[63]

Despite their unbroken record of failure, the filibusters received financing for their piratical ventures, rarely lacked for recruits from across the South and the panned-out western gold fields, and generated enthusiastic receptions upon returning stateside from their campaigns. While applauded in the South as well as in some quarters in the North, filibusterism and conspiratorial gambits such as the Ostend Manifesto prompted opinion north of the Mason-Dixon line to conclude that the militant national chauvinism, first unleashed in Mexico, now threatened to spiral out of control.

Manifest Destiny thus produced only an ephemeral legacy of good feelings. While the nation had staked its claim to the entire white man's continent, the vast new territories immediately brought into sharp relief the ultimate contestation over identity between the "Slave Power," the southern planter aristocracy, and "free soil" unionists. Both North and South embraced racial modernity, including a consensus on Indian removal, and both condemned abolition of slavery as the worst sort of extremism. Finally, both embraced the cause (with complete absence of irony) of the United States as manifestly a rising empire of liberty. Despite these commonalities, they had no solution—other than an internecine war of incomprehensible scope—to resolve the sectional divide and the psychic anxieties that pervaded the Jacksonian-antebellum era.

At the dawn of the antebellum era, a romantic literature had evolved, an American Renaissance that initially reflected the boundless optimism of the rising republic. Between 1823 and 1841 Cooper produced the "Leather-stocking tales," featuring the Daniel Boone—like hero Natty Bumppo and evoking nostalgia for the passing of the frontier amid the modernizing market society. Edgar Allan Poe virtually invented the genres of mystery and horror. Themes of uniqueness, greatness, and providential destiny echoed through the early novels, stories, and poetry of Whitman, Longfellow, Nathaniel Hawthorne, and Melville. "We Americans are the peculiar, chosen people, the Israel of our time," Melville wrote. "We bear the ark of the liberties of the world."[64]

By the late 1840s, however, the ebullience of the Young America movement within romantic letters had transformed into a deep foreboding over the crass materialism of the market society and the frontier violence of the Indian and Mexican wars. In *The Scarlet Letter* (1850), Hawthorne brilliantly exposed the fear and intolerance that, while rooted in Puritan society, yet prevailed across the land. He sought personal transcendence from a spiritually empty life by joining the commune at Brook Farm, one of the myriad utopian experiments that sprang up at this time. Melville emerged as "the great debunker of Young America," which he had once exalted but now condemned through the "black pessimism of Moby-Dick," the allegory of Captain Ahab's monomaniacal and self-destructive obsession with the great—and white—whale (1851). Henry David Thoreau decried U.S. violent aggression and declined to pay taxes that supported war and slavery. Stung by the nation's lust for war, Ralph Waldo Emerson concluded in 1847, "No act of honor or benevolence or justice is to be expected from the American government." Poe, found writhing in the death throes of agony on the streets of Baltimore in 1849, had drunk himself to death at age forty.[65]

The transformation of Manifest Destiny and the Young America movement from an almost messianic faith in a glorious national future to one of dark foreboding "helps us to understand the manic psychology of the antebellum period," Edward Widmer notes. By the 1850s Young America, having "aged dramatically," now signified "a spirit of restless expansionism and ugly greed." The exemplars of national destiny had "lost control of the rhetorical juggernaut they created." Like the Puritan "cittie on a Hill," Young America had fallen from God's grace and into the grasp of a "dangerously aggressive, unstable nationalism."[66] The epic writers of the era, like Jefferson and Adams in their last years, fully grasped the peril that lay ahead.

CHAPTER 3

Reunite and Conquer

Like a massive avalanche, the Civil War thundered across the national landscape and left a mountain of debris in the path of the "empire of liberty." It would take more than a generation to clear the way sufficiently for the nation to fully "heal" and reassert a revived imperialism extending well beyond the antebellum conception of merely continental "destiny." Even during this interregnum, however, the ongoing conquest of "merciless Indian savages" continued and, despite the end of slavery, the exaltation of whiteness gained renewed momentum.

The Civil War and the subsequent industrial era unleashed profound domestic dislocations over the sectional divide, the corporate revolution, mass immigration, rapid urbanization, farmer unrest, and deep divisions fostered by racial, gender, ethnic, and class hierarchies. Those dislocations brought challenges to cultural hegemony, yet Americans ultimately powerfully reaffirmed their national identity and assuaged psychic crisis by choosing war.

Few grasped the connection between foreign aggression and domestic unity more fully than Secretary of State William H. Seward. Less than two weeks before the Confederacy opened fire on Fort Sumter Seward proposed to head off the impending internecine struggle by starting a war with one or more nations among Britain, France, Russia, and Spain. Such a conflict might "wrap the world in flames" while inspiring North and South to put aside their differences for the sake of national unity against a foreign enemy-other.[1]

As Seward had feared, the empire of liberty itself went up in the flames of a murderous civil war. The aggressive foreign war that Seward had sought to unify the nation would be deferred until the turn of the century. While the contradictions were too profound to be put aside in 1861, the significance of Seward's proposal rested not just in its desperation but moreover in the recognition that ultimately "domestic tranquility" depended to a substantial degree on identity-driven enemy-othering and foreign war.

Before focusing its aggressive drives abroad the United States confronted contradictions flowing from the most reactionary elements of national identity. The Civil War was a rebellion in Union discourse alone, though such an interpretation endures in the usable past. The South had ample precedent for its insistence that state-rights federalism, or Confederate nationalism, legitimately represented "America." From the first presidential election in 1788 to 1836, proslavery southerners controlled the executive branch for all but the two one-term, repudiated presidencies of John and John Quincy Adams. Beginning in 1836, pro-South northern "doughfaces" (because, critics charged, their views could be molded like dough) such as Martin Van Buren and Franklin Pierce, along with the southern slaveholders John Tyler, James K. Polk, and Zachary Taylor, maintained the proslavery presidency. While southern elites shared Myth of America discourse and beacon of liberty patriotic national identity with the North, they did so within a framework in which sovereignty rested ultimately with the states. Thus a genuine power struggle, rather than a rebellion against a legitimate unitary authority, erupted over the principle of a strictly federal versus a consolidated national government.

The unprecedented scope and violence of the Civil War underscored that the Myth of America was the driving force within the imagined community. Only by viewing the nation as the sacred product of providential destiny could such a mammoth bloodletting have been justified on both sides. While it was Abraham Lincoln who in 1862 told Congress, "We shall nobly save, or meanly lose, the last, best hope on earth," Confederate leaders insisted that they too fought to preserve liberty.

The federal victory in the Civil War decisively confirmed the permanence of the Union—the lexicon literally changed from the United States "are" to the United States "is"—and ultimately produced an even more powerfully ensconced hegemonic national identity than ever before. Thus, for all its bloodshed and lingering regional divisions, the ultimate legacy of the Civil War was political unity, material expansion, and a revival of national destiny under God.

3. *Our Heaven Born Banner* (1861) by William Bauly. This pro-Union print made from the painting features a lone Zouave sentry safeguarding the nation from a promontory at the break of dawn. The sentry's rifle and bayonet provide the staff for the American flag, illuminated by the dawn. The print responded to a highly publicized Confederate insult to the flag at Fort Sumter at the outbreak of the Civil War. Courtesy of the Library of Congress.

By rejecting the Confederate alternative of "a house divided," the United States emerged from horrific conflict "touched by fire," as Oliver Wendell Holmes put it, yet ultimately renewed in its national-imperial purpose.

The sacrifices of war had been profound: more than 3 million men went into military service; more than 1 million of them, out of a total population of 32 million, became casualties, including a death toll of 620,000, nearly as many dead as in all other U.S. wars (before and after) combined. Throughout the defeated South, plantations, farms, homes, stores, towns, railroads, and factories lay in ruins.

Despite a long tradition of mythical discourse of the Civil War as a crusade for freedom, any student scratching the surface of history quickly learns that the North's primary motivation at the outset was to maintain the Union rather than to destroy slavery. A Northern wartime ditty crudely but aptly captured the predominant outlook:

A willingness to fight with vigor,
For loyal rights, but not the nigger.[2]

Lincoln, the Illinois "railsplitter," born in a log cabin and thus heir to the Jacksonian "self-made man" tradition, embraced racial modernity and, like Jefferson, could not envision the "black" and "white" "races" living together on the continent. However, he viewed slavery as wrong and favored the venerable solution of colonization of African Americans to resolve the historical problem of racial incompatibility.

Lincoln's devotion to the Union was nothing short of sacred, and he would embrace any solution—from emancipation to ongoing southern servitude—as long as the *modus vivendi* would preserve the national union sanctified by Myth of America discourse.[3] While only African Americans and a tiny minority of abolitionists and "radical" Republicans in the North challenged white supremacy, the blood sacrifice of war ultimately led to the repudiation of slavery as incompatible with national identity. The efforts of abolitionists, black and white, and the blood of Yankee soldiers thus ushered in renewal, rebirth, and regeneration through unparalleled internecine violence. Unrelenting abolitionist agitation and African American resistance finally received confirmation from Lincoln's proclamation freeing slaves in the Confederate states as of January 1, 1863.

Putting his astonishing literary talents on display at Gettysburg, Lincoln powerfully reaffirmed the Myth of America. The "great civil war" that now roiled the nation would determine whether the project of "our fathers . . . a new nation, conceived in liberty . . . can long endure." Be it "highly resolve[d]," Lincoln intoned from the battlefield, "that these dead shall not have died in vain; that this nation, under God, shall have a new birth of freedom; and that government of the people, by the people, for the people, shall not perish from the earth." As he honored the courage and sacrifice of white men on both sides, Lincoln ignored African Americans. In subsequent generations the Civil War became a historical spectacle—a source of popular obsession with generals, battles, and imagery that often perpetuated the romance of the Lost Cause and allowed masses of sympathizers to remain not merely "Confederates in the attic" but often Confederates right out in the open as well.[4]

The kaleidoscope of Civil War imagery—the bloody lane and cornfield at Antietam, the Emancipation Proclamation, Mathew Brady's photographs, the "Battle Hymn of the Republic," Lincoln at Gettysburg, Sherman's march to the sea, Grant and Lee at Appomattox, and the final Shakespearean tragedy at Ford's Theater—all redefined and ultimately "hallowed," the meaning of America. The Civil War permanently transformed the Constitution, as the Thirteenth, Fourteenth, and Fifteenth amendments brought the promise, though not the actuality, of African American male citizenship and equal protection under the law.

Consolidation and Corporate Capitalism

The Union victory not only affirmed Myth of America identity; it also ignited an age of industrialization that unleashed economic and social upheaval. The massive Union war effort brought not just the defeat of the South, "but the defeat of the whole Southern economic and political system, and the triumph of a state-fostered industrial and financial complex in the North."[5] The Civil War thus ushered in precisely what the Jeffersonians and Jacksonians had sought to avoid through "anxious aggrandizement" and expansion of slavery— high tariffs, subsidies for internal improvements, a national banking system, and other aspects of consolidated federal power. The American system approach to national expansion, championed by Quincy Adams and Henry Clay but fought off by Jackson and John C. Calhoun in the antebellum years, triumphed in the Civil War.[6]

Although hegemonic discourse persistently affirms the shibboleths of laissez-faire, unprecedented Union borrowing and government purchasing ignited the industrial age. During the Civil War, as in the world wars of the twentieth century, the federal government burgeoned to previously unfathomable proportions, culminating in a $1.2 billion budget in 1865. The first truly national currency, national banking system, prolific federal borrowing, new taxes, and protective tariffs spurred unprecedented wartime production that carried over into postwar industrial growth. With the government as the largest purchaser, the iron, textiles, shoe, and meatpacking industries took off during the war. Massive military contracts and orders fueled dynamic postwar urbanization and business growth, especially in burgeoning Midwest cities. Heavy Union wartime investment in railroads spurred the dominant industry of the industrial era. Banking, investment, steel, and other industries flourished as they financed and built more than two hundred thousand miles of railroad track by 1893, compared to thirty-five thousand at the end of the Civil War.[7]

The legacy of the Civil War ultimately affirmed a pattern evident throughout U.S. history: there was no business like war business. The relationship between war and economic growth, though typically elided by nationalist discourse, richly informs the modern history of the United States. War fueled the industrial economy and gave rise to vast fortunes in the hands of economic elites who orchestrated corporate consolidation. Huge profits flowed into relatively few hands, as John D. Rockefeller (oil), Andrew Carnegie (steel), Gustavus Swift (meat packing), and Henry Havermeyer (sugar), among several others, employed vertical and horizontal integration, destroyed competition, repressed labor, and skirted pathetic attempts at government regulation through bribes, lobbies, trusts, and holding companies.

Minimized in history through the trope of panics, the two lacerating depressions of the industrial era created massive disruption and debilitating consequences radiating throughout the economy. The crash of 1873 forced closure of the New York Stock Exchange for ten days, railroad stock plummeted by 60 percent, and thousands of businesses went bankrupt, producing widespread unemployment. The depression of the 1890s was even worse.

The depressions underscored that the self-regulating market was, as Karl Polanyi brilliantly explained in his classic work, "a stark utopia." Absent direction, manipulation, and oversight, the economy would function haphazardly and ineffectually. Hegemonic forces thus exploit the market in pursuit of self-interest, with sufficient trickle-down effect to maintain social stability while warding off government regulatory intervention. "Laissez-faire was not a method to achieve a thing," Polanyi explains, "it was the thing to be achieved."[8]

Liberals and reformers invariably affirmed Myth of America identity and thus proved powerless to challenge the corporate consolidation and cultural hegemony. By perpetuating the myth that political freedom, civil rights (for white men), and the rule of law would ensure a just society, "liberals played a critical role in legitimating corporate capitalism and politically insulating it from democratic challenge," Nancy Cohen explains. Polanyi was even more blunt in referencing "liberals, whose minds habitually missed the true characteristics of the world they were living in."[9]

Social Darwinist and laissez-faire discourse provided "a rather unsubtle justification of existing hierarchies of wealth and power."[10] Weak presidencies and ineffectual reforms characterized the era. Corporate attorneys brushed aside such putative reforms as the Interstate Commerce Commission (1887) and the Sherman Antitrust Act (1890). The Pendleton Act (1883) gave halting start to civil service reform, yet its attack on local political elites such as city bosses served to check the power of the men whose machines often delivered jobs and a degree of empowerment to the underclass.

The industrial era produced a dramatic disparity of wealth tied in with the rigid racial, class, and gender hierarchies of Gilded Age society. Seven-eighths of all families controlled only one-eighth of national wealth. In 1889, seven-tenths of national wealth belonged to one three-hundredth of the population, comprising a permanent upper class.[11]

Immigration as Legitimizing Discourse

In the national narrative of immigration, historical disavowal plays a critical cultural role in affirming Myth of America identity. Well before the Revolution, future Founding Fathers such as Franklin and Jefferson expressed fears that nonwhite and non—English speaking immigrants would undermine American homogeneity. In so doing they engaged in historical amnesia by failing to acknowledge that they themselves were the immigrant invaders of the continent. The patriotic narrative of immigration obscured continuous xenophobic reactions, from the Revolutionary era through the nativist outburst beginning in the 1840s. Nativism has not been completely repressed in nationalist discourse but rather has been depicted as an aberration and thus "is almost never acknowledged as a driving force behind much of the nation's immigration policy."[12]

Despite the two Gilded Age depressions the dynamic industrial economy created jobs, luring a massive influx of new workers. That 23.5 million new immigrants, mostly young men from eastern and Mediterranean Europe, entered the country between 1880 and 1921 suggests that the nation did indeed prove hospitable to the "huddled masses." At the same time, however, the discourse elides the duality of a history of xenophobia as well as xenophilia.

Chinese sojourners in the second half of the nineteenth century neatly capture the duality of foreign immigration policy. Industrial capitalism welcomed the Chinese "coolies" for the cheap labor they provided in constructing the western railroads before nativists turned on "the treacherous, almond-eyed sons of Confucius" and summarily cut off immigration under the Chinese Exclusion Act (1882). Chinese, who comprised 90 percent of the Central Pacific Railroad workforce, did most of the backbreaking labor of laying track across the Sierras, only to encounter racial violence and demands for their expulsion from the country. "We do not let the Indian stand in the way of civilization so why let the Chinese barbarian?" observed the New York governor and onetime presidential candidate Horatio Seymour. President Rutherford B. Hayes also linked the "pernicious" Chinese "labor invasion" with "our experience in dealing with the weaker races—the Negroes and Indians."

In the face of such a virulent discursive barrage, the "heathen Chinee" of Bret Harte's popular poem did not stand "a Chinaman's chance" within U.S. culture. "No matter how good a Chinaman may be," advice columns warned, "ladies never leave their children with them, especially little girls." Using gendered discourse to demean the Chinese, the California governor in 1869 averred, "We ought not to desire an effete population of Asiatics."[13]

As the exclusionary immigration law drove out the "rat-eating Chinaman," Mexican-Americans assumed many of the onerous labors, such as mining and road building, associated with "winning the West." Though many Mexican-Americans assimilated or resisted effectively, discriminatory "greaser laws" and violence rendered them second-class citizens through much of the West and Southwest. "Bereft of political power, subject to a capricious system of justice, and pushed off private and communal lands," David Weber notes, "they had truly become foreigners in their native land."[14]

While the nation celebrates itself for opening its arms—as powerfully represented by the Statue of Liberty and by Emma Lazarus's poetic allusion to "your tired, your poor, your huddled masses yearning to breathe free"—the reference to "wretched refuse" in the next line hints at the xenophobic reception that greeted many immigrants. The "native" and predominantly white labor force, plagued by the constant threat of unemployment, often rallied against the threat of competition from cheap immigrant labor.

Opened in 1892 as a modernist immigrant-processing station, New York's Ellis Island reflected a shift from raw nativism to the application of medicalized disciplinary knowledge to incoming immigrants. Ellis Island was not merely an open-armed receiving station for the huddled masses, but a laboratory of inspecting, testing, probing, drugging, and accepting and rejecting immigrants.[15]

The Specter of Radicalism

Industrialization required that most of the immigrants gain entry into the country yet shuddered over the menacing European ideas of unionism, socialism, and anarchism that many brought with them. Cultural containment of these radical threats prevailed throughout the industrial era. During the Civil War troops fresh from Gettysburg arrived in New York City to put down worker unrest, fused with anticonscription rioting, in what remains the largest urban uprising in U.S. history. Although the Union went to war under the discursive banner of "free labor, free men," in actuality it linked labor unrest with unpatriotic disunity in wartime, a legacy that allowed industrialists "to wrap their burgeoning power in the bunting of patriotism." The Lincoln administration suffused suspension of habeas corpus, the demand for loyalty oaths, arbitrary arrests, and suppression of publications with a discourse of preserving freedom—a model adopted by future wartime governments into the twenty-first century.[16]

Myth of America discourse condemned organized labor as radical collectivization in violation of the laws of modern political economy. Labor combinations, as they were called, were unnatural and had to be contained, whereas corporate consolidation represented progress and the natural and inevitable evolution of modern society. In the wake of the Paris Commune of 1871, labor resistance could now be labeled communistic or anarchistic and a threat to patriotic unity rather than being perceived as an effort to redress the overweening power of corporate capital and the widening disparity of wealth. The "red spectre of the commune" often appeared discursively linked with the persistent threat of "Negro riots" or Indian uprisings that threatened to turn the prairies "crimson" with the blood of innocent settlers.[17]

Hegemonic discourse equating organized labor with subversion enabled management to win virtually all the major struggles of the era. Already weakened by the crash of 1873, which put men out of work and thus deprived labor of money to organize, labor lost in the Great Strike of 1877, the first attempt at a nationwide walkout in U.S. history. In the same year that Northern armies withdrew from the South, granting home rule, the government employed troops to put down the riot and delivered a major setback to labor. The Haymarket affair a decade later, which included a bomb explosion, undermined labor in the minds of the middle class and ushered in the almost complete triumph of corporate capitalist hegemony. While the *New York Times* denounced strikes as "combination[s] against long established laws," Americans sided overwhelmingly with management when it employed Pinkerton strikebreakers from Pittsburgh to Coeur d'Alene. As another paper editorialized, in a revealing blending of race and class anxieties, "If the master race of this continent is subordinated to or overrun with the communistic and revolutionary races, it will be in grave dangers of social disaster."[18]

Nothing symbolized the cultural hegemony driving the containment of radicalism better than federal invocation of the Sherman Antitrust Act—a failed effort to regulate *corporate* power—to halt the Pullman strike in Chicago in 1894. Some two thousand troops and five thousand federal marshals put down what was referred to as a rebellion fomented by the lower classes. The union organizer Eugene "Dictator" Debs, who had offered to end the strike if workers were given their jobs back, spent six months in prison, from which he emerged a dedicated socialist. Debs lost an appeal to the Supreme Court, which ruled that "the strong arm of the government may be put forth to brush away all obstructions to the freedom of interstate commerce."[19]

Hegemonic discourse condemned organized labor and made its repression the single exception to the nation's virulent opposition to state intervention in the marketplace. Management authority over workers, like God's supervision of man, had been ordained by nature. "Strikes began with Genesis," one management official explained. "Cain was the first striker and he killed Abel because Abel was the more prosperous fellow." "Agitators" had no right to speak for workers, whose needs would be provided for by the "Christian men to whom God in His infinite wisdom has given the control of the property interests of the country."[20]

Farmers suffered an even more decisive political defeat than laborers under industrialization, a process that culminated in the pivotal presidential election of 1896. Before deciding on "fusion" with William Jennings Bryan and the Democrats, Populists had won several local and state campaigns and threatened to become a viable third party, one that sought to rein in railroad, banker, and corporate power in the interests of debt relief and higher income for farmers and workers. The Republican urban industrial constituency viewed the

Populist Democrats, as they did the radical workers, as a menace to the new order of sound money and progress in the midst of the worst depression to that point in the nation's history. Corporatist Republicans triumphed under William McKinley in 1896 and held the presidency for twenty-eight of the next thirty-six years.

Whiteness and Masculine Solidarity

The nation's identity-driven exaltation of whiteness drove the marginalization of farmers, workers, women, and immigrants. Absent reunion between northern and southern white males, the renewal of imperial foreign policy in the 1890s would not have been possible. National identity thus shattered the promise of Reconstruction through the revival of a master race discourse that simultaneously obscured class and income hierarchies among white men. In order fully to reconstitute Myth of America identity after the Civil War, white men from the South had to be reincorporated within the imagined national community. At the same time, white supremacy precluded the threat of a coalition of blacks and poor whites in the South rising as a challenge to Bourbon-Redeemer hegemony.

Cultural hegemony framed advocates of black equality as a radical Republican minority. The *Cincinnati Enquirer* captured popular sentiment with the pithy, yet chilling observation at the Civil War's end: "Slavery is dead, the Negro is not. There is the misfortune." Those who sought to transcend the culturally constructed barriers of race met with resistance, often violent, and ultimately their efforts sank beneath a great swell of white supremacist discourse. "The slave went free; stood for a brief moment in the sun; then moved back again toward slavery," as W. E. B. Du Bois put it.[21]

In a remarkable testament to the power of representation, the national narrative that forged reunion represented postwar Reconstruction as a phenomenon that had victimized *whites*. The Reconstruction myths, which prevailed as the nation's usable past until the 1960s, anchored the sectional reconciliation rooted in whiteness. Widespread northern acceptance of the Reconstruction myths, which centered on "black rule" over the downtrodden Confederacy and simultaneous exploitation by northern carpetbaggers and southern scalawags, all accomplished under a pitiless Yankee occupation, reaffirmed the United States as a white man's country.[22]

The psychic crisis of the 1890s reinvigorated American identity through racial othering. During this decade massive African American disfranchisement occurred in concert with the establishment of the Jim Crow system of legalized segregation in the South. Pronounced phobias projecting violence and rapaciousness onto African Americans spurred an upsurge of racial violence in the 1890s, as white mobs lynched at least one thousand African Americans, typically in front of cheering crowds amassed to witness the beating, burning, genital mutilation, dismemberment, and various other tortures that accompanied these cultural rituals. "Even by American standards it was a troubled time in American race relations," Paul T. McCartney observes.[23]

The triumph of Jim Crow underscored the essential continuity of racial modernity. The African American other—as well as the Indian, ethnic, female, and radical other—naturalized the discourse equating whiteness with Americanness, bridging the sectional divide and paving the way for the revival of imperialism.

The massive fallout from the Civil War raised the specter not only of racial equality but also of women's rights, which in some ways constituted an even more palpable threat insofar as women, unlike African Americans, outnumbered men. The Civil War apotheosized male honor and "warrior patriotism," gendered discourses that exalted men while marginalizing women. "White Civil War women achieved at best mixed success in their progress toward the emancipatory goals," Drew Gilpin Faust concluded. Feminists and suffragists of the era, including Susan B. Anthony and Elizabeth Cady Stanton, argued that the war had "created a revolution in woman herself," but the calculated exclusion of women from the Fifteenth Amendment's expanded constitutional guarantee of voting rights demonstrated that patriarchy remained arguably more deeply ensconced than racial modernity, as even black men received de jure voting rights still denied to women. Moreover, the separate sphere embodied in the "cult of domesticity" contained women culturally while perpetuating the English common law tradition of "civil death" with respect to legal and political rights.[24]

God and Country

The postbellum agenda of national reconciliation, grounded in reaffirmation of America as the white man's country, received critical support from the pulpit. Echoing Alexis de Tocqueville, the Briton James Bryce found through his Gilded Age travels that "Christianity is in fact understood to be, though not the legally established religion, yet the national religion."[25]

During the Civil War, the profoundly religious Lincoln left a deep imprint on the national consciousness by linking the "salvation" of the Union—a "new birth of freedom . . . under God"—with providential destiny. As the war continued, Northern Christians came to view abolition as divinely ordained. The assassination of Lincoln provided a martyr, a veritable Christian saint for the Union cause. Adding to the aura of the tragic event, the assassination occurred on Good Friday, "the slaying of the second Father of our Republic on the anniversary of the day on which He was slain."[26]

Also affirming Christianity at the core of identity was Thanksgiving, made an official holiday during the Civil War. Thanksgiving was "exclusively an American day," noted the *New York Times,* a national holiday that affirmed that God had overseen the survival of the Pilgrims and the birth of a New Israel on North American shores. Thanksgiving mythology depicted harmonious relations between the European settlers and Indians, who had helped the Pilgrims to find food, thus eliding ethnic cleansing. "God bless America" became a common invocation in prayer and public ceremony while the "Battle Hymn of the Republic" ("Glory, Glory Hallelujah") linked the Lord with the eventual Union triumph. During the Civil War Congress voted to imprint the motto "In God We Trust" onto the nation's coins, reaffirmation for all citizens of the "special relationship [that] existed between their nation and their God."[27]

The Civil War thus affirmed righteous violence while strengthening the bonds fusing national and providential destiny. Tens of thousands of African Americans had long since embraced Christianity, a religion, after all, founded by victims of Roman oppression, and now the jubilee of abolition could be interpreted as deliverance to the biblical Promised Land. The defeated Confederacy could also relate to powerful Christian traditions of affinity for the downtrodden and of martyrdom.

While scores of Christian missionaries offered typically paternalist support and assistance to freed slaves, Protestantism remained sutured to whiteness. Prominent northern antebellum antislavery proponents, including Henry Ward Beecher and his more famous sister, the author Harriet Beecher Stowe, "implored northern audiences to forget past sectional strife, to forgive former Confederates for the war, and to forge a new sense of national solidarity with southern whites." Beecher's acquiescence to Jim Crow was so forthright as to prompt Frederick Douglass to vow that if "Mr. Beecher were my slave, and I had a rawhide, I could take this opinion out of him in less than a half an hour."

Dwight L. Moody, a former shoe salesman turned evangelist and architect of the Third Great Awakening in the 1870s, preached "the gospel of reconciliation" before millions of citizens, often at segregated revival camps. Beecher and Moody were merely the most prominent of "a coterie of white Protestant leaders joined together to authorize and sanctify the northern embrace of southern whites." The Women's Christian Temperance Union (WCTU), which became the largest women's organization in the country (it had almost two hundred thousand members by 1900), embraced sobriety and suffrage but not racial tolerance. WCTU leaders often demonized the black, ethnic, and Catholic other to promote their divinely ordained causes, thus affirming the glorification of whiteness.[28]

A national patriotic boom followed by a "splendid little war" in 1898 capped off the era of reconciliation and revival. In the last two decades of the nineteenth century a fervid new regime of patriotic representation emerged, as manifested in a new cult of the American flag and reverence for national holidays, historic sites, national monuments, symbols, songs, sermons, prayers, hymns, paeans, parades, fairs, speeches, ceremonies, reunions, and social organizations. These pervasive cultural phenomena synthesized a common national identity and established boundaries as to acceptable, and thus also unacceptable, ways of viewing origins, history, values, attitudes, and modes of behavior within the imagined community. Ritual and culture provided disciplinary knowledge, which was internalized by the public, and reinforced a staunchly patriotic nationalist worldview. After traveling across the nation, Charles Dudley Warner observed in 1889, "For the past ten years there has been growing in this country a stronger feeling of nationality, a distinct American historic consciousness."[29]

The patriotic boom fostered "an ideology of sameness and an ideology of obligation." The Grand Army of the Republic (GAR), organized to memorialize the Union victory and sacrifice, became an instrument of national patriotism. The GAR drove the agenda that established Memorial Day, formerly Commemoration Day, as a national holiday in the years immediately following the Civil War. The South embraced Memorial Day as an opportunity to honor the Confederate dead while simultaneously opposing Reconstruction and the emancipation legacy. Monuments evocative of the Lost Cause sprang up throughout the South. Monument building, statuary, and cemetery memorials flourished across the country in the two generations following the Civil War. Gradually, these material manifestations fostered a common, rather than regional, sacred identity, bringing North and South together, a process that culminated at Gettysburg in 1913 as fifty-three thousand aged Confederate and

Union veterans met at the epic battlefield site in common commemoration. Excluded, African American soldiers held a smattering of "separate but equal" Union veteran and Emancipation Proclamation commemorations.

Nothing illustrated the national patriotic revival better than the cult of the flag. The GAR as well as both the Sons and the Daughters of the American Revolution proved instrumental in spreading national reverence for Old Glory. These groups, joined by a new American Flag Association, practiced and promoted public singing of the "Star-Spangled Banner," backed laws in several states that criminalized misuse or abuse of the flag, and made flying of the flag mandatory on warships, at military installations, and in classrooms and outside of schools and public buildings across the country. The GAR acquired and distributed flags to ensure that "the national colors adorned the desk of every principal of every public school."[30]

Fetishistic rituals affirming patriotism displaced anxieties and forged unity within postbellum society. "Nationalism takes shape through the visible, ritual organization of fetish objects—flags, uniforms, airplane logos, maps, anthems, national flowers, national cuisines and architectures as well as through the organization of collective fetish spectacle—in team sports, military displays, mass rallies, the myriad forms of popular culture," Lauren Berlant explains. Through compulsive displacement of anxieties onto the "impassioned objects," the fetish offers a sense of control, relief, and community.[31]

Through ritual and fetish the nation-state—though invisible, intangible, and ultimately imagined—exercised a powerful hold on national consciousness. Rituals included the singing of the national anthem and "My Country 'Tis of Thee" with hats off and hands held over hearts; ceremonial presentation of the flag (folding, unfurling, raising, etc.); commemoration of Flag Day; and common public recitation of the Pledge of Allegiance (written in the early 1890s).[32]

The "renaissance of patriotism" not only bridged the sectional divide but also internalized Myth of America identity within the minds of the millions of new immigrants. "Native" citizens noted that the newly arrived Europeans possessed "neither the language nor traditions nor habits nor political institutions nor morals in common with us." Immigrants could scarcely escape being swept up by the patriotic culture, however, as its rituals served the purpose of "acquainting our adopted citizens with the fact that we have a body of traditions and attaching them to those traditions."[33]

The patriotic boom thus facilitated unity within a sharply more diverse, dynamic, and mobile society as the United States transitioned from localized "island communities" into an integrated, modern industrial nation. Heritage and myth played an increasingly important role in affirming American identity, as government and private groups displayed unprecedented commitment to such historic sites as Plymouth Rock, Mount Vernon, Bunker Hill, and the Hermitage, along with Gettysburg and other Civil and Revolutionary War battlefields. The Washington Monument, completed in the late 1880s, preceded turn-of-the-century national park "monumentalism," as spectacular natural sites, particularly in the West, also became part of a distinct national community.[34]

"Winning" the West

Nothing was more American than ethnic cleansing of Indians, which culminated in the West during the industrial era. While the crisis over slavery had once threatened national expansion, the Union triumph removed all obstacles and replaced them with incentives, such as the Homestead Act of 1862 and unprecedented mobility for settlement through the burgeoning railroad network.

Not even the most powerful Indians, the Sioux of the Northern Plains, could hope to withstand the identity-driven quest to win the West. Even the high point of Indian resistance, in 1876 at Little Big Horn, served only to reignite the exterminationist impulse. Prior to Little Big Horn, Christian humanitarianism had spurred President Ulysses S. Grant's "peace policy," which approached the Indians of the Great Plains and Rocky Mountain region "with a Sharp's Carbine in one hand and a Bible in the other." The peace policy confronted Indians with an ultimatum: retreat to the least desirable land, set aside for reservations, whose administration was rife with corruption and inefficiency, or face destruction. When Indians resisted, Civil War veterans like the ironically named William Tecumseh Sherman (who had some experience with this style of warfare) pledged to "prosecute the war with vindictive earnestness against all hostile Indians until they are obliterated or beg for mercy."[35]

Embracing the noble savage stereotype, General George A. Custer admired Indians' "proud majesty" but also viewed them as "cruel and ferocious" vermin who "infested" the Plains. His Seventh Cavalry had already conducted a campaign of indiscriminate murder and mutilation at a village called Washita, an incident similar to the infamous Sand Creek massacre of Cheyenne men, women, and children in the eastern Colorado territory in 1864. Whites were not alone in their willingness to commit atrocities in the race war, as Indians proved by slaughtering 462 Minnesota settlers in 1862 and as Sitting Bull demonstrated in his reception of the Seventh Cavalry. The general's Crow scouts, who were well aware of the bellicosity of the Sioux, pleaded with Custer to turn back, but he drove his army into the Little Bighorn valley in the Black Hills on June 25, 1876. The bodies of the 265 cavalrymen were found on a hillside, stripped naked, mutilated, their hearts staked to poles.

Custer's "last stand" constituted the Pearl Harbor or September 11 of the Gilded Age generation and elicited the same paroxysms of regenerative violence those events would unleash against the nation's savage enemy-others. Bold headline news of the western "MASSACRE" stunned the nation and, salting the wound, marred patriotic celebration in the centennial year. The Sioux victory constituted an incomprehensible assault on mythical culture: savagery over civilization, red over white, satanic evil over Christian good.[36] Little Bighorn belied the representation of *Rescue,* the Horatio Greenough sculpture placed on the Capitol steps in 1853, depicting a towering frontiersman subduing a tomahawk-wielding Indian while a woman and child cower in the background (see fig. 1).

Only a wave of regenerative violence could reassert the triumphant meta-narrative of progress inherent in Myth of America identity. The *Richmond Enquirer,* among countless such editorials, called for a "war of extermination," noting that whenever a "barbarous and uncivilized race comes into constant contact with a supreme and civilized one, the inferior . . . passes out of existence."[37] A series of Supreme Court decisions followed in the Jefferson—Jackson tradition of stripping Indians of both millions of acres of land as well as due process. Other newspapers and prominent individuals linked the Sioux with "dangerous classes" of labor radicals and the "communistic" Molly Maguires, who mounted a guerrilla resistance to the brutal working conditions in the nation's mines and coalfields.

Indian conquest culminated militarily after Little Bighorn: bureaucratically with the General Allotment Act of 1887; and symbolically at Wounded Knee, South Dakota, in 1890. The Allotment, or Dawes Act, perceived as humanitarian reform, compelled all Indians, regardless of their cultural diversity, to end their "nomadic barbarism" by moving onto individual 160-acre plots provided to male heads of households. The assimilationist efforts amounted to an internal colonialism that complemented segregation of African Americans. Some Indians embraced assimilation but most echoed the words of one Sioux, who averred, "We can talk and work and go to school like white people but we will still be Indians." Some in Congress sniffed out the underlying effect of the allotment program—freeing up "surplus" Indian land for sale. The Colorado senator and former interior secretary Henry Teller declared the Dawes Act should have been entitled, "A bill to despoil the Indians of their lands and make them vagabonds on the face of the earth." Finally, at Wounded Knee, fighting erupted as soldiers attempted to disarm a Sioux band, ending with the slaughter of 150 Indians, at least a third of whom were women and children, along with 25 cavalry deaths. As the armed struggle over the continent between the Euro-Americans and the indigenous population at last came to an end, the Indian population had fallen to a low of some 250,000—perhaps 100,000 fewer than when the Civil War began.[38]

Female reformers like Helen Hunt Jackson, the author of the classic *Century of Dishonor* (1881), might be expected to bemoan Indian conquest, but men who did so risked being dismissed through gendered tropes as "squaw men." Women were active in missionary and educational work among Indians but scarcely influenced national policy, considered beyond woman's proper domestic sphere. Under Myth of America hegemony, women, Indians, African Americans, Mexican Americans, southeastern European immigrants, and Asians had a common status—separate and unequal.

The Imperial Wars

The cultural work of national reconciliation, conjoined with the psychic anxieties of the industrial era, left the United States poised to launch the imperial wars. The trope imperial wars offers a more inclusive referent than *Spanish-American War* for a conflict that embroiled the United States and Spain, but also Cuba, Puerto Rico, Hawaii, Guam, Samoa, and the Philippine archipelago.

Rather than constituting a "new diplomacy" replacing an "old" or "isolationist" foreign policy, the imperial wars constituted a *revival* of the identity-driven interventionist paradigm that had been derailed by the sectional crisis and the tumult of industrialization. Having failed to provoke a foreign war to head off the Civil War, Seward had tried to pick up where Manifest Destiny left off as he envisioned annexation of Canada, Cuba, Greenland, Haiti, Hawaii, Iceland, the Dominican Republic, and the Virgin Islands. Seward ultimately achieved only a portion of his ambitious diplomatic agenda, but the portion was large, namely, Alaska, which he purchased in 1867 for $7.2 million but only after, in the spirit of the times, paying substantial bribes to both Russians and U.S. congressmen.

Fear of racial amalgamation, memories of Confederate-style filibusterism, and the Grant administration scandals precluded any hope for a quick revival of Manifest Destiny. Public revelation of the scandals "tarnished expansion" and precluded pursuit of Seward's broader imperial agenda. In 1870, the Senate rejected a Grant administration treaty annexing Santo Domingo (as the Dominican Republic was then called), denounced by critics as a "filibustering project" that would undermine the purity of the white republic. James G. Blaine, who served as secretary of state in the 1880s and again in the 1890s, was the leading Republican internationalist after Seward, and he vigorously pursued an expansionist agenda, but the Civil War legacy of the "bloody shirt" and other postwar dislocations hamstrung most of his efforts.[39]

Asia-Pacific expansion received broad support from traders, missionaries, and naval power advocates, all of whom were imbued with visions of Myth of America destiny. Fervent Protestants, perceiving a personal and national mission to save souls across the globe, traversed the Pacific. "A nation with the truth of God, a nation in covenant with God," intoned the Reverend David Gregg, "that is what the world needs for the true peace and progress and good of all nations." Commander Matthew C. Perry, commanding a fleet of smoke-belching "Black Ships," informed the "weak and semi-barbarous" people of Japan that it was God's will that they open trade with the United States. The number of U.S. missionaries in China climbed from 513 in 1889 to some 1,300 in 1905. Trade with China and Korea grew while exports to Japan alone tripled from 1894 to 1897.[40]

There being still only minimal foreign investment in China, the Open Door reflected not the drive for capitalist expansion so much as an opportunity backed by the considerable missionary community in the "Orient" to spread Americanism around the globe. The benign trope of an Open Door elided identity-driven imperial ambition. Delivered to fellow Western moderns in 1899 and 1900, the Open Door diplomatic notes sought to preclude the European imperialists from closing the door into China before the United States could assert its own identity in Asia.

The United States thus competed with the "white" European nations in a modernist imperial thrust to lay claim to the nonindustrial tricontinental world of Asia, Africa, and Latin America. In the century following the 1815 Concert of Vienna, direct European control expanded from 35 percent to 85 percent of the earth's landed space. The industrial revolution laid the foundation for global colonialism, as the new era of steel, oil, and modern finance capitalism drove the quest for natural resources, markets, and coaling stations for naval and merchant ships and offered sites for spreading Christianity, acting out desire, and manifesting prestige.

While condemning Old World European aggression, the United States pursued hegemony in Latin America. Frequently attacking a continuing British presence in the hemisphere, the United States withdrew its prior support for joint construction of a trans-isthmian canal and made various plans to proceed unilaterally with the project. In a sharp dispute over the border between Venezuela and British Guiana in 1895, the administration of Grover Cleveland revealed the remarkable breadth of the U.S. hegemonic vision in a message to Whitehall, which read in part, "Today the United States is practically sovereign on this continent [South America], and its fiat is law upon the subjects to which it confines its interposition."

Myth of America identity still fostered belligerence toward Great Britain, a phenomenon known as "pulling the lion's tail," but increasingly the shared, albeit mythical, Anglo-Saxon racial superiority spurred the English-speaking nations toward rapprochement. Despite high tensions during the Civil War, London had declined to recognize the Confederacy. The United States and Britain thus avoided conflict and began jointly to assume the "white man's burden" of establishing hegemony over darker-skinned subaltern peoples across the globe. The British approved the subsequent U.S. war with Spain while the United States backed the British Raj in India and the Boer War in South Africa. "The downfall of the British Empire I should regard as a calamity to the race and especially to this country," Theodore Roosevelt declared in 1899.[41]

Secretary of State Richard Olney's assertion that the United States was "practically sovereign on this continent" revived "traditional Canadian fears" of Yankee hegemony. In the midst of a border dispute in 1896–97 following the discovery of gold in the Yukon Territory, Senator Henry Cabot Lodge dismissed the Canadians as a "collection of bumptious provincials." Roosevelt asserted that his nation "regards the Canadian with the good-natured condescension always felt by the free man for the man who is not free." Diplomacy resolved the border dispute (in Washington's favor) between the "good natured" and fellow white, mostly Protestant "cousins."[42]

Choosing War

As in the case of the Oregon Treaty in 1846, the United States thus found a modus vivendi with British imperialism while choosing war with the more vulnerable Catholic Spaniards ensconced in nearby Cuba. A declining empire, Spain had weathered the ten-year Cuba Libre struggle from 1868 to 1878. Confronted with renewed guerrilla resistance in the late nineties, Madrid responded with a brutal policy of *reconcentración* of the population into prison camps. In New York especially, the competing "yellow press" offered sensational accounts of Cuban brutalities, reflecting a militant national identity and the revival of Manifest Destiny aggression. On February 15, 1898, an explosion tore apart the battleship *Maine,* killing 265 sailors.

Long conditioned by patriotic culture to Remember the Alamo, militants now urged the public to "Remember the *Maine,* to hell with Spain." Without questioning why the warship was provocatively moored in Havana harbor, the press and public overwhelmingly assumed Spanish culpability, ignoring the possibility that the ship's bituminous coal bins may have ignited from internal causes. (The precise cause of the *Maine* explosion, whether a bomb or an internal mishap, remains disputed.)

Discourses fusing gender, race, and providential destiny permeated the ensuing drive to war. Obsessed with manhood, honor, and chivalry, "jingoes" (a British euphemism to avoid blasphemous utterance of Jesus) sought a cathartic war. They affirmed manhood by calling on the nation to save the Cuban damsel from her Spanish ravisher. By feminizing Cuba, gendered discourse underscored the inherent weakness of women, who were subject either to domination or liberation under male authority, thus helping to contain the New Woman at home. As would often occur in wartime, gendered language thus reified patriarchal hegemony on the home front.

Jingoists, led by the inimical Roosevelt, perceived the United States as having passed through adolescence and at last arrived at the time to "put aside childish things and assume the functions of manhood." Roosevelt combined northeastern aristocracy, which made him an effective spokesman for advancing civilization, with an overdetermined cowboy manliness, which enabled him to exalt violent aggression in the conquest of new frontiers. Having famously overcome his own exaggerated asthmatic youth through manly pursuits "out West," Roosevelt glorified the "strenuous life" and the nation's "lusty youth." Profoundly concerned that the improvements of everyday living in the industrial era had rendered the country soft, Roosevelt lusted for war, which he later described as "a great thing" because it "brought us a higher manhood."[43] "Idleness and luxury have made men flabby," the *North American Review* asserted, and "a great war might help them to pull themselves together."[44] Prominent jingoes such as Albert Beveridge concurred, declaring that war would provide "millions of young Americans with a virile manhood." The war even brought forth a "flurry of enthusiasm for masculinizing images of Jesus."[45]

The gendered discourse placed intense pressure on McKinley to choose war over diplomacy with Spain. When McKinley kept diplomatic lines open after the *Maine,* including the possibility of peaceful mediation, critics called into question his "backbone."[46] The *New York Journal* looked for "any signs, however faint, of manhood in the White House." Charging McKinley with pursuing a "weak, ineffectual, pusillanimous policy," the *Chicago Tribune* declared, "The people want no disgraceful negotiations with Spain." Newspapers and congressmen received thousands of letters from belligerent citizens. "I wish to God we had a [*sic*] Andy Jackson" in the White House, one of them declared. "The debate over [McKinley's] backbone shows that gendered ideas about leadership limited the range of politically viable options available to him," Kristin L. Hoganson explains.[47] Ultimately, "The Major" realized that taking charge of foreign policy was the only way to ensure that he would not become another in the long series of ineffectual Gilded Age presidents. By grasping, however haltingly, the significance of foreign policy, McKinley laid claim to the imperial presidency and would soon begin to censor dissemination of news from the battlefield.

As the United States moved toward mounting a war against them, the Spanish agreed to end the odious *reconcentrado* and declare an armistice with the Cuban rebels. Madrid soon realized, however, that nothing less than humiliating withdrawal and capitulation, and possibility not even that, would satisfy the Yankee militants. As on numerous other occasions—1846, 1964, and 2003, for example—the United States actively pursued war. With the jingoists clamoring to "wipe out the stain Spain has put on our Flag," the House voted overwhelmingly for war in April 1898, but the count was only 42–35 in the Senate, foreshadowing the subsequent anti-imperialist movement. Ritualistic patriotic unity prevailed at the time, however, as the Congress stood as one and sang the "Battle Hymn of the Republic."

The drive to affirm national identity rallied not only jingoists but also humanitarians, who championed the nation's destiny to save Cuba from a decadent European empire. The margin in the Senate would have been even narrower, and the measure might possibly have failed, in the absence of an amendment by Senator Teller in which the United States renounced any plans to annex Cuba. By pledging that Cuba would be liberated and turned over to "its people," the Teller Amendment won over senators who insisted they wanted to help the Cubans but not to engage in imperialism, which they thought to be un-American. Moreover, the amendment satisfied those who saw no place for the racially mixed Cubans under the American flag. Racial modernity thus ignited a humanitarian paternalism as well as deep-seated fears of an amalgamation undermining the purity of the imagined community.

While not oblivious to racial or imperial motives, the usable past of the Spanish-American War has long obscured the extent to which fear of a truly independent Cuba motivated the decision to go to war. Narratives at the time and many since focused on humanitarian motives to liberate Cuba, but beneath the discourse was a U.S. drive for hegemony. An independent Cuba, with a population of 1.6 million people, one-third of African descent, located only ninety miles from Florida, would defy the hegemony inherent in the Monroe Doctrine. Just as the founding patriarchs had rejected independence for the "black republic" of Haiti, racial modernity precluded acceptance of Cuba independent of the civilized hegemony staked out under the Monroe Doctrine.[48]

Less responsive to strategic motives than to the emotional affirmation of national identity through external aggression, most of the public greeted the declaration of war with overwhelming enthusiasm. Just as the volunteers had flowed to Texas to fight in the Mexican War, more than one million men immediately turned out to fight the war against Spain. "It was the apotheosis of patriotism," Secretary of War Russell Alger declared.[49] Communities across the nation prayed, rang church bells, hung out patriotic bunting, and proudly packed their young men off to war.

The stunning news of Admiral George Dewey's destruction of the Spanish fleet in Manila Bay on May 1 electrified the nation. Focusing squarely on the *Maine*, Cuba, and the Spanish general Valeriano "Butcher" Weyler, most Americans undoubtedly did not realize that Spanish colonialism extended to the Philippines, nor could they pinpoint the location of the Southeast Asian archipelago. Ignorance of geography did not dissuade one hundred thousand citizens from pouring into New York's Madison Square for a delirious, impromptu celebration of the nation's arrival as a global power, a display mirrored in other communities across the nation.

Equally ecstatic was Emilio Aguinaldo, the leader of the Philippine insurgency against Spanish colonialism, who promptly declared the archipelago an independent nation "under the protection of the mighty and humane" United States, "the cradle of genuine liberty." Myth of America discourse proved so powerful that even distant rebel leaders like Aguinaldo and, later, Vietnam's Ho Chi Minh held out hope that the language might constitute a genuine reflection of American identity. Aguinaldo declared he had attentively read over the Constitution and had found no "authority for colonies." A U.S. general had reassured him as well, noting, "In 122 years we have established no colonies. I leave you to draw your own inference."[50] Aguinaldo learned a bitter lesson on the workings of discourse, however, as the United States landed twenty-five hundred troops in Manila—the nation's first ever nonwestern military landing—and denied the Philippine rebel any role in taking the Spanish surrender.

While McKinley alluded to "commercial opportunities to which American statesmanship cannot be indifferent," it was the arrival of the nation as a world power that thrilled the president and the public. The celebration of militant national identity led Americans to conclude that not only the Cubans and the Filipinos, but Puerto Ricans, Samoans, and Hawaiians as well were unfit for self-government. "We need Hawaii just as much and a good deal more than we did California," McKinley proclaimed. "It is manifest destiny."[51]

The powerful religious component of national identity drove imperial aggression. "God marked the American people as His chosen to finally lead in the regeneration of the world," Beveridge proclaimed. Under "God's hand," the war had evolved as part of the "eternal movement of the American people toward the mastery of the world." While long recognized as the most outspoken imperialist, the Indiana senator reflected the mainstream, as he well represented the popular Middle American worldview. Millions of citizens doubtless concurred in Admiral Dewey's assessment that "the hand of God" had enabled his triumph in Manila Bay without a single seaman dying in the attack.[52] The entire sixteen-week war against Spain ended with 345 U.S. combat deaths, though 2,565 others perished, mostly from disease.

McKinley himself famously appealed to the nation's missionary impulse with a moving testament to a group of Methodist ministers. Ignoring the fact that the Philippines has been Christianized for centuries, McKinley explained that it had come to him through prayer: "There was nothing else for us to do but to take them all, and to educate the Filipinos, and uplift, and civilize, and Christianize them."

Manifest Destiny thus turned conquest into a benign providential mission, thereby absolving the nation of responsibility for the massive violence that ensued. McKinley depicted his nation as devoid of aggressive inclinations, as he repeatedly emphasized "the responsibility *that has been put upon us*" (emphasis added). "In the providence of God, who works in mysterious ways," McKinley declaimed, "this great archipelago was put into our lap." The public consented to a popular interpretation that the United States, as Roosevelt put it, had "been forced by the exigencies of war to take possession of an alien land" which it would proceed to govern with "disinterested zeal for their progress."[53]

Following the lead of Josiah Strong, whose jeremiad in *Our Country* (1885), became the best-selling text of the era, McKinley seamlessly melded Protestantism and patriotism. "Piety and patriotism go well together," he declared in a New Jersey speech. Discourse linking the nation's destiny with the hand of God permeated McKinley's wartime speeches. "Love of flag, love of country, are not inconsistent with our religious faith," he advised, "and I think we have more love for our country and more people love our flag than ever before."[54]

While tropes of gender, race, and religion permeated national discourse, the imperial wars flowed from a marriage between the imperial moment and the perennial psychic crisis. The sense of crisis resonated among contemporary observers, including Strong, who pronounced the United States the "most nervous" country in the world, and Frederick Jackson Turner, who wondered with the closing of the frontier what would become of the nation's "restless nervous energy." The sources of psychic distress included the long shadow of the sectional crisis; the threats of African American and female advancement; waves of new and more foreign immigrants; labor and urban unrest replete with fears of radicalism, socialism, and anarchism; the angry and emotional Populist revolt; the severely depressed economy of the 1890s; and the closing of the frontier, the fountainhead of national identification.

War—like nothing else—offered cathartic deliverance from national anxieties in the wake of the myriad dislocations of the industrial era. "A bourgeoisie feeling enervated and fearful of lower-class unrest," argues T. J. Jackson Lears, sought "moral regeneration through military adventure." As a Mississippi senator explained on the eve of conflict, a "wholesome war . . . will have a purgatorial effect upon this nation and we will come out of it, like the Phoenix from its ashes, renewed and with glory." The Spanish-American War, David Trask avers, "released pent-up emotions that had been building up among the American people."[55]

Innumerable references confirm that the deep wound the Civil War inflicted *among white men* had at last been healed. The people should be "grateful to God for the reunion between North and South which has been brought by this war," one minister declaimed. "The Civil War is over at last and all its an-

THE CRADLE OF LIBERTY.

4. *The Cradle of Liberty* (1876) by Currier and Ives. The Union victory in the Civil War ultimately affirmed the imagined community and the Myth of America. This lithograph symbolizes the nation's power, patriotism, and justice. Courtesy of the Library of Congress.

tagonisms are forgotten." A Kentucky congressman, referring in charming bluegrass fashion to "the late unpleasantness" of the sectional divide, declared that the people of his commonwealth "will be glad as citizens of a common country to touch elbows with the men of Massachusetts . . . for the honor of our country." New words to an old song reflected the link between the two wars, as people gathered to sing "Hang General Weyler to a Sour Apple Tree as We Go Marching On."

The trope "splendid little war"—advanced by John Hay, who in his capacity as Lincoln's private secretary remembered the Civil War well—underscores the sense of psychic relief. Foreign policy affirmed national identity by projecting and channeling wrenching internal anxieties onto external enemy-others. The war prompted widespread acknowledgment that "imperialist nationalism could be the solvent of social conflict." War offered catharsis, regeneration through violence, patriotic bonding, and emotional reaffirmation of national destiny, under God. Advancing a motif that would become hegemonic in the Cold War—bipartisan foreign policy—a Missouri congressman declared, "Divided we may be, among ourselves, upon questions of domestic policy, as to our relations toward other nations we present an unbroken front."[56]

The imperial wars thus illuminated a pathology embedded within the imagined community: violent external aggression ultimately responded to profound *internal* anxieties. The prominent New South editor Henry Watterson acknowledged that the imperial wars flowed from domestic anxieties but added, "Anything is better than the pace we were going before these present forces were started into life." By engaging in the "exchange of domestic dangers for foreign dangers," Watterson acknowledged, "we risk Caesarism, certainly, but even Caesarism is preferable to anarchism."[57]

The imperial wars reflected continuity with Indian conquest, the Patriotic War, and the invasion of Mexico. The United States *chose* to engage in all of the major nineteenth-century wars, initiating three of them through formal congressional declarations of war. National militancy responded to a high degree of internal anxiety, as the psychic crisis functioned not as an ephemeral phenomenon but rather as a drive inherent within identity.

Mythical discourse drove external violence, which cemented the corporate cultural hegemony that had arisen during the industrial era. With the national community uniting emotionally behind the providential mission of destroying foreign enemies, the internal divisions of region, race, gender, ethnicity, and class could be put aside. The intoxicating discourse of national destiny en-thralled Americans, thus obscuring hierarchies based on wealth, power, race, and gender. By choosing war, the United States carved out the cultural space re-quired to culminate the long ordeal of reunion and to renew the nation's impe-rial identity.

CHAPTER 4

Imperial Crises

W hile the imagined community sought in war cathartic release from myriad internal anxieties, the externally focused fin de siècle violence brought only temporary relief. War functioned like an alcoholic binge, elevating the national mood to unnatural heights, only to produce the inevitable hangover in its aftermath. The "splendid" euphoria of victory gave way to bitter recriminations over the U.S. invasion of the Philippines, which contravened Myth of America discourse depicting the United States as a virtuous beacon of liberty and champion of self-determination. Critics savagely condemned imperialism in the Philippines, inciting a national debate and necessitating development of new, discursively more benign approaches to a yet hegemonic foreign policy. "The more successful we are in making the Filipinos our subjects by force of arms," averred former interior secretary Carl Schurz, "the more will our triumph corrupt our morals, tarnish our honor and undermine our free institutions of government." "What American ever dreamed," an Illinois congressman declaimed, "that within four years of our denunciation of Weylerism in Cuba our generals in the Philippines would be following the notable and brutal methods of that Spanish dictator?"[1]

Despite such criticism, so-called anti-imperialists had so deeply internalized Myth of America identity as to render their opposition contradictory and ultimately ineffectual. Anti-imperialists viewed the imperial wars and especially the Philippine invasion as a fundamentally discontinuous and unAmerican foreign policy that eroded crucial distinctions between the virtuous United States and the corrupt Old World of Europe. Under this frame, the

United States was a noninterventionist republic that advocated self-determination for all while avoiding "entangling alliances." Patriotic discourse thus elided the nation's continuous history of violent aggression and conquest of Indians, slaves, and Mexicans.

In November 1898, six months after Admiral Dewey's triumph in Manila Bay, the Anti-Imperialist League, chartered in Boston, denounced the extension of sovereignty over "foreign territory, without the free consent of the people thereof . . . in violation of constitutional principles, and fraught with moral and physical evils to our people."[2] The league featured such luminaries as Grover Cleveland, Schurz, Andrew Carnegie, Charles Francis Adams, Stanford president David Starr Jordan, and the labor leader Samuel Gompers. Rallying behind the liberating discourses of the Declaration of Independence, the Farewell Address, and Lincoln's eloquent invocations, the league organized in most major cities and collected fifty thousand signatures. Angry, articulate, and skillful at invoking the nation's sacred texts in their behalf, the anti-imperialists proved impossible to ignore.

As the Anti-Imperialist League focused its opposition on the peace treaty with Spain, Emilio Aguinaldo and his Filipino followers—declining to assume their assigned role as "little brown brothers"—took up violent resistance on February 4, 1899. The war with Spain had ended and Hawaii, Guam, Cuba, and Puerto Rico had been effectively assumed, but a bitter guerrilla war in the Philippines had only just begun.

The tropes of rebellion and insurrection—depicting the actual residents of the archipelago as somehow external to their own land—attests to the power of language to create meaning. The war began, Secretary of War Elihu Root explained, when Aguinaldo, "a Chinese half-breed, attacked in vastly superior numbers our little army." Root's racialized depiction of Aguinaldo reversed popular representations of the Filipino leader before the insurrection, when newspapers often described him as a courageous freedom fighter. After the outbreak of fighting, the press no longer described Aguinaldo as white or handsome, and photographs showed him wearing peasant garb rather than a suit, the attire of leaders of civilized countries.

As in Iraq in the twenty-first century, the United States first liberated the country and then asserted it could not leave because the subject people lacked the capacity to govern themselves. Once the "savage" Filipinos had "attacked," a manly nation "cannot withdraw," as one senator explained, and "give over to Manila to loot, pillage, and rape." Noting that the average Filipino male was five feet six inches tall and weighed a mere 125 pounds, imperialists asserted a child-like dependency. Senator Albert Beveridge advised that "in dealing with the Fil-ipinos we deal with children." Editorial cartoons and magazine articles gen-dered the Philippines as a land of "dusky Venuses" who were "sexually desirable, feminine women" who would make "a good wife"—in contrast with the in-creasingly assertive New Woman at home. In short, the United States could not leave the defenseless, childlike, feminized archipelago either on its own or vul-nerable to European colonization. "In the end," McKinley averred, "there was no alternative."[3]

Under the poetic license of Rudyard Kipling's "white man's burden," the United States thus launched an atrocious "savage war for peace." The nation dis-patched 126,468 troops, 4,234 of whom died, as compared with the astonishing slaughter of some 250,000 Filipinos—an estimate that "appears conservative." A lopsided ratio of at least 15 Filipinos killed to every 1 wounded illuminated the homicidal Yankee campaign as "race-making and war-making . . . intimately connected."[4] U.S. commanders, 90 percent of whom were veterans of the Indian wars, issued direct orders to the troops not to take prisoners, thereby enabling, as one Briton in Manila described it, "simple massacre and murderous butchery." Commanders gave orders to "burn and kill the natives" and employ "the fear of God" to break their will to fight. A brigadier general advised his troops "to kill and burn, the more you kill and burn the better you will please me."[5]

Under U.S. cultural perceptions the Filipinos had launched an irrational guerrilla resistance against the advance of civilization and were no longer owed "the restraints that defined civilized war." U.S. soldiers thus sought to "blow every nigger into nigger heaven" and allowed that the islands would not be pacified "until the niggers are killed off like the Indians." Another wrote home, "I am in my glory when I can sight my gun on some dark skin and pull the trig-ger." U.S. soldiers sometimes "hacked to pieces" their victims and "went in and killed every native we met, men, women, and children. It was a dreadful sight." The fighting men "have been relentless," the *Philadelphia Ledger* acknowledged in November 1901, "and have killed to exterminate men, women, and children, prisoners and captives, active insurgents and suspected people, from lads of ten up, an idea prevailing that the Filipino was little better than a dog." "We come as a Christian people to relieve them of the Spanish yoke," an army general wrote to his wife, "and bear ourselves like barbarians." As U.S. soldiers fought a race war on a distant archipelago, white mobs besieged African Americans at home in cities such as Akron, Wilmington, New Orleans, and New York.[6]

U.S. foreign policy thus mirrored the domestic identity from which it sprang. In its savagery the Filipino conflict reflected continuity with the Indian and Mexican wars and foreshadowed an exterminationist style of warfare that would be waged against Japan and in another twentieth-century "savage war for peace" in Indochina. In all cases, the nation sought affirmation of Myth of America identity by conquering racially inferior, heathen foes—whether Algonquians, Apaches, Mexicans, Filipinos, "Japs," or "Viet Cong"—while carrying out the carnage under modernist tropes of spreading civilization, progress, and freedom.

As the "race war" in the Philippines abated, racial classification keyed the occupation as the U.S. "Anglo-Saxons" supervised creation of new provinces that "territorialized race." Occupiers and collaborators "racialized religion" by creating Catholic enclaves that insulated elite Filipinos from their own putatively racially inferior brethren. "Racial formation was the product of intense contestation and dialogue," Paul Kramer explains, "a joint American-Filipino venture situated inside a broader and evolving colonial project."[7]

News of the savage campaign in the Asian archipelago shattered the official discourse of "benevolent assimilation." The Anti-Imperialist League and other critics exploded with rage. "We talk of civilizing lower races, but we have never done it yet," the Yale professor William Graham Sumner declared. "We have exterminated them." The Negrophobe South Carolina senator "Pitchfork" Ben Tillman delighted in the advantages accruing to Dixie, noting that as a result of the "shrouds of murdered Filipinos, done to death because they were fighting for liberty," northern Republicans could no longer "dare to wave the bloody shirt and preach a crusade against the South's treatment of the negro."[8]

Imperialists denied launching an aggressive war, employing tropes of insurrection, rebellion, and even betrayal stemming from the "inbred treachery" of the Filipino bandits. The war thus reflected the "barbarous cruelty among uncivilized races" whose very resistance constituted a "crime against civilization." Discourse focused on Filipino "massacres" while ignoring the far more widespread U.S. atrocities. Americans justified the campaign by comparing it with the nation's long history of warfare against the "merciless Indian savages." William Howard Taft, named imperial governor of the Philippines in 1901, noted that the islands could be subdued and administered "as we govern the Indian tribes."[9]

Myth of America cultural hegemony marginalized anti-imperialists as elite, feminine, and subversive of national destiny. Militant nationalism targeted elitist New England "mugwumps" such as the septuagenarian Massachusetts "half-breed" Republican Senator George F. Hoar, describing such foes as "grey-beards" who lacked manly vigor, "generally over-ripe and decayed citizens," "aunties," "squaw men," and "old women with trousers." Impelled by the same gendered discourse used to spur the nation to war over Cuba, imperialists declared that the country needed "patriotic Americans, not a lot of old women and decrepit politicians in their dotage."[10] Militant discourse thus reified gendered stereotypes of feminine weakness, marginalizing women and war protesters and staking out foreign policy as masculine terrain.

Vaulted into the presidency as a result of McKinley's assassination in 1901, Theodore Roosevelt led a different charge from the one his Rough Riders had executed at San Juan Hill—a frontal assault against anti-imperialist subversion on the home front. A romantic historian who grasped core national identity more fully than the anti-imperialists, Roosevelt viewed the call to "abandon the Philippines to their own tribes" as incompatible with the nation's historical trajectory. The "cravens and weaklings" opposed to fighting in the Philippines logically ought to feel "morally bound to abandon Arizona to the Apaches." "Every word that could be said for Aguinaldo could be said for Sitting Bull." Likewise, Henry Cabot Lodge argued that to condemn the Philippine invasion one would have to condemn the "forefathers" for "ever having settled in these United States." Roosevelt and Lodge offered a telling point, as the anti-imperialist movement had not emerged in opposition to conquest of virgin land, winning the West or against Manifest Destiny. As Richard Drinnon points out, "Many or most of those in what was loosely called the anti-imperialist movement were really liberal imperialists who could not bring themselves to recognize they lamented the passing of a country that never was."[11]

Anti-imperialists harbored the same racial modernity as their opponents, yet they argued in behalf of racial purity rather than conquest. U.S. atrocities in the Philippines included widespread rape, one solider describing his mission to "kill all the men, fuck all the women, and raise up a new race in the islands." Anti-imperialists, however, frequently cited their fears of a miscegenation that would undermine the "American race" as a result of the "lust of empire" and the "lechery of world conquest." Fusing tropes of race, sex, and gender, anti-imperialists feared that "the vigorous blood, the best blood" would now be contaminated by its mixing with "the daughters of Filipino 'niggers.'" E. L. Godkin decried annexation of the islands as not only unconstitutional but also a threat to incorporate "alien, inferior, mongrel races." Schurz dubbed the Filipinos a "large mass of more or less barbarous Asiatics." Ever elusive in his "anti-imperi-alism," William Jennings Bryan opposed annexation yet endorsed coaling sta-tions and a protectorate for the Philippines. The model progressive Robert La Follette feared anarchy would follow withdrawal from the Philippines, adding that the archipelago also offered a "great market" for trade.[12]

Their own contradictions helped defeat the anti-imperialists, yet it was coming of age patriotic nationalism inspired by anxiety-assuaging splendid victory that drove the conquest and annexation of the Philippines. Thus, with an inappropriateness that can only be described as Orwellian, the United States formally selected the date of July 4, 1902, to declare the end of the Philippine in-surrection. In actuality, fighting and atrocities lasted until 1914, mostly against the Moros (Muslims) of the southern archipelago.

While officials promised eventual independence (no date was set) and re-ferred only to territories or dependencies, the nation born of anticolonial re-bellion was now indisputably engaged in colonialism. The imperial wars, cul-minating in the conquest of the Philippines, did not reflect a change in national identity—rather, its reaffirmation—but it did increase the nation's interna-tional power and prestige as naval bases, coaling stations, and trade ports stretched from Hawaii to Subic Bay in the Philippines and throughout the Car-ibbean.

In Hawaii, which, like the Indian territories, had been devastated by disease following the arrival of the British explorer James Cook in 1778, the *haole* (West-erners) gradually assumed authority through a "slow, insinuating invasion of people, ideas, and institutions. . . . The mutilations were not only physical, but also psychological and spiritual." After the United States overthrew the Hawai-ian monarchy in 1887, a colonial sugar oligarchy took power under a "discourse that portrayed the conceptions of government, economics, education, and ideals as the only proper and 'realistic' models," Jonathan Osorio notes. Anti-imperialists fought off Hawaiian annexation in 1893 but the United States seized control of the volcanic islands amidst the euphoric imperial thrust of 1898.[13]

The most striking development in East Asia, Japan's emergence as an indus-trial-military power, defied Western perceptions of Asiatic inferiority rooted in racial modernity. Despite his penchant for racist bellicosity, Roosevelt re-sponded to Japan's stunning victory in war over Russia in 1905 (yellow people were not supposed to prevail over white people) by brokering the peace arrangements at Portsmouth, New Hampshire. Concerned that the vulnerable Philippines remained "our heel of Achilles,"[14] Roosevelt oversaw the Root-

Takahira Agreement (1908) by which Washington and Tokyo acknowledged the other's Asian possessions. Nevertheless, a "Pacific estrangement" between the two powers remained palpable and set them on a course of imperial rivalry that would culminate in the obliteration of Hiroshima and Nagasaki.

Japan bitterly resented Western racial modernity, including U.S. efforts to limit Japanese immigration and travel to Hawaii and California, where the San Francisco school board mandated segregation of the "Japs" within public schools, a reflection of the "yellow peril" that had prevailed since the wave of Chinese immigration culminating in the Exclusion Act of 1882. Roosevelt intervened against the school board while negotiating voluntary limits on Japanese immigration, yet at the same time the Rough Rider president sent the appropriately monikered Great White Fleet to Yokohama, an ostensibly friendly visit which nonetheless underscored growing U.S. naval power behind the emerging "empire on the Pacific."[15]

Caribbean Hegemony

The United States cemented its Caribbean hegemony unimpeded by other nations and also free of the "emotional" opposition engendered by the Philippine conquest. The exaltation of whiteness and spreading progress drove popular consent. Like Aguinaldo, the Cubans discovered they had been dupes of the Yankee discourse. "None of us thought that [U.S. intervention] would be followed by a military occupation of the country by our allies, who treat us as people incapable of acting by ourselves, and who have reduced us to obedience," the Cuban leader Máximo Gomez declared in June 1899. "This cannot be our ultimate fate after years of struggle."[16]

The denigration of the Cubans to which Gomez referred proved crucial to establishing hegemony as well as to promoting the usable past of splendid military triumph. The war effort was more chaotic than triumphant, however, as U.S. forces had lacked food, supplies, provisions, facilities, proper command and communications, and medicine even as tropical disease ravaged the ranks. Only two days after his victory at San Juan Hill, Roosevelt implored Washington to send food and ammunition. On July 7 the Rough Rider declared that "the mismanagement has been beyond belief" and the inept war effort "has brought us to the very verge of disaster." "Our incompetent conduct of the Spanish-American War was unbecoming a nation on the eve of becoming a world power," concluded two government historians, one an army officer, in a 1969 assessment. "Military management," they averred, was "more than inefficient; it was downright stupid."

Amid the confused campaign Cuban rebels initially welcomed the Yankees and went on to play decisive roles as fighters, scouts, guides, and interpreters. Spain's General Weyler flatly declared that without the Cubans "the Americans would not have been able to effect their landing, attack the city of Santiago de Cuba with success, and secure its surrender." Triumphant discourse elided the Cuban contribution while celebrating the nation's providentially destined victory.

Denigrating the Cuban role mattered, as to have acknowledged the Cubans as competent in war might suggest they were equally competent to govern themselves. "Both officers and privates have the most lively contempt for the Cubans," noted the famous war correspondent Stephen Crane. U.S. forces often precluded Cubans from a more active role in the fighting and denied them the right to participate in liberating Santiago by claiming that they would loot, plunder, and pillage. General Calixto García, whom Weyler cited as the driving force behind Spain's defeat, responded bitterly, "We are not savages who ignore the principles of civilized warfare."

In 1898 and for the most part ever since, the splendid war narrative wrote the Cubans out of their own history. "In the historical literature of the 'Spanish-American War,'" Louis Perez notes, "Cubans all but vanished." As a result, "Americans remembered 1898 as something done for Cubans; Cubans remembered 1898 as something done to them." Myriad histories described the war as not merely splendid but also "short and glorious," a "picnic," a "colorful war" with "comic opera overtones," a "dazzling venture," a "thing of charging rough-riders and flashing sabers." While Myth of America identity sanctioned corporate domination of allegedly uncivilized nations, many historical accounts omitted reference to the thirty- to fifty-million-dollar U.S. investment in Cuban sugar plantations and railroads.[17]

After eighty years, the Monroe Doctrine had become so naturalized that the public supported McKinley's declaration that "until there is complete tranquility in [Cuba] and a stable government inaugurated military occupation will be continued." Precluded by the Teller amendment from annexing Cuba, Root devised the Platt Amendment (1901), which granted Cuba nominal independence while providing the United States with the "right to intervene for . . . the maintenance of a government adequate for the protection of life, property, and individual liberty." The United States also secured coaling stations and permanent bases for occupation forces. Senator Orville Platt of Connecticut explained that since the Cubans "are like children," Americans had to "be in a position to straighten out things if they get seriously bad." As General Leonard Wood wrote privately to Roosevelt, "There is, of course, little or no independence left in Cuba under the Platt Amendment." Rather than effecting a "Cuba libre," the United States occupied the island with more troops than had fought there during the war itself.

The putative anti-imperialists revealed the extent to which they, too, hallowed the Monroe Doctrine and imperial identity by mounting virtually no opposition to the denial of Cuban independence. The Democratic Party platform in 1900 made imperialism "the paramount issue of the campaign" and asserted, "No nation can long endure half republic and half empire." However, the party's two most eminent anti-imperialists, Bryan (who again lost decisively to McKinley) and Cleveland, both endorsed the Platt Amendment. Senator Hoar also praised the Platt Amendment as "eminently wise and satisfactory."[18] The imperial wars thus underscored the hegemony of Myth of America identity, which invariably beat back counterhegemonic discourses.

Finally rid of Spain but now confronted with the stark reality of the U.S. occupation, Cuban leaders could only protest and resist. When they did just that and refused to ratify the Platt Amendment, Root, dripping paternalism, charged the Cubans with being "ungrateful and unreasonable" and threatened that in the future Washington "will not quite be so altruistic and sentimental" in its dealings with the islanders. In the end, the titular Cuban leadership concluded it had no choice but to accede to the demand to incorporate the provision in the new constitution. As they adjusted to U.S. hegemony, Cuban factions sometimes requested Yankee intervention to stave off their own domestic opposition. Nonetheless, the Platt Amendment remained a neuralgic issue in Cuban politics, one that rebels and nationalists rallied around for decades. Fidel Castro invoked the *platista* legacy when he came to power in 1959 by acknowledging the late nineteenth-century rebels "who had fought thirty years and not seen their dream realized," those who had "initiated the war for independence that we have completed."[19]

While largely overshadowed by events in Cuba and the Philippines, Puerto Rico became a test case in securing legal sanction for Caribbean hegemony. Following the landing in July 1898 at Guanica Bay and the ouster of the Spanish, the United States ultimately designated the island an unincorporated territory, neither a state nor an autonomous country. Roosevelt and other officials applied the usual paternalist discourse to the "pathetic and childlike" islanders. The United States had no desire to annex the racially mixed island, much less offer statehood, but the compact colonial state, more modernized than Cuba, proved conducive to hegemony. In the landmark "insular cases" between 1901 and 1910, the Supreme Court upheld the constitutionality of Caribbean colonialism by ruling that territories such as Puerto Rico did not have to be accorded full citizenship rights.[20]

The ultimate symbol of U.S. hegemony over Central America and the Caribbean was the Panama Canal, which resulted from Yankee intervention. When the Colombian Senate rejected his canal treaty, Roosevelt denounced the "contemptible little creatures" and authorized a coup by Panamanian elites, who effected secession from Colombia under the protection of a U.S. gunboat. The subsequent treaty provided the United States with "all the rights, power and authority" within a ten-mile canal zone strip as well as the right to intervene "at its discretion." Panama received ten million dollars, annual rent, and nominal independent status. Completed in 1914, the Panama Canal was a spectacular feat of modern engineering, transportation, and commerce—but also a potent symbol of Yankee hegemony throughout Latin America.

Through his apotheosis of war and his contempt for a wide array of foreign "monkeys," "creatures," "ungrateful wretches," "Anthropoids," and "Chinks," Roosevelt was the very incarnation of racialized U.S. aggression. The Rough Rider president, ironically so revered at home as to have the benignant teddy bear named for him, affirmed U.S. hegemony in his 1904 Corollary to the Monroe Doctrine, which he draped in tropes of masculinity and modernity. Roosevelt announced that the United States would intervene in the Western hemisphere on behalf of all "civilized" nations to correct "chronic wrongdoing" or "impotence" on the part of "backward" nations.[21]

The Roosevelt Corollary marked the beginning of a significant transition from territorial aggrandizement and direct intervention to the discursively more benign Dollar diplomacy. Indirect imperialism, conducted under such paternalist tropes as protectorate and dependency, enabled the United States to control trade and security while securing the Caribbean Sea as an "American lake." Dollar diplomacy reflected a "discursive mapping of the world, hierarchical, gendered, and racialized" at the root of diplomacy from the imperial wars to the onset of the Great Depression.[22]

Unable to substitute "dollars for bullets," the Taft administration in May

1910 sent in the Marines, ostensibly to end fighting among Nicaraguans, a "most worthless, useless lot of vermine," according to one Marine officer, "even worse than our 'Little Brown brothers' the Filipinos." The United States seized control of Nicaraguan finances, backed by twenty-seven hundred Marines at the apogee of occupation in 1912, and followed the same pattern in neighboring Honduras. The "relationship of guardian and ward," Taft averred, "indicates progress in civilization."[23]

Modernist discourse fueled imperialism while at the same time affirming corporate cultural hegemony at home. An emphasis on "sound money," masculinity, professional expertise, and racial modernity undergirded both domestic and foreign policy. Forces of disorder, anarchy, and socialism would be contained in both the domestic and foreign contexts. The manly, racialized foreign policy thus complemented containment of the domestic threats posed by socialists, populists, the New Woman, peace reformers, and advocates of African American equality.

Cultural hegemony meant that a critical mass of Americans consented to national foreign policy as they internalized the binary tropes of civilization and primitivism that affirmed imperialism. Race, gender, and Social Darwinist and millennial expectations of human evolution structured the discourse of civilization. Under this discourse, only white or Anglo-Saxon races had evolved past savagery to the civilized stage. Race, conjoined with manliness and providential destiny, obscured the inequalities of class, which had threatened to divide white men in America since the seventeenth century and which proved particularly menacing throughout the tumultuous industrial era.[24]

A series of international exhibitions, attended by millions of citizens from 1876 to 1916, reinforced cultural hegemony. "The directors of the expositions offered millions of fairgoers an opportunity to reaffirm their collective national identity in an updated synthesis of progress and white supremacy," Robert Rydell explains.[25] In the wake of industrial depressions, violent class conflict, and racial and gender anxieties, the fairs reaffirmed the superiority of U.S. institutions, material progress, subordination of inferior races and primitives, and containment of women. At the World's Columbian Exposition, held in Chicago's neoclassical White City in 1893, the historian Frederick Jackson Turner pronounced that after "crossing a continent, winning a wilderness," the nation's continental frontier was now closed.[26]

An identity-driven mythology of the Old West arose to assuage national anxiety over the closing of the frontier. Beginning in 1882, William "Buffalo

Bill" Cody launched a popular touring Wild West show, a spectacle that purported to reveal the true story of "gradual civilization of a vast continent," once a "Primeval Forest, peopled by the Indian and Wild Beasts only." Like Turner's romanticized past, Buffalo Bill's Wild West show represented the West as mythic national space, "a space in which history, translated into myth, was reenacted as ritual."[27]

Like the Wild West shows circulating across the country, the White City prominently displayed subjugated Indians. Subjected to ridicule and displayed in the full regalia and "proud majesty," Indians appeared as defeated savages who had now given way to inevitable and divinely sanctioned progress. By the turn of the century the genre of Western literature, beginning with Owen Wister's *The Virginian* (1902), depicted the West as the site in which the free (white) man could redeem his rugged individualism and masculine virtue, which may have been stifled, as they were in the Virginian, through an upbringing in the civilized, lawyerly, and soft society of the East. These same masculine anxieties underlay Roosevelt's cultivation of personal manliness on a Western dude ranch as well as the popularity of Boone and Crocket clubs, which reified the nation's heroic frontier mythology, and the rise of manly sports like boxing and football. Medieval fantasies featuring knights and maidens joined the Westerns in fueling the dime novel industry. These narratives sanctioned violent regeneration, the Westerns typically culminating in a cathartic shoot-out marking the triumph of civilized forces over Indian primitives or outlaw villains. Women and children invariably served as props to legitimate the hero's violence as he protected them from savagery and lawlessness.

While representation eased psychic crisis over the closing of the frontier, similar phenomena unfolded with respect to the New South. Two years after the White City exhibition, the "mulatto" educator Booker T. Washington "electrified" his white audience at the Cotton States International Exposition in Atlanta, sending them into a "delirium of applause" by rejecting the quest for African American social equality as "the extremist folly." With the New South needing African American labor to break its dependence on northern industry, Washington offered an ideal solution in which "the Negro" could help rebuild the South and pursue industrial education and job training while accepting a status of political and social subjugation. Meanwhile, minstrel shows traversed the nation, amusing audiences with myriad depictions of childlike African American racial inferiority.[28]

Exhibitions naturalized binaries of white and colored, civilization and progress in concert with the unfolding of "an age of American dominance in international affairs." The Pan-American Exposition in Buffalo in 1901 followed an explicit design "to justify, by means of the most available object lessons we can produce, the acquisition of new territory." While reluctantly concluding that displaying Aguinaldo himself was "not practical," planners ensured that many actual Filipinos appeared in various displays as primitives incapable of self-governance. In the Louisiana Purchase exhibition in St. Louis in 1904 and in other fairs before World War I, hundreds of Filipinos, alternatively depicted as indolent, fierce, or monkeylike, provided a staple display to reinforce the otherness of "barbaric tribes" in contrast with the advance of Western civilization. The Darkest Africa display at Buffalo similarly represented Africans, some of whom were played by African Americans even though, as one organizer complained, "the darkies of the South do not take kindly to the public rogue box." An Old Spain display described Mexicans as having "no ingenuity" and "absolutely lacking in mechanical skill."[29]

In their exaltation of whiteness, coupled with tropes of civilization, progress, and the inevitable march of manly empire, the series of exhibitions affirmed identity and imperial foreign policy for the millions of citizens who attended or read about them. Financially supported by federal and local governments, the exhibitions solidified the alliance between industrial capitalism and imperial foreign policy, marginalizing African Americans, women, and radicals at home while sanctioning intervention against primitives abroad. The fairs glorified empire as a means of encouraging consensus and white male solidarity across class lines, a solidarity that helped fend off challenges to corporate hegemony.

The exhibitions, museum exhibits, and myriad other cultural manifestations enabled Americans to internalize imperialism as an integral component of national identity. An increasingly literate society, fueled by a new mass media of newspapers, magazines, romantic cowboy tales and other dime novels, reports from various battlefronts, travel and missionary accounts, hunting and adventure stories (most famously Roosevelt's postpresidential African safari), all perpetuated the dominant binary of civilization and primitivism. The unique combination of savagery and civilization drove the popularity of Edgar Rice Burroughs's *Tarzan*, published in 1911. Though raised among the apes, Tarzan was a displaced aristocrat by birth, a white man who thus became, through "natural selection," the "king of the jungle." An intoxicating combination of power and sexuality, civilization and homicidal violence, the "ape man" introduces himself to an ultimately submissive Jane, as "TARZAN, THE KILLER OF BEASTS AND MANY BLACK MEN."[30]

While historians have long framed the first generation of the twentieth century as the Progressive Era, many of the changes of the period ultimately reinforced rather than challenged corporate hegemony. Progressives sought to replace the drift of laissez-faire (itself shrouded in mythology) with the mastery of a rational society supervised by professionals determined to implement a wide range of pragmatic middle-class reforms. The profound impact of the Darwinian revolution lay behind the Progressive movement, as evolution underscored that human life was not predestined but rather could be shaped and managed by scientific rationalism within a progressive society. Progressive reform could undermine the appeal of anarchists and radical laborers and check the virtually unfettered power of the Gilded Age business and banking moguls.[31]

The consolidation of wealth and power had accelerated during the industrial era, as a tiny percentage of the population—1 to 2 percent comprising landed elites, financiers, and corporate executives—controlled more than half the nation's wealth.[32] Settlement house workers, muckraking journalists, and various reformers focused increasing attention on how "the other half lives," contrasting the plight of the poor with the abuses of virtually unregulated corporate power. The huge gap between rich and poor, unemployment and labor agitation, child labor abuses, dangerous working conditions and on-site accidents remained sources of simmering class resentment. Workers resorted to strikes at an accelerating rate, peaking at 3,648 in 1903, rendering the United States "the most strike-torn nation in the world."[33]

Some Progressives forged critical links between corporate power at home and a world divided between civilization and primitivism. Progressives sought moral redemption through domestic reform and benevolent paternalism abroad. They thus criticized Dollar diplomacy, which had not only failed to replace bullets with dollars—that is, the Marines repeatedly "had" to be landed in Cuba and Nicaragua—but also reflected negatively on bankers and corporate elites at a time when Progressives had begun to subject the great men of high finance to unprecedented scrutiny. Progressives viewed industrial combinations and central banking as inevitable products of maturing capitalism, yet they sought to rein in the worst abuses of the system and to establish the ultimate authority of government over imperious financiers long symbolized by J. P. Morgan.

Significantly, however, while implementing a wide range of domestic reforms, Progressives also sought to redeem the world. Following the lead of John
Bassett Moore, an international lawyer, and Carnegie, who promoted the concept of a league of nations, peace internationalists conducted various congresses and cheered the treaties signed at The Hague in 1899 and 1907, which endorsed arbitration and the creation of a world court. Peace internationalists
received support from church organizations, overwhelmingly Protestant, as
they sought to build a world order rooted in consultation, arbitration, adjudication, and avoidance of war. Such groups as the American Peace Society, the
Carnegie Endowment for International Peace, and the League to Enforce Peace
reflected mainstream progressive values and included prominent establishment figures such as Root, Taft, and Woodrow Wilson.[34]

Despite their advocacy of peaceful internationalism, the vast majority of
these Progressives deeply internalized Myth of America identity, which led
them, ironically, to prove highly amenable to foreign intervention. Just as they
sought to regulate capitalism through modest government trust busting and
various social reforms, Progressives advocated rational management of the
new empire. Progressives rejected isolationism, much less any such radical
"new freedom" as turning over Cuba, Puerto Rico, or the Philippines to their
own racially inferior people. Uniformly white, professional, and appealing to
the middle class, the reformers enabled the widespread domestic racial violence
during the progressive era, including a spike in the popular southern ritual of
lynching.

No one seemed better suited to carry out progressive reform than Wilson—
and no one would better symbolize the progressive penchant for foreign intervention. As an educator, former president of Princeton University, southerner
by birth but governor of New Jersey, the pious son of a Presbyterian minister,
Wilson seemed the perfect embodiment of religious redemption and secular
modernity.

Myth of America identity drove Wilson to embroil the United States in a
series of interventions, beginning with the Mexican Revolution. By 1910, the
United States controlled 75 percent of Mexico's mines and 50 percent of its oil
fields, while typically representing the country as a land of indolent males taking their siestas under large sombreros while señoritas appeared as dark-eyed,
passive beauties. Following the ouster of Porfirio Diaz in "the most honest election in the history of the republic," the United States conspired to overthrow his
successor, Francisco Madero. One of the conspiratorial generals, Victoriano

Huerta, ordered Madero's murder, an act that spurred disorder in Mexican politics and left Washington embroiled in a turbulent social revolution.[35]

Although both Wilson and his secretary of state, Bryan, appeared to possess impeccable anti-imperialist credentials, they had deeply internalized the Myth of America, and these two reverent men especially believed in the nation's providential mission to redeem mankind. Wilson and Bryan thus set about with remarkable fervor not merely to influence but essentially to dictate the outcome of the Mexican political imbroglio. Like Spain's Weyler in fin de siècle Cuba, Huerta was described as a "butcher," an "Ape-like old man, of almost pure Indian blood" who could not be allowed to remain in power. "Usurpations like that of General Huerta menace the peace and development of America," Wilson explained. "It is the purpose of the United States therefore to discredit and defeat such usurpations *whenever they occur*" (emphasis added).[36] National identity precluded the nation from seriously considering Senator Joseph Bristow's (R-Kansas) "radical" proposal that "the Mexican people should be permitted to fight out their own domestic troubles the same as we did from 1861[to] 1865."[37]

Following the "Tampico incident,"[38] the United States invaded Veracruz, Mexico's principal port. Marines and navy blue-jackets took the city, killing at least 126 Mexicans and wounding more than 200, compared with 17 U.S. dead and 63 wounded. The "progressive" occupiers instituted municipal and much-needed sanitary reforms, outlawed the "so-called sport" of bullfighting favored by the "Spigs," and instituted medical screening of prostitutes—a logical step in view of the suddenly furious increase in demand for their services. As in Cuba, no matter how worthy the U.S. reforms, the national humiliation inherent in the military invasion and occupation overshadowed whatever modernist progress came with it.

When Wilson, albeit reluctantly, recognized the Constitutionalist Venustiano Carranza as president of Mexico, the enraged "bandit" Pancho Villa terrorized the U.S. border in retribution, conducting, among other offensive actions, a notorious bloody raid on Columbus, New Mexico, in March 1916. Invoking what foreign policy "realists" would later call credibility, U.S. officials immediately decided to hunt down Villa, as to do otherwise "would ruin us in the eyes of all Latin Americans," who "like children," would "pile insult upon insult if they are not stopped when the first insult is given." The six-thousand-man punitive expedition under General John J. Pershing penetrated deep into Mexican territory, oblivious to nationalist sentiment and thus ensuring an inevitable clash with Carranza's army, which came at Carrizal in June and left fourteen U.S. soldiers dead. "Despite his sometimes blind stupidity in dealing with Mexico," Lester Langley notes, Wilson at this point did at least reject his secretary of war's call for a reprise of the 1846 military assault on Mexico City and instead agreed to negotiations that culminated in the withdrawal of U.S. forces in 1917.[39]

Haiti, the other major site of pre–Great War U.S. "moral" intervention, lacked Mexico's powers of resistance and, as its residents were black, came under more extreme racial violence in the course of a nineteen-year U.S. occupation. The United States, which had opposed the republican revolution against France, infiltrated Haiti economically and engaged in eight incidents of "gunboat diplomacy" prior to the twentieth century. "Misbehavior" in "the dusky little republic" spurred another Marine invasion in July 1915. Even as he welcomed the "extraordinary advances" of "the Negro race" the Virginia-born and Georgia-raised Wilson embraced segregation and the Reconstruction Myths, as reflected in his delight in screening *Birth of a Nation* in the White House. Wilson had employed racial modernity in supporting annexation of the Philippines, explaining, "The principles of the Declaration of Independence do not require the immediate surrender of a country to a people like this." Haiti perplexed Bryan, as reflected in his remark, "Dear me, Niggers speaking French!"[40] The United States established a puppet government in Port-au-Prince, seized the customhouses, supervised financial institutions, instituted forced labor, sponsored road building and other internal improvements, and encouraged social reforms in the now-well-established modernist framework inherent under Caribbean hegemony.

As the Marines conducted an ongoing guerrilla war with rural insurgents, dubbed Cacos, they manifested continuity with the nation's history of searching out to destroy Indian savages, Mexican mongrels, Filipino goo-goos, and now Haitian "savage monkeys." The racial violence inherent in national identity led to the killing of some 11,500 Haitians over the length of the occupation. Although U.S. soldiers tended to view Haitians as inferior to the Negroes at home, as in past wars they often linked the domestic and foreign racial violence. One soldier, for example, delighted in "steadying down on my job of popping at black heads much as those behind the 'hit the nigger and get a cigar' games at American amusement parks." Though rarely discussed, rapes of Haitian women occurred frequently.[41]

The manly domination of savage enemy-others in Haiti flowed from an identity-driven modernist discourse of advancing civilization. U.S. journalists did not "take the trouble to examine into the facts" of the brutal occupation, Oswald Garrison Villard observed, adding that "a watchful, well-informed, intelligent, and independent press was . . . sorely lacking."[42] Coinciding with the Haitian intervention, the United States, in effect, engaged in a neomodernist version of the slave trade by purchasing the Virgin Islands and their predominantly black residents from Denmark for twenty-five million dollars in 1916.

Redeeming the Globe

The Great War that erupted in Europe in 1914 overshadowed the Caribbean interventions and ultimately brought an end to the Progressive Era. Consistent with the venerable discourses of Washington's Farewell Address and the Monroe Doctrine, the United States initially sought to avoid "entanglement" in the European bloodletting. However, within months of the eruption of the "guns of August" in 1914, Myth of America identity, enhanced by the nation's newly assumed status of world power, began to hew out a path that would lead to direct intervention in World War I.

Despite the absence of threat to U.S. security, national identity, fused with domestic anxieties, eventually drove the nation to choose war. The gradual path to intervention in the Great War traversed a familiar narrative, beginning with the shocking sinking of the luxury liner *Lusitania* (1915), which provoked patriotic memories of the *Maine* explosion; the ultimate inability of diplomacy to protect neutral rights at sea; and the Zimmermann Telegram (1917), in which Germany offered Mexico the opportunity for revanchism in return for joining a war against the United States.

Most Americans sympathized with Great Britain—now its partner in assuming the white man's burden following a century and a half of rapprochement. The cultural affinity for the English cousin over the German "Huns" and their Central European allies led the United States ultimately to put aside blatant British violations of neutral rights and to focus overwhelmingly on German depredations and particularly the sensational *Unterseeboot,* or submarine, attacks on allegedly neutral shipping. Berlin could hardly consider the Atlantic trade benign, however, as the Triple Entente instituted a blockade in an attempt to starve the Central Powers into submission. The British stored munitions even in the hold of the *Lusitania,* which traversed the war zone in spite of German warnings, including advertisements in the New York newspapers.

While opposition remained formidable, support for intervention grew steadily under a discursive regime of preparedness. The term emphasized national defense when the ultimate objective was offensive engagement in the European war. The preparedness movement featured speeches, parades, rallies, and filmic depictions of spike-helmeted Huns invading a U.S. city. While hundreds of thousands marched for preparedness in 1916 in all major cities, the Plattsburg movement championed universal military training, a step toward the coming national draft.

Influential white male internationalists longed for the cultural renewal of manly violence against external enemy-others. Men such as Roosevelt, Root, Lodge, and Henry Stimson joined British and French propagandists on behalf of the Allied cause.

Recognizing that it was but a short step from preparedness to direct intervention, a wide array of peace activists, internationalists, and feminists countered the interventionists from 1915 to April 1917. The American Union Against Militarism worked closely with the Women's Peace Party, the American Church Union, and other antiwar groups. Perceiving the call to arms as a mortal threat to domestic reform, socialists and staunch progressives accused capitalist elites of marching toward war to reap greater profits. The preparedness movement provided a mere cover for "the commercial, industrial, and imperialistic schemes of the great financial masters of this country," La Follette charged.[43]

Professing after the *Lusitania* sinking that one could be "too proud to fight," Wilson initially stood against the rising tide of militancy and proved politically adept by securing modest preparedness programs while fending off calls for large-scale militarization. As a progressive, Wilson remained wary of a big army and the potential fusion of industry and finance into a government-orchestrated war machine. He also expressed concern that if the United States became embroiled in the European carnage all of "white civilization" might be threatened and world leadership lost to the yellow hordes of Asia. Madison Grant's bestseller *The Passing of the Great Race* (1916) reflected profound racial anxieties on the eve of U.S. intervention.

Appalled by the staggering destructiveness of the European stalemate, Wilson called for an end to the war based on "peace without victory," which Roosevelt promptly derided as "national emasculation." The real emasculation, however, was occurring day after blood-soaked day, as ultimately some ten to thirteen million young men died—two thousand a day at one point in 1916—in the trenches of Verdun, the Somme, at Gallipoli, and across the eastern front as well. Increasingly hemmed in by the Allied blockade and weary of diplomacy with Washington, Germany responded to Wilson's "peace without victory" speech of January 22, 1917, by launching all out submarine warfare in a calculated effort to defeat the allies before the United States could intervene and make a difference in the war.

Several factors implicated in Myth of America identity now propelled the nation toward direct belligerence. Broad consent fell in behind the view that as the most moral and advanced nation in the world, a model society of Christian individualism and virtue, the United States had an obligation to intervene to save Europe and lead the world. How could "America" assume its preordained place of world leadership while remaining aloof from the most destructive conflict in history? By 1917 progressives including Wilson increasingly saw the senseless carnage of the Great War no longer as a reason to stay out but rather as a call to intervene in order to save Western civilization.[44] Conditioned by a usable past emphasizing the moral superiority of their own imagined community, millions of citizens came to link providential national destiny with intervention to redeem the world.

The anguished scholar within Wilson deplored the resort to war, yet the drive to reaffirm Myth of America identity prevailed. Seemingly providentially, the Russian Revolution of February 1917, in which a provisional government replaced the tsarist autocracy, transformed Russia into a "fit partner" in Wilson's crusade to make the world "safe for democracy." The prospect of a "democratic Russia," soon to be shattered by the October Bolshevik Revolution, thus fueled Wilson's conviction that intervention would lead to nothing less than a globe transformed in America's image. Millennialism saturated Wilson's eloquent thirty-six-minute address to Congress on April 2, 1917, generating widespread support affirming national identity and spurring overwhelming votes for a declaration of war by 82–6 in the Senate and 373–50 in the House of Representatives.[45]

As in every major U.S. war, domestic anxieties underlay the decision to engage in cathartic external violence. The wave of violence against African Americans and fears of the "passing of the great [white] race" reflected deep-seated neuroses over racial formation inherent in national identity. At the same time, by 1913 women had full voting rights in nine Western states and partial rights in twenty-nine more and now pressed for full national suffrage. Some women were becoming more open about sexuality, as Margaret Sanger launched a public campaign for birth control. With the modern feminist movement arising behind the irrepressible surge of millions of New Women, the specter of gender equality threatened culturally constructed patriarchy.

As an exclusively male phenomenon, in terms of actual combat, war exalted masculinity and vaulted manliness to the epicenter of national attention while containing femininity within a marginalized separate sphere. War revived manly discourse, tropes of chivalry, and the pure excitement inherent in the risk of death. "How can one enjoy life without this highly spiced sauce of danger?" wondered the aviation hero Eddie Rickenbacker.[46] Men longed to be part of jubilant victories evoking memories of marching into the halls of Montezuma, stirring triumph in the Battle of New Orleans, and in the splendid victory over Spain. Interventionists saw in war a tonic for the complacency of a society increasingly preoccupied with commercialism and consumerism, with drink, dances, movies, bicycle rides, and other carefree entertainments that failed to inculcate a strenuous masculinity in young men.

Women like Fanny Garrison Villard perceived the significance of gendered discourse and the pressures that tropes of manliness placed on men to support the war. "The fear of being called peace-at-any-price men makes cowards of them all," she noted with ironic insight. At the same time, the term *pacifist,* which emanated from Europe at the turn of the century, functioned as an epithet in a culture that viewed opposition to war as subversive. While the academic intellectual Wilson might be viewed as exempt from crude appeals to manliness, in actuality the president "was imbued with a masculine-Christian crusader spirit." In remarks before the Pittsburgh YMCA in 1914, for example, Wilson expressed "an exquisite combination of contempt and hate" for "the moral coward." The president concluded, "Be militant!"[47]

Still exalting manliness and war, Roosevelt declared, "No nation ever amounted to anything if its population was composed of pacifists and poltroons, if its sons did not have the fighting edge." Unlike future U.S. politicians who willingly sent masses of young men to war while keeping their own safe at home, the aging Rough Rider inculcated the fighting edge in his own son, Quentin. In the course of a mission the young aviator burned alive in his aircraft, sinking Roosevelt into depression six months before his own death in 1918.[48]

In addition to gender and racial anxieties, class antagonisms and labor strife remained palpable on the eve of war, as reflected most brutally in the 1914 Ludlow massacre. In an incident reminiscent of the Homestead strike and Wounded Knee, National Guardsmen summoned in behalf of the Rockefeller-owned Colorado Fuel and Iron Company opened fire on striking United Mine Workers and their supporters, killing some sixty persons, mostly women and children. At the same time, prewar reforms such as direct democracy, a national income tax, including progressive levies against wealthy elites, and government regulation of banking, industry, and finance all targeted laissez-faire, the shibboleth that had enabled the corporate-industrial elite to function as the virtual "lords of creation" during the Industrial Age.[49] By contrast, intervention in the war promoted the fusion of business and industry and higher profits from war production and brought an end to the progressive reform movement. U.S. exports spiraled from just over two billion dollars in 1913 to more than six billion dollars in 1916.

The Christian and millennial traditions fueled the drive toward intervention. Pastors described the Germans as a "pack of hungry, wolfish Huns" and decried the "rape" of Belgium. "The clergy did not have to be duped" into war, Conrad Cherry notes. "They drew upon their own religious traditions of Israelite war, holy crusade, and 'just war' theory in order both to ground their pro-war arguments and to give shape to their militant rhetoric." A clergyman advised his congregation, "This conflict is indeed a crusade, the greatest in history—the holiest." The nation's most popular evangelist, Billy Sunday, declared that "the fight between America and Germany" paralleled that of "Hell against Heaven." The YMCA, National Catholic Council, and Jewish Welfare Board joined in wartime unity. Many U.S. Jews embraced the war in support of the British Balfour Declaration promising a Zionist homeland. Irving Berlin, a Jew, wrote "God Bless America" during the Great War, though it did not become a popular anthem until the next world war.[50]

Intervention thus flowed broadly from the cultural hegemony of militant nationalism. Crucially, progressives—including the public philosophers John Dewey and Walter Lippmann, Gompers, the African American intellectual W. E. B. Du Bois, the feminist Carrie Chatman Catt, and millions of others supported the war they thought would make the world safe for democracy. Du Bois, Catt, and others concluded that intervention would create jobs and advance the causes of racial and gender equality. Senator Hiram Johnson of California, remembered mostly as a postwar "isolationist," explained his support for intervention through mythical discourse as "our destiny must be the ultimate destiny of world democracy." Gompers declared simply, "The hopes of the world can be expressed in the ideal—America."[51]

Just as they engineered change at home through rational, pragmatic reforms, progressives followed Wilson's lead in a protean campaign to reshape the world and usher in a new diplomacy that would achieve nothing less than to "make the world itself at last free." The anti-interventionist Randolph Bourne observed that a "peculiar geniality" linking intervention and national redemption drowned out voices of restraint and appeals to traditional diplomacy. Oswald Villard pleaded in vain for the United States to remain aloof from the war as "the one great beacon-light of a nation unarmed and unafraid." The U.S. Socialist Party, refusing to follow the lead of its European comrades into war, instead "held true to its international principles and bravely passed an antiwar resolution."[52]

Whereas Socialists and progressives such as La Follette had sought to restrain the power of wealthy financial-industrial elites, the reinvigoration of national identity through war instead ushered in a new corporatism. The nascent militarization of the economy began with the National Defense Act of 1916, but then evolved swiftly in the wake of direct intervention. The rapid conversion to war production as well as the demands of training, equipping, and transporting some two million men "over there" spurred unprecedented collusion between government and industry. Under the Wall Street financier Bernard Baruch, the War Industries Board (WIB) set high prices to encourage production and rewarded the largest firms, thus promoting centralization of industry. Profits soared in the arms, shipbuilding, chemical, and other war industries. Justice Department antitrust activities virtually ceased, as the Webb-Pomerone Act of 1917 specifically exempted exporters from antitrust laws. "The Wilson administration had clearly demonstrated its willingness to place the power of government at the disposal of private capital," David Kennedy notes.[53]

Intervention in the Great War thus gave birth to the modern military-industrial complex that would fully flower in the second half of the century (see chapter 7). The WIB represented the powerful forces that populists and the more radical progressives had sought to curtail, though in other respects the WIB was an "extension and an elaboration of the government-business regulatory alliance that began emerging during the Progressive years." In any case, the WIB "concentrated further power in Washington" and proved to be "rife with conflicts of interest, profiteering, and other malfeasance."[54]

While the war did create new opportunities for women and African Americans, an intense reaction against them responded to that very progress. Thousands of female nurses and clerical and service workers directly supported the armed services, and even more joined war industries. "For every fighter a woman worker," urged one mobilization poster. Women inevitably encountered wage discrimination, sexual harassment, and other forms of resistance from male workers and even from unions, though thousands of women were able to join worker associations.

As many women had anticipated, the war at last culminated the seemingly endless campaign for suffrage, yet not without bitter resistance to the end. Exploiting the pervasive Wilsonian discourse linking the war and democracy, the National Women's Party picketed the White House, scuffled with intolerant war zealots, and found themselves hauled to jail (more than two hundred were arrested) and force fed during hunger strikes. Women already voted in seventeen states, and their labor was crucial to the war effort, so Wilson finally relented and endorsed the Susan B. Anthony amendment in 1918, which Congress eventually approved and the states ratified as the Nineteenth Amendment in 1920.[55]

The war not only changed the status of women but also compelled the society to grapple with the perennial "Negro problem." Hoping for the best from the war, Du Bois in 1918 urged African Americans to "close ranks shoulder to shoulder with our fellow white citizens." The war brought two dramatic changes: 367,000 black men entered the armed forces, albeit in segregated units and often as mess boys and in other menial roles; and the Great Migration spurred an infusion of some 750,000 African American workers into northern cities. While lynchings (eighty-five were recorded in 1915), beatings, church burnings, rapes, and other violence remained unexceptional in the South, the violent reaction within armed forces training camps and in industrial cities stunned the nation. Riots that killed scores of people erupted in Chicago, Houston, St. Louis, Tulsa, and other cities, as white soldiers and workers resisted the black infusion and the newfound opportunities for which African Americans proved willing to fight. While the National Association for the Advancement of Colored People (NAACP), the Urban League, and other organizations flourished in mounting resistance to racial violence, the Wilson government proved indifferent. Deeply disillusioned, Du Bois concluded that his country was "yet a shameful land."[56]

As throughout U.S. history, war encouraged intolerance of those who failed to support external aggression and thus became subversives despite the ostensible rights of freedom of speech and expression. In June 1917, only a year after his "He kept us out of war" reelection campaign, Wilson declared, "Woe be to the man or group of men that seems to stand in our way." Following the con-

5. "Honor the Brave" (May 1917). U.S. government war poster. Created in May 1917, shortly after U.S. intervention in the Great War, the poster solemnly honors the dead across the nation's history of warfare. Memorial Day emerged as a national holiday after the Civil War and became a force of reunion and patriotic unity, as symbolized by the Union soldier and the Southern gentleman marching side by side at the center of the image. Courtesy of the Library of Congress.

gressional vote for intervention, Root averred, "We must have no criticism now."[57] What began as a campaign of persuasion turned to one of propaganda and then of compulsion and then of countersubversion and punishment.

With the country now committed to fighting its first total war since the Civil War, most Americans demanded full investment in the cause on the part of all citizens. "What we had to have was no mere surface unity," explained the progressive journalist George Creel, appointed head of the Committee on Public Information (CPI), "but a passionate belief in the justice of America's cause that should weld the people of the United States into one white-hot mass instinct with fraternity, devotion, courage, and deathless determination." The CPI served as a "relentless publicity machine" justifying intervention and war aims by distributing millions of posters, pamphlets, press releases, exhibitions, advertisements, and succinct public addresses by a trained force of seventy-five thousand Four-Minute Men. Sticking to their abbreviated script, these militants addressed audiences in the millions in schools, churches, and union halls as the government-sponsored propaganda campaign drove an agenda of patriotic conformity.[58]

In a testament to the broad internalization of Myth of America hegemony, including gendered conceptions linking manhood and national service, no reprise of the widespread Union draft riots occurred as some 24 million men registered. The nation mobilized an army of 4.5 million men behind the progressive trope of military service, which trumped the selective component of the Selective Service Act (1917). Despite campaigns against "slackers," the establishment of local boards under the national draft legislation enabled favoritism based on class, as unknown thousands of well-connected men managed to stay "over here" while common workers shipped out.

Visions of unity and racial purity underlay the wartime revival of nativism. CPI persuasion and propaganda promoted not only mobilization but also a protean vision of national unity in representing the war as "a wonderful chance in this country to weld the twenty-five or thirty races which compose our population into a strong, virile, and intelligent people . . . a splendid race of new Americans." Instead of "division into race groups," Lodge averred, the war "will unify us into one Nation, and national degeneracy and national cowardice will slink back into the darkness." With some 4.6 million immigrants from Germany and the Austro-Hungarian Empire residing in the United States, an anti-German propaganda campaign compelled allegiance to their adopted land while manifesting itself in popular culture through the renaming of German foods, banning Beethoven, burning German books, prohibiting teaching of the language, and assaulting and on occasion murdering insufficiently patriotic German-Americans. "Coerced affirmations of loyalty frequently sufficed," notes Richard Steele, "but on scores of occasions in communities throughout the nation the nonconforming and the unlucky were tarred and feathered, painted yellow, dunked, ridden out of town, beaten, whipped, hung to unconsciousness, and occasionally murdered by mobs acting in the name of patriotism."[59]

Nothing better underscored the relationship between war and affirmation of national identity than the call for eliminating "hyphenate-Americans." Under hegemonic nationalist discourse, ethnic identity, war criticism, and left wing or radical politics violated the premise of "100 percent Americanism." Only in a nation in which mythical discourse had been so profoundly internalized could repression of these groups be openly and energetically pursued amid a campaign to make the world "safe for democracy." Thus the anti-German campaign and generalized xenophobia melded with attacks on labor and radicalism, all within the cauldron of a rising wartime national security state.

The war shattered the vision once held by Wilson and other progressives of unions and industry working in concert to transcend the Gilded Age history of class conflict. Although the war brought near full employment and rising wages, inflation and awareness of windfall corporate profits spurred unprecedented labor unrest and more than three thousand strikes annually from 1914 to 1920. Wilson supported conservative unionism, embodied by the American Federation of Labor under Gompers, which in return supported the war and the campaign to marginalize "radical" labor. Wages might rise and unions could flourish—as long as workers embraced the war effort.

With nearly a quarter of the labor force walking out at one time or another in 1919, the Wilson administration used every means at its disposal—antilabor propaganda, revocation of mail permits, injunctions, indictments, infiltration, arrests, warrantless searches, phone taps, vigilante assaults, and strikebreakers. The nation employed "a vast and unprecedented network of domestic surveillance and control organizations to monitor and silence critics of the war, labor activists, and radicals." Police and state militia repression of a national steel strike delivered a blow to labor everywhere, as workers from other industries fell in line. A government back-to-work order, described by the once-compliant Gompers as "so autocratic as to stagger the human mind," ended the largest coal strike in U.S. history.[60]

Work stoppages combined with the shattering impact of the Bolshevik Revolution to spur the Red Scare, which constituted "the greatest single assault on constitutional rights that had ever taken place in the United States."[61] The trope of a mere scare minimizes the depth and dramatic impact of the repression, which drove the left out of U.S. politics.

The twin pillars of repression—the Espionage Act of 1917 and the Sedition Act of 1918—enabled the assault on workers, immigrants, and the left as well as on the constitutional guarantee of free speech. The first act provided a wide berth to interpretations as to actions considered treasonous or disruptive of the military effort and also allowed revocation of mailing privileges. The Sedition Act outlawed any comments deemed disloyal or subversive, even those delivered in private and even mere expression of contempt or scorn for the government. Only the Armistice in November 1918 prevented a flood of repressive prosecutions. Similar assaults on free speech had occurred during the Quasi War and the Civil War but not on this scale.

The Red Scare spurred a burgeoning federal political police force to inaugurate a campaign of countersubversion that would persist into the twenty-first century. Under the direction of Attorney General A. Mitchell Palmer and a twenty-four-year-old lawyer obsessed with radicalism, John Edgar Hoover, the Justice Department ordered raids in thirty-three cities and twenty-two states. The Senate Judiciary Committee subsequently condemned the illegal raids, conducted in part in response to a bombing attempt on Palmer's home in June 1919.

With Socialist Party membership growing by almost a third from 1918 to 1919, government at all levels, with enthusiastic public support, responded with repression. The "dragnet arrests" of January 1920 hauled in more than four thousand suspected radicals, as "virtually every leader of every local community organization was taken into custody." "The public was ecstatic," Geoffrey Stone notes. The *Washington Post* opined against "hairsplitting over infringement of liberty" in deference to ridding the country of radical influence. Although the "Palmer raids" emanated from Washington, "state and local governments exceeded the federal government in the virulence of their antiradical activities." The Red Scare was "whipped-up by bizarre vigilante organizations such as the self-styled American Protective League," Robert Latham adds.[62]

The purge achieved the desired effect, as some three thousand alleged radicals were deported after the Palmer raids and local prosecutions. The Red Scare gutted the International Workers of the World (the Wobblies) and resulted in the deportation of the anarchist Emma Goldman and the jailing of the Socialist leaders Victor Berger and Eugene Debs—Debs had garnered 6 percent of the popular vote for president in 1912 but now condemned the "capitalist war." The government banned a meeting in Minneapolis of the People's Council, a prominent Socialist organization, intercepted its mail, beat its members, and denied them their passports to attend an international conference in Stockholm. Convinced, particularly in the wake of the Bolshevik triumph, that domestic disorder represented a mortal threat to their power, the "Anglo-Saxon elites in the national establishment," Alan Dawley concludes, determined to meet the perceived threat "not by compromising with industrial workers, promoting racial justice, or furthering social reform, but by cracking down on discontent."[63]

Wartime repression targeted not only workers, immigrants, and radicals but also African Americans, Jews, women, and noncompliant progressives. Belligerent nationalists branded A. Philip Randolph, the NAACP, and other mainstream African American organizations as radical, thus encouraging vigilante violence, rebirth of the Ku Klux Klan, and a "rapid retreat of the federal government in race matters." Once African Americans arrived over there, Army authorities "campaigned strenuously to convince French soldiers and commanders not to treat darker-skinned U.S. soldiers as equal" through such means as shaking hands, praising them, dining with them, or, worst of all, allowing them intimacy with French women.[64]

Anxieties about the erosion of gender hierarchy at home emerged powerfully during the war and the wartime repression. The press condemned the social worker Jane Addams, as much a national hero as any woman could have been before the war, for her peace activism. Militarists worried that the country might become "a nation of Jane Addamses." One newspaper dismissed Addams and Congresswoman Jeanette Rankin as "a couple of foolish virgins" as a result of their opposition to the war. A judge sentenced the Socialist activist Kate Richards O'Hare to five years in prison under the Espionage Act for declaring that the nation treated women like "brood sows" to bear children to be sent off to war and "made into fertilizer."[65]

Guilty of a spectacular political misjudgment, progressives who had embraced the war as an opportunity to redeem the world as well as their own society instead witnessed the disintegration of their movement. Wilson and the progressives sought in militarism a revival of national unity only to find instead a deepening of internal divisions and exacerbation of anxieties. As progressives hoisted the banner of patriotic nationalism, Dawley explains, "they did not foresee the cruel trick history had in store, that in seeking to capture nationalism for their own ends, they turned out to be its captives."[66] Rather than uniting the public behind a "new freedom" at home and abroad, the war discredited progressives and their cause and brought to power the very conservative forces they had sought to contain. Like the anti-imperialists at the turn of the century—and liberals generally throughout U.S. history—the progressives ultimately failed because of their unwillingness to call into question Myth of America identity.

With their two-term president and a majority of progressives having embraced intervention, anti-interventionists had been marginalized and branded as subversive. Addams, Bourne, the Villards, and perhaps especially La Follette, who consistently "stood against the gale of super-patriotic support for the war," proved powerless against what the Wisconsin progressive described as "a new spirit of intolerance that challenges the right of any man to utter his independent judgment." Forced into silence during the war, Addams later recalled, "Within a year after the war began the old causes were . . . abandoned like war trenches on the Western Front and we found ourselves fighting in the last ditch for the primary bases of democratic society, the civil liberties proclaimed in the Declaration of Independence." Max Eastman concluded, "In nations as well as individuals hysteria is caused by inner conflict." War, John Dewey belatedly discovered, "compels all nations, even those professedly the most democratic, to turn authoritarian and totalitarian."[67]

Militant national identity thus destroyed the Progressive Era and gave rise to an emergent military-industrial complex and national security state. White supremacy, authoritarianism, xenophobia, and repression of the left flourished during the war to make the world safe for democracy.

CHAPTER 5

Choosing War

Going to war in 1917 brought deliverance from domestic anxieties and reaffirmation of Myth of America identity through externally focused violence. National patriotism soared as the arrival of two million U.S. troops made a difference in the war, affirming the nation's identity as a divinely sanctioned redeemer nation. The tumultuous welcome accorded Wilson in London and Paris, complemented by the emotional homecoming of U.S. troops, thus inspired another brief yet splendid new era of good feelings.

The Fourteen Points—the most powerful representation of Myth of America discourse since Lincoln and the Civil War—electrified domestic and international opinion. With the war ending on the basis of the president's eloquent appeal for "open covenants" and "a just and stable peace," who could doubt the arrival of the United States at the pinnacle of world leadership? The cathartic emotion of war and deliverance, however, obscured the fatal obstacles lying squarely in the path of peace.

As celebration of the Armistice and the doughboys' return ebbed away, psychic anxieties resurfaced powerfully over both domestic concerns and the League of Nations fight. On the home front, citizens grappled with the sweeping changes of Prohibition, economic conversion to peacetime, changing gender roles and sexual mores, the Great Migration and racial upheaval, strikes and labor unrest, immigration, "100 percent Americanism," and the assault on the left and erosion of constitutional rights in the Red Scare. At the same time, following his triumphant arrival in Paris, Wilson came to the edge of a great chasm lying between the discursive vision of a world made safe for democracy and European power politics. At Versailles, the president stepped directly into the abyss.

Wilson's Myth of America millennialism grated on the Allied leaders, especially President Georges Clemenceau of France, who found that "talking to Wilson is something like talking to Jesus Christ." In defiance of Wilson's call for "peace without victory," the Allies had already formulated secret treaties and decided on a Carthaginian peace that would saddle Germany with a debilitating reparations bill. As Harold Nicolson, a British delegate at Versailles, later explained, the British, French, and Italians noted "that the United States in the course of their short but highly imperialistic history, had constantly proclaimed the highest virtue while as constantly violating their professions and resorting to the grossest materialism." The "doctrine of self-determination" had not been applied "to the yellow man or to the black" nor to "the Red Indians or even the Southern states." The Allied leaders "observed that, almost within living memory, the great American Empire had been won by ruthless force. . . . Can we wonder that they preferred the precisions of their own old system to the vague idealism of a new system which America might refuse to apply even to her own continent?"[1]

The subsequent rejection of the Versailles Treaty by the U.S. Senate reaffirmed Myth of America unilateralism by rejecting the multilateral League of Nations. The war destroyed the reformist impulse of the Progressive Era and returned to power the same corporatist elite that had triumphed under William McKinley in 1896. Supposedly pragmatic progressives such as John Dewey and Walter Lippmann, who had embraced intervention as a means to advance both the nation and the world, had failed to grasp that national identity ultimately precluded egalitarian reform. The war brought a virtual end to trust busting and enabled consolidation of industry and guaranteed profits. "The radicalism which had tinged our whole political and economic life from soon after 1900 to the World War period has passed," a thankful Calvin Coolidge intoned.

The "roaring" prosperity of the 1920s benefited the middle and upper classes, which strengthened spontaneous consent behind Myth of America hegemony. The sweeping social change of the "roaring twenties"—the proliferation of radios, movies, vaudeville, jazz, mass advertising, automobiles, appliances, gadgets, baseball and other national sports—preoccupied the white middle and upper classes, who benefited most from rising wages and increased leisure time. Union membership declined from 5.1 million in 1920 to 3.6 million in 1929, as "scientific management" brought efficiency to the mass production assembly line. Continuing a long-term trend, farmers' percentage of national income fell from 16 percent in 1919 to 9 percent in 1929, as rural and urban poverty persisted.

Anxieties over race, gender, religion, and immigration reaffirmed national identity. The latest in a continuous series of religious "awakenings" emerged in the 1920s in response to perceptions of declining spirituality in a material age and the growing independence of women, now equipped not only with suffrage but also with birth control, which appeared to hail a new age of "sexual anarchy." The renascent Ku Klux Klan made restoration of female purity a chief objective, in addition to putting back in "their place" African Americans grown "brazen" and "uppity" as a result of wartime geographic and social mobility. While usually perceived as an extremist group, the Klan, once stripped of its flamboyant robes and rituals, actually reflected *mainstream* racial modernity, Protestant intolerance, patriarchy, and xenophobia.[2] The eugenics movement flourished, as millions of citizens touted mythical Anglo-Saxon superiority while exalting the purity of the Aryan race in contrast with the threats posed by blacks, Jews, Mexican-Americans, hyphenates, and Asians. While the Scopes "Monkey Trial" in 1925 delivered a broadside to fundamentalist discourse, to be sure, the evolution controversy at the same time rallied Christian conservatives, who used their churches, Bible schools, radio programs, and other means to defend religious tradition from the "diabolical" secular assault.[3]

Xenophobia permeated postwar culture, as the nation embraced the most sweeping immigration restriction in its history in 1924. The Johnson-Reed Act belied the national mythology of xenophilia—the United States as an open-armed haven for freedom-seeking immigrants—by sharply reducing the influx of new immigrants from eastern and southeastern Europe. The legislation naturalized the binary between good (English and Swedish, for example) and bad (Russians, Jews, Greeks) immigrants. Significantly, however, although the 1924 law created the U.S. Border Patrol, it enabled the inflow of Mexican migrant workers as a source of cheap labor for emergent agribusiness and other industries. Enabling migrants to work while excluding them from citizenship proved ideal, as a government report explained, because while the "migrants are providing a fairly adequate supply of [cheap] labor," the Mexican was "less desirable as a citizen than as a laborer."[4]

The myth of isolationism notwithstanding, the United States maintained the largest peacetime army in its history and possessed a navy arguably second to none. The National Defense Education Act of 1920 provided for a general staff to coordinate strategic planning and rapid mobilization for war. The Foreign Service, reorganized and professionalized under the Rogers Act (1924), trained a core of diplomats who would serve for generations. White male Protestant elites dominated the Foreign Service, which excluded women, blacks, and Jews throughout the interwar period. Another elitist organization, the Council on Foreign Relations, formed during the twenties as an establishment forum on world affairs.[5]

Until the autumn of 1929 the Republican internationalists marked progress in resurrecting a U.S.-led liberal (capitalist) hegemony out of the ashes of the Great War. Although the bitter legacy of the war led to an abandonment of crusading, make-the-world-safe-for-democracy Wilsonianism, the United States facilitated private economic and cultural initiatives and worked closely with private sector corporations, banks, and high finance to manage the postwar debt reparations triangle among the former belligerents. The nation thus conducted an internationalist foreign policy that historians have variously described as "informal empire" or "independent internationalism" or "empire without tears" but hardly isolationist.[6] Widespread cultural influence began with the arrival of the doughboys, continued with wartime food relief, and then exploded in the 1920s as tourists, artists, musicians, writers, expatriates, and movies flooded Europe. "There is no country where the power of the dollar has not reached," a *New York Times* reporter in Europe declared. "There is no capital that does not take the United States into consideration at almost every turn. . . . Isolationism is a myth."[7]

The Negation of Everything American

Myth of America identity fueled enemy-othering of Bolshevism, a consistent foreign policy overshadowing the entire interwar period and squarely contradicting the myth of isolationism. Not since the calumniation of the "merciless Indian savages" had the nation identified a demonic enemy whose very existence defied national identity. As a rival teleology advocating class struggle and promising the worldwide triumph of Socialism, Marxism directly contravened the Myth of America. The United States thus strove not merely to contain Bolshevism but to destroy it. The Marxist ideology not only vilified capitalism, it foreordained its destruction and sponsored a radical international organization, the Comintern, to push the process along. In addition to fomenting revolution against capitalism, "godless Communists" also condemned religion in the most heretical terms—it was merely the "opiate of the masses," sniffed the inimical Karl Marx. The Bolshevik dictatorship violated Western precepts of liberal pluralism, notably electoral politics and a putatively free press.

The devastation of Europe in the Great War heightened fears of the spread of the Bolshevik poison. After first reacting cautiously to the Bolshevik Revolution, Wilson embraced virulent anti-Communism and launched an undeclared "secret war" in Russia. The United States and the Western allies intervened directly in northern Russia and in Siberia, where Japan also intervened, both during and after the Great War. The Allies backed reactionary forces in the ensuing Russian civil war. The "Reds" won, however, and the Allied intervention of 1918–20, which included 14,000 U.S. troops (175 of whom died on Russian soil), succeeded only in generating long-term enmity and fuel for generations of anti-Western propaganda.

On his fateful nationwide speaking tour, Wilson described Bolshevism as "*the negation of everything American*" (emphasis added).] The president thus echoed the overwhelming majority of diplomats and presidential advisers, including Secretary of State Robert Lansing, who decried "atheistic Bolshevism" as a threat to "life, property, family ties, and personal conduct, all of the most sacred rights." Driven by such sentiments even after the withdrawal of troops from Russia, Wilson continued to send military aid to the White armies and to enforce an undeclared blockade of Russia.

Decrying Bolshevism as "the poison of disorder, the poison of revolt, the poison of chaos," Americans often linked domestic reformers and marginalized groups with the red threat. Progressives, socialists, feminists, and African Americans defied cultural hegemony by condemning the unsanctioned Russian intervention. Feminists pointed out that the Bolsheviks had promptly awarded women suffrage and called for gender equality, while the United States had continued to withhold the vote. Similarly, Wilson feared that because the wartime experiences had "gone to their heads," African Americans "returning from abroad would be our greatest medium in conveying Bolshevism to America." Some associated Bolshevism with "free love" as well as the threat of an overweening Jewish influence flowing from the new immigration of the past generation. Herbert Hoover, for example, noted the "very large majority of Jews" associated with "Communistic outbreaks." "The Protocols of the Elders of Zion," bogus documents that purported a global Jewish conspiracy, gained widespread credence at this time.

"Godless Communism" thus appeared as the preeminent binary in forging, affirming, and policing hegemonic conceptions of national identity. Targeting the USSR as the primary national enemy-other, the United States refused to conduct diplomacy with Bolshevism and sought to isolate the contagion by surrounding it with hostile regimes, a *cordon sanitaire*. Foreign Service diplomats viewed the Soviet Union as a "pariah regime" bent on world conquest and insisted that no diplomatic initiative emanating from the Kremlin could be taken seriously.[8]

The shattering impact of the Great Depression encouraged new thinking, however, prompting Franklin D. Roosevelt to recognize the Soviet Union in 1933, a news event overshadowed by the simultaneous end of Prohibition. Trade and cultural ties with Russia had increased in the 1920s, and some Americans flirted in the midst of the Depression with an attraction to Soviet state planning. Such views never came close to gaining ascendancy, however, and achieved even their limited popularity only as a result of the crisis of U.S. capitalism. Moreover, brutal Stalinist collectivization and the Kafkaesque Moscow purge trials stunned Americans such as William Bullitt, the first ambassador to the USSR, and ultimately reaffirmed virulent anti-Communism. Recognition ignited opposition, especially within the State Department, where an intense anti-Communism never abated throughout the Depression, war, and Cold War years. Diplomacy with the Soviets thus proved anomalous, a product of the exigencies of the Depression and subsequent world war.

Peace Internationalism

Despite U.S. repudiation of the League of Nations, a marginalized yet determined internationalist peace movement asserted itself throughout the interwar period. In the wake of the Great War (and the passing of Theodore Roosevelt) discourses exalting the manly virtues and splendid conquests of war rang hollow. Bitter memoirs, journalistic accounts, war stories, histories, literature, films, and speakers condemned the senseless violence of the Great War and the inequities of the Versailles Treaty. The Women's International League for Peace and Freedom (WILPF), demonized as subversive during the Red Scare, revived under the tireless leadership of its national secretary, Dorothy Detzer, after her arrival in Washington in 1923. WILPF, the American Friends Service Committee, the Carnegie Endowment for International Peace, the National Council for Prevention of War, and myriad church and pacifist groups lobbied in the wake of the shockingly destructive Great War for disarmament, arbitration, and other efforts to prevent a future conflict.

Myth of America discourse rarely credits peace advocacy for accomplishments in world politics, instead disdaining such activists for their putative naïve idealism. The idea of a league of nations emerged first in the peace and disarmament movements. Internationalists advocating peace and disarmament had taken part in the 1899 and 1907 congresses at The Hague, which created the Permanent Court of International Justice, or World Court. Within the Congress, so-called peace progressives condemned the Carthaginian peace and tangle over wartime debts and reparations; intervention and nonrecognition of the Soviet Union; and U.S. imperialism in Latin America and the Caribbean. Many of these senators joined the peace advocates in encouraging at least informal participation in the league and membership in the World Court.

While the narrative of isolationism implies a self-obsessed ignorance and contempt for engagement in world affairs, all of these activists expressed keen interest in foreign policy. Advocacy of international peace, justice, arbitration, nonintervention, and anti-imperialism had little to do with isolation but instead represented an *alternative yet activist* foreign policy paradigm. However, the postwar patriotic narrative, which drove militant global intervention, naturalized the pejorative trope isolationism rather than the benign noninterventionism or the laudatory "peace progressivism."[9]

Peace activism threatened national identity by putting international accord ahead of American unilateralism. While the overwhelming majority of peace advocates shared the perception of the United States as the leading force in international redemption, they wanted the nation to lead the world to peace, disarmament, and international law rather than toward unilateral intervention and militarism. "Pacifists in the twentieth century fundamentally have been internationalists," Timothy Smith points out. A member of the National Council for the Prevention of War warned against "too much isolationism" and "not enough of an appreciation of the necessity of international cooperation, if peace is to be attained and maintained. . . . The issue we face is not 'neutrality' or war. The third course is 'cooperation for peace.'"[10]

Peace activists often opposed individual policies such as the nonrecognition and isolation of Russia and condemned allies such as Britain and France for their colonial domination of dark-skinned, non-Western peoples. Some peace activists sharply condemned U.S. imperialism in the Caribbean and Central America, thus violating the sanctity of the Monroe Doctrine. Peace proponents applauded the Washington Treaty, negotiated by Secretary of State Charles Evans Hughes in 1921–22. The Four-, Five-, and Nine-Power treaties partially contained a nascent naval arms race, endorsed the Open Door in

China, and elicited great power support, including Japan, for the status quo in East Asia. While approving the treaties, peace progressives called for a still broader disarmament by noting, "The world-wide limitation of armies is as important as the limitation of navies."[11]

Peace internationalists often forged the vital link between domestic and foreign policy by advocating reform and justice at home as well as abroad. Their ranks included liberals, feminists, Socialists, clergy, experts on international law, pacifists, and various reform-minded citizens. Critics from the American Legion, Daughters of the American Revolution, and the Hearst press, among many others, often condemned peace advocates for their progressive views on domestic issues, such as economic justice, worker and women's rights, and support for farmers. Mainstream critics sought to discredit the *domestic* policies of peace-minded groups through the use of *foreign policy* tropes such as "pink," "parlor Bolsheviks," and "unmanly pacifists. "The peace movement needs in it more men who chew tobacco," one activist acknowledged.

The usable past echoes condemnation of the peace movement, not only through the trope of isolationism but also through the timeworn binary of realism and idealism. Realist discourse blended seamlessly with Myth of America identity. The realist emphasis on power and self-interest served to marginalize peace internationalism. Even Progressives such as Lippmann asserted that "pacifists in Britain and America were a cause" of the Second World War as a result of their idealistic quest for world peace. Scores of realist scholars have echoed Lippmann's charge, thus creating an ironclad "lesson of the past." "This thesis permeates both popular thinking and scholarship . . . from the 1950s to the present post—Cold War era," notes Cecilia Lynch, and serves a cultural mission "to disparage peace movements and dissent and legitimize interventionist policies."[12]

Although they remained marginalized, peace internationalists and domestic reformers gained cultural space when the Great Depression delivered a staggering blow to national identity. The Crash brought declining production, loss of earnings, mass unemployment, bank failures, falling exports, trade disputes and protectionism, and ultimately the rise of fascism, imperial rivalry, and a second world war. The nation's Gross National Product fell from $98.4 billion in 1929 to almost half as much within three years. Nearly fifteen million people lost their jobs. The first of many low points came in 1929, when the "Bonus Army" of World War I veterans demanding early payment of their service bonus encamped for months in Washington in groups of homemade shacks that were dubbed Hoovervilles, only to be violently driven out, their camps put to the torch by the same army in which they had once served. Roosevelt revived spirits with his brilliance at radio communication and a spate of New Deal programs, but his decision to torpedo the London Economic Conference and delink the dollar and gold in 1933 marked the breakdown of the liberal world system.

The national economic calamity revived Progressive Era discourses critical of the overweening power of big business. The gold-based "sound money" system, apotheosized since the 1896 campaign, and discourses exalting banking, finance, investment, and foreign loans all fell into disrepute. Much of the public blamed bankers and speculators, the former icons of the New Era, for the Crash. In 1933, after highly publicized hearings, a congressional committee declared that reckless speculation in securities constituted "one of the most scandalous chapters in the history of American investment banking." Roosevelt was a privileged neoaristocrat and thus far from a Socialist, yet he condemned "economic royalists" for impeding reform.[13]

While the Crash threatened to undermine cultural hegemony, an international crisis emerged following Japanese aggression in Manchuria in 1931. The Stimson Doctrine, named after Secretary of State Henry L. Stimson, pronounced U.S. nonrecognition of the Japanese puppet state of Manchukuo. Tokyo soon launched a punitive assault on Shanghai, the center of Western economic interests, and parted company with the League of Nations, which it denounced as a racist Western organization. A Pacific arms race ensued. With militant Japanese expansion in Asia, and Adolf Hitler representing the worst imaginable German revanchism, an explosive international environment prevailed throughout the depression years.

Noninterventionists and peace activists feared that the deteriorating international environment, combined with the anxiety of "economic royalists," would lead to renewed U.S. militarism. Peace progressives turned to the history and memory of World War I to forge a usable past against the revival of intervention. A revisionist literature asserted that the war had profited wealthy elites while undermining democracy at home. By emphasizing the wartime secret treaties, the failure of Wilsonian self-determination, the disillusion and discord at home, including the Red Scare, these writers produced a formidable challenge to intervention and enemy-othering inherent in national identity.[14]

Nothing did more to spur noninterventionist discourses than the Nye Committee hearings (1934–36), which investigated what would later be known as the military-industrial complex (MIC). Detzer and other peace internation-alists had lobbied for such an investigation since the end of the Great War. Less well known, however, the American Legion and other conservative groups also initially backed the investigation. Finally, under the stewardship of Gerald Nye, a Wisconsin-born progressive Republican and North Dakota senator, the Sen-ate Special Committee Investigating the Munitions Industry (SSC) convened in April 1934.

The post—World War II patriotic narrative dismisses the Nye Commit-tee—"among the most significant congressional investigating agencies in American history"—as an example of a naïve isolationism, an indulgence in foreign policy idealism, a progenitor of appeasement. "The committee has been painted in negative tones by most scholars and writers," Paul Koistinen points out. "Seldom has a conscientious and accomplished investigating body been treated as shabbily by history."[15]

In the course of two years the SSC conducted the most thorough analysis in U.S. history of the relationship, driven by militant national identity, between war, banking, and industry. Amassing thirty-nine volumes of evidence totaling fourteen thousand pages of hearings, interviews, reports, and press releases, the SSC documented "some of the very worst suspicions" about the munitions makers. Despite efforts by the munitions makers to sanitize their files and ob-struct the investigation, the SSC found that the industry had "evaded or ig-nored laws and treaties by gun running, selling illegally through intermedi-aries, and falsifying documents." Prior to U.S. intervention in the Great War, bankers, munitions makers, and public officials "perpetuated war scares" and "relied on bribery . . . as a standard business device." By grilling the financier and War Industries Board chairman Bernard Baruch, the SSC brought to light World War I price fixing and "shameless profiteering." War industries threat-ened to withhold their product until the government met their price, a practice the SSC fittingly but subversively labeled "the strike of capital."

The SSC assiduously avoided any charges of conspiracy, yet it revealed "an unhealthy alliance" between munitions makers and government forming "a self-interested political power which operates in the name of patriotism and satisfies interests which are, in large part, purely selfish." The SSC fueled coun-terhegemonic peace progressivism by revealing the critical nexus between al-lied loans and the decision to intervene in the Great War. A committee majority urged outright government ownership of munitions industries, steep taxes on war profits, and strong regulation of the shipbuilding industry.[16]

By the time it concluded its work in June 1936, the SSC had offered nothing less than a prescient analysis of the dangers of the MIC. The SSC revealed to Americans the self-interest and collusion between banking, war industries, the national military, and their political supporters. Its findings had profound implications for U.S. history that would carry into the twenty-first century.

The SSC could not have commanded the national spotlight for two years and offered such an incisive counterhegemonic analysis under conditions other than those of high anxiety fostered by the Great Depression and the bitter memories of World War I. Eventual U.S. intervention in World War II, followed by the prolonged Cold War, followed by the war on terror reflected the normal climate of Myth of America hegemony that would preclude wide currency of a subversive analysis such as that offered by the historic SSC.

Although Congress enacted *none* of its recommendations for strict controls of war-related industries, the SSC, the peace movement, and the World War I revisionists had fostered an atmosphere conducive to the passage of neutrality legislation designed to distance the nation from direct intervention in the growing international crises of Europe and Asia. The first such law, passed in 1935 in the midst of the SSC investigation, banned travel in a war zone as well as loans and arms sales to belligerents, reflecting the popular perception that the absence of such restrictions had sucked the nation into the Great War. Roosevelt reluctantly signed the legislation while chafing over the erosion of the imperial presidency in foreign affairs.

Compatibility with Fascism

Despite opposition from some peace internationalists, Myth of America identity proved compatible with fascist and militarist regimes throughout the 1930s. By 1930 U.S. firms had loaned Benito Mussolini's fascist regime in Italy more than $460 million while direct investments accounted for another $121 million. In 1933 Roosevelt declared he was "deeply impressed by what [Mussolini] has accomplished" and said, "I am keeping in fairly close touch with that admirable Italian gentleman." Following the initial outcry, "once the crisis of the Italo-Ethiopian War had passed, good relations with Rome were restored," David Schmitz points out. "Italian fascism was perceived as meeting all the qualifications for U.S. support: promise of political stability, anti-Bolshevism, and increased trade with the United States."[17]

Although many Americans expressed contempt for Nazism, the United States conducted a robust trade with Germany, carried out by such firms as

DuPont, Union Carbide, Standard Oil, and IBM, among others. These corporations, backed by Roosevelt, ignored a State Department protest that the Nazis employed the capital provided by U.S. corporations "for the maintenance of the German industrial program and . . . for German rearmament" designed to facilitate "aggressive measures."[18] Until the fall of 1938, when the *Kristallnacht* pogrom made it impossible to ignore the maniacal anti-Semitism inherent in Nazism, actions against Jews little concerned the United States, as many Christians shared to varying degrees a generalized suspicion and often hostility toward the Jewish "race." But, perhaps above all, at the root of appeasement was the virulent anti-Bolshevism the West shared with the fascist regimes. Hitler spewed hate for Communists and Jews alike; indeed, he typically conflated the two.

The U.S. response to the Spanish Civil War (1936–39) underscores the nation's identity-driven affinity for fascism and militarism. The Spanish right, which coalesced under General Francisco Franco, rejected the electoral victory of the leftist Popular Front and struck against it in July 1936. Although conventional diplomatic practice sanctioned trade and arms shipments to the legitimate government in such cases, the United States, Britain, and France declined to aid the Loyalist government. This policy, aptly characterized by Douglas Little as "malevolent neutrality," facilitated Franco's victory in the spring of 1939.[19]

Franco's authoritarian regime ultimately proved more compatible with Myth of America identity than the democratically elected government of Spain. As early as 1931 diplomats feared "widespread Bolshevistic influences," though fewer than one thousand members belonged to Spain's Communist Party. One diplomat, invoking the trope of original sin, warned of Spain falling into "the coils of the communistic serpent."[20] Such dark suspicions appeared to be confirmed by the Loyalist takeover and occupation by armed workers of the holdings of the Spanish subsidiary of International Telephone and Telegraph. The specter of Bolshevism appeared even more real when the Soviet Union responded to German and Italian support of Franco by sending its aid and war materials to the Loyalists in Barcelona. On April 1, 1939—a mere three days after his forces took Madrid—the United States accorded Franco diplomatic recognition.

Only the marginalized left and a smattering of peace progressives advocated an antifascist foreign policy. The Socialist Norman Thomas secured a private meeting with Roosevelt to emphasize the actual nonneutrality of Washington's position in Spain. Detzer demanded justification for an arms embargo enforced against the Spanish Republic but not applied to "all the secondary supplying countries." The supposedly isolationist Nye introduced a joint resolution calling for repeal of the embargo. Neither Nye nor William Borah, another supposed isolationist, called for direct intervention on behalf of the Loyalists, but they emphasized that the embargo ultimately benefited Spanish fascism. Sharply opposed by Roosevelt, Nye's resolution died in committee.[21]

Under national identity the only alternative to appeasement—entering into a collective security arrangement with the Soviet Union, the primary enemy-other—was a cultural impossibility. Thus the Spanish Civil War cemented the Western diplomacy of containing Bolshevism by appeasing fascism. U.S. policy, as Arnold Offner explains, "reinforced Anglo-French appeasement and served to secure Franco's victory."[22]

Despite Stalin's draconian domestic policies, the Soviet dictator rejected the Trotskyist call for world revolution, which he called an "idiotic slogan," in deference to "socialism in one country," by which he meant breakneck industrialization and ruthless liquidation of all political opposition. Foreign Minister Maxim Litvinov worked tirelessly to promote the Popular Front of coalition politics with capitalist states. Despite these efforts anti-Communism remained the primary concern of England, France, and the United States, even as the Nazis launched a massive remilitarization and fascist Italy invaded Ethiopia in 1935. "There are only two governments in Europe capable of being a real victor. One is Germany, and the other is Russia," the diplomat Breckenridge Long declared. "I shudder to think of a Russian domination of Europe."[23] In Britain Winston Churchill and others expressed a preference for fascists like Mussolini over "the bestial passions of Leninism."[24]

The 1938 Munich Conference marked the apogee of appeasement and gave rise to the "Munich syndrome," which obscured Soviet efforts to deter fascist aggression by securing collective security arrangements with the West. The Cold War narrative emphasized "unmitigated Soviet perfidy," as manifested in the Nazi-Soviet Pact, Michael Carley points out, while obfuscating "the Anglo-French rejection of numerous Soviet initiatives to improve relations . . . or to create an anti-Nazi coalition, especially during the period 1935–1938." Peter Boyle concurs, noting that the United States backed Britain and France in rejecting "strenuous efforts by Stalin and Litvinov" to forge "a collective front against Hitler." Thus at "the root of failure of Anglo-Franco-Soviet cooperation against Nazism was anti-communism."[25]

The 1939 Nazi-Soviet Pact brought an end to appeasement; moreover, by fusing communism with fascism the alliance created cultural space within the United States for the nation to move toward intervention. Plenty of evidence existed to make the case that both regimes were "evil" and thus deserving of a manly, providentially sanctioned U.S. response. Nazi and Soviet aggression, as the two powers divided Eastern Europe in 1939, thus revivified the martial spirit within Myth of America identity and eroded support for strict neutrality.

The historic American affinity for the fellow white, British cousins fueled the rising national militancy. Churchill, whose mother was American, inspired sympathy as he embodied heroic resistance in the Battle of Britain. In 1941 polls showed that Britain was the European country that the U.S. public liked best. During the Blitz, Hitler's bombing assault on London, Edward R. Murrow and other broadcasters vividly reported on the besieged island outpost of Anglo-Saxon civilization. Many Americans came to see the war as a great moral cause for all of Western civilization.[26]

The Good Neighbor Discourse

Following the outbreak of World War II in 1939, Latin America became a critical site in the revival of militant national identity leading to direct U.S. intervention. Diplomacy toward Latin America thus takes on an importance that transcends hemispheric relations alone. The consistent pattern of U.S. hegemony also underscores the compatibility between the Myth of America and militarist regimes.

Given the compartmentalization of modern scholarship, historians and other academics typically analyze Latin American diplomacy independently, as a separate subfield, thereby divorcing U.S. hegemony from mainstream diplomacy. Thus the interwar period could be labeled isolationist even as the United States supervised and occupied hemispheric protectorates in Cuba, Haiti, Puerto Rico, and Panama. The United States reinforced quasicolonial authority over the Dominican Republic, Nicaragua, and the West African nation of Liberia. Puerto Rico remained a U.S. possession with no prospect for self-determination, as underscored when police opened fire on a nationalist demonstration in the 1930s, killing seventeen and wounding hundreds. The overriding purpose of initiatives such as the Jones Act of 1917 bestowing U.S. citizenship upon Puerto Ricans was to undercut advocates of outright independence for the island.[27]

At the end of World War I, prolonged military occupation of Haiti and Santo Domingo had generated opposition, especially by progressive magazines such as the *Nation* and the *New Republic*. Congressional hearings on the Haitian occupation publicized incidents of murder, torture, and rape. Many progressives who had endorsed supervision over various "backward" and "dependent" states before the war now condemned such action as imperialistic. Dollar diplomacy increasingly fell into disrepute as "anti-imperialists in both the United States and in borrowing countries began to forge a transnational cultural movement that challenged claims about mutual benefit and progress with a narrative about exploitation and destruction," Emily S. Rosenberg explains. Interventionists fired back at critics with tropes of "parlor bolshevists" and "revolutionary propagandists" as a broad debate over imperialism emerged.[28]

Domestic opposition, Latin American resistance, and the onset of the Depression ushered in the "good neighbor policy." At the Havana Conference of 1928, the Latin delegates resolved, "No state has a right to intervene in the affairs of another." The good neighbor policy, first advanced by peace progressives and only then embraced by Hoover and Roosevelt, elided an actual foreign policy of relentless support for the reactionary dictatorships and oligarchies that often courted U.S. hegemony to gain power and profit.[29]

The Roosevelt administration, no less than his Republican predecessors, carried out a continuous foreign policy of hegemony rooted in Euro-American modernity and propounded as doctrine since the Monroe presidency. Bitter relations with Mexico, now exacerbated by the specter of Bolshevism, continued after the Great War. Myth of America identity had long held that the United States, as the racially superior modernist nation, should enjoy unimpeded access to Mexican land and resources. The essential problem, Ambassador James Sheffield explained, was Mexico's "Latin-Indian mind, filled with hatred of the United States.[30]

By scripting Central America and the Caribbean as being under Bolshevik threat, the United States underwrote the suppression not only of radical but also even of merely liberal reformers. As Mexicans sought to gain control of their resources, "with increasing certainty the United States evaluated the Mexican Revolution's policies as Communist-inspired," Daniela Spenser notes. Coolidge insisted on the "undeniable fact that the Mexican government today is a Bolshevist government." While Mexico had indeed drawn inspiration from Leninist anti-imperialism, Soviet foreign policy proved heavy-handed in Mexico, which broke off relations with the USSR in the late twenties. By that time J. Edgar Hoover had infiltrated Mexico with propaganda and forged documents purporting to show Russian plans to instigate a Communist revolt in Mexico.[31]

Despite the lack of Soviet influence over Mexico, the Bolshevik enemy-other remained at the forefront of popular and official U.S. consciousness. President Lázaro Cárdenas defied the United States by turning away from an earlier agreement, speeding up the tempo of the land reform program, and seizing additional property claimed by Americans. On March 18, 1938, Cardenas nationalized the four-hundred-million-dollar oil industry, which prompted Secretary of State Cordell Hull to call for a showdown with "these communists down there."[32] The United States cut off all loans and economic aid for five years, until the desire for hemispheric solidarity against Nazi Germany overwhelmed all other considerations and a modus vivendi emerged.[33]

The weaker Central American and Caribbean nations could not offer as much resistance and thus fell under almost complete Yankee domination. Despite the pervasive discourse of spreading democracy and being a good neighbor, Myth of America identity empowered dictators who understood they would receive support as long as they cooperated with creditors, investors, and corporations. In Haiti, pressure exerted not only by the Haitians themselves, but also by other Latin Americans, African Americans, and peace internationalists compelled the United States to bring an end to the bloody military occupation of 1915–34. Hegemony and dependence continued, however, as the United States crushed a peasant rebellion, kept a tight rein on Haiti's finances, and facilitated the rise of the postwar dictatorships of François "Papa Doc" Duvalier and his son, Jean-Claude "Baby Doc." In the adjacent Dominican Republic, occupied by U.S. Marines from 1916 to 1924, a dictatorship under Rafael Trujillo received U.S. support by adhering to the dictates of dollar diplomacy. The U.S. military trained the constabulary, and neither it nor the mainstream press displayed concern when in 1937 Trujillo's troops carried out genocide against some ten thousand to twenty-five thousand Haitian migrants looking for work in the Dominican sugar fields. Washington maintained financial supervision until World War II.[34]

Imperial anxiety accelerated over instability in Nicaragua, where the charismatic rebel leader Augusto César Sandino defied U.S. hegemony. The United States withdrew from Nicaragua in 1925, following fifteen years of direct military occupation, but in the absence of a Trujillo clone there, the Marines were sent back the following year and reached a peak of fifty-six hundred in 1929. Sandino refused to accept a U.S.-brokered political settlement, explaining, "Eighteen years of American meddling in Nicaragua have plunged the country deeper into economic misery."

The failure of thousands of U.S. Marines to hunt down Sandino or stop his raids made a mockery of the United States and a legend of Sandino. When the journalist Carleton Beals accomplished what the Marines could not—he found Sandino and published several articles based on their interview—Stimson denounced the "revolutionist propaganda [which] had quite seriously warped the accuracy of American news." The State Department closely monitored Beals's journalism, referred to him as an "alleged American citizen," intercepted his mail, and started a file on him headed "Anti-American Activities."[35]

By 1931 Stimson called for an end to the occupation, citing the deaths of several Marines in Sandino's periodic raids, its high cost in the midst of the Depression, and the embarrassing parallels between U.S. actions in Nicaragua and the Japanese invasion of Manchuria denounced under the Stimson Doctrine that same year. With the foreign intervention at an end, Sandino promptly declared an end to his rebellion and paraded triumphantly into Managua, where he and his followers received amnesty. However, in February 1934, the U.S.-trained Guardia Nacional under Anastasio Somoza arrested Sandino as he left a dinner party with the president, took him to a Managua airfield, and shot him to death. Many of his followers met the same fate.

The United States trumpeted the Somoza family dictatorship as a good neighbor and a model for all of Central America. Somoza proved ideal: he embraced U.S. hegemony in return for personal power and profit, spoke fine English, had lived in the United States, and was an avid baseball fan. He and his two sons ruled and plundered the country for the next forty-three years.[36]

Hegemonic U.S. identity drove a similar outcome in El Salvador, where the charismatic nationalist Agustín Farabundo Martí, a young intellectual more radical than Sandino, sought to liberate all of Central America by means of socialist revolution. After the State Department warned of a "serious situation in Salvador resulting from the Communistic outbreak," the United States applauded the Salvadoran oligarchy, which killed the so-called bolshevist Martí and slaughtered perhaps thirty thousand of his followers in 1932. The bloodbath created stability because the left had been exterminated, earning prompt U.S. recognition of the military regime that had carried it out. Under U.S. supervision, the coffee oligarchy continued to displace peasants from the land in order to expand the plantations.

In Guatemala, the dictator Jorge Ubico caved in to pressure and agreed to conduct trade on U.S. terms, including abrogating a most-favored nation agreement with Great Britain. U.S. forces had intervened six times in Honduras by 1925 and conducted a continuous occupation of the Panama Canal Zone. Costa Rica, always the most stable Central American country, required less direct policing, though its economy, too, became dependent on the United States. Bananas and coffee dominated the exports of all the Central American countries; northern markets and U.S. corporations could make or break them. In Costa Rica, for example, in 1929 coffee and bananas represented seventeen million of the eighteen million dollars total export revenues.

U.S. foreign policy thus fostered dependency. Oligarchy and terror helped to preserve "a social-economic system in which 2 percent of the population in four of the five Central American nations controlled the land and hence the lives of the other 98 percent," Walter LaFeber explains.[37]

Long perceived as destined to enter the U.S. orbit, Cuba, the largest Caribbean island, remained under Yankee hegemony. Since Spain's ouster, the United States intervened repeatedly under the Platt Amendment until 1925, at which time Gerardo Machado, a "reformed cattle thief," became president. Embarking on a tour of the United States, Machado pledged his fealty to Coolidge and assured bankers and businessmen that their investments were safe in Cuba, whose government he modeled along the lines of Mussolini's fascist regime. When the Depression brought a collapse in sugar prices, undermining Machado's authority, he countered dissent with repression, which only deepened the resistance. Roosevelt backed the diplomat Sumner Welles's decision to oust Machado, who left the island for good.[38] Livid over continued instability in Cuba, Welles on at least two occasions specifically requested a U.S. Marine landing, but Roosevelt refused to authorize a blatant violation of the good neighbor discourse.

The United States denied recognition to Ramón Grau San Martén, a surgeon and anatomy professor at the University of Havana, as his array of domestic reforms, including woman's suffrage, rights for labor, and hostility to foreign ownership threatened U.S. hegemony. The United States allied instead with reactionary militarists more compatible with U.S. identity. The man Beals promptly dubbed the "new Machado" was Fulgencio Batista, the head of the Cuban armed forces. Beals accurately reported that the United States now backed "an illegal government which looked legal," reflecting an "interventionist attitude not one whit different" from that which existed before the good neighbor policy. Batista soon assumed direct authority over Cuba, which he ruled for more than two decades. The "failure to establish normal relations with Grau enabled Batista to rise," Irwin Gellman notes, and "diplomatic ties consolidated his power." The United States "was able to contain the forces of social revolution, mitigate the effects of nationalist reforms upon its interests, and actually tighten its control over Cuban developments," Jules Benjamin observes.[39]

By the onset of World War II, the United States had succeeded as never before in establishing the hegemony over its southern neighbors that the Monroe Doctrine had prophesied more than a century before. In collusion with local strongmen—dubbed "the good neighbor of tyrants" by the Peruvian leader Haya de la Torre—the United States cemented a hegemonic relationship that kept most Latin American nations in debt, dependent on northern markets, and limited in their economic diversification and trade with European nations.[40]

As he moved toward intervention in World War II, Roosevelt dramatically exaggerated the Nazi threat to Latin America. The president invoked the Monroe Doctrine's "no-transfer" clause (of any American state to a European power), winning the approval of the Latin American states at the Havana Conference in the summer of 1940.[41] Roosevelt also negotiated the "destroyers for bases" deal in which the United States received ninety-nine-year leases for naval and air bases in seven British possessions in the Americas, from Newfoundland to Trinidad, with Bermuda in between, in return for supplying Britain with fifty naval destroyers.

Gaining new bases and expanding national influence flowed from Myth of America identity and thus received public consent. Roosevelt unilaterally extended the Monroe Doctrine to Greenland and Iceland, states more European than American. The United States landed troops on Iceland, in the first military expedition outside the Western Hemisphere since World War I, while extending the "neutrality zone" a thousand miles from U.S. shores, acts of "hemispheric defense" that Roosevelt insisted did not require congressional approval. "The people seem to regard Iceland as an island off the coast of Maine," the noninterventionist senator Robert Taft complained.[42]

Unable to rule the English Channel, Hitler could hardly rule the Atlantic, much less occupy and control such a vast region so far from Germany, yet fears of a Nazi assault on Latin America accelerated. Americans responded to charges that Hitler was fomenting coups in Latin American states and possessed elaborate plans for their administration. The persistent "warning of invasions, surprise attacks, and fifth-column revolts in Latin America," Gellman points out, "excited peoples' emotions" and helped to revivify militant national identity.[43]

Psychic Crisis

In keeping with a continuous pattern over the sweep of U.S. history, intensified anxiety eventually culminated in an identity-driven renewal of warfare. The psychic crisis, which inheres in identity (see appendix D), became acute in the midst of the Depression, the New Deal, the rise of counterhegemonic peace activism, and foreign aggression in Europe and Asia.

The seemingly insoluble economic collapse shattered Myth of America identity of the nation's providential destiny to lead the world as the exemplar of modernist progress. The can do American spirit had given way to despair. Social legislation, factory laws, unemployment insurance, and unions arose under the New Deal to provide social protection in the wake of the free fall of the market system. Roosevelt acknowledged the depths of the Depression, declaring that "one-third of a nation" remained "ill-housed, ill-clothed, and ill-fed." By his second term the nation confronted the ignominy of a recession within a prolonged depression.[44]

While the Depression overshadowed everything, the rise of European fascism, Soviet collectivization, and Japanese militarism also defied the nation's providential destiny to lead the world. As the German command economy roared to life behind militarism, the Soviets industrialized rapidly, though at horrific human costs not fully grasped in the West, on the basis of a series of five-year plans. With free enterprise and the "magic of the marketplace" discredited by the Crash, many saw "no alternative but either to remain faithful to an illusionary idea of freedom and deny the reality of society, or to accept that reality and reject the idea of freedom," as Karl Polanyi put it in 1944. "The first is the liberal's conclusion; the latter is the fascist's."[45] While many clung to the shibboleths of classical theory, Roosevelt, lacking a sophisticated grasp of economics, never evolved a systematic or consistent program.

Even though Roosevelt sought to preserve capitalism, the New Deal incited widespread anxiety of an un-American creeping socialism. Roosevelt's domestic program had brought a dramatic expansion of federal authority, ranging from promotion of electric power to programs for artists and musicians. The president had condemned "economic royalists" while empowering an elite intellectual brain trust. The New Deal focus on domestic relief, reform, and recovery contravened the nation's rugged individualism. New Deal programs such as the National Recovery Act, with its Blue Eagle codes, appropriated patriotic symbolism, normally the provenance of warfare, and applied it in a domestic context.

While Myth of America identity inscribed Bolshevism as the nation's primary enemy-other, the Communist Party USA (CPUSA) achieved unprecedented growth and legitimacy as a result of the crisis of capitalism. Labor militancy, notably in the sit-down strikes, earned workers unprecedented federally sanctioned rights to collective bargaining. The New Deal era proved so subversive as to recognize Indians as a separate culture under the Indian New Deal. In California, the socialist writer Upton Sinclair, the famous muckraker, nearly won the governorship through an EPIC campaign—End Poverty in California—that rallied the emotional support of millions of ordinary people. A massive financial infusion, in which spending reached as much as ten billion dollars during the Depression, funded an anti-Sinclair campaign that narrowly enabled the Golden State to avoid falling under the "Crimson banner."[46]

The CPUSA campaigned openly for the rights of workers, women, and African Americans at a time when "stark racial binaries structur[ed] U.S. life and law."[47] Roosevelt, often retreating to Warm Springs, Georgia, in the Democratic "solid South," did little to advance African American equality. The president did, however, appoint a Jew to his cabinet, Treasury Secretary Henry Morgenthau, and Jews joined other agencies as well, which provoked bitter condemnation of the "Jew Deal" threat to Anglo-Saxon Christian hegemony.

The Depression–New Deal era produced a crisis of masculinity. With as much as one-third of the male workforce jobless during the economic collapse, men lost the ability to fulfill the role of family provider, causing an emasculating loss of confidence, depression, and a spike in suicides. Millions of men literally lost strength during the Depression, as sickness and malnourishment became so pervasive that from 1940 to 1945 the armed forces rejected one-third of all men after physical examination following induction. The New Deal Civilian Conservation Corps reflected anxieties about proper socialization of male youth during the Depression, while numerous writers expressed fears of the nation becoming soft, often by contrast with a powerful, thrusting Germany. A social worker, Harry Hopkins, served as the president's closest adviser. Inside the State Department Welles and a few other homosexuals or alleged homosexuals, later demonized as "lavender boys," threatened masculine identity. Fears mounted over the appearance of growing female empowerment as Secretary of Labor Frances Perkins became the first female cabinet officer, and Eleanor Roosevelt spoke her mind on issues of national and international policy.

Despite continuing opposition owing to memories of the failed crusade in the Great War, militant national identity gradually drove the nation toward direct intervention in World War II. By the time of the destroyers-for-bases deal, prointervention groups trumpeting militant identity exerted influence across the country. Backed by some three hundred local chapters, the Committee to Defend America by Aiding the Allies sponsored rallies and speakers, stressed the putative Nazi designs on Latin America, and distributed such films as *It Could Happen Here,* which depicted a German invasion of the United States. The pro-British Century Group lobbied tirelessly for aid to Britain and for the United States to fulfill its destiny as a world power by taking a role in the war.

Nationalist anxiety centered on the prospect of increased radicalism both at home and abroad. The nation's identity precluded a noninterventionist continentalist foreign policy centered on Western Hemisphere trade and defense, as advocated by Charles A. Beard, among others. "We would never be satisfied to be bottled up in the American continent," the diplomat William Phillips declared. If the economy remained stagnant or deteriorated because of Nazi domination of European markets, capitalism could give way to a regimented economic order at home, presumably directed by New Dealers, women, Jews, and socialists. The diplomat Pierrepont Moffat feared "the probability of ultimate Bolshevism," while John Foster Dulles warned of "social revolution." Free trade internationalists such as Hull believed the United States would be forced to adopt "regimentation of an ever increasing scale."[48]

Despite the bitter struggle during the "great debate" of 1939–41, both interventionists and noninterventionists—like the turn-of-the-century imperialists and anti-imperialists—embraced Myth of America identity. The vast majority of noninterventionists perceived the United States as a chosen nation, under God, and a model for all the world, whereas Europe, by contrast, remained a seething cauldron of Old World corruption, a continent seemingly destined to embroil itself in an endless series of aggressive wars. By remaining disengaged from the European war, they reasoned, the United States could pursue its mission to provide the world with a model of democratic government. Noninterventionists thus invoked Washington's Farewell Address and Quincy Adams's Fourth of July speech to insist that the nation must avoid "entangling alliances" or going in search of "monsters to destroy." Most noninterventionists, however, shared mainstream racial modernity and thus supported hegemony over Latin America.[49]

Memories of the slaughter and devastating trench warfare of World War I remained vivid. "We cannot re-conquer a continent without wholesale death," advised the *New York Times* military correspondent Hanson Baldwin, an Annapolis graduate with three years of active service. Some noninterventionists predicted as many as a million U.S. casualties in the event of war. In September 1940 anti-interventionists formed the America First Committee (AFC), headquartered in Chicago but with offices sprouting across the country. Most AFC members concurred with Nye, who accused Roosevelt of steering the country "straight into a war of European power politics." Roosevelt denied the charge, declaring during the 1940 campaign, "Your president says this country is not going to war."[50]

Choosing War

As in World War I, the United States, as the world's providentially destined beacon of liberty, could scarcely sit out the great battle for the soul of Western civilization. Secretary of War Stimson went to the heart of the matter with his observation in May 1940 that "without real cooperation on our part toward securing victory we would have little influence at the end." Military production would not be sufficient to meet the Nazi threat "until we got into the war ourselves."[51]

The same month Roosevelt won reelection to an unprecedented third term, Admiral Harold Stark presented "Plan Dog" (naval slang for the fourth of a series of options, or option D), which became the U.S. war strategy. Plan Dog called for concentrating efforts on defending the British cousin and then defeating Nazi Germany in Europe. The memorandum warned that the United States did not have the naval power or military forces sufficient to fight in both Europe and the Pacific, but that the defeat of Germany was a vital "national interest."[52]

By a wide majority Congress passed the Lend-Lease Act as HR 1776, a trope implicitly demonstrating the connection between foreign policy and national identity by invoking the original "fight for freedom." Appealing to the nation's heritage in a fireside chat on December 29, 1940, Roosevelt declared, "Never before since Jamestown and Plymouth Rock has our American civilization been in such danger as now." Calling on the public to display "the same spirit of patriotism and sacrifice as we would show were we at war," the president called on the nation to serve as the "great arsenal of democracy." The fireside chat reached 76 percent of the public, either directly or indirectly, and met an overwhelmingly favorable response. "Mr. Roosevelt has brought the country along step by step in a masterly way," the banker Thomas Lamont observed.[53]

A national campaign against alleged subversives, as typically occurs when the nation goes to war, followed approval of lend-lease. AFC members condemned lend-lease, which they viewed as unconstitutionally enabling the president to make war at his own discretion. "I would not give such powers to the Archangel Gabriel," Oswald Garrison Villard declared. The noninterventionist senator Burton Wheeler (D-Montana) bluntly labeled lend-lease "the New Deal's triple A foreign policy; it will plow under every fourth American boy."[54] Although he called Wheeler's comment the most "dastardly, unpatriotic thing that has ever been said," Roosevelt had done his part to bring about the acrimony by impugning the patriotism of those who disagreed with his foreign policy. Continually invoking the term popularized in the Spanish Civil War, Roosevelt condemned "appeaser fifth columnists" and critics who employed "certain techniques of propaganda, created and developed in dictator countries."[55]

By far the most captivating opponent of lend-lease and hence the target of a determined countersubversive assault was the aviation hero Charles A. Lindbergh, who testified for almost five hours against H.R. 1776. As the first man to fly solo from New York to Paris (a feat he accomplished in May 1927), the "Lone Eagle" still enjoyed tremendous prestige and celebrity, flowing also from his marriage to Anne Morrow and from the repercussions of the "crime of the century," the sensational kidnapping and murder of their infant son in 1932. Noting that Britain had survived the Nazi bombing in relative close proximity, Lindbergh explained that German bombing could not by any means be extensive enough to serve as prelude to an invasion of the United States. Writing in the *New York Times,* Baldwin agreed that Lindbergh "obviously was right."[56]

By countering efforts to portray aid to the Allies as homeland defense, the highly publicized testimony of the aviation hero undermined Myth of America identity. Interior Secretary Harold Ickes labeled Lindbergh the "No. 1 Nazi fellow traveler" and the "first American to raise aloft the standard of pro-Nazism." Lindbergh left himself vulnerable by declining publicly to condemn Nazism and by making a stereotypical reference to Jews as a separate "race" during a highly publicized AFC rally in Des Moines. His variant of anti-Semitism was widespread in the prewar United States, as reflected in the 1924 immigration law and in polls showing that at least a third of the public favored Jewish exclusion. Nevertheless, as Geoffrey Smith notes, Lindbergh undermined the move-ment, as "non-interventionists were everywhere on the defensive, explaining that they were not Nazis."[57]

As enemy-othering reinvigorated militant national identity, the nation moved toward direct involvement in the world war. The media and public opinion turned in favor of intervention, as the "great debate" proved one-sided in newsreels and motion pictures. The public, including millions of illiterate citizens, soaked up newsreels that promoted intervention and disdained airing of competing viewpoints. "For all practical purposes, the [motion] picture industry has become a servant of the Roosevelt administration in respect of foreign, naval, and military designs," Charles and Mary Beard declared. In Hollywood Jack Warner led the way as the major studios offered to produce "simplistic one-sidedly interventionist propaganda."[58]

A renewed Nazi blitzkrieg in April 1941 helped interventionists to relegate subversive critics to the margins. The Nazis overwhelmed Greece and Yu-goslavia in a matter of days while they continued to rain bombs on London, striking the House of Commons. Newspapers brought maps of Europe dark-ened by fresh waves of Nazi conquest. Hitler, however, changed the course of war on June 22 by launching an ultimately fatal campaign against his most hated enemy, the Soviet Union. Operation Barbarossa, the greatest land inva-sion in history, bogged down after the fall of Kiev, as the Soviets, despite mas-sive losses, continually rebuilt defensive lines and fought tenaciously.

The diplomat Joseph Grew vividly exemplified identity-driven enemy-oth-ering when he called Barbarossa "the best thing that could have happened. Dog eat dog. Let the Nazis and the Communists so weaken each other that the democracies will soon gain the upper hand or at least will be released from their dire peril." By late July the Nazis had failed to take Leningrad or Moscow, and the *New York Times* described German losses as "staggering." The Luftwaffe had suffered great losses during the blitz as the German campaign utterly failed to break British morale, prompting Hitler to cancel Sea Lion, a planned cross-channel invasion of the British Isles.[59] Roosevelt could no longer plausibly em-phasize any immediate Nazi threat to the Americas. Moreover, Barbarossa re-duced the chances that an incident would bring the nation into the war, as "Hitler was determined to avoid war with the United States until victory in Russia was assured." In June 1941 the fuehrer ordered, "Every incident involving the USA is to be avoided."[60]

In a historic meeting aboard ship off the Newfoundland coast near Argentia Bay, the two "Anglo-Saxon" leaders Roosevelt and Churchill forged an enduring bond that would carry them through the war together. Together the two men sang hymns in a somber Sunday morning shipboard service. Churchill reported to his cabinet on August 19 that Roosevelt had promised that "he would wage war, but not declare it, and that he would become more and more provocative. If the Germans did not like it, they could attack American forces." Roosevelt had indicated that "everything was to be done to force an 'incident.'"[61] Roosevelt thus rejected the advice of Stimson, Hopkins, and others who urged him to seek a congressional declaration of war rather than a secret policy of manipulation that raised, as Stimson put it, "a grave question of constitutional relations between the President and Congress—a relation which went to the very fundamentals of free government." The first incident came on September 4, when the U.S. warship *Greer* fired on a Nazi submarine it had stalked. Much as Polk had instigated the war with Mexico in 1846 and then blamed it on Mexico, Roosevelt told a Navy Day audience, "We have wished to avoid shooting. But the shooting has started. And history has recorded who fired the first shot."[62]

Although committed to the "Europe-first" strategy established under Plan Dog, the United States ultimately went to war through the "back door" that opened when the Japanese attacked Pearl Harbor. The United States and Japan had a long and troubled history, one exacerbated by U.S. racial exclusion policies in the western states and under the 1924 immigration law. Under racial modernity the Western powers viewed themselves as the only peoples sufficiently civilized to possess the right to hold colonies thousands of miles from their shores. The westerners seemed determined to contain Japan while clinging tenaciously to their colonies, including British Hong Kong, India, Burma, and Malaya; French Indochina; the Dutch East Indies; Portuguese Timor; and the United States in Guam, Hawaii, and the Philippines.

In the U.S. cultural imaginary, the Chinese represented a benevolent mass of simple humanity who worked the "good earth," to use the novelist Pearl Buck's phrase, whereas Japan remained the yellow peril. (After Pearl Harbor, *Life* ran an article entitled "How to Tell Japs from the Chinese.")[63] Following the establishment of Manchukuo in 1931, Japan asserted under the Amau Doctrine of 1934 its own special "mission" (*shimei*) in China in which Tokyo represented itself as engaged in saving China from the threat of Communism. With the U.S. frontier having closed, China offered a romanticized vision and a site for manifesting U.S. prestige and visions of providential expansion. Missionaries, traders, naval strategists, politicians, journalists, and publishers, and the China lobby broadened public support for Generalissimo Chiang Kai-shek and his English-speaking wife, invariably described as being beautiful and charming during her frequent U.S. visits. While declining to invoke the neutrality law to come to the aid of an elected government in Spain, the United States proved willing to come to the aid of a corrupt Chinese "nationalist" regime.[64]

The "China incident" of 1937, a brutal Japanese military assault that spiraled out of control in the aptly characterized "rape of Nanking," placed Japan and the United States on a collision course of competing imperial identities. Vastly overconfident about its own imperial destiny, Japan badly miscalculated, as its invasion aroused a determined Chinese resistance: "Unable to maintain control of the vast rural countryside . . . the Japanese armies in China soon found themselves hopelessly frustrated, both militarily and politically." Japan resorted to murderous assaults, chemical warfare, and "annihilation campaigns," killing as many as 2.7 million noncombatants. On September 27, 1940, Japan, increasingly gripped by militaristic fanaticism, signed the Tripartite Pact, which sanctioned German and Italian aggression in Europe in return for a similar nod to Japan's New Order in Asia.[65]

The United States denounced Japan's aggression, yet for a long time sought to avoid war in Asia under the Europe-first dictates of Plan Dog. The Americans and the British responded sharply, however, to Japan's "Southern advance" into Indochina, as Washington froze Japanese assets and cut off its access to oil. Roosevelt ordered the Filipino armed forces put under direct U.S. command, pledged to send B-17 long-range bombers to Manila, and appointed General Douglas MacArthur to command U.S. forces in East Asia. The actions by the West heightened the sense of panic in Japanese ruling circles as a result of the country's dependence on oil.[66] Undermined by Western economic sanctions and with nearly one million troops bogged down for a fourth year in China, Japan grew more desperate. Decoded Japanese government messages left little doubt that Japan would use force to break what it perceived as encirclement, but they also showed that Tokyo might be willing to negotiate. Indeed, Prime Minister Fumimaro Konoe had initiated unofficial conversations between Hull and Nomura Kichisaburo, but the talks went nowhere. The United States proved unwilling to consider any proposal that would sanction Japan's aggression against Indochina, even for the short term, or which would lead to a permanent "violation" of the Open Door in China.

The United States had already chosen a path to war rather than aggressive pursuit of a diplomatic settlement. During the Argentia Conference in August, Roosevelt and Churchill agreed that mounting Axis aggression could be stopped only by force. By October 1941 the United States conducted an undeclared naval war in the Atlantic, extended maximum possible aid to the USSR, bolstered Hawaii and the Philippines, and confronted Japan with economic sanctions and an inflexible negotiating posture.

Myth of America identity, especially racial modernity and U.S. destiny to become an Asian power, precluded a negotiated settlement with Japan. Seeking to avoid war with the United States, Konoe proposed a direct summit with Roosevelt, but Washington rejected the proposal. "Rightly or wrongly," Ian Nish observes, "the American reply to Ambassador Nomura on 2 October seemed to ignore the Japanese proposals and came close to breaking off negotiations for a Konoe-Roosevelt summit after fifty days of exchanges on the subject." The November talks between Hull and Nomura, who desperately sought to avoid war, offered a last-gasp opportunity. On November 26 the Roosevelt administration precluded virtually any hope of a negotiated settlement by demanding that Japan "withdraw all military, naval, and police forces from China and from Indo-China." The demand for unilateral concessions offered no face-saving formula to Tokyo, which could only mean war. The Japanese military pushed for war, and Emperor Hirohito approved the ill-fated plan for a quick and decisive series of strikes to try to win the war or at least gain concessions before Japan ran out of resources.[67]

Japanese air and naval forces slammed into U.S.-occupied Hawaii early Sunday morning, December 7, 1941, killing 2,323 Americans and crippling the Pacific fleet, yet igniting the imagined community for violent retribution as nothing else could have done. Attacks on Singapore, Guam, the Philippines, and Wake Island followed. On December 8, with only one dissenting House vote, Congress declared war on Japan. Hitler gratuitously declared war on the United States on December 11, although the Tripartite Pact did not obligate him to do so. Italy followed blindly in Hitler's wake.

Now thoroughly marginalized, noninterventionists promptly disbanded their organizations and denounced Japan's aggression, but they did not abandon their conviction that the United States had brought on the war. "Our principles were right," the AFC national committee declared. "Had they been followed, war could have been avoided." All agreed, however, that the only course, now that the nation's Pacific imperial outpost had been attacked, was, as Senator Wheeler advised, "to lick hell out of them." The United States, in the "righteous might" invoked by Roosevelt in his stirring "day of infamy" war address, proceeded to do just that.

The diplomat Chester Bowles was but one of many noninterventionists who now abandoned the cause, yet insisted, "We will be proven right historically." History, however, "has not been kind to the anti-interventionists of 1939–1941," Justus Doenecke notes. "For years, except in the occasional scholarly studies, they have been perceived in the most negative of terms." Yet the noninterventionists had argued convincingly that the United States had not been compelled to go to war but had *chosen* to enter onto the path to conflict in both Europe and Asia. Anti-interventionists had "insisted that the nation had choices," Michael Sherry explains, "and that reaction itself was a choice, one triggered not by (or only by) the dictates of national safety but by conniving allies, imperial ambitions, a misplaced democratic idealism, the New Deal's failure to bring recovery, or a devious President."[68]

Under the hegemonic usable past, the United States—isolationist, idealistic, and allegedly a reluctant belligerent—entered World War II only because of the Japanese assault on Pearl Harbor on the "day of infamy," December 7, 1941. The "infamy framework" reflects "a tradition of national history in which World War II makes its appearance on December 7, 1941," Emily S. Rosenberg explains. [69] This frame obscures critical knowledge on such issues as peace internationalism, imperialism, enemy-othering of anti-Bolshevism, and support for European fascism and Latin American militarism, as the Myth of America discourse ensured that the nation would strive to spread civilization and freedom around the globe.

Rather than isolationism, racial modernity and providential destiny inherent in Myth of America identity drove U.S. foreign policy in East Asia. Clearly the United States had not threatened war with Britain over its imperialism in India or with France over its domination of Indochina or with the Netherlands over its subjugation of the Javanese. National identity appeased allied imperialism while choosing war with Japan as it modernized and sought to take a leading role in the "great game" in its own "neighborhood." This discussion should not minimize Japan's murderous aggression, its crude and cynical pan-Asianism, its political instability marked by a spate of assassinations, and its own violent xenophobic insecurities. Moreover, Japan, in the final analysis, did start the war through its ultimately suicidal assault on Pearl Harbor.

Nevertheless, the "infamy frame" provides a hegemonic national narrative that obscures U.S. cultural identity, Japanese fear of encirclement, the Western double standard on Asian imperialism, Roosevelt's machinations, and Washington's unbending negotiating position, all of which recede from causation in deference to the totalizing trope of the perfidious sneak attack. The national patriotic narrative obscures the possibility that the Pacific War, and thus intervention in the world war, was not inevitable or unavoidable.[70] Myth of America identity impelled the United States to condemn and confront Japanese imperialism in East Asia—a foreign policy that led directly to the Pacific War. Had the United States actually been isolationist rather than determined to extend its hegemony across the Pacific, the attack on Pearl Harbor would very likely never have occurred. The nation chose to confront Japan, principally over its invasion of China, and that confrontation, combined with Japanese aggression, led to war.

The iron hegemony of the World War II good war narrative condemns arguments such as these as "revisionist" heresy. History considers the counterfactual argument that U.S. intervention might have been avoided reckless, subversive, and unhistorical. Many historians have so deeply internalized the empiricist "noble dream" that they either do not realize or do not acknowledge that the hegemonic arguments to the contrary—that the war was necessary, that the United States had to go to war, and that the war produced a better world and thus was a good war—are equally founded upon the counterfactual assumption that things would have turned out much worse absent intervention.

The point is not that U.S. entry into World War II was necessarily wrong or mistaken but rather to unpack the hegemonic interpretation in order to broaden inquiry into the coming of the war, the war itself, and its profound consequences. Destabilizing the hegemonic usable past challenges the marginalization of noninterventionists and peace activists as the subversive and failed architects of appeasement or at best of the misguided diplomacy of isolationism. For decades these narrative frames have empowered the U.S. warfare state at the expense of quests to advance an alternative hegemony of peaceful internationalism. Counterhegemonic inquiry thus enables a more complete analysis of the impact and repercussions of the war, both at home and abroad, including the intimate connection between World War II and the Cold War (see chapter 6).

As the most economically advanced exemplar of modernity—racially superior, providentially destined, and determined to revivify its masculine strength—the United States went to war in an identity-driven quest to see its way of life prevail in Europe and Asia. As throughout Euro-American and U.S. history, war powerfully reaffirmed the imagined community through external violence against evil enemy-others. Amidst the renewed psychic crisis of the insoluble Great Depression and the New Deal, a cleansing war could wash away the legacy of liberal reform and rebuild the bulwarks of patriotism, profits, and, at long last, economic recovery through the expedient of military Keynesianism.

CHAPTER 6

Wars Good and Cold

With Myth of America identity buoyed by victory in Europe and Asia, the United States demanded universal acceptance of its providential mission to shepherd the "Free World." When the USSR, the other triumphant power to emerge from World War II, rejected the scripted teleology of U.S. global hegemony, the Soviets *reemerged* as the primary external enemy-other. The "Cold War" entailed not merely defensive "containment" of communism, but rather a renewed quest to "roll back" and defeat the communist movement.

Framing the Cold War as a postwar phenomenon facilitated placing the onus for the conflict on "Soviet expansionism." This frame elides the extent to which identity driven Bolshevik enemy-othering prevailed throughout the interwar period. It also obscures that the renewed Cold War flowed from the failure of World War II to deliver on the promise of a "liberated Europe" or of a "democratic China." Rather than ushering in an idyllic "American Century," the "good war" instead brought a renewed Cold War, hot war in Korea, enduring militarization, decades of U.S. global intervention, increased support for dictatorships abroad, and counter-subversive campaigns against reformers at home. Conventional representation thus leaves substantial disciplinary knowledge to unpack on both World War II and the Cold War inextricably linked with it.

The Sunday morning Japanese "sneak attack" on Pearl Harbor could not have been more perfectly calculated to spur consent within the imagined community. "The war came as a great relief," *Time* acknowledged, as "Japanese bombs had finally brought national unity." Tokyo's assault on the U.S.-occu-

6. "Americans Will *Always* Fight for Liberty" (1943), poster produced by the Office of War Information. The image underscores a militant national identity in which Americans "*always*" fight for liberty." As they march off to the European and Asian theaters of World War II, the soldiers acknowledge the memory of men of the Continental Army, thus affirming that both the Revolutionary War and World War II—and indeed all American wars—are to be internalized as fights for liberty. Courtesy of the Library of Congress.

pied islands ignited a "war without mercy" that lurched toward annihilation of the savage Asiatic foe. Pearl Harbor—like the Alamo and Little Big Horn before it as well as the September 11 attacks sixty years later—spurred the righteous violence embedded in cultural identity.[1]

By uniting the national community, ending the Great Depression, and enabling the United States to achieve its "destiny" of global hegemony, World War II cemented itself within the discursive usable past as the good war. As two-thirds of U.S. men aged eighteen to thirty-four served, the war became a model of patriotic duty handed down to future generations of sons, grandsons, and great-grandsons. World War II, in short, serves as "the nation's most commonly agreed upon moral reference point."[2]

Countless representations over the years reinforced this monolithic interpretation of World War II. These include iconic images, such as the photograph from 1945 of U.S. soldiers raising the flag on Iwo Jima's Mount Suribachi; the photographs of victory parades from Times Square to San Diego; myriad personal accounts of World War II, such as Studs Terkel's oral history *The Good War* and Stephen Ambrose's *Band of Brothers;* and enshrinement of a monumental vision of World War II in Washington. Hollywood productions glorifying the good war began with the wartime propaganda films and carried into the twenty-first century with such films as *Saving Private Ryan* and *Flags of Our Fathers.* As Gary Gerstle points out, heroic representations of World War II "traffic in nationalist nostalgia for an era before Vietnam, when the United States fought a good war . . . and white men ruled America."[3]

Likewise, the Cold War, a phrase popularized by Walter Lippmann in his 1947 book of the same title, has been internalized within patriotic national identity as a righteous triumph of freedom over totalitarianism. The Cold War consensus precluded critical analysis for a full generation until the crisis over U.S. intervention in Indochina in the 1960s created the cultural space that enabled revisionists to challenge the hegemonic frame placing exclusive blame for the Cold War on the Soviet Union and Communist fanaticism. A determined counterassault against the revisionist interpretation gradually rebuilt the bulwarks of nationalist hermeneutics.

By the 1990s the end of the Cold War brought a revival of patriotic discourse trumpeting U.S. victory and moral superiority. The argument that the United States and its Western allies won the Cold War, as reflected in the complete collapse of Soviet Communism, revived the unambiguous orthodox interpretation and at the same time powerfully reaffirmed Myth of America identity. Hegemonic interpretation branded Cold War critics as "unrealistic, misguided, wrong . . . duped and disloyal" apologists for Joseph Stalin. "With the apparent popular consensus that the United States won the Cold War," Timothy Smith notes, "the critics appear even less credible" than the 1960s revisionists.[4]

Myth of America identity thus generates a tenacious defense of the Cold War narrative, as any acknowledgment of the constructed nature of the conflict posed the threat that it could be deconstructed. Such deconstruction might undermine cultural hegemony and threaten to redirect the national focus onto domestic reform movements and peace internationalism. The Cold War thus carried such high stakes as to generate substantial disciplinary knowledge, marginalization of subversive critics, and vigilant policing of the patriotic narrative.

Although deeply embedded in national consciousness, the Cold war is nonetheless a cultural construction devoid of ontological status. Simply put, the Cold War always was and still is a narrative discourse, not a reality. While the Berlin Wall, nuclear weapons, and the deaths of millions of people were all too real, to be sure, the way in which these phenomena are framed and interpreted can only be determined by representation. The Cold War, as Alan Nadel puts it, was a period marked by "general acceptance . . . of a relatively small set of narratives by a relatively large portion of the population."[5]

The constructed Cold War reflected continuity within national identity and foreign policy rather than a postwar phenomenon brought on by Soviet expansionism. The Cold War can be understood as "another episode in the ongoing production and reproduction of American identity through the practices of foreign policy, rather than as simply an externally induced crisis," David Campbell explains.[6] The Soviet Union and Communism thus merged into the long line of enemy-others dating back to Indian conquest and critical to the reaffirmation of the mythically rooted imagined community.

The half-century campaign against Communism provided an almost ideal "evil empire" as the focus of foreign policy militancy backed by domestic consent. "The Soviet could be represented as the grand 'other' of a Western-centric order," Robert Latham explains.[7] Culturally conditioned by the wartime crusade against the Nazis and the "Japs," Americans embraced the renewal of Soviet enemy-othering in short order. Like the Nazis, but unlike the Japanese or "Red" China, the Russians were "white," hence racial modernity played less of a role than in most previous conflicts. Yet the "Communist menace" performed the same cultural function as a litany of previous enemies of the national community.

The Cold War powerfully affirmed cultural hegemony that the good war had first reestablished following the anxiety-ridden interregnum brought on by the Depression and the New Deal. Both the good war and the Cold War revived elite white male authority while precluding the return of New Deal liberal reform and peace internationalism. The Cold War construction generated a postwar national security state and military-industrial complex, accompanied by a thoroughgoing purge of the left, thus powerfully reinforcing cultural hegemony and marginalizing critics, reformers, and proponents of cooperative internationalism.

As a working definition for this narrative, the Cold War can be seen as the constructed competition between two modernist teleological discourses—liberalism (inclusive of capitalism) and Marxism-Leninism. Virulent hostility and militarization animated both of these discourses, yet both stopped short of driving the two empires into direct military conflict. At the same time, the Cold War reaffirmed cultural identity and policed domestic hierarchies in the name of national security. The Cold War thus constituted a global foreign policy phenomenon with profound domestic implications.[8]

From "Grand" Ally to Renewed Enemy-Other

Only the U.S. decision to define Germany and Japan as the nation's primary enemies relegated the Soviet Union and Communism temporarily to the back burner. The World War II alliance was grand precisely because it constituted a discontinuous *mariage de convenance,* with Adolf Hitler presiding. After extending lend-lease aid to Russia following the Nazi invasion in June 1941, Franklin D. Roosevelt sought a much closer association, one that would lead the Kremlin to support a postwar order compatible with liberal modernity. In no small part because of his own political skills, Roosevelt succeeded in sustaining the Grand Alliance through the war, but peaceful coexistence with Communism ultimately proved incompatible with U.S. national identity. Thus for the second time in a generation a U.S. president would wage war in Europe and fail to achieve his grand design for a new world order.

The Atlantic Charter complemented by the Four Freedoms established a wartime discourse commensurate with the Myth of America, including freedom of the seas, free trade, collective security against aggressors, and other ideals reminiscent of Wilson's Fourteen Points. Roosevelt's Four Freedoms (from want, from fear, of speech, and of worship) resonated with Americans and millions of world citizens who wished to pursue these same goals in their own countries. On January 1, 1942, twenty-six nations signed the Declaration by United Nations, committing themselves to the principles of the Atlantic Charter. Americans thus mobilized for war armed with the faith that their chosen nation was leading the world into a new era of liberal progress under God.

Mutual trust anchored relations between the putatively Anglo-Saxon English-speaking cousins, but Stalin distrusted his Western partners and charged, "The Atlantic Charter was directed against the USSR." Roosevelt strove to reassure Stalin, U.S. aid poured into the USSR, and the United States acted as the "great arsenal"—though hardly, in Stalin's case—"of democracy." Although the United States subsidized the Allied war effort, Roosevelt reneged on an impetuous pledge to open in the near term a second front in Europe to relieve the Nazis' military pressure on the retrenching Soviets.[9]

The wartime strategy of unconditional surrender reassured Stalin but also fit squarely with a continuous identity-driven U.S. history of exterminating devilish foreign enemies. Just as past generations had conducted ethnic cleansing of Indians, chosen war with Mexico, and hunted down the Filipino "goo-goos" and Haitian "Cacos," this generation's "rendezvous with destiny" would culminate in the total defeat of the aggressors in Europe and Asia. Spurred by a trope deliberately appropriated from the Civil War hero U. S. Grant, Americans rallied around the culturally rooted campaign to achieve victory without quarter. Meanwhile, the Soviet people could bear the brunt of Nazi aggression and perish at the mind-bending rate of ninety dead Soviet soldiers to every one U.S. combat death.

Later called one of the "great mistakes" of the war by the *New York Times* military correspondent Hanson Baldwin, unconditional surrender shored up the Grand Alliance while at the same time, however, encouraging Germany and Japan to prolong the war as long as possible. The strategy nonetheless achieved Roosevelt's aim of maintaining the unlikely alliance while minimizing U.S. casualties.[10] The problem with unconditional surrender, as Baldwin pointed out, was that it ultimately enabled the Soviet Union to extend its own hegemony halfway across the European continent. The more ground the Red Army gained, the more pregnant Allied discussions became about the ultimate political fate of liberated areas.

Wartime enemy-othering of the Nazis and the "Japs" left little cultural space to focus enmity on Communism. The Office of War Information (OWI) promoted Allied war aims while Hollywood affirmed the global crusade by emphasizing the demonic character of the Axis. As misguided fellow European whites under the sway of a fanatic leader, the Germans fared much better than the Japanese. "It was a rare film that did not employ such terms as Japs, beasts, yellow monkeys, nips or slant-eyed rats," as Hollywood became "a compliant part of the American war machine." OWI supervision of Hollywood "represents the most comprehensive and sustained government attempt to change the content of a mass medium in American history." Domestic wartime propaganda not only promoted the good war, it set the stage for the Cold War revival by depicting the Soviet Union and "Uncle Joe" Stalin as a trustworthy ally and fit partner in forging a new world order.[11]

The discursive regime of the Grand Alliance remained intact through the Yalta Conference of February 1945, which kept alive a dying president's vision of a postwar order overseen by the "four policemen": the United States, Britain, the USSR, and "nationalist" China. Stalin signed on to the Yalta "Declaration of Liberated Europe" and pledged to support the postwar United Nations Organization and to join in the Pacific War raging against a receding but still fierce Japanese resistance, an important agreement for the casualty-conscious Americans prior to a successful test of an atomic weapon. Roosevelt declared that the Yalta Declaration of Liberated Europe meant the elimination of "spheres of influence and balances of power and all the other expedients which have been tried for centuries—and have failed." Roosevelt's characteristically ebullient discourse notwithstanding, the Yalta accords represented "the best the Big Three could do to hold their alliance together, and it was not enough," as Lloyd Gardner concluded after a careful reconstruction. The partition of Europe had been largely accomplished *before* the [renewed] cold war began."[12] By the end of his life Roosevelt had to realize that he had taken the country into a war to "liberate Europe," yet the outcome of the war in east-central Europe was the displacement of Nazi power by Soviet hegemony.

The Soviets were not inclined to accept passively the extension of liberal modernity throughout liberated Europe for the rather obvious reason that it was anathema to Marxist-Leninist ideology, Soviet security needs, and Stalin's dictatorial personality. The self-proclaimed generalissimo embraced a straightforward spheres-of-influence approach, hardened by Marxist teleology. He meant to restore the tsarist empire and preclude as best he could the emergence of hostile regimes on the Soviet borders. Well aware that in the previous war the

Western powers had sought to cordon off Bolshevism, if not destroy it, Stalin intended to erect his own "sanitary" buffer zone. "This war is not as in the past," he told his Yugoslav comrades. "Whoever occupies a territory also imposes on it his own social system. It can be no other way." Along these lines, V. M. Molotov asserts in his memoirs that Roosevelt "miscalculated" the U.S. ability to sway the USSR with reconstruction aid, and "they woke up only when half of Europe had passed from them. . . . They certainly hardened against us but we had to consolidate our conquests."[13]

While the Soviets clearly anticipated some sort of sphere of influence, recent scholarship finds "growing evidence of a relative restraint of the Soviet Union outside its sphere of influence, and of Stalin's caution in the management of crises in the year after the war." Even in Poland, Stalin initially *discouraged* Polish Communists' efforts to establish a Marxist regime. In recent years historians have found that Soviet "policy toward Poland went against establishing the basis of a future communist system."[14] Stalin also restrained the ambitions of Bulgarian Communists until 1947. Burned by surprisingly stiff resistance during the invasion of Finland following the Nazi—Soviet Pact, Stalin now settled for a "soft sphere"—"Finlandization" in Western Cold War tropology—and showed only passing interest in Scandinavia. Stalin tried to hold back Yugoslavian Communism under the "revisionist" Marshal Tito; "rebuffed continuing Greek Communist pleas to support an all-out armed drive for power on their part"; supported the Gaullist coalition in France; urged Italian comrades to compromise with the right wing; long anticipated a unified Germany and thus held back into 1948 the German Marxists who sought to push ahead with communization. In East Asia, Stalin even went along with U.S. support for the so-called nationalist regime despite the growing power of the Chinese Communist Party, a deviation for which he later personally apologized to Mao Zedong.[15]

A contradiction apparently existed within Stalin's violent pathology. On the one hand, as leader of the Communist world, his duty was to expand the Marxist-Leninist creed. On the other hand, he became threatened by other prominent Communist leaders—hence his liquidation of internal rivals, such as Nikolai Bukharin and Leon Trotsky, whom he, respectively, had executed after a show trial and hunted down and assassinated in Mexico. The obvious intellectual superiority of Bukharin, Trotsky, and others over him apparently fed Stalin's insecurities about the potential influence of foreign Communists as well, including Tito and Mao.

The extent to which Stalin may have been willing to compromise declined in concert with the hardening of Western positions, particularly after the war ended. What emerges, then, is "a shifting period of uncertainty and ambivalence" followed by "a decisive acceleration of a crystallization process in the Soviet sphere, at the same time as the same process was occurring in the West."

Churchill's discontinuous diplomacy underscores the fundamentally constructed character of the Cold War. During a late-night meeting in the Kremlin in October 1944, Churchill and Stalin entered into the famous "percentages agreement," dividing Europe into prospective spheres of influence. In a telegram to Roosevelt, Churchill explained that the Moscow percentages agreement could serve as a guide to the postwar settlement in countries threatened by civil wars in which "probably you and I would be in sympathy with one side and U.J. [Uncle Joe] with the other." During the war Britain thus proved "more willing than the United States not only to accept but to endorse an expanded Russian sphere of influence."[16]

By March 1946, however, when he delivered the famous "iron curtain" address in Fulton, Missouri, a discursive regime of religion, race, and gender drove Churchill to summon the West to confrontation with the Soviets. He called for "Christian civilization" and the "English-speaking world" to mount a manly response to the Communist challenge. Idolized in the United States since the Battle of Britain, though defeated by the Labour Party at the polls, Churchill now asserted that the Soviet Union sought "totalitarian control" of Eastern Europe. Stalin responded that Churchill had revealed himself as a "firebrand of war" whose apotheosis of the "English-speaking world" was redolent of Hitler's racial theories. The new president, Harry Truman, shared Churchill's views, however, and soon dressed down Molotov and told aides he was tired of "babying" the Soviets.

American-Century Unilateralism

Myth of America universalism precluded the United States from accommodating an extended Soviet sphere of influence. As God's chosen nation, the leading white modernist power in the world, the United States, most Americans believed, had an obligation to assume world leadership and spread its way of life across the globe. Before U.S. intervention in World War II, Henry Luce, the publisher of *Time-Life*, reaffirmed hegemonic national identity with the popular trope of the "American Century," the title of his 1940 bestseller. Much as John O'Sullivan had trumpeted Manifest Destiny and the war on Mexico in the mid–

nineteenth century, Luce, a century later and with no greater subtlety, called on the United States to "exert upon the world the full impact of our influence, for such purposes as we see fit and by such means as we see fit." Invoking Myth of America destiny, Truman similarly intoned after the war, "Now this great Republic—the greatest in history, the greatest the sun has ever shone upon—is charged with leadership in the world for the welfare of the whole world as well as our own welfare."[17]

Imperial hubris accelerated in the wake of the atomic bombings of Japan and victory in the good war. As noted in my discussion of the *Enola Gay* exhibition in 1995[18] (see note 27 in the introduction), Myth of America identity renders illegitimate any interpretation other than that the United States had to use the bomb to bring an end to the war. Considering, very likely accurately, that its enemies would have used the bomb had they developed it first, the United States did not hesitate to unleash two attacks on Japan within three days in August 1945.

The perpetual and circular debate over the decision to drop the bombs reflects the futility of historians' efforts to prove their case or reveal "the truth" about such issues. Scholars and patriotic nationalists have long insisted that the bomb ended the war, as nothing else could have, and saved the nation from suffering massive casualties, for which they even constructed a mythical figure of five hundred thousand and even one million men. Critics respond that a modification of unconditional surrender enabling the emperor to remain on the throne as a purely symbolic figure—a condition that Washington acceded to even after the two atomic attacks—could have led to a negotiated end of the war with a Japanese nation that clearly was already defeated; thus the dropping of the bombs would have proved unnecessary. Revisionists, subjected to withering attacks within the hegemonic culture, have long argued that the "real" reason for use of the bombs was to bring a rapid defeat to Japan in order to deter increased Soviet influence in postwar Asia. Such influence would have flowed from an expanded Kremlin role in compelling Tokyo's surrender. Such debates, while productive of critical knowledge, at the same time underscore the constructed essence of historical discourse, as none of these interpretations can be proven as true.

That the United States became the first nation to develop and employ the atomic bomb could only serve as powerful cultural reaffirmation of Myth of America identity as the world's chosen nation. Thousands of references, issued from the White House and from pulpits across the nation, reflected the widespread view that God had provided the United States alone with the ability to harness the "very power of the Universe" and to retain sole possession of the bomb. The first atomic test blast had been named, after all, for the Holy Trinity. The bomb was thus "sacred" and "the greatest thing in history," declared Truman, the middle-American president reflecting a middle-American consensus.[19] Despite such glorification of the ultimate weapon, the U.S. military seized photographs and film and suppressed information for decades about the grotesque impact on the ground in Hiroshima and Nagasaki.

The power of the bomb, both symbolic and real, obscures the extent to which Hiroshima and Nagasaki represented continuity rather than discontinuity in the wartime Allied bombing campaign. Pearl Harbor generated "a rage bordering on the genocidal" within the imagined community, John Dower notes. Near the end of the war distinctions between military and civilian targets had already eroded to such an extent that the military did not think twice about incinerating eighty thousand to a hundred thousand Japanese civilians in a single night of firebombing. During the interwar period a "winged gospel" had emerged perceiving the airplane as a "mechanical god" that would "usher in a dazzling future, a virtual millennium." With the onset of World War II the "winged gospel" morphed into a "technological fanaticism" perceiving airpower as a transcendent force in modern warfare. The punishing "conventional" air raids and firebombing of Germany and Japan flowed from a lethal combination of this fanatic faith and demonization of the wartime enemy-others. As military analysts counted the number of sorties and projected the level of unseen destruction, the human repercussions of the relentless aerial campaign gave way, as Michael Sherry points out, to a "long erosion of moral scruples during the war."[20]

Myth of America identity precluded consideration of multilateral control of nuclear weapons under UN auspices. International control would have defied the mystical faith that Providence had provided America alone with the "winning weapon." The Baruch Plan, set forth in 1946 by the man who presided over the original military-industrial complex in the Great War, called for retention of the atomic monopoly while the USSR and other powers turned over all fissionable material and submitted to international inspections. The neuralgic Soviets could be counted on to reject both internal inspections as well as the proposal to give up their own research and materials while Washington retained its monopoly until the very last stage of the proposed control process. The Kremlin summarily rejected the Baruch Plan and almost surely would have pursued a nuclear weapons program under any circumstances.[21]

Militant national identity drove Cold War foreign policy, as nothing less than a "preponderance of power"—a "world environment hospitable to U.S. interests and values"—could be accepted. Preponderance also meant establishment of a worldwide military base system and other efforts to "relentlessly preserve our superiority on land and sea and in the air." "As long as we can out-produce the world, can control the sea and can strike inland with the atomic bomb we can assume certain risks otherwise unacceptable," declared Secretary of Defense James Forrestal in 1947, two years before his suicide, which came after delusions in which he saw Russian troops creeping across the grounds outside his hospital window.[22]

The obsession with enemy-others was a national rather than an individual pathology, however, as reflected in the Truman Doctrine of April 1947. Depicting a binary world of good and evil, the president declared, "It must be the policy of the United States to support free peoples who are resisting attempted subjugation by armed minorities or by outside pressures." Backed by broad public consent, the Congress approved four hundred million dollars in military aid to Greece and Turkey, yet the Soviets had little connection with the Greek left, which bid for power after leading the wartime anti-Nazi resistance. Despite the trope of "free peoples," Truman sent money to reactionary monarchists, who ultimately came to power in Greece. Turkey fended off the left as well, enabling a right-wing regime in Ankara to enter the "free world" alliance.

The Truman Doctrine and the Marshall Plan that same year affirmed the identity-driven pursuit of U.S. postwar hegemony in Europe and beyond. The Marshall Plan of loans and assistance proved successful, ultimately bridging the "dollar gap" by providing the West Europeans with the capital they needed to purchase U.S. products. The European Recovery Program, along with the newly established Washington-dominated and -headquartered World Bank and International Monetary Fund, powerfully affirmed U.S. global hegemony.[23]

During Stalin's characteristic late-night peregrination in the Kremlin, U.S. economic might must have appeared as a fearful specter. Rather than lapsing back into depression, as the Marxist-Leninist ideology projected, the United States emerged from the war as an unparalleled colossus. While the Soviet Union lay in ruins, the United States was unscathed. The Soviets understood that U.S. financial power and its vibrant consumer culture had more appeal to the war-ravaged nations of east-central Europe than the USSR could offer. The Kremlin precluded Czechoslovakia from joining the Western trading bloc and in 1948 orchestrated a coup that culminated in the death of the liberal Czech leader Jan Masaryk. Sovietization followed in Prague.

Born and raised in Middle America in a town called Independence, Truman responded by calling on "moral God fearing peoples [to] save the world from Atheism and totalitarianism."[24] The Czech coup revived bitter memories of Hitler, whose aggression had gained decisive momentum through the partition of Czechoslovakia at Munich in 1938. U.S. citizens and West Europeans thus forged in their minds a powerful link between Nazi and Soviet behavior, an image of "red fascism" bolstered by the relatively new trope of totalitarianism.[25] The analogy submerged critical distinctions: both Hitler and Stalin were dictators, but Hitler was rash and gloried in war, whereas Stalin, however ruthless with his domestic enemies, pursued a cautious foreign policy reflecting a determination to avoid war with the West.

The cloaking of Stalin in SS garb put to rest the Uncle Joe trope and unambiguously established the Soviet Union as the nation's premier enemy-other. Indeed, the remarkable change in American representations of the Soviet Union from the good war to the Cold War underscores the extent to which culture shapes perception within the framework of national identity. Put another way, the dramatic shift shows that culture makes history and constructs reality.

Psychic crisis—the combined impact of depression, war, and a renewed Cold War—hardened enemy-othering and created a cultural climate conducive to militarization while simultaneously precluding a revival of New Deal reform and peace internationalism. The North Atlantic Treaty Organization (NATO) was a logical product of Western militarization, the fusion of the Hitler—Stalin image, and the identity-driven fixation with enemy-others. NATO's putative purpose was collective security, as the signatory nations of Western and Mediterranean Europe agreed that an attack on one would be tantamount to an attack on all. As a security organization, NATO would have been an excellent mechanism to contain *Hitler,* as George Kennan pointed out, but the vision of a *Soviet* blitzkrieg was a chimera.

The last thing the war-ravaged USSR and the cautious Stalin wanted to provoke was another all-out war with the West. "In 1945 and the following years, Stalin was far from thinking of marching the Soviet Army westwards to the Atlantic," Alexander Dallin notes.[26] The huge Red Army may have appeared menacing, but Marxist doctrine held that capitalism would collapse of its own contradictions. Marxist-Leninists advocated agitation, propaganda, and subversion, but not direct military invasion of capitalist states.

This point can hardly be overemphasized: the "Soviet threat" to West European and ultimately U.S. security was a Cold War construction. Yet the public, conditioned by memories of Hitler, internalized the specter of a Red Army invasion, which prevailed for generations. "Distortions of understanding are deeply implanted in the public mind," lamented Kennan, the architect of containment who had turned Cold War critic. "Great masses of people in this country and in Europe," he explained in 1983, "have now been taught to believe that the Soviet leadership has been obsessed, ever since World War II, with a desire to invade Western Europe, and has been 'deterred' (gnashing its teeth, we must suppose, in frustration) only by the threat of nuclear retaliation." Ultimate "victory" in the Cold War reaffirmed the constructed Soviet military threat, as William Perry, Bill Clinton's defense secretary, declared that NATO "achieved its founding purpose of deterring attack from the Warsaw Pact."[27] Perry apparently did not know that NATO was founded six years prior to the Warsaw Pact.

Choosing War in East Asia

In the United States, the triumph of the Chinese Communist Party in October 1949 shattered long-held romanticized Western illusions about the emergence of a democratic China. Indeed, the tropes of fall and loss affirm Myth of America universalism and the scripting of China as a site for fulfilling U.S. destiny. Americans had backed the loser in the Chinese civil war. The defeated Chiang Kai-shek and his corrupt regime, which Roosevelt had projected as one of the "four policemen" of the postwar era, retreated to Taiwan (Formosa). The birth of the People's Republic (PRC) ended any hope of China's anchoring the American Century in Asia, thus provoking a powerful domestic backlash rooted in identity-driven disillusionment.[28]

The Sino-Soviet Pact (1950) uniting the world's most populous and physically largest nations against U.S. hegemony triggered psychic crisis in the United States. Despite the almost hysterical fears of monolithic Communism, the Sino-Soviet alliance, much like the Grand Alliance, lacked deep roots. Confronted by increasingly militant U.S. "imperialist" opposition, Mao felt forced to ally with the USSR even though Stalin had scarcely supported the Chinese revolution and Mao bitterly resented "Stalin's rude and contemptuous treatment" of him. Stalin also rejected Mao's calls to turn Mongolia over to China and to help in reclaiming Taiwan from Chiang. Under the alliance Stalin did pledge to come to China's aid in the event of a direct U.S. or Japanese attack on the mainland. Nevertheless, the alliance peaked in the midfifties and fell apart completely as Mao condemned the Soviets for advocating peaceful coexistence with the West and being "frightened in the face of imperialist aggression" during the Cuban missile crisis in 1962.[29]

Having thoroughly internalized Myth of America identity, few U.S. citizens—and relatively few Western historians even today—stopped to consider that Washington's domination of Japan was far more direct than that of the USSR in any of its "satellites." While the Japanese occupation, unlike the extension of U.S. power in Western Europe, could hardly be called "empire by invitation," liberal modernity had proved compatible with the one Asian nation that, patterning itself after the West, modernized and industrialized in the prewar era.[30] Thus, contrary to Roosevelt's expectations, it was Japan, not China, that anchored the expansion of capitalist modernity in East Asia after the war.

The postwar reorientation of Japan proved successful and, together with the Marshall Plan, reflected the establishment of a hegemonic liberal modernity under U.S. supervision in the industrialized centers of Europe and Asia. The U.S. occupation focused on economic recovery and stability, which required going easy on scores of industrialists and other leaders who had been complicit in Japan's wartime aggression but were now needed to promote order and economic development. Emperor Hirohito remained on the throne, albeit as a figurehead, and the occupation forces carried out only seven executions for war crimes. Unlike the Nuremberg trials, which forced Germany to confront, at least to some extent, its responsibility for the war and genocide, Japan under U.S. supervision never had to answer for its annihilation campaigns, POW slave camps, and mass rape and sexual exploitation of Chinese and Korean "comfort women." As a result, many Japanese today elide the nation's history of aggression even as the country remilitarizes for the first time since World War II.

The United States thus placed a higher priority on economic integration and establishment of Japan as a base of U.S. militarism in Asia than on reforming Japanese society. By the time the San Francisco Treaty of 1952 formally ended the occupation, the United States had established 132 military installations in Japan, 90 percent of them on Okinawa, and continued to occupy Japan into the twenty-first century. Overall, the Japanese people and Japan's new leadership embraced U.S. hegemony and made the most of it. By the 1970s a de-

militarized Japanese economy was outcompeting the United States in key industries, such as automobiles and electronics.[31]

Building around Japan, the United States sought nothing less than global
hegemony, including incorporation of the entire "great crescent" of Asia into
the free world orbit. While the advanced Japanese economy would serve as the
industrial center, the vast region of Southeast Asia, including Malaya, the East
Indies, Indochina, and the Philippines, would serve as markets and provide raw
materials. Under this neocolonial framework, security planners perceived the
nexus between Japan, Southeast Asia, and the United States and its European
trading partners as vital to the success of the postwar order centered in New
York and Washington. This project, however, collided squarely, and with profound consequences, with decolonization and the rise of nationalism across
Asia as well as in Africa and Latin America (see chapter 8).

Despite the remarkable success of the United States in reorienting Japan,
the perceived loss of China in 1949 combined with the Soviets' successful testing of an atomic bomb the same year defied the teleology of U.S. global destiny
under God, thus heightening national anxiety to levels that typically sought relief through violent catharsis—and yet another war. Drunk with a euphoric
sense of destiny following victory in the two-front war, Americans internalized
the perception that any deviation from liberal universalism under U.S. leadership violated the free world mandate.

The drive to internationalize Myth of America hegemony led to the culminating event of the formative years of the revived Cold War, direct intervention
in the Korean civil war. That conflict would prove to be the "only hot war between the United States and another Great Power during the Cold War and
brought with it periods of extraordinary tensions and danger." Until the time it
actually erupted, Americans could scarcely have imagined their country fighting a major war on a craggy Asian peninsula the vast majority of them would
have been unable to pinpoint on a map. Korea had neither vital natural resources nor overwhelming strategic significance. What Korea did have, along
with China, Greece, Yugoslavia, and many other states, was a postwar power
struggle between Communist insurgents, advocates of a U.S.-style liberal-cap-
italist world order, and diverse groups in between. It was hardly surprising that
the onetime "hermit kingdom," occupied and exploited by Japan for half a century, would be left divided and struggling to find its way in the postwar world.[32]

As in the case of Pearl Harbor, the Korean War patriotic narrative typically
associates the conflict with a perfidious attack launched by an evil enemy-other

with neither warning nor honor. According to this rendering of the past, a previously reluctant United States then rose to a redemptive defense of freedom. This pattern of historical mythmaking sanctifies these conflicts and elides consideration of antecedents and of all complexity. For most of the public, then, the Korean War began on June 25, 1950, when the North Korean Communist Kim Il Sung "invaded" South Korea. This frame buries pertinent issues, such as the nonexistence of any such entities as a North or South Korea (essentially there had long been one Korea) as well as the conceptual problem of invading one's own country.

By viewing the Korean conflict as a product of monolithic Communism— that is, by blaming it directly on the Kremlin and the Chinese—Americans were blind to the fact that the Korean War was fundamentally a civil war between domestic factions. Although Kim was a dedicated Marxist-Leninist and, as such, sought and, after much hesitation, received clearance from Stalin for the assault on his domestic enemies, the conflict became an international war only as a result of the U.S. decision to intervene directly. Only that decision transformed a civil war into a bitter, terribly destructive, and profoundly significant Cold War conflict.

Thus, as with most U.S. wars, Myth of America identity impels a patriotic narrative. Bruce Cumings argues, in contrast with the conventional focus on June 1950, that "the Cold War arrived in Korea in the last months of 1945" when U.S. forces occupied the southern half of the country. While poor peasants comprised the vast majority of Korea's population, a tiny oligarchy coalesced around an obdurate, Princeton-educated Christian elite, Syngman Rhee, who emerged as the prototypical U.S. client. As the CIA acknowledged, "The extreme Rightists control the overt political structure in the US zone." Meanwhile, Kim began to establish a police state of his own north of the 38th parallel.

Belying the standard narrative of a war started solely by Kremlin-backed North Korea, U.S. officials on the ground understood that Rhee, possessed of an "inflated ego," intended no less than Kim to unite the peninsula under his authority. "The South Koreans wish to invade the North," U.S. officials reported, adding that Rhee vowed to "do it" even if it "brought on a general war." The United States backed the southern side as part of the great crescent strategy and to advance American Century universalism in East Asia. Thus the U.S. military helped Rhee hunt down political opponents and lodge them in concentration camps. By 1949 hundreds of Koreans had died in clashes between opposing forces, particularly in the center of the country.[33] While the focus on June 25, 1950, offered a narrative reifying Cold War binaries, civil war came to Korea not because it was part of the international Communist movement but as a result of political divisions in a country long ravaged by conflict.

Among its myriad consequences, the Korean War ended any hopes of the UN emerging in the short term as a genuine international peacekeeping organization. The United States rejected an opportunity to attempt to establish the UN, headquartered in New York, as the pivot of a new multilateral cooperative internationalism. While forging close economic and military ties with fellow European white modernist states under the Marshall Plan and NATO, the United States allowed the UN to "devolve into a Cold War sideshow." Henry Wallace, marginalized in part because he championed the UN over unilateralism, insisted "America's opportunity" to lead "a world crusade in the name of the brotherhood of man" had been sacrificed to a "crusade in the name of hatred and fear of communism."[34]

With the Soviet Union boycotting the Security Council over the UN's refusal to seat Red China, the United States gained international sanction for its unilateral invasion of Korea. "In 1950," Cumings avers, the UN "General Assembly was a legislature more amenable to Truman's policies than the U.S. Congress."[35] The UN sanctioning of the intervention also enabled Truman to employ the banal trope "police action," even though officials understood from the outset that achieving a successful outcome would require a prolonged military effort at substantial cost, with a large number of casualties and profound implications for domestic economic priorities. Congress and the public consented to the police action, however, as the Cold War binary blended seamlessly with national identity. The UN imprimatur notwithstanding, the subsequent campaign was indisputably a U.S. war, planned and waged by U.S. commanders and soldiers and with the U.S. taking 90 percent of the casualties on the "allied" side.

After *choosing* war, Americans rallied behind General Douglas MacArthur, a national hero since making good on his "I shall return" pledge, made when he was forced to abandon the Philippines, which he had left vulnerable to Japanese attack even after Pearl Harbor. MacArthur's carefully staged return carried over into his acceptance of Japan's surrender, followed by his tenure as supreme commander of the occupation in Tokyo. After he pulled off a precarious amphibious landing at Inchon on the Korean coast in September 1950, the reputation of the general-hero, known for his aviator sunglasses and signature corn-cob pipe, reached its apogee. Following the successful landing, U.S. forces reversed the course of the war and eventually sent Kim's army reeling back toward the Chinese border.

At this point, the pathology of U.S. imperial nationalism prevailed, leading to what Kennan called at the time "an absolutely unbelievable and stupendous military blunder."[36] Seared by criticism over the putative loss of China, Truman and Secretary of State Dean Acheson opted to silence the many critics, especially the Republican ones, who excoriated containment as a "panty-waist" strategy inconsistent with the nation's manly, providentially sanctioned destiny of unambiguous victory over evil enemy-others. Rather than settling for the status quo ante, the United States sought "liberation" of the Korean peninsula to deliver a staggering blow to the world Communist movement. As U.S. forces surged north in the fall of 1950, China girded for a massive intervention.

The decision to "liberate" Korea, even at the risk of starting a wider land war in Asia, underscores a profound internalization of Myth of America universalism. Even so it is difficult to understand how U.S. officials could have been so obtuse—if only they had stopped to imagine, for example, how they might have reacted to hostile forces marching toward the Rio Grande!—but disrespect for China, which was not only red but yellow, and thus racially inferior, and the towering prestige of the general-hero MacArthur, who insisted China would not intervene, led to the disastrous campaign for liberation. Reaching the height of banality, the *New York Times* chimed in, explaining that China could hardly feel threatened by the prospect of "a free and united Korea."[37] Such comments highlight the deeply internalized perceptions of innocence ingrained within mythically rooted national identity.

In November hundreds of thousands of Chinese troops slammed into the U.S. and South Korean forces. The Chinese intervention turned the war into a bloody stalemate, with myriad pernicious consequences, not least the devastation and permanent (thus far) division of Korea itself. Ridden by anxiety at the prospect of another dramatic setback vis-à-vis Communism in Asia, Truman publicly contemplated using atomic weapons, which the Joint Chiefs of Staff advised might blunt the Chinese attack. Although the front eventually stabilized under General Matthew Ridgway, both sides remained wounded and obdurate; fighting continued for two more years to little effect. Truman sacked MacArthur, yet the general—like the failed filibusterers of the antebellum period—returned home to a hero's ticker-tape parade. The PRC rejected a negotiating opportunity in January 1951 only to suffer punishing losses in a U.S. offensive a few months later. Kim, backed by Stalin, had launched the June 1950 assault convinced he would win quickly; Rhee, too, had believed he could unite the peninsula; Mao thought he could punish the imperialists; and the United States had been overwhelmed by hubris. In the final analysis, as William Stueck notes, "the war is laden with miscalculation on all sides."[38]

Until the massive U.S. invasion of Indochina a generation later, the Korean War was the largest and bloodiest global conflict of the postwar era. The war was "a virtual holocaust," as more than two million Korean *civilians* died along with hundreds of thousands of combatants on all sides. The war featured savage fighting and atrocities, especially after the Chinese intervention. Some of the clashes, such as that at No Gun Ri, where possibly hundreds of fleeing refugees were mistakenly killed by U.S. forces, went unreported for decades. The United States liberally employed napalm and, as in World War II, bombed relentlessly, targeting dams—whose destruction unleashed flooding that washed away whole villages—as well as people. U.S. airpower alone killed at least one-ninth of the entire Korean population, an astonishing statistic. Perceiving themselves as defenders of liberal order against a "red foe that scorns all rules of civilized warfare," as *Collier's* put it, "nervous American troops are ready to fire at any Korean." Incorporating the trope "gook" into the military lexicon, soldiers joined South Korean police in the "slaughter of hundreds of South Korean civilians, women as well as men," the *New York Times* reported. The Korean War thus joined previous Pacific wars as another "war without mercy" against savage Asiatic foes. Equally ruthless North Korean forces reciprocated with atrocities of their own, including the slaughter of thousands of civilians, who were dumped into mass graves, and the execution of hundreds of U.S. POWs through the expedient of a bullet to the head.[39] Incompatible with a glorious national past, the Korean intervention became the "forgotten war," overshadowed by the triumphalism of the good war before it and the Indochina War of the next generation.

Driven by Myth of America hegemony and obsessed with worst-case scenarios of a red tide enveloping the globe, the United States had declined to let a small, relatively inconsequential country determine its own fate. The disastrous quest for liberation in Korea reflected the persistence of the World War II legacy of ultimate victory and securing the unconditional surrender of evil foes. Even as a Soviet and Chinese ally, Korea would not have fundamentally altered the world "balance of power" that foreign policy "realists" exalt. But given the gospel of the Cold War binary, allowing Korea to go Communist in defiance of national identity would have precipitated a domestic political bloodbath. The war brought frustration in any event, as much of the public viewed limited war—the failure to utterly destroy savage enemies—as un-American.

While the patriotic historical narrative generally regards the Korean War as a successful containment or at worst a stalemate—unfortunate yet necessary to preserve U.S. "credibility"—the conflict in many respects constituted a defeat for the United States. The Korean War "worked rather well" for both of the great Marxist regimes, Odd Arne Westad notes.[40] Stalin got to watch the United States bleed while avoiding war. Despite its massive losses, an estimated nine hundred thousand casualties, China emerged as a world power, its Communist regime and ties with the USSR solidified, its reputation among non-Western countries for standing up to the United States heightened. That pattern continued later in the decade as the PRC periodically shelled the offshore islands of Jinmen and Mazu across the Taiwan Straits despite U.S. threats to employ the nuclear option. Washington thus remained deeply embroiled in the dispute between China and Taiwan, a potential *casus belli*, into the twenty-first century. The United States also sent troops to South Korea on a (thus far) permanent basis, perpetuating the intervention in Korean politics. The United States backed authoritarian regimes in Seoul for decades until democracy gradually emerged. U.S. militarism menaced an insecure North Korean regime, which remained a dictatorship under Kim's son and successor, Kim Jong Il.

Combating Godlessness

While the Korean War reinforced the trope of Communist fanaticism, the U.S. decision to conduct a major war in a small country on the other side of the world flowed from its own fanatical obsession with combating evil. In recent years scholars have begun to analyze religiosity in a Cold War context, yet the subject remains dramatically understudied. "It is hard to emphasize adequately the importance of religion at the height of the cold war," Nadel notes. "Throughout the popular culture and political rhetoric of Cold War America," Thomas Doherty adds, "religion stood as a sturdy pillar in the anticommunist fortress sustaining one nation, 'under God.'"[41]

Imbricated within Myth of America identity, intense religiosity was not new to the Cold War but rather "deeply imbedded in the thought and character of the American people." While Woodrow Wilson's religiosity is well known, less attention has been focused on Roosevelt's wartime religious appeals. "The world is too small to provide adequate 'living room' for both Hitler and God," the president declaimed on January 6, 1942, in an address to Congress. The

Nazis threatened to implant "their new German, pagan religion throughout the world—the plan by which the Holy Bible and the Cross of Mercy would be displaced by 'Mein Kampf' and the swastika and the naked sword." Thus in World War II the nation fought "to cleanse the world of ancient evils, ancient ills. . . . We are inspired by a faith that goes back to . . . Genesis: 'God created man in His own image.' We are fighting, as our fathers have fought to uphold the doctrine that all men are equal in the sight of God." In October 1943 the theologian Reinhold Niebuhr urged Christians not to "turn the other cheek" but rather to embrace the "historic mission" of the "Anglo-Saxon world" to stand against the Axis powers.[42]

Religious appeals drove the Cold War binary of a millennial struggle between good and evil. Seth Jacobs interprets the Cold War as "an all-consuming religious crusade against an adversary who rejected God's universal moral law and sought to enslave humanity under an atheistic creed." Most Americans, M. J. Heale notes, "were both propertied and Christian, so that both elites and citizens at large were likely to be allergic to 'atheistic communism.'" Niebuhr's "Christian realism" carried over from the good to the Cold War and played a critical role in rallying religious support for a tough-minded response to "godless Communism." Whereas Niebuhr was a Christian intellectual, populist appeals from the Catholic bishop Fulton J. Sheen and the Southern Baptist Billy Graham reached audiences numbering in the tens of millions. Both used the new medium of television to great effect in the 1950s, Graham's emotional televised crusades carrying into the twenty-first century. The popularity of these Christian militants overwhelmed the pacifism of A. J. Muste and other Christian peace internationalists.[43]

The 1950s, sometimes viewed as the most religious decade of the twentieth century, represented another in a series of great awakenings intrinsic to national identity. From 1940 to 1959 official membership in a church or synagogue rose from 49 percent to 69 percent of the population. In its 1955 Christmas issue, *Time* referred to the "unprecedented revival in religious belief and practice everywhere in the U.S., as faith in God, prayer, belief in the divinity of Jesus, and the Bible as the literal word of God soared throughout the decade." Film provided a powerful medium for representing biblical narratives through epic Hollywood productions such as Cecil B. DeMille's *The Ten Commandments* (1956).[44]

Truman and Eisenhower perpetuated the tradition of Roosevelt and Wilson and virtually all of their predecessors in linking the fate of the United States with God's divine plan. Truman repeatedly depicted the Cold War as a "moral, God-fearing" cause, while Eisenhower launched a tradition of White House prayer breakfasts and declared, "The forces of good and evil are massed and armed and opposed as rarely before in history . . . freedom is pitted against slavery, lightness against the dark." Eisenhower added "one nation under God" to the Pledge of Allegiance on Flag Day, June 14, 1954, and two years later sanctified "In God We Trust" on coinage as the nation's official motto. Few, however, could match Secretary of State John Foster Dulles in depicting the Cold War as a moral struggle between good and evil. Dulles's religiosity not only predisposed him to rule out negotiations, neutralism, or any "moral compromise" with godless Communism, it also, Jacobs argues, led him to support Asian leaders who lacked popular support in their own countries, namely, Chiang, Rhee, and Vietnam's Ngo Dinh Diem, collectively described by Dulles as "Christian gentlemen who have suffered for their faith."[45]

The Christian trope of a crusade against "godless tyranny" in Eastern Europe fueled a U.S. Cold War campaign of psychological warfare. "Contrary to the general perception at the time," Westad points out, "it was the United States that was the propaganda master of the Cold War, in terms of both effort and resources spent." Assisted by East European émigrés, the United States and its allies beamed propaganda through the Voice of America, the CIA-funded Radio Free Europe (RFE), Radio Liberation, Vatican Radio, and Radio in the American Sector (of Berlin). Organizations such as the Crusade for Freedom, also covertly funded by the CIA, staged propaganda displays and sent leaflets behind the "iron curtain" in balloons, which burst at high altitudes and rained down their cries for resistance. Spies entered the so-called captive nations, almost invariably to be captured and executed after being betrayed by Soviet moles who had penetrated the Western governments.[46]

While Western tropes like iron curtain and totalitarianism offered constant reaffirmation of the U.S. crusade for freedom, psychological warfare at the same time prompted the Soviets and their allies to clamp down even harder. They did so ruthlessly, purging dissidents and executing fallen Communists after sensational, choreographed show trials. Increasingly and murderously paranoid, Stalin orchestrated another wave of purges at home in response to the chimerical "doctor's plot" just months before his own death in March 1953. Stalin's successors inherited mounting opposition to Soviet hegemony and outright resistance in East Germany, where workers struck and others called for an end to the Communist Party dictatorship. Western and émigré propaganda fueled the uprising, but Soviet forces crushed the East German revolt in June 1953.

A similar scenario played out throughout the Soviet empire, most spectacularly in Hungary in the wake of the stunning denunciation of Stalin by his ultimate successor, Nikita S. Khrushchev. In a supposedly secret speech delivered before the Twentieth Soviet Communist Party Congress in February 1956, Khrushchev bitterly denounced "the crimes of the Stalin era." Not illogically, Hungarians responded by throwing out their own neo-Stalinist leader, replacing him with a reform prime minister, Imre Nagy. Nagy, however, lost control of the situation, as "liberationists," dramatically encouraged by the CIA/RFE radio propaganda, demanded the withdrawal of Red Army troops.

As Myth of America identity demanded ultimate victory over evil enemies, Eisenhower, Dulles, and a host of psychological warriors hoped to exploit the Hungarian unrest to trigger a meltdown of the Soviet empire. Hungarian reformers accelerated their resistance in Budapest in the fall of 1956, tearing the red stars off of public buildings and toppling a gigantic statue of Stalin. Citing their own obsessions with credibility and falling dominoes, the Soviet leaders told Nagy, "If we withdraw our troops from Hungary and Budapest . . . the imperialists will interpret it as weakness on our part and will attack." Concluding "we have no other choice," Khrushchev sent more than sixty thousand Red Army troops in November 1956 to brutally put down the rebellion, killing thousands and executing some three hundred Hungarians, including Nagy.[47]

Rather than achieving liberation, psychological warfare thus merely cemented and quite possibly prolonged Soviet hegemony. Alternative scenarios to the way this history unfolded are endlessly debatable, but the diplomatic record shows that the United States relentlessly rejected opportunities to attempt to negotiate a settlement of Cold War issues in both Europe and Asia. Determined to win the Cold War rather than negotiate with evil, the United States chose economic sanctions, militarization, psychological warfare, and covert intervention over diplomacy.[48]

Myth of America identity precluded meaningful negotiations with godless Communists, just as the nation had eschewed diplomacy with merciless Indian savages and mongrel Mexicans and conducted saturation civilian bombing in pursuit of unconditional surrender of the Japs. "Hostility to the United States was, by definition, hostility to progress and righteousness, and therefore was, by definition, illegitimate," Frederick Logevall explains. The United States "had no meaningful diplomacy with Communist adversaries through long stretches of the Cold War" as a result of the cultural perception that the demonic reds possessed an "omnivorous and insatiable appetite for power," hence "the only language they understood was deterrence and preponderant military force."[49]

Despite his eloquent yet fundamentally propagandistic "Chance for Peace" speech on April 16, 1953, Eisenhower prioritized militarization, psychological warfare, and especially covert operations even as he eschewed negotiations. Eisenhower rejected insistent pleas from the now more flexible Churchill, once again serving as British prime minister, to conduct a summit with the new Soviet leadership. As for those new leaders, Eisenhower advised Churchill, in a vividly gendered trope, "Russia was a woman of the streets and whether her dress was new, or just the old one patched, it was certainly the same whore underneath."[50] Yet the Kremlin defied such demonizing discourse and displayed flexibility. As two scholars note, "Between 1953 and 1955 cease-fires were achieved in Indochina and Korea; the Soviet and Chinese governments indicated their willingness to normalize relations with Japan; an Austrian peace treaty was signed; and the heads of the American, British, and French governments met in Geneva with their Soviet counterparts at the first Cold War summit conference."[51] Khrushchev and Nikolai Bulganin sent unmistakable signals as they even dropped by the U.S. embassy on July 4 to pay their respects to the imagined community.

When the French defeat at Dien Bien Phu in 1954 forced the summit in Geneva, the United States steadfastly opposed any sort of negotiated settlement, as Dulles did not share Khrushchev's enthusiasm for the "spirit of Geneva" or for a thaw in the Cold War. Opposed to conducting diplomacy with Communists as a matter of moral principle, Dulles refused even to shake hands with China's top diplomat, Zhou Enlai. By the late 1950s U.S. obdurateness and a series of East–West crises—the Hungarian intervention, Khrushchev's issuing of an ultimatum over the Western enclave in Berlin, the Cuban Revolution, and illegal U-2 overflights of Soviet airspace, culminating on May 1, 1960, in the shoot-down of a U.S. plane—all conspired to preclude any real "chance for peace." The usual stereotypes of Khrushchev as mercurial and bombastic are not without foundation, yet in the conventional Cold War narrative they invariably overshadow the Soviet leader's keen interest in reform and his call for "peaceful coexistence" with the West.[52]

Unpacking the Discursive Regime

As identity-driven foreign policy proved more conducive to psychological warfare and militarization than to negotiations, the curtain across the heart of Europe indeed became increasingly iron. The U.S.-led crusade for freedom left the Soviets with two choices—capitulation to a hostile anti-Communist alliance, drawing it closer to Soviet borders, which of course was no choice at all, or hardening of Communist Party authority through violent repression of liberalizing tendencies. As the War Resisters League astutely noted, "Aggressor governments do not suddenly become peaceable merely because menacing foreign opposition appears; on the contrary, its mere presence enables them to intensify the anxieties of their own peoples and strengthen their dictatorial systems." Despite the logic of these arguments, hegemonic Cold War discourse condemned critics and peace internationalists as subversive.[53]

Any meaningful unpacking of the Western Cold War narrative requires acknowledgment that U.S.-sponsored militarization, including NATO, undermined the prospect of amelioration of Soviet hegemony. To be sure, NATO complemented Western European economic integration and psychic recovery from the bitter wartime trauma, thereby promoting cohesion and confidence. However, little appreciated at the time or since, NATO also undergirded Soviet hegemony over Eastern Europe. The Kremlin could never really consider a pullback of its forces and allow for liberalization, or "Finlandization," of the East European regimes, so long as those states could be expected to enter straight into a hostile military alliance targeting the USSR. Just as Communist Party authorities had projected all along, the East European states, led by the Baltic republics, immediately joined NATO after the Soviet empire disintegrated in 1989–91.

The putative crusade for freedom thus functioned primarily to reify Myth of America identity while consigning the peoples of Eastern Europe to Soviet-backed authoritarianism. Had the West adopted a less confrontational and less militarized approach on east-central Europe, Khrushchev might well have been willing to allow substantial reforms to unfold rather than take the draconian step, which he sought to avoid, of direct intervention in Hungary. The Austrian treaty and the olive branch extended to Tito in Yugoslavia reflected the Kremlin's new thinking in the wake of the historic denunciation of Stalin, but the United States resolutely opposed negotiations in deference to liberation and unconditional surrender of the godless enemy-other.

The argument sketched out above is, of course, scandalously heretical within the discourse of what is called the free world. To the extent criticism and alternative narratives are even acknowledged they are bitterly attacked as the worst sort of left-wing revisionism. Cold War orthodoxy rejects any explanation of this history other than that the Soviet Union was an evil, dictatorial power that took every opportunity to engage in repression of other peoples in defiance of the civility of the U.S.-led free world. Advocacy of liberation was the only possible Western response short of capitulation or Munich-style appeasement. Under this interpretive frame, NATO has been considered virtually sacrosanct, a vital pillar of postwar containment.

At this point we have come full circle on Eastern Europe and the culturally constructed Cold War. The renewed and intensified East–West conflict evolved from the wartime strategy urging the Soviet Union to enter the heart of Europe in the context of rolling back the Nazis. The United States rejected a spheres-of-influence arrangement along the lines of the Churchill–Stalin percentages agreement because such an arrangement defied American Century universalism. Any "substitute for victory" would have vindicated the prewar "isolationists," who had repeatedly predicted that the nation would fail, as it had in World War I, to make the world safe for democracy. Indeed, some noninterventionists accurately predicted the outcome that occurred, arguing that U.S. intervention in World War II might defeat the Nazis only to result in the extension of Soviet power into the heart of Europe. In that event, "having saved the world from Nazism should we not be morally obligated to go on and save it from Bolshevism?" queried the *Saturday Evening Post* in November 1941.[54]

This discussion suggests that the crucial turning point in this history was not the mythical "Yalta sellout" or the emergence of the Cold War after 1945, but rather U.S. intervention in the proverbial good war. One of the outcomes of the Cold War was its chilling effect on virtually any attempt to interrogate the trope of World War II as the good war. With the nation continuously mobilized for war and confronting "evil" adversaries in the USSR, Red China, Korea, Vietnam, Cuba, and elsewhere, the unambiguous good war narrative became sacrosanct. The purge of the left and the rebirth of many isolationists as "Asia-first" Cold War interventionists buried the legacy of noninterventionism and peace internationalism.

World War II brought victory, ended the Great Depression, reintegrated Western Europe and Japan, and ushered in a putative golden age of prosperity and consensus. Hollywood immortalized the conflict in scores of heroic war movies—films in which a Russian soldier was nowhere to be seen, even though the USSR bore the overwhelming burden of defeating the Nazis. The public honored the war, the 405,000 U.S. dead (291,557 in combat), and another one million who suffered injuries. Perspectives that might defy the hegemonic good war paradigm—racial oppression at home and abroad, the relentless bombing campaign against civilian targets, propaganda, censorship, war profiteering, military Keynesianism, fueling of the military-industrial complex, and a purge of the left—all gave way to a national narrative that powerfully reaffirmed the righteousness of the crusade.[55]

The monolithic good war interpretation flows in part from the legacy of the Nazi Holocaust. Surely a war fought against such a demonstrably evil enemy had to be just. Yet the United States did not enter the war over the fate of European Jews and rejected any deviation from established military strategy, including moderation of unconditional surrender, to come to the aid of these victims. On December 17, 1942, the Allied command issued a statement confirming that the Germans were carrying out "Hitler's oft-repeated intention to exterminate the Jewish people in Europe. From all the occupied countries, Jews are being transported, in conditions of appalling horror and brutality, to Eastern Europe." The Allies realized that Poland had emerged as "the principal Nazi slaughterhouse" and that "the ghettos established by the German invaders are being systematically emptied of all Jews."[56] Although four million more Jews died after 1942, my point is not to insist that the Allies could have brought a swift end to the slaughter, but rather to suggest that the celebration of World War II as a moral crusade obscures the actual Western nonresponse to genocide.

The sheer mass horror of the Nazi Holocaust, with its refuse piles of naked, emaciated human bodies, brought powerful cultural affirmation of the righteousness of World War II. By defeating the perpetrators of the Holocaust, the Allies became liberators, which at the same time had the salutary effect of effacing their own past crimes against humanity through enslavement, ethnic cleansing, imperialism, colonialism, and saturation bombing of civilian targets. The triumphant representational regime erected around the wars "good" and "cold" also obscures a continuous history of postwar U.S. military interventions as well as the cultural hegemony of the warfare state.

Perhaps only now, after the passing of the "greatest generation," can World War II be broadly analyzed.[57] We will never know what would have transpired had the noninterventionists won the great debate, obviated war with Japan, and thus headed off U.S. intervention in World War II. It is possible that the world situation could have been worse, perhaps much worse, than it turned out. It is also possible that it could have been better.

Although such counterfactual scenarios are, of course, purely speculative, the critical point is that Myth of America identity demands a hegemonic interpretation of both the wars good and cold as the courageous response of free men against the forces of evil. Monolithic historical interpretation narrows the boundaries of intellectual inquiry and establishes disciplinary knowledge that limits analysis, not only of these foreign policy conflicts but also, crucially, of who benefited from the contingent decisions that were made. Proponents of the hegemonic narrative cannot prove that U.S. global intervention made for a better world any more than a counterfactual scenario can prove that the foreign policy was fatally flawed. However unsatisfying, such uncertainty is an inescapable component of the art of historical discourse. What is crucial to understand, however, is that Myth of America identity, and its orthodox intellectual defenders, insist that they alone grasp the truth and that the nation, under God, employed its righteous might in the wars good and cold. This narrative constitutes hegemonic nationalist discourse and nothing more.

CHAPTER 7

Militarization and Countersubversion

The "good" war powerfully reaffirmed national identity by resurrecting the imagined community in the wake of the debilitating Great Depression. Massive government spending, grounded in the fiscal policy outlined by the Briton John Maynard Keynes, the preeminent economic thinker of the twentieth century, fueled the war effort and economic recovery. The unparalleled deficit spending belied classical economic theory and underscored the failure of laissez-faire either to end the Depression or fund the massive war effort. While free enterprise remained integral to the discourse of capitalism, the Depression and the war had shown that the "magic of the marketplace" could not anchor modern liberalism. A mixed economy, including substantial government "pump-priming," thus emerged as the foundation of advanced capitalist societies.[1]

The critical point, however, is that the nation embraced federal spending *for militarization* while rolling back the limited New Deal social welfare state. As Keynes explained, "It seems to me politically impossible for a capitalist democracy to organize expenditure on a scale necessary to make the grand experiment which would prove my case [for recovery through deficit spending]—except in war conditions." The implications of Keynes's comment are profound: the United States had become dependent on government financing of a warfare state.[2]

If the solution to the economic crisis was Keynesianism, Myth of America identity ensured that is was military Keynesianism rather than a "socialistic" expansion of the New Deal. Militarization brought an end to the Depression, whereas the New Deal had not, but only because wartime expenditures dwarfed Roosevelt's prewar domestic spending. The war had shown that the nation could spend its way out of the Depression through massive pump priming, yet it would do so only in the name of war. "Forging links among government, business, science, and other partners," Michael S. Sherry explains, the war demonstrated the "attractions of militarization—prosperity, power, [and] victory."[3]

While national identity remained continuous in U.S. history, perceptions of the role of the military had thus changed dramatically. The founding patriarchs associated standing armies with British occupation and tyranny. Subsequent generations carried forward the tradition of opposition to a large military establishment, which might undermine democracy and create a "garrison state." In 1940 the United States had a modest armed forces establishment and a public that opposed involvement in another European war. A decade later the nation was the world's preeminent economic and military power, and its navy and air force were second to none; until August 1949 it enjoyed a monopoly on atomic weapons and considered the entire world as falling under its legitimate foreign policy jurisdiction. Although millions of citizen soldiers returned to civilian life after World War II, the country never demobilized culturally, economically, or as the world's preeminent arms trafficker. Victory in the two-front good war vaulted the prestige of the military to unprecedented heights.

The United States had affirmed its manliness, racial superiority, and destiny to lead the "free world" while at the same time entering into a (thus far) permanent epoch of militarization. The war affirmed the strength of the nation's fighting men, many of whom had been unemployed and emasculated by the Depression, and sanctified militarization through the defeat of the seemingly invincible Nazi war machine. Defeat of the "Japs" affirmed racial superiority and sanctified aerial bombardment and the legitimacy of employing atomic weapons. In view of these triumphs, opposition to militarization became un-American.

The Cold War and militarization became mutually reinforcing, as the former provided a constant source of enemy-othering to justify the unbridled expansion of the latter. Just as the Depression spawned the New Deal, war and Cold War spawned the national security state (NSS), a "state within a state" with a "unified pattern of attitudes, policies, and institutions." Drawing its lifeblood from the culturally rooted binary of the Communist enemy-other, the NSS girded for "perpetual confrontation and for war." The National Secu-

rity Act of 1947 reorganized the foreign policy bureaucracy to wage the revivified Cold War, as it created a National Security Council (NSC) to draw up plans
for global hegemony; the CIA; and a new Department of Defense, with a cabinet-level secretary, to coordinate the four service branches under a new Joint
Chiefs of Staff. National security was the basis for, in essence, an expanded and
militarized civil service. Similarly, the State Department, which numbered 974
employees in 1939, counted four times that many by the end of the war.[4]

The trope of national security, which came into use during the prewar great
debate over intervention, offered linguistic sanction for the drive for a militarized global hegemony. National security and "defense" policy elided an aggressive foreign policy committed to exporting American Century universalism,
including corporate capitalism, to every corner of the globe. The language reflects not deliberate deception but rather the degree to which Americans had
internalized their own identity-driven discursive regimes of anti-Communism, militarism, and providential destiny.

Built during the war, the Pentagon, the world's largest office complex, became the new epicenter of American power. Three times the size of the Empire
State Building, a virtual city-state unto itself, the new concrete and limestone
edifice contained offices, command centers, cafeterias, recreation facilities, and
hospitals. Washington, D.C., burgeoned during the war, as did other regional
centers of militarism, especially California and the rising Sunbelt states. For
scores of communities, cities, states, and regions, the link between military production and prosperity was palpable and addictive.

The wars good and cold afforded the cultural space for the emergence of an
archipelago of U.S. military installations encircling the globe. Beginning with
the destroyers for bases agreement with Great Britain in 1940, the United States
secured air and naval bases in Newfoundland, Bermuda, the Bahamas, Jamaica,
St. Lucia, Trinidad, Antigua, and British Guiana. Triumph across the Atlantic
and the Pacific added bases in Okinawa, the Philippines, Iceland, Greenland,
the Azores, Saudi Arabia, Diego Garcia, and North Africa. "We are going to
maintain the military bases necessary for the complete protection of our interests of world peace," Truman declared at war's end. "Bases which our military
experts deem to be essential for our protection, and which are not now in our
possession, we will acquire."[5]

Few texts reflect Myth of America hegemony, the NSS, and Cold War militarization better than NSC document number 68 (1950). Like previous national
security documents, but now with a more apocalyptic tone in the wake of the

"loss" of China and the Soviet atomic test, NSC 68 depicted a death struggle between "the integrity and vitality of our free society" and "slavery under the grim oligarchy of the Kremlin." NSC 68 affirmed the essential binary between the "free world" and "a new fanatic faith, antithetical to our own, [which] seeks to impose its absolute authority over the rest of the world." At stake was nothing less than "the fulfillment or destruction not only of this Republic but of civilization itself."[6]

NSC 68 and the U.S. invasion of Korea cemented the identity-driven warfare state over the social welfare state. NSC 68 endures as a monument to Cold War culture because it embodied mythical discourse, conjoined with the new ethos of national security, and called, moreover, for unbridled militarization to win a holy war between good and evil. The ultimate manifestation of military Keynesianism, NSC 68 advocated dramatic increases in defense spending—spending at whatever levels officials deemed necessary—to win the epic struggle. Following Truman's approval of the policy paper on September 30, 1950, the defense budget soared during the Korean War from $13 billion in 1950 to $48.7 billion in 1953.[7]

The bitter Korean War "militarized the cold war as never before." Prior to the Korean invasion, NATO consisted of fourteen "undermanned, poorly equipped, largely uncoordinated army divisions, only two of which were American." Three years later, fifteen well-armed divisions existed in a rearmed West Germany alone, as U.S. defense spending had more than doubled as a percentage of GNP. Ground and air bases, port facilities, communications complexes, and integrated planning under U.S. supervision attested to the militarization of the ostensibly North Atlantic alliance, which in actuality extended into the Near East through the inclusion of Greece and Turkey. After Korea and NSC 68, Washington transformed a "paper commitment" into a pledge "to keep major forces on the continent permanently and take the lead in coordinating their operations with NATO partners." By 1952, 80 percent of U.S. aid to Western Europe consisted of security assistance.[8]

In the wake of the Korean War, the United States established permanent bases in Japan and South Korea, committed the nation to fight Communism across the vast reaches of Southeast Asia, and ensured a generation of enmity with the PRC by interposing the U.S. Navy between the mainland and Taiwan, which Beijing viewed as a renegade province.[9] Cold War militarization in Asia ignited the Japanese economy and paved the way for dynamic economic growth in South Korea and Taiwan. Economic growth spurred by wartime production thus bolstered military Keynesianism abroad as well as at home and fueled the spread of corporate capitalism throughout the world.

Enemy-othering at the core of national identity marginalized opposition to militarism that emerged both at home and abroad. On the domestic front, fiscal conservatives mounted opposition to open-ended security commitments as well as open-ended costs. Conservatives ultimately accepted rearmament, following yet another great debate, in return for a tacit understanding that militarization would preclude a revival of the socialistic New Deal and fend off threats posed by national health, farm subsidies, rent controls, the union closed shop, and other reforms.

Both militarization and brinkmanship encountered opposition in Western Europe yet U.S. hegemony won out, the discourse of a unified "Atlantic community" notwithstanding. The Eisenhower "New Look," which blatantly threatened to use nuclear weapons in war, "was self-consciously hegemonic because it aimed to make American strategic doctrine the only choice of NATO as a whole," Andrew Johnston explains. Pressure from Washington forced Allied acceptance of first use of nuclear weapons, as John Foster Dulles rejected the European call for a strategy of using nuclear weapons only in response to attack, declaring simply yet chillingly, "Our plans might not be purely defensive."

As Providence had provided the United States alone (until 1949) with the nuclear option, the nation reserved the option of using the "winning weapon" should it become necessary to defeat evil enemies. Both Truman and Eisenhower threatened to use the bomb whereas Dulles, Johnston notes, believed that "in the hands of a confident nation, brandishing apocalyptic power was supremely moral." Dulles's moral militancy assuaged the domestic right wing while keeping the "Reds" unsure as to U.S. intentions, including the prospect of meeting "Communist aggression" with "massive retaliation." The Korean stalemate, including bloody battles with the "Chinese hordes," encouraged the emphasis on nuclear weapons, which could destroy hordes without exacting commensurate U.S. casualties.

Use of the ultimate weapon promised to deliver the psychic satisfaction of liberation rather than the demasculinizing frustrations of limited wars for containment, such as in Korea. The first-use option meant that the nation might strike at its own choosing rather than leaving the initiative in the hands of enemy-others. Oblivious to the implications of his own punishing World War II bombing campaign against civilian targets, General Curtis LeMay expressed the frustration of many through the metaphor of poker, declaring that the United States "always just called the bet. We ought to try raising sometime."[10]

The MIC Ascendancy

The military-industrial complex (MIC) profoundly impacted U.S. society and foreign policy. The United States devoted massive resources and energies—radiating throughout the society, including the economy, politics, education, and culture—on preparations for war, planning for war, and engaging in war. The MIC germinated with the expansion of federal power in the Civil War, followed by naval expansion in the late nineteenth century, and came of age in the Great War, as the War Industries Board (WIB) dramatically expanded government-sponsored collusion with "defense" industries. Despite the onset of the Depression, corporations, businesses, trade associations, and the armed services continued to grow during the interwar period. The Roosevelt administration increased spending for air and naval power, especially after Munich, but it was lend-lease and the drive to serve as the "great arsenal" that ultimately unleashed militarization. By 1941 defense spending rose to 13 percent of GNP, whereas it had been less than 1.5 percent for most of the 1930s.

The full-blown MIC became "a permanent fixture of American life" as the United States entered into the World War II crusade against the enemy Axis. When Roosevelt self-referentially proclaimed that "Dr. Win the War" had replaced "Dr. New Deal," most New Dealers believed the nation could revive the reform spirit after victory. Thus New Dealers, like the Progressives of the previous generation, did not foresee how much war would change society, undermine the reform impulse, and ultimately lead to a hegemonic militarized postwar order. Despite the insights gleaned from the penetrating Senate Special Committee (SSC) investigation of the "unhealthy alliance" between government and war industries, the same system of command economy, guaranteed profits, and enhanced corporate power emerged in the Second World War.[11]

The hegemonic Cold War binary of the communist enemy-other created cultural space for the NSS and the MIC to flourish. Under the prevailing tropes depicting the USSR and "Red" China as implacable godless foes, virtually any and all weapons were justified. With gendered discourses of masculinity prevailing, congressmen risked being labeled "soft" on communism if they opposed funding a new weapons system. Defense industries, especially in California but across the country as well, employed sizable proportions of engineers, physicists, and mathematicians, thus lending white-collar support to the MIC. Labor not only offered little challenge but patriotic postwar unions embraced the MIC, which created jobs for tens of thousands of blue-collar workers.

Militant national identity drove the military into a position of "extraordinary power and influence," enabling the emergence of what Sidney Lens termed *a new form of militarized "private socialism"* [emphasis added]. The triumph of the MIC "signaled trouble for America," Paul Koistinen argues, as "the corporate community-armed forces partnership repeatedly demonstrated that it could operate in ways that served the interests of the partners at the expense of the nation's immediate and long-run interests."[12] While advancing a command economy, the dominant troika of corporate power, the armed services, and national security elites buried the New Deal and precluded the reemergence of a regulatory state that might threaten militant cultural hegemony. These developments continued a trend born in the Civil War, empowered through the industrial era, culminating in the 1896 election, advanced during the imperial wars and especially through intervention in World War I. Throughout modern U.S. history, war and militarization proved integral in the cultural process of marginalizing farmers, feminists, minorities, reformers, and peace progressives.

With violence and warfare imbricated within national identity, the United States prioritized military rather than domestic-orientated research and development. Prior to Pearl Harbor, sparse federal funding for science focused mainly on agriculture. During and after the war, however, massive federal funding for science, coordinated by the Pentagon and the new National Science Foundation after 1950, fueled militarization. Expenditures on defense, space, and energy-related research comprised more than three-fourths of all federal spending on science and technology, with medical research comprising most of the remainder.[13]

More than any previous war, World War II suggested that the quality rather than quantity of weapons could prove decisive, a mindset underscored by Hiroshima and Nagasaki. Moreover, the "success" of the bomb and the emphasis on air power in World War II raised the possibility that technology could save the lives of U.S. servicemen through advanced military hardware (and ultimately software as well). Jet aircraft, guided missiles, and radar joined atomic weaponry as breakthrough technologies that made a difference in winning the war. Discoveries in nuclear physics, aerodynamics, and supercomputing produced a series of breathtaking "advances" in military technology. Successful testing of the hydrogen bomb in 1952 was followed by inter-continental ballistic missiles, silent and thus invulnerable nuclear submarines, warp-speed jet aircraft as well as massive bombers, missiles with multiple warheads, sophisticated satellite, microwave, and laser technology, and myriad additional innovations.

The wars "good" and "cold" brought universities into the militarized culture. Under Vannevar Bush, the architect of wartime science policy, the Massachusetts Institute of Technology (MIT), Harvard, Caltech, and others received millions of dollars in federal funds to back the war effort. Federal appropriations approximately doubled after Korea, as Johns Hopkins, California-Berkeley, Stanford, Chicago, most of the Ivy League schools, and myriad state universities across the country received funding for military related applied and classified research. The bulk of defense funding, however, went to a few elite institutions, led by Boston's MIT, which was dubbed "the Pentagon on the Charles."[14]

With militant national identity and the Cold War campaign against enemy-others determining the nation's priorities, militarization rather than an open-ended pursuit of knowledge dominated the research agenda. The Defense Department became the single largest patron of science, a testament to the triumph of militarization. Perceived military needs determined what scientists and engineers studied, designed, and thought. Scientists understood that funding readily available for military research and development (R&D) would not be available for humanitarian research. Moreover, the Cold War and concerns about espionage undermined scientific internationalism, a broad sharing of knowledge as a spur to research and advancement. By tightening the bonds between the university and the state, the MIC prioritized dependency and secrecy rather than open presentation, publication, and academic freedom. The symbiotic relationship between the academy and the MIC thus produced, as Stuart Leslie notes, a "profound skewing of research agendas."[15]

The entire "alphabet soup" of the NSS joined myriad private foundations in funding military R&D. In addition to the State and Defense Departments and the four armed service branches, the Atomic Energy Commission (AEC), NSC, CIA, FBI, the National Security Agency (NSA, created in 1953), the National Aeronautical and Space Administration (NASA, 1958), the Defense Intelligence Agency (DIA, 1961), and numerous other agencies sponsored university and scientific research. The Ford Foundation, Carnegie Fund, various Rockefeller groups, the Social Science Research Council, think tanks such as the RAND (for research and development) Corporation, and other foundations collaborated as well in the emergence of an "academic national security complex." The MIC thus forged "astonishing levels of collaboration between the universities, the foundations, and the intelligence arms of the American state."

Generations of scientists, professors, and graduate students devoted their research to finding new ways to destroy the Communists. At MIT, for example, the top secret Project Troy devised means to promote instability inside the Soviet Union and the nations behind the "iron curtain." At Harvard and Columbia, Russian research centers secretly funded by the CIA probed weaknesses in the Soviet system while promoting orthodox interpretations of the Cold War. With scientific research dictated by "the requirements of the national security state," Leslie notes, academic programs and corporate products became "so skewed toward the cutting-edge performance of military technology that they had nothing to give the civilian economy."[16]

The militaristic culture, conjoined with the modernist faith in technological progress, paved the way for congressional funding of virtually every new weapons system that could be devised. The MIC thus enabled a massive rearmament, everything from handheld firearms and machine guns to nuclear, biological, and chemical weapons. With noninterventionists and peace progressives politically moribund, Congress facilitated the expansion of the MIC.

As the providentially sanctioned leader of the free world, the righteous nation legitimized its role as the leading arms manufacturer and global arms dealer. Producing more weaponry than even its inflated projection of need could justify, the MIC fueled the militarization not merely of the United States but also of the planet. As the great arsenal took shape in the war, the United States produced more than 40 percent of world munitions output by 1944. The percentage continued to grow, and by the twenty-first century comprised about half of the world's armaments. The "millions of weapons produced over the long-haul," Paul Pierpaoli avers, "add nothing to the nation's economic potential" but rather have resulted in "many lost economic opportunities."[17]

The defense establishment emphasized enemy capabilities, such as the chimerical threat of a Soviet assault on Western Europe, while virtually ignoring Soviet intentions, such as their overwhelming focus on homeland defense and exertions to avoid war with the West. Intelligence agencies produced estimates of enemy capabilities that virtually ensured congressional funding for new weapons systems. Interservice rivalry among the four armed service branches also fueled the MIC, as each sought funding for bases, weapons, and strategic priority in national security planning.

While condemning most federal regulation and public welfare programs as creeping socialism, Myth of America identity sanctifies corporate welfare for militarization. The MIC "turned many defense contractors into quasi-nationalized industries sustained for reasons of state policy, as opposed to market competitiveness," Alex Roland explains. "The intimate working relationship between the military services and the defense industry invited outright corruption." MIC-driven corporate welfare and corruption occurred under the veil of Cold War secrecy, many weapons systems being funded, developed, and even rendered obsolescent before the public became aware of their existence. The news media, overwhelmingly compliant during the Cold War, rarely probed the rampant waste, fraud, and corruption built into the MIC. Boeing, Lockheed, General Dynamics, and scores of other contractors joined more mainstream corporations, such as General Motors and General Electric, in the pursuit of the easy-to-come-by federal largesse for militarization.[18]

While disciplinary knowledge and a campaign of countersubversion marginalized critics of the MIC, condemnation emanated from an unlikely source, the former general-turned-president Dwight D. Eisenhower. In his penetrating farewell address in 1961, Eisenhower neatly encapsulated the entire phenomenon, which he had come to understand all too well. The president warned, in now-historic yet unheeded words, against "the acquisition of unwarranted influence, whether sought or unsought, by the military-industrial complex." As public policy threatened to become "captive of a scientific-technological elite," the "potential for the disastrous rise of misplaced power exists and will persist." Eisenhower grasped the "almost insidious penetration of our own minds that the only thing this country is engaged in is weaponry and missiles." As "the government contract becomes virtually a substitute for intellectual curiosity," the nation's scholars had become "dependent on federal employment, project allocations, and the power of money." In sum, "a permanent armaments industry of vast proportions" menaced national life.

The MIC address was Eisenhower's finest, albeit last, hour, as the president's "admonitions were late." In the eight years of his presidency "the government had spent over $350 billion on defense, allocating seventy-seven cents of every budget dollar for military-related purposes."[19] Moreover, Eisenhower had chosen as his secretary of state Dulles, a perfervid anti-Communist whose version of Christianity precluded diplomacy with "godless communism," thus entrenching militarization. Eisenhower's own desire to get "more bang for the buck" led to an escalatory policy of "massive retaliation" dependent on an expanded nuclear arsenal.

Deeply conflicted, Eisenhower advocated strategic sufficiency, yet the MIC developed its runaway identity under his purview. The Soviet launch of the first satellite, Sputnik, in 1957 produced a hysterical response even though the blast had not altered the "strategic balance." Democrats, angling for a return to the White House, charged that Eisenhower, somnambulate, had allowed a "missile gap" to emerge, thus rendering the country vulnerable to a first strike by the demonic Soviets. Eisenhower knew from covert U-2 overflights of the USSR that the actual missile gap favored the United States, the nation that asserted the right to first use of nuclear weapons, and which remained far superior in air and especially naval power.[20]

Unable to command the debate, Eisenhower settled for having the last word as he left office. The hero of Normandy had acknowledged through his address that a hegemonic culture of militarization dominated U.S. foreign policy. Eisenhower in effect embraced the view of the Nye Committee, whose analysis of World War I and warnings about the threat posed by the fusion of military and industrial power had been engulfed by the wars good and cold.

By the 1960s the Cold War binary, the NSS, and the MIC had become so thoroughly internalized within culture as to exercise absolute authority over foreign policy and national priorities. After riding the missile gap and charges that the Republicans had been soft on Communism to the White House, John F. Kennedy launched an immediate military buildup that carried through the Indochina wars. The U.S. defense budget regularly exceeded the entire GNP of most West European nations. In the 1960s defense spending exceeded the total of all personal income taxes; accounted for one-quarter of public works; and subsidized a large segment of manufacturing jobs and one-third of all research in the United States. As Harold Lasswell had warned, the time had indeed arrived when "the specialists on violence" had become the most powerful group in society."[21]

Countersubversion

As the nation militarized, a culturally driven campaign of countersubversion marginalized, disciplined, and virtually silenced voices of dissent. The misleading trope of a Red scare suggests an ephemeral phenomenon, while the subsequent trope of McCarthyism reframes a broad cultural campaign into an episodic witch-hunt conducted by a single alcoholic rogue politician. Both referents obscure the intimate connection between countersubversion and national identity: they have been *continuous* throughout national history. "Red

Scares have been part of the American political process," the British scholar M. J. Heale explains, "not aberrations or the products of mindless hysteria or the spawn of gifted demagogues."[22] A focus on the Red scares as two discrete postwar phenomena also insulates the iconic liberal Roosevelt and other architects of substantial *interwar* efforts to denigrate, slur, harass, and defeat opponents of militant intervention. The usable past thus clouds the essence of a continuous campaign flowing from Myth of America identity, which torpedoed progressive reform initiatives while empowering militarist hegemony.

The discontinuous New Deal reforms, which emerged in a climate of Depression-driven desperation, came under attack throughout the 1930s. In its very essence of being new, the New Deal threatened cultural hegemony, and thus Roosevelt's program and the progressive causes associated with it proved ephemeral. Well before the onset of World War II, virulent right-wing critics such as Charles Coughlin and Gerald L. K. Smith savaged the New Deal as communistic and labeled Roosevelt a dictator. The American Legion and other patriotic organizations, born in World War I, refired the engines of countersubversion, especially as another European war loomed.

The psychic crisis of national identity during the Depression created cultural space not only for the New Deal, but also for the emergence of a vibrant left. Communist Party USA advocacy became more open as its membership grew from 12,000 in 1932 to 80,000 in 1939. The CPUSA evolved into the "institutional center of a large, influential, and uniquely American radical political movement," Kate Wiegand notes, as it "regularly channeled thousands of grassroots activists into a whole range of respected political causes including the civil rights and union movements." The CPUSA condemned racism and defended, when no one else would, the so-called Scottsboro boys, who were threatened with execution on trumped-up and racially motivated rape charges in Alabama. By advocating women's equality and including women in its membership activities, the CPUSA also spurred the feminist movement.[23]

By the late 1930s the gradual abandonment of the New Deal and the drift toward intervention abroad undermined the Depression-fostered, limited toleration of counterhegemonic discourse. J. Edgar Hoover bridged the countersubversive movement between the two wars. Obsessed with Bolshevism since 1917 and an architect of the Palmer raids at the end of World War I, Hoover and the newly reorganized FBI (1934) became a federal anticrime force but also a vast bureaucracy dedicated to repressing the left. Under the New Deal and then especially during World War II, Hoover solidified his half-century reign as arguably the most powerful single individual in the nation. Until well into the postwar era, The Director strove single-mindedly to repress progressives, Communists, African Americans, Mexican-Americans, feminists, Indians, and homosexuals.[24]

Well before World War II Roosevelt dismissed the standard set in 1919 by Supreme Court Chief Justice Oliver Wendell Holmes calling for constitutional protection of free speech unless it posed a "clear and present danger."[25] Asserting his right to investigate groups promoting "false teaching contrary to our democratic ideals," Roosevelt "frequently used Hoover to dig up information on people or groups with no better rationale than that he was curious." The president grew increasingly anxious and intolerant in 1938, as conservatives began to seize the initiative by defeating his Court reorganization proposal and to savage the New Deal for its failure to bring recovery. Roosevelt's "routine" use of federal power against his political foes revealed "a president little concerned about civil liberties."[26]

Not content to attack dissenters through propaganda alone, the administration unleashed Hoover's FBI. Illegal wiretapping, infiltration of anti-interventionist groups, interference with the mails, harassment and barring of speakers, and a wide variety of formal and informal censorship escalated during the great debate. The House Committee on Un-American Activities, established in 1938, encouraged the tendency to equate dissent with disloyalty. "The guns of reaction are booming," warned the American Civil Liberties Union (ACLU). The Smith Act of 1940, which outlawed membership in any group advocating the overthrow of the U.S. government, anticipated postwar campaigns against radicals.

Under Roosevelt's direction, Hoover conducted an exhaustive probe of the America First Committee and prominent noninterventionists such as Gerald Nye and Charles Lindbergh. Despite the complete absence of foreign influence in the committee, harassment, intimidation, and allegations of unpatriotic behavior characterized the administration's response to noninterventionists.[27]

As anti-Bolshevik enemy-othering gained renewed momentum in the context of the Spanish Civil War, a new House Un-American Activities Committee (HUAC) strove to police deviations from the patriotic consensus. By investigating individuals "associated with various liberal and Communistic groups," HUAC blurred distinctions between progressive reforms, the New Deal, and Communism, the better to tar them all with the broad brush of subversion. Following the Nazi–Soviet Pact and the outbreak of World War II, Roosevelt undermined civil liberties by initiating federal wiretapping of alleged subversives and "fifth-columnists"; ninety-two bugs were in place by 1941.[28]

Direct involvement in World War II ensured the triumph of the NSS and the MIC while setting in motion a thoroughgoing purge of the left. Hoover consolidated unprecedented power during the war, as the FBI sprawled from a force of 898 to one of 4,886. Like the Pentagon, the NSS, and the MIC, the FBI needed an almost perpetual state of war—thus it embraced the renewed Cold War—in order to secure and consolidate its dramatic wartime expansion. Hoover worked in concert with the burgeoning defense establishment, as Secretary of War Henry Stimson urged the FBI to conduct a "ruthless" and "relentless" campaign of bugging, break-ins, and searches.[29]

Identity-driven racial modernity and intensified wartime enemy-othering produced the internment of some 130,000 first- and second-generation Japanese-Americans. The military simply presumed, rather than investigated, alleged disloyalty within the unassimilated Japanese-American community. Internment of the "inscrutable Orientals" showed that "Dixie had no corner on the market of discrimination." Driven by enemy-othering, but not by race, and thus on a smaller scale, the nation also harassed and interned Italian- and German-Americans. Americans offered little opposition. In April 1942 *Life* sounded the drumbeat with the feature "Voices of Defeat," offering incendiary accounts of people and organizations deemed subversive.[30]

The wartime leadership of the liberal ACLU supported the curbs on civil liberties. Freda Kirchwey of the *Nation* endorsed suppression of speech perceived as supporting "the fascist offensive" by declaring that the words "should be exterminated exactly as if they were enemy machine-gun nests." The ACLU banned the CPUSA and the German Bund from holding membership in its organization, while the Supreme Court upheld expulsion of Jehovah's Witnesses from Pennsylvania schools for declining to pledge the flag. David Riesman and other liberal intellectuals cited the precedent of Lincoln's actions in the Civil War to justify wartime suppression of free speech. The Holmes standard of clear and present danger thus gave ground broadly to widespread suppression of free speech justified under the trope of national security.[31]

Careful to demonstrate that they were loyal Americans, liberals embraced the NSS and the work of rooting out subversion. Arthur Schlesinger, Jr., and other Democrats, in apotheosizing the "vital center," impugned the patriotism of Henry A. Wallace and the few other politicians who continued to advocate progressive reform at home and peace internationalism abroad. The CPUSA openly supported Wallace, lending apparent credence to attempts to link his effort to revive domestic reform with Communist subversion. While Wallace called for diplomacy rather than confrontation with the Soviets, as well as international cooperation and commerce, hegemonic national identity called for eradicating rather than negotiating with evil enemy-others.

Discourses challenging the Myth of America, which carved out a modest cultural space during the Depression-era psychic crisis, could not function in the postwar era. Wallace's abject showing—he received just 2.4 percent of the vote in 1948—revealed the absence not merely of a domestic Communist threat but also of even a progressive threat. By the late 1940s, the peace movement "was limited to pacifist groups, some feminist groups, and a small group of liberal internationalists," Timothy Smith observes. The former Idaho senator Glen Taylor, Wallace's running mate, lamented a climate in which it had become "almost a traitorous act to criticize any of the policies which are taking us down the road to militarism." A WILPF spokeswoman condemned militarization as "one of the most alarming trends in contemporary life" while *Christian Century* charged that NATO "will hand over to the military services actual control" of foreign policy. The countersubversive campaign overwhelmed these voices of dissent.[32]

Truman's shift to the "vital center" and his embrace of aggressive Cold War policies played well in Peoria, as his upset electoral victory in 1948 showed. Truman had not completely abandoned the New Deal, but most of his laundry list of Fair Deal domestic reform proposals was hung out to dry by Republicans and conservative Democrats. The NSS discursive regime effectively linked progressive reform and the New Deal legacy with Communism, isolationism, and appeasement. Myth of America identity consistently linked unionism, national health care, welfare programs, and progressive politics with the enemy-other of godless Communism.

The loss of China followed by the U.S. invasion of Korea fueled the national campaign of countersubversion. Millions of Americans responded to the charge that demon enemies within had betrayed the United States and the Christian Chinese nationalist leader Chiang Kai-shek. The Republicans seized the high ground of patriotic identity out of their frustration over being deprived of the White House ("twenty years of treason"), first as Roosevelt's repeated whipping boy and then, compounding the frustration, suffering a humiliating defeat in 1948 to the relative novice Truman.[33]

With noninterventionism completely discredited in the wake of the wars good and cold, the loss of China enabled those tarred with the prewar brush of isolationism to return to the fold of militant national identity. Enemy-othering of Red China allowed these former isolationists to morph into "Asia-first" non-Communists. In close association with the powerful China lobby, the Asia-first Republicans charged that the Democrats had allowed spies and the "striped pants boys" in the State Department to "sell China down the river." The Asia-firsters now had an issue—China and internal subversion in a single package—and an iconic hero, Douglas MacArthur, particularly after the outbreak of war in Korea and the successful Inchon landing.[34]

The anxiety-ridden enemy-othering that burned over the nation after the fall of China and the Korean invasion created a cultural climate conducive to the visible demagoguery of McCarthy and the devastating countersubversion of "Hooverism." Enjoying almost complete freedom from oversight, Hoover constructed an internal security empire, a secret political arm of the NSS. Americans celebrated FBI successes in crime fighting against bank robbers and kidnappers—though not against the Mafia, which flourished in the postwar years.[35] The FBI investigated and exposed as many present or former CPUSA members and other radicals as possible, typically causing them to be summarily fired from their jobs and to cease their political activities as a prerequisite to reconstructing their lives. FBI agents employed wiretaps, rifled trash, intercepted mail, broke into homes and offices, leaked damaging information, supplied the IRS with tips against alleged radicals, and committed other illegal acts in the absence of executive or congressional oversight. Truman once referred privately to the FBI as the Gestapo but he, like all presidents, declined to challenge Hoover, the tough-minded leader of the nation's "G-men."[36]

The pervasive reach of cultural countersubversion played out in congressional legislation and sensational investigations ranging from New York to Hollywood. Aided by, among others, Ronald Reagan, an FBI informant through his association with the Screen Actors Guild, Congress investigated the alleged Communist sympathies of hundreds of actors, directors, and screenwriters, calling many of them to Washington beginning in 1946 for televised hearings to answer whether they were now or ever had been members of the Communist Party. Some Hollywood figures declined to testify or "name names," for which they were jailed or, more typically, found themselves deprived of work after being placed on the Hollywood blacklist.

The trope of McCarthyism clouds understanding as to just how deeply countersubversion pervaded the culture and complemented national identity.

At universities, ostensibly centers and symbols of intellectual freedom, the campaign against the left was as pervasive as the MIC. Aided by FBI informants, including William F. Buckley at Yale and Henry A. Kissinger at Harvard, universities investigated and dismissed faculty for radicalism while undermining freedom of thought. Universities offered little resistance, as federal agents typically were "an invited guest in campuses and quadrangles, and there is precious little evidence that the universities objected to, or even thought much about, the price that was being exacted," notes Sigmund Diamond, who was dismissed from Harvard on trumped-up charges by Dean McGeorge Bundy. Harvard also allowed its Russian Research Center to be compromised by informants affiliated with the FBI and CIA. Countersubversives infiltrated not just the elite institutions but universities across the country.[37]

Even though only ten states, according to FBI estimates, counted more than one thousand bona fide Communists, state and local governments determined to root them out to defend national security. "Little HUACS" sprang up all over the country beginning in the 1930s. Newly mandated loyalty oaths swept through the states, affecting as much as 20 percent of the workforce from 1947 to 1957, forcing thousands out of jobs, and costing millions of dollars in state and FBI loyalty investigations.[38]

Internal enemy-othering transcended the "Communist threat" to simultaneously repress labor, women, homosexuals, African Americans, and other minorities. "Precepts of class, race and religion were militating against the emergence of a genuinely multicultural society," Heale observes. "The red scare politics of the 1940s and 1950s were an expression of a kind of political fundamentalism" rooted in "traditional American political culture" and reflecting the "*normal operation of American politics*" [emphasis added].[39]

The intensity of local countersubversive campaigns varied by region and state, but everywhere they targeted potential threats to Myth of America cultural hegemony. Especially in the Midwest, "eruptions after about 1935 owed much to a conservative reaction against labor advances and New Deal reform." In Michigan, site of the famous sit-down strikes, defenders of hegemonic national identity drove out the New Deal administration of Governor Frank Murphy. In California "inquisitors stalked the state for an extraordinary three decades." In the South, anti-Communism often fused with militant segregation and Protestant revivalism, as reflected in Billy James Hargis's Christian Crusade. Florida mandated the course "Americanism vs. Communism" in school curriculums, and Arkansas adopted a like program of "Democracy vs. Communism." Anti-Communism began to be used as a weapon to defend segregation in the South, "but in northern cities too white homeowners sometimes sought to protect their neighborhoods from African American incursions by invoking the red menace."[40]

The countersubversive movement brought roaring to the surface the profound identity-driven social anxieties over gender and sexuality. While China was unambiguously red, many domestic subversives were labeled pink, suggesting borderline or covert radicalism but also a color associated with femininity. The campaign against pinks thus simultaneously linked assertive women with Communist sympathizers. The "powerful political consensus that supported cold war policies abroad and anticommunism at home fueled conformity to the suburban family ideal," Elaine Tyler May points out.[41]

Cultural hegemony associated progressive social welfare programs such as national health, public housing, and child care with the menace of femininity and moved aggressively to contain them. "Anti-communist attacks on women in government and policy circles curbed both feminism and the social democratic potential of the New Deal," Landon Storrs argues. Domestic containment of feminism during this time proved so pervasive as virtually to obscure the existence of the women's movement between the achievement of suffrage and the "second wave" of activism normally associated with the publication of Betty Friedan's *The Feminine Mystique* in 1963. "The lack of a visible women's movement allowed most people to believe that disgruntled women were simply neurotic malcontents," Wiegand explains. Countersubversion forced many activist women with ties to Old Left radical organizations, including Friedan, to quell their activism until the emergence of the New Left in the 1960s.

World War II offered an opportunity to reinvigorate masculine identities through the exercise of power abroad, simultaneously reinforcing "hegemonic militarized masculinity" on the domestic front. Wartime propaganda posters depicted bare-armed servicemen with bulging muscles and promoted an image of revivified national strength reinforced by victory over the Axis. While German strength remained respected, wartime discourse exalted white manhood through invidious contrast with Japanese males, depicted as subhuman jungle dwellers and dishonorable kamikaze fanatics. Moreover, as *Time* warned in its 1942 "Portrait of a Japanese," the immoral "Jap" has "raped Chinese girls and can't help wondering what white ones would be like." While "intersections

between wartime discourse of race and masculinity were often complex, lay-
ered, and contradictory," Christina Jarvis notes that true manhood and whiteness typically appeared inseparable.[42]

The white masculinity inherent in Myth of America identity carried into
the postwar era, as reflected in the GI Bill of Rights (1944). As the New Deal
withered and died, this single public welfare program thrived, as Congress allocated more than $7 billion a year to it in 1947–50—"more than triple all other
spending on social welfare, health, housing, and education." The GI Bill helped
ensure that "America's fighting men" could anchor the nuclear family by re-
suming their patriarchal role as educated or trained and employed heads of
households. Rosie the Riveter could return to her proper domestic sphere.[43]

The "Father Knows Best"–June Cleaver representations between the late
forties and early sixties marginalized women, who had grown more assertive as
a result of taking on new roles in wartime and in the process acquiring increased confidence and independent-mindedness. The emphasis on conformity and the nuclear family associated with the 1950s often featured sharp anxiety about female influence, as exemplified in Philip Wylie's well-known rant
against the emasculating influence of "destroying mothers." "The conformity
and masculinity crises were never far apart," K. A. Cuordileone observes.[44]

National identity fostered an extraordinary linkage between countersubversion and the demasculinizing forces of femininity, homosexuality, and "deviant" behavior. "The hyper-masculinity of national policy" in World War II
and the Cold War led to "a politics resistant to postmodern complexities of
gender, sexuality, or race," Suzanne Clark argues. Postwar discourse featured
"excessive scorn for the feminine," anxiety over perceived threats of "sentimentality," "pantywaist" diplomacy, "political sterility," "fatal weaknesses," "dark
impulses," "perversion," and other tropes that served to demonize or contain
women, leftists, pinks, and lavenders.

A "tough-minded realism" reminiscent of Theodore Roosevelt's exaltation
of warfare and the "strenuous life" permeated hegemonic discourse. The Democrats strove to "masculinize the liberal reform tradition" with their move toward the vital center and away from the New Deal legacy of empowered social
workers at home and elitist, striped-pants diplomats "selling out" the nation
abroad. The Alger Hiss case brought an outpouring of such discourse as well as
homophobia. Whitaker Chambers, Hiss's accuser, "confessed" his former Communist sympathies as well as his homosexuality. Countersubversive discourse
plagued the 1952 presidential campaign of Adlai Stevenson, who was perceived

as a classically effete liberal "egg-head." Richard Nixon, who rode the Hiss case to national prominence, ruthlessly derided "Adlai the appeaser" while Hoover secretly launched an "ugly whispering campaign" alleging Stevenson was a homosexual. The Director kept a file on Stevenson labeled "Governor of Illinois—Sex Deviate." When Stevenson ran again in 1956, the popular journalist Walter Winchell declared, "A vote for Adlai Stevenson is a vote for Christine Jorgensen," referencing the first recipient of a sex change operation (from man to woman). Buckley's *National Review* charged liberals with "definite antagonism toward all strenuous ideals of life."[45]

Alfred Kinsey's research into sexual practices, asserting a much wider incidence of homosexuality than believed, combined with the fear of "communist penetration" to excite a wave of identity-affirming homophobic discourse. The Lavender Scare—a fear that homosexuals posed "a threat to national security and needed to be systematically removed from the federal government—permeated 1950s political culture," David K. Johnson argues. A vicious campaign intended to root out suspected gays and lesbians ensued. "Can [you] think of a person who could be more dangerous to the United States of America than a pervert?" asked Senator Kenneth Wherry of Nebraska. As both homosexuals and Communists remained closeted, "you can't hardly separate homosexuals from subversives," he added. While the Senate launched an investigation under the heading "Employment of Homosexuals and Other Sex Perverts in Government," Billy Graham and other Cold War clergymen praised the endeavors aimed at "exposing the pinks, the lavenders, and the reds who have sought refuge beneath the wings of the American Eagle." Ultimately, then, as Cuordileone argues, "sexual containment was necessary for the containment of Communism," as both were deeply implicated in the nation's identity.[46]

Linking countersubversion with cultural anxiety destabilizes a patriotic narrative, which insists that anti-Communism responded to genuine threats to national security. In the 1990s, amid a climate of unbridled nationalist self-congratulation following "victory" in the Cold War (see chapter 9), nationalist scholars exploited newly released documents to justify the campaign of domestic containment. Their efforts reflect the production of disciplinary knowledge as well as the "noble dream" that historians can unveil the curtain on historical truth through new documentary evidence. Although they are the ones challenging traditional historical interpretation, the authors label those who question their interpretation revisionists, the standard term for denigrating and thus policing perceived left-wing scholarship.

The New McCarthyism studies exploited documents showing a much higher level of Soviet espionage activity in the United States than previously thought. The Venona transcripts made public a highly classified U.S. intelligence program beginning in the 1940s that succeeded in intercepting and deciphering portions of Soviet diplomatic cables. The intercepted cables revealed the Soviet espionage activity in the United States, including code names and detailed activities of both Soviet and U.S. citizens. Ironically but also revealingly, this information began to filter out of the former Soviet Union before the U.S. bureaucracy disgorged the Venona records.[47]

The reluctance to release the new documents reflected not only the usual free world obsession with secrecy, but also the embarrassing revelation that Congress and Hoover's FBI had focused so much on the perceived threat of domestic *subversion*—the absurdity that a relative handful of CPUSA members might overthrow the intensely nationalistic United States—that they overlooked a good deal of actual *espionage*.

While the Venona documents revealed new evidence of Soviet espionage, the effort to exploit them to justify countersubversion, even to rehabilitate McCarthy, underscores the critical role of history in affirming patriotic identity and ordering and reordering domestic hierarchies. The New McCarthyism frame elides pertinent information, including the fact that most of the spying took place during the war, when the Soviet Union and the United States were allies and working toward the same immediate ends. Moreover, as Jessica Wang points out, espionage is "something that states do," an exploit perpetrated "by almost all countries, including the United States." Maurice Isserman calls for a greater sense of proportion regarding espionage, warning, "*Espionage* is one of those words, along with *treason* and *disloyalty*, that summon up powerful emotions—understandably so—but also make it difficult to draw the distinctions necessary for exploring historical complexities."[48]

The narrative of the New McCarthyism illustrates how Myth of America identity marginalizes the left and reformers in both history and History. These narratives display indifference to the trail of "human wreckage" left in the wake of the crusade, which "blighted thousands of lives, careers, and marriages." For every genuine spy such as Klaus Fuchs or Julius Rosenberg, hundreds of people "guilty" only of "ideological deviation" became victimized. For every well-known victim, hundreds of obscure men and women lost their jobs, homes, and lives solely on the basis of their past leftist affiliations. The countersubversive campaign became a nightmare of families divided, blacklists compiled, books burned, hearings held on trumped-up charges, constitutional rights denied, and in some respects most odious of all: intense pressure to ensure the misery of others by naming names. Moreover, as Ellen Schrecker points out, one cannot account for "a world of things that did not happen: reforms that were never implemented, unions that were never organized, movements that never started, books that were never published, films that were never produced. And questions that were never asked."[49]

The anxiety-ridden outburst of postwar countersubversion reaffirmed militant national identity while simultaneously smashing the left. Although liberals had moved themselves to the "vital center," they failed to comprehend that the center now became the left, and hence they left themselves with little room to maneuver. Thus, as Schrecker notes, "the overall legacy of the liberals' failure to stand up against the anti-communist crusade was to let the nation's political culture veer to the right."[50]

Hegemonic national identity ensured that peace remained a suspect cause and that there would be no diplomacy with Communist enemy-others. The anxiety-ridden paroxysm of countersubversion purged the nation of peace internationalists who posed a threat to militant national identity. The left not only advocated alternatives to Cold War militancy, it might also have advanced the causes of progressive reform and racial and gender equality. The subversives truly were a threat—not to "national security" but to national identity.

CHAPTER 8

Neocolonial Nightmares

I n the postwar era, the "Third World" emerged as a staging ground for violent reaffirmation of U.S. cultural identity. As a white, modernist, and
manly nation, under God, the United States inscribed the non-Western
world as an arena of "backward" and "developing" peoples and lands. The Myth
of America sanctioned the projection of militant national identity across the
globe, usually with devastating consequences for indigenous peoples. The Second Indochina War, however, exposed the pathological contradictions inherent in the nation's identity and its neo-colonialist foreign policy.

The Cold War intensified violent conflict in the Third World, yet the
North–South struggle sprang from deeper roots. The global struggle reflected
the ongoing process of hegemonic Western modernity projecting itself onto
various cultures on the three continents of Africa, Asia, and Latin America. This
history may be conceptualized under the framework of postcolonialism within
a tricontinental geographic setting. "Postcolonial cultural critique involves the
reconsideration of this history," Robert J. C. Young explains, "particularly from
the perspectives of those who suffered its effects, together with the defining of
its contemporary social and cultural impact."[1]

Postcolonial historical analysis recognizes the hybridity inherent within
neocolonialism, as opposed to the rigid binaries of the North acting out its desires on a passive South. As international relations must always encompass intercultural relations, both the modernist and tricontinental peoples displayed
agency through collaboration, resistance, absorption, cooptation, and myriad
other forms. Nevertheless, with the United States and other modernist powers

viewing Third World nations as sites or subjects of their neocolonialist projections, this history necessarily involves a substantial focus on the actions and perceptions of the imperial powers.

As imperialism emerged out of the Industrial Revolution, the tricontinental world provided access to raw materials and guaranteed markets and ultimately sites for the Western nations, including the United States, to exercise power, act out desire, and project prestige.[2] The Great War dramatically weakened European suzerainty and left the United States poised for "inheritance of empire." However, as Secretary of State Robert Lansing warned Woodrow Wilson, the U.S. wartime discourse of "self-determination" was "loaded with dynamite" as it posed "the danger of putting such ideas into the minds of certain races." The United States safeguarded Latin American hegemony against self-determination and collaborated with European powers in the "mandate" system, a perpetuation of colonial rule in Asia and Africa. Tricontinental nationalists such as Vietnam's Ho Chi Minh left Paris not only disillusioned with the failed promises of Wilsonian self-determination but also with a growing appreciation of J. A. Hobson's and V. I. Lenin's theory of imperialism.[3]

While the United States sought to distance itself from the legacy of European colonialism, the nation relentlessly pursued a neocolonial foreign policy in Asia, Africa, and Latin America. With the Cold War struggle between good and evil serving as the primary frame, the United States viewed opposition to its postwar foreign policy, including "neutralism," as irrational, subversive and susceptible to violent repression. The nation's emergence as the world's preeminent global power coincided with the massive postwar wave of decolonization. "Only regimes that accepted American hegemony in foreign policy and in development strategy were seen as viable," Odd Arne Westad explains.[4]

Neocolonialism, rather than decolonization, ultimately proved compatible with Myth of America identity. In collaboration with oligarchs and militarists who often "waged war on their own peasant populations,"[5] the United States suppressed tricontinental liberation struggles. The nation often avoided direct intervention by assisting regimes in carrying out terror and oppression, yet Myth of America universalism was so deeply internalized that the United States repeatedly intervened with massive military force on sites thousands of miles from its own shores.

The hegemonic Cold War narrative posits a mythic turning point in which the United States reluctantly abandoned its ideals of decolonization for a "realist" policy of containing Communism. But the United States had never followed such a self-denying idealism with respect to self-determination of other cultures. National identity drove a violent hegemony shrouded by discourse and continuous throughout the nation's history. Thus the United States, rather than teetering between the choices of decolonization and intervention, idealism and realism, acted after World War II much as it always had. The world had changed as a result of World War II, to be sure, but national identity had been revivified by American Century unilateralism rather than remade by the war. Identity-driven U.S. foreign policy was violently reactionary and continuous rather than forward-looking and idealistic.[6]

While benign discourses depicted the United States as engaged in promoting modernization and progress in the free world, the nation's militant identity made it a lethal force in countless global interventions. Modernization theory held that scientific and technical rationalism could effect a social transformation of societies framed as developing or backward. The national security and academic security complexes invested heavily in modernization. "Compliant scholars and research analysts accumulated information on Third World development and dissent in the interests of U.S. foreign policy," Irene Gendzier explains, including counterinsurgency and destabilization programs."[7]

However sincere U.S. intellectuals and policy planners may have been about modernization, the militarization of foreign policy overwhelmed such considerations. By 1958 the United States had agreed to train and equip forces in more than seventy countries, had formal security commitments with forty-three of them, and some 1.5 million troops posted in thirty-five nations.[8] The United States continued to oppose UN multilateralism in deference to invasive unilateralism in defiance of international law, which prohibits intervention by one state into the affairs of another for the purpose of changing the latter's policies or conditions.[9] Postcolonial intervention unfolded indirectly whenever possible, yet the drive for global hegemony and the determination to uphold manly credibility led to direct U.S. intervention as well, culminating in the debacle in Southeast Asia. Despite this history of militarism, nationalist discourse reached Orwellian dimensions as some Eurocentric realist scholars characterized the Cold War as an era of the Long Peace, eliding the massive violence of postcolonial history.[10]

Hegemony and Repression South of the Rio Grande

The persistent drive for hegemony over Latin America underscored the imperial continuity of U.S. foreign policy before and after World War II. "Since the promulgation of the Monroe Doctrine of 1823," Young points out, "Latin America has been subject more than any other region in the world, even Southeast Asia, to neo-colonialism in the form of U.S. imperialism: military, political and economic."[11] Although not without resistance, to be sure, Washington established varying degrees of great power authority throughout the Western Hemisphere. While the largest states, Mexico, Canada, Argentina, and Brazil, offered generally more effective resistance than the vulnerable Central American and Caribbean states, the United States pursued hegemony over all, and all mounted a corresponding resistance. Cuba under Fidel Castro would emerge as the most neuralgic point of resistance.

Following World War II, the identity-driven Cold War fueled neocolonialism. The wartime Four Freedoms had inspired Latin American nationalism, while at the same time the inclusion of the USSR in the Grand Alliance offered legitimization for the left, spurring the growth of unions and of the Communist Party throughout Latin America. Improved postwar relations with Argentina's Juan Perón, whose neutrality in World War II had angered the United States, affirmed that military dictators offered the most reliable allies against the left and that the Cold War sanctioned support for such regimes.

Determined to fend off any meaningful UN internationalism, which might threaten U.S. hegemony over the region, in 1947 the United States forged the Treaty of Rio de Janeiro. "We have preserved the Monroe Doctrine and the inter-American system," the Republican and supposedly isolationist senator Arthur S. Vandenberg averred. While the United States represented the Rio pact as an anti-Communist alliance, Vandenberg underscored the nation's determination to exercise "a complete veto" of any changes in the hemisphere. The "collective security" treaty against nonexistent external threats to the region thus reinforced U.S. hegemony.

The lighter-skinned generals and oligarchs that the United States invariably backed stood to profit directly from U.S. hegemony. Yet millions of other Latin Americans hoped that closer ties with the Yankee colossus would lead to economic progress. At the time, per capita income hovered around $250 annually, while the average Latin American lifespan was forty-three years. Despite the discursive references to hemispheric solidarity since the Monroe Doctrine, the United States placed priority on postwar European and Japanese recovery and showed little genuine interest in privations south of the border. As the United States implemented the Marshall Plan, Truman responded incongruously and yet revealingly when asked why no equivalent program would be forthcoming for Latin America as in Europe. "There has always been a Marshall Plan in effect for the Western Hemisphere . . . known as the Monroe Doctrine," he declared.

Myth of America identity led to U.S.-backed repression typically carried out by the Yankee-armed and -trained military and police forces in collaboration with oligarchic powers. When resistance and calls for reform emerged, the United States invariably viewed them as subversive, Communistic, and a threat to national security. As postwar foreign policy became increasingly militarized, most U.S. economic assistance went into the Latin American military forces under the Mutual Security Program. Other investments went into extractive industries and thus did little to provide for long-term growth and stability.

Multilateral agreements proscribing intervention meant nothing to the United States, which repeatedly intervened, both directly and indirectly, throughout the region. The nation thus ignored the new Organization of American States (OAS), which replaced the defunct Pan-American Union and declaimed, "No State or group of States has the right to intervene, directly or indirectly, for any reason whatever, in the internal or external affairs of any other State." The Rio Treaty and the OAS "gave the appearance of collective decision-making on the continent," Laurie Johnston notes, "but the extent of U.S. power subverted any notion of equal partnership."[12]

Beneath the benign discourse of being a good neighbor, Americans viewed themselves as superior to the putatively hot-blooded, racially mixed Latin Americans. Truman, who, like most Americans, knew little about the region, decided the Latin Americans were, like the Jews and the Irish, "very emotional." John Foster Dulles concurred, noting "You have to pat them on the back and make them think you are fond of them." In a notoriously contemptuous report following a tour of the region in 1950, George F. Kennan asserted that despite the "inordinate splendor and pretense" of the Latin American capitals, there was "no other region of the earth" in which "nature and human behavior could have combined to produce a more unhappy and hopeless background for the conduct of human life." As Latin Americans would not be sophisticated enough to fend off un-American radicalism on their own, the United States "must concede that harsh governmental measures of repression may be the only answer." The United States subsequently sanctioned militarist repression through training in various internal security techniques.[13]

The Cold War binary of good and evil drove the CIA intervention in Guatemala in 1954. Jacobo Arbenz, a reformer who had risen through the military to assume the presidency in a legal election in 1951, attempted to implement a broad range of desperately needed reforms in the small country plagued by grinding poverty. In addition to redistributing land to peasant farmers, Arbenz broadened voting rights, established a minimum wage, and promoted literacy and health care programs. As the United States deemed government-initiated measures to spread social and economic equality Communistic and un-American, the CIA covert operation, encompassing psychological warfare backed by a naval blockade and air support, drove Arbenz from power. With the coup under way, Majority Leader Lyndon Johnson condemned the "flagrant" effort by "the Soviet Communists" to "penetrate the Western Hemisphere." Amid the rigid orthodoxy of the post–Korean War period, only a single "maverick" member of Congress, the North Dakota senator William D. Langer, voted against the concurrent House and Senate resolution. The compliant U.S. press tarred Arbenz as a Soviet-backed radical and treated the story as if "brutal Guatemala was bullying the long-suffering United States." Moreover, as Piero Gleijesus observes, "the discreet works of the CIA were of no concern to patriotic journalists."

The U.S.-backed military government took back the redistributed land that had offered hope to half a million peasants, returned the oligarchy to power, and launched a reign of terror. In 1999 a thirty-five-hundred-page UN-sponsored "truth commission" report detailed the two generations of ferocious and indiscriminate violence carried out by the U.S.-backed Guatemalan regime. The report condemned the United States for training, covert assistance, and overall complicity in the slaughters and "disappearing" of some two hundred thousand Guatemalans.[14]

While oligarchs and militarists willingly colluded with the United States, masses of Latin Americans resented U.S. hegemony. Many, such as Che Guevara, who had witnessed the Guatemalan repression, turned to the left and devoted their lives to combating U.S.-backed repression. Because U.S. hegemony worked against economic and social progress, resentment flared, as Vice President Richard Nixon discovered when an angry crowd rocked his limousine during a visit to Caracas in 1958, an incident that shocked the otherwise oblivious North American public.

Although no state had more reason to resent historic Yankee hegemony than Cuba, Myth of America discourse has demonized Fidel Castro so thoroughly as to virtually foreclose any alternative reading of Cuban history. Castro rose to power behind a renewed sense of *la patria*, defense of the homeland, which targeted the United States, through its decades of intervention, as "the sworn enemy of our nation." Castro mounted a guerrilla opposition that drove out Fulgencio Batista, a light-skinned military dictator long backed by the United States, sugar-producing corporations, Cuban oligarchs, and the Mafia, which operated profitable casinos and brothels in Havana. When Castro legalized the Communist Party, ousted moderates, summarily tried and killed some five hundred opponents of the Revolution, outlawed foreign ownership, denounced U.S. imperialism in a speech at the UN in September 1959, and signed a commercial agreement with the Soviet Union, his days were numbered as far as Washington was concerned.[15]

Concluding that only a "mad man" could so blatantly defy the United States, Eisenhower broke off diplomatic relations, while the CIA launched Operation Mongoose to eliminate Castro. Livid over the "perfect failure" of the CIA-backed assault by exiles at the Bay of Pigs only three months into his presidency, John F. Kennedy and his brother Robert proceeded "absolutely like demons" with a variety of "nutty schemes," as CIA director Richard Helms put it, to assassinate Castro. In 1975 the Senate Church Committee found "concrete evidence" of eight plots to kill or discredit Castro.[16]

Determined to display his manly resolve to both the Cubans and the Soviets, Kennedy proved willing to risk nuclear war. Foreign policy "realists" laud Kennedy's handling of the Cuban Missile Crisis in October 1962 as a reflection of "cool judgment," his "finest hour" as the nation confronted the "greatest peril." According to this discursive regime, Kennedy went "eyeball to eyeball," forced Khrushchev to "blink first," and then, as Kennedy himself put it, "I cut his balls off." Stripped of the macho, patriotic discourse, the imposition of the Caribbean blockade—a unilateral act of war—and the decision to go on national television to demand dismantling of the sites should be considered reckless, given the stakes, especially as Kennedy himself viewed the chances of nuclear war as one in three.[17]

The hegemonic narrative of Cold War history precludes all but a smattering of "revisionists" from calling into question the U.S. right to force the missiles out of Cuba because their presence, as one moderate British scholar put it, "destabilized the international situation and imperiled world peace." Under this putative realist frame, nuclear weapons aimed at Russia from various European sites anchored a stable world balance of power. whereas missiles in Cuba, which had been invaded by the United States, were inherently destabilizing. This standard narrative condemns the Soviet–Cuban effort to emplace the missiles in secrecy and confront the West with a fait accompli as a reflection of the evil mendacity inherent in Communism. This frame elides U.S. violence and mendacity in secretly attempting to assassinate Castro and other foreign leaders.[18]

Rather than building goodwill through the abortive Alliance for Progress, Kennedy oversaw military takeovers of six Latin American countries during his one-thousand-day presidency. The process continued under Johnson, who claimed to understand Latin Americans because he was a Texan, though the opposite was more likely to be true. Determined, like all U.S. leaders, to show his toughness, Johnson explained that the Latinos only understood brute force. In 1964 the administration blamed "left-wing agitators" for riots that erupted against U.S. imperial occupation of the Panama Canal Zone, the one area as sensitive as Cuba. Myth of America identity fueled CIA intervention in tiny Guiana in the early sixties, bringing to power Forbes Burnham, a bigoted neo-fascist, over Cheddi Jagan's democratic Marxist reform government.[19]

Larger interventions in Brazil and the Dominican Republic prompted more public attention but virtually no protest from Americans. In Brazil the reformist government of João Goulart moved to expropriate corporate holdings, limit the repatriation of funds taken from foreign-owned industries, broaden ties with labor and Communist governments, and promote global disarmament. The United States colluded with the Brazilian military to foment a coup that toppled the government while scripting the action as an effort to save Western Christian civilization from radicalism. As in Panama in 1903, a U.S. carrier task force fitted out for the occasion but did not have to take a direct role to bring off the coup. Johnson proffered immediate recognition, sent his "warmest regards," and finished with an Orwellian flourish by congratulating the perpetrators of a military coup for upholding "constitutional democracy." The new Brazilian leadership "became a close ally of the United States in intervening elsewhere in Latin America."[20] Authoritarian rule and oligarchic "free market" capitalism dominated Brazilian life until 1985.

Determined not to appear weak by allowing "another Cuba" and "another situation like that in Vietnam," Johnson poured twenty-four thousand U.S. Marines into the Dominican Republic in 1965, thus shattering the thirty-year tradition of avoiding direct U.S. military intervention. The situation arose after the CIA colluded in the assassination in 1961 of Rafael Trujillo, formerly a compliant dictator. When the social democrat Juan Bosch came to power in a free election, the United States backed a military coup led by a leader so pliable as to be dubbed *el americanito*. When Bosch attempted to retake his own government in 1965, Johnson dispatched the marines to oust him and empower the usual combination of militarists and oligarchs to bring stability, a euphemism for repressing social reform.

With Myth of America hegemony at the helm of a continuous foreign policy, it mattered little which party occupied the White House, as Nixon and Henry A. Kissinger demonstrated in the Chilean intervention in 1973. Great power diplomacy anchored the "Nixinger" foreign policy worldview. Kissinger, the most celebrated Eurocentric realist in recent history, believed that "the axis of history starts in Moscow, goes to Bonn, crosses over to Washington, and then goes to Tokyo. What happens in the South has no importance."[21]

But despite their vaunted realism, Nixon and Kissinger invested most heavily in credibility, a pathological obsession with maintaining the nation's masculine status as the world's preeminent superpower virtually no matter what the cost. The socialist reformer Salvador Allende, a physician, defied Yankee hegemony by winning the Chilean presidential election in 1970 and launching a program of land redistribution and nationalization of resources, especially abundant copper. The CIA had funneled millions into the electoral campaign against Allende in covert support of another candidate. "That son of a bitch Allende," Nixon thundered. "We're going to smash him." While employing sanctions and trade tactics designed to "make the economy scream," the administration pumped millions into an anti-Allende propaganda fund and more than tripled direct assistance to the Chilean military.

A neofascist regime headed by General Augusto Pinochet proved more compatible with the identity-driven U.S. foreign policy. The junta bombed the national palace in Santiago on September 11 and overthrew Allende, who committed suicide during the assault. Pinochet then inaugurated a "Caravan of Death" by rounding up, torturing, and murdering more than three thousand supposed leftists (including three U.S. citizens) and imprisoning thousands more. Before his death in 2006 Pinochet would be charged with crimes against humanity. In June 1976 Kissinger had reassured Pinochet, "We are sympathetic with what you are trying to do here. . . . We want to help, not undermine you." Three months later Michael Townley, a U.S. citizen and CIA asset, carried out a terrorist car bombing in Washington, D.C., in collusion with the Chilean secret police, the Dirección de Inteligencia Nacional (DINA), killing a Chilean diplomat who had backed Allende along with yet another U.S. citizen. The United States sought to cover up its complicity with a foreign government in carrying out a terrorist act on Embassy Row, a half mile from the State Department.

Time, Newsweek, the *New York Times,* and the *Washington Post* proved compliant as they quoted unnamed "intelligence officials" as having "virtually ruled out" the responsibility of the Pinochet regime for the murders.[22]

Right-wing dictatorships complemented Myth of America identity because they resonated manly militancy, represented light-skinned elites, stood for oligarchy and corporate power, and usually received backing from the Catholic Church because of their cultural conservatism. Rather than merely responding to perceived threats, the United States worked proactively with Latin American military dictatorships in Operation Condor, a campaign of repression of the Latin American left encompassing terror, torture, and assassination. Plan Condor sought to stamp out left-wing dissent in Argentina, Bolivia, Brazil, Paraguay, and Uruguay. U.S.-backed military dictators such as Pinochet and General Alfredo Stroessner, who came to power in 1954 and ruled Paraguay for thirty-five years, disappeared thousands of reformers and political opponents.

The United States affirmed the compatibility between Myth of America identity and right-wing repression by providing the Latin American dictators with staunch political, technical, logistical, and direct operational support. Americans green-lighted not only the Chilean intervention, but also the Argentine generals' "dirty war" campaign of disappearing thousands of reformers. The United States backed the Paraguayan and Uruguayan regimes through ongoing training in counterinsurgency and police state techniques at the Georgia-based School of the Americas. Americans coordinated repression from a headquarters in the Canal Zone and often employed Cuban exiles as extranational forces in the counterinsurgency dirty wars.[23]

Imperial Decolonization

While the United States would be unable to establish in Asia and Africa anything approaching its postwar hegemony over Latin America, Myth of America identity nevertheless drove a foreign policy of militant neocolonialism throughout the two continents. Intervention flowed from national identity rather than from a discontinuous or defensive diplomacy brought on by "Communist expansionism" during the Cold War. Western efforts, fundamentally reactionary, could not long repress the postcolonial drive for decolonization. As UN membership spiraled from 51 to 126 nations from 1945 to 1968, the quest for at least nominal national independence proved irrepressible.

The United States quickly abandoned its wartime discourse of decolonization. It did so not merely for purposes of solidifying alliances and containing

Communism, the conventional explanation, but because modernist hegemony over colored subalterns was more compatible with national identity than support for democracy. Profound anxieties over racial upheaval within the United States itself paralleled the challenge to the international color line and reinforced neocolonialism.

The nation's identity-driven discourses trumpeting self-determination initially inspired hope throughout Asia and Africa that the United States would champion postwar decolonization. During the war Roosevelt condemned European colonialism as being incompatible with the Atlantic Charter and the Four Freedoms. At the same time, national security elites sought to break down the British imperial preference system and other trade barriers. Churchill led a bitter European resistance, however, and declared he would brook "no suggestion that the British Empire is to be put in the dock and examined by everyone to see if it is up to standard." The British prime minister's son, Randolph, chimed in, querying the journalist Walter Lippmann, "Why do you always worry about our niggers? We don't worry about yours."[24]

Toward the end of the war Roosevelt abandoned the call for self-determination of the colonies in deference to a trusteeship system that actually differed little from the post—World War I mandates. The policy, paradoxically, albeit aptly, described by two scholars as "the imperialism of decolonization," essentially featured a discourse of anticolonialism but a foreign policy of neocolonialism. The West promised gradual emancipation of the colonies while the United States and its European allies maintained control of their commerce and used them as strategic assets and sites for military bases. "The package as a whole," Victor Pungong notes, "represented only a marginal improvement on the mandates system and was a far cry from hopes of an anti-imperial revolution that Rooseveltian idealism had generated." As the United States "established itself not as the champion of freedom but as a major obstacle to those seeking genuine independence, a sometimes-intense anti-American sentiment took shape around the globe," Michael Hunt notes.[25]

Orientalism and Oppression in the Middle East

In no area of the world would anti-Americanism stemming from U.S. neocolonialism have a more wrenching impact on the United States than in the so-called Middle East. In part Washington collaborated in an "inheritance of empire" from its fellow white modernist British cousin. The Truman Doctrine replaced British power in the Mediterranean, but following World War II London also withdrew from Burma, Egypt, India, Palestine, and most of the Middle East. The identity-driven Cold War provided a frame for the expansion of U.S. global power from the Mediterranean into the Middle East. As the self-pro-claimed leader of the free world, the United States had to intervene to prevent even a single country from going Communist, or else the world would disinte-grate "like apples in a barrel infected by one rotten one," as Dean Acheson put it.[26]

National identity produced Orientalist prejudices, anti-Communism, cor-porate expansion, and growing support for a Jewish homeland. The persistence of the myth of isolationism obscures surprisingly deep-seated connections with the Middle East, beginning with the struggle with the North African "Bar-bary pirates" in the early national period. By 1840 more Americans traveled to Egypt than citizens of any other country except Britain, as U.S. society experi-enced a "craze about Egyptology in the nineteenth century." In the post–Civil War years U.S. entrepreneurs conducted a profitable trade with the Ottoman Empire, including massive quantities of Turkish opium. Americans returned home with commodities such as carpets, colorful décor, and kitsch depicting harem scenes, desert oases, flying carpets, and the like.[27]

Americans also frequently expressed Orientalist prejudices by establishing binaries between Islam and Christianity. *Turk* and *Mohammedanism* emerged for the othering of Middle Easterners in opposition to the civilized, modern Christian culture of the West. No one performed these linguistic acts better than Theodore Roosevelt, who declared it was "impossible to expect moral, intellectual and material well being where Mohammedanism is supreme." Demonizing binaries also emerged from accounts of missionaries. The vast ex-tent of their global travels in the nineteenth century, including the Middle East, is "truly remarkable" and "belies arguments of historians who view the culture of this period as insular."[28]

Zionism proved compatible with U.S. Christian culture, as millions identi-fied with the desire to reoccupy the biblical Holy Land. "Like colonialism else-where," as Ilan Pappe points out, Zionism "was a European movement, with people entering Palestine for the sake of European interests, not local ones. The locals were seen as a commodity or an asset to be exploited for the benefit of the newcomers or an obstacle to be removed."[29] In 1918 Roosevelt declared it would be "entirely proper to start a Zionist State around Jerusalem." It was one of the few issues on which he and his devout rival Wilson agreed. Wilson's own man-date commission, however, issued a prescient warning in 1919 that the Zionist project would violate Palestinian self-determination and invite violent tumult in the region. By the end of the Great War, the Jewish population of the British Mandate of Palestine had grown to 12 percent of the total. It took World War II and the Nazi Holocaust, however, to provide the decisive impetus to the Zionist movement.

As the wartime Allies confronted the Zionist question, Franklin Roosevelt found himself conflicted, just as he had been on the broader issue of colonialism. Although a longtime Zionist, Roosevelt observed prophetically that as European Jews poured into the region "the millions of surrounding Arabs might easily proclaim a Holy War and there would be *no end of trouble*" [emphasis added]. Roosevelt's death left the matter in the hands of Truman, also enamored of biblically motivated Zionist sympathies but less appreciative than Roosevelt of the consequences. In 1947 the UN partitioned Palestine into a binational state, one Jewish and one Arab.

Determined from the outset to drive out enough Arabs to create a Jewish-dominated Israeli state, the Zionists won support from Truman despite sharp protests from his advisers, the British, and oil companies. Genuinely horrified by the Holocaust, yet also aware of the political benefits of winning over the growing population of U.S. Jews, Truman decided to recognize the new state of Israel in 1948. "My soul [*sic*] objective in the Palestine procedure has been to prevent bloodshed," Truman proclaimed, yet his support of the independent Jewish state ensured more, not less, bloodletting, as war had already erupted between Zionists and Palestinian Arabs opposed to the establishment of a Jewish state.[30]

Anti-Communist enemy-othering, more than anti-Semitism, underlay the opposition to Zionism within the State Department. Anti-Semitism flourished in the prewar years, as the 1924 immigration law classified Jews as members of "the Hebrew race," as opposed to "the Caucasian race," and millions of citizens embraced stereotypes of Jews as usurious moneylenders, killers of Christ, and fundamentally as others who refused to fully embrace the imagined national community (never mind that the immigration law excluded them). Only after World War II did the change in immigration law and inclusive references to a U.S. Judeo-Christian religious heritage become widespread. While Jews remained others, the Nazi Holocaust created the cultural space necessary to bring Jews into the fold of national consensus.

Support for Zionism strengthened the good war discourse and distanced the United States from its nonresponse to the Holocaust. "America could not stand by while the victims of Hitler's racial madness were denied the opportunity to build new lives," Truman declared. "For the Americans, and for many postwar European leaders, Israel was first and foremost expiation for the Holocaust," Westad argues.[31]

The horror of the Holocaust overshadowed a vicious Israeli campaign of ethnic cleansing designed to rid the nascent Jewish state of as many Palestinians as possible. Israel wiped out 370 Palestinian villages, driving out some 700,000 Palestinians and leaving a minority of only 160,000. In September 1948 Jewish extremists assassinated a Swedish diplomat appointed by the UN, which had condemned the Israeli aggression and called for repatriation of Palestinian refugees as well as the internationalization of Jerusalem. As they would do on many occasions, the Israelis stonewalled the UN and perpetuated the campaign of ethnic cleansing. "Repatriation of an Arab population would threaten the colonial nature of the Zionist project and ethnographic character of the state of Israel," Nur Masalha explains.[32]

Despite lingering anti-Semitism within the United States, Zionism affirmed Myth of America identity. The United States and Israel were both products of "white" European modernity and each had been "chosen" for errands into the wilderness to redeem lands in the possession of heathens for the Kingdom of God. U.S. Christian culture featured pervasive imagery of the Holy Land and fostered support for its redemption under the modernist European Jews. The emergence of the U.S.–Israeli "special relationship" thus rested on firm, if often unspoken, cultural ground.

U.S. support for Israel ultimately flowed from identity- driven Orientalist and neocolonialist representations of Palestinians and Arabs. European colonialism had long depended on naturalizing imagery of Arabs as backward, decadent, treacherous, and untrustworthy. Nineteenth-century literary and artistic works established a binary between "vigorous, active, masculinized, and morally upright" European civilization and "a decaying, demasculinized, deviant, or spiritual Orient."[33] Orientalist discourse and cultural mapping, rooted in European colonialism and perpetuated by postwar neocolonialism, established a frame that enabled U.S. and Western support for the Israeli civilizing mission into the Arab wilderness. The seizing of land and conducting of ethnic cleansing of native subalterns paralleled the historic trajectory of the United States itself.

U.S. cultural affinity for Zionism proved strong enough even to trump concern by the oil companies and strategic planners that recognition of Israel would jeopardize exploitation of Middle East oil supplies. Indeed, this development underscores the notion that economic decisions emerge within boundaries established by cultural identity. The United States sought to exploit Middle East oil supplies because it had the right, as the most advanced and "free" country in the world, not because corporate oil executives pulled the strings of national policy behind closed doors.[34]

The internalization of Myth of America identity, including Orientalist and gendered discourses, drove the overthrow of Iran's Mohammed Mossadegh in a CIA-sponsored coup, the first outside the Western Hemisphere, in 1953. Feminized for wearing gowns, for crying in public, for possessing an "oriental mind," the "dizzy old wizard," as *Time* referred to the septuagenarian Iranian leader, could not be allowed to practice state socialism or drift into the "Soviet orbit." Under such circumstances, Dulles averred, the "free world would be deprived of the enormous assets represented by Iranian oil" and "if Iran succumbed to the Communists there was little doubt that in short order the other areas of the Middle East, with some 60 percent of the world's oil reserves, would fall into Communist control." Thus Eisenhower authorized the CIA coup that succeeded in driving Mossadegh from power and replacing him with the royal regime of Shah Reza Pahlavi. The United States thus "stifle[d] a developing country's nationalism in favor of traditional European-style imperialism," Mary Ann Heiss points out.[35]

Despite the Eisenhower administration's refusal to back the Anglo-French-Israeli invasion of Egypt in the Suez crisis of 1956, U.S. officials shared Orientalist perceptions of Gamal Abdel Nasser, whom Dulles characteristically condemned as an "evil influence." The administration agreed that Nasser "had gone too far" by nationalizing the European-built canal, yet Eisenhower forced the invaders to withdraw for "double-crossing us" by not informing Washington in advance of the assault on Suez. Nevertheless, the United States supported—with no apparent sense of irony—Britain's condemnation of Nasser's "insidious" suggestion "that the oil of the Arab countries should be exploited by the people of the area and not by foreigners."

Masculine anxieties, deeply implicated in the cultural construction of the Cold War narrative, played out in the Middle East. Following an antimonarchical coup in Iraq in 1958, Eisenhower dispatched U.S. Marines to Lebanon and issued his own doctrine essentially forbidding Communism in the Middle East. Explaining the doctrine in terms of masculine anxiety over credibility, Dulles insisted, "Turkey, Iran and Pakistan would feel—if we do not act—that our inaction is because we are afraid of the Soviet Union."[36]

By the outbreak of the Six-Day War in 1967, Americans had internalized "images of noble Israelis surrounded by unruly Arabs," essentially creating "a hierarchy of race and culture in which the Arabs ranked far below the Israelis." From *The Sheik* in 1921 to the long epics *Exodus* and *Lawrence of Arabia* in the early 1960s, Hollywood became a reliable source of Orientalist imagery. Even the "best and the brightest" of national security elites indulged in Orientalist slurs, as when William Bundy referred to Arabs as "rug merchants."[37] The United States thus inherited from Europeans, but then affirmed and reinforced within its own culture, perceptions of Arabs as "basically, irrecusably, and congenitally 'Other,'" as Edward Said, the classic theorist of Orientalism, put it. Moreover, within the "polarity that was set up between democratic Israel and a homogeneously non-democratic Arab world, the Palestinians, dispossessed and exiled by Israel, came to represent 'terrorism' and little beyond it."[38]

These cultural perceptions underlay unconditional support for Israel in the Six-Day War. Opinion polls showed an almost twenty to one ratio of pro-Israel sympathy in the conflict. By this time, the Palestinian Liberation Organization (PLO), founded in 1964, had begun to launch attacks against Israel with the backing of Nasser, who declared, "Since Palestine was usurped by the sword, it must be regained by the sword." Israel went on the offensive on the morning of June 5, 1967, and in short order seized Gaza, the West Bank, and East Jerusalem, humiliating its Arab foes. The takeovers created tens of thousands of additional Palestinian refugees.

By the time of the Six-Day War the MIC had led the way to a thoroughgoing militarization of the region. While a U.S. war raged in Indochina, the navy patrolled the Middle East from its global network of bases. Arms sales strongly influenced foreign policy all over the globe and especially in behalf of Israel, which received Hawk surface-to-air missiles from the Kennedy administration in 1962 in return for an Israeli pledge, which Tel Aviv promptly violated, to allow inspections of Israel's Dimona nuclear power plant. The Johnson administration "moved to make Israel eligible for almost any conventional weapon in the American arsenal" in an ultimately futile effort to preclude the Jewish state from cultivating nuclear weapons. Israel prevaricated about its top-secret nuclear program and refused to sign the 1968 Non-Proliferation Treaty.[39]

Cultural affinity for Israel proved so powerful that the United States overlooked and attempted to cover up a vicious Israeli assault on the *Liberty,* a U.S. naval intelligence vessel on a reconnaissance mission off the Sinai coast during the Six-Day War. While the usable past encourages citizens to Remember the

Alamo and Remember the *Maine*, it also ensures that few remember the *Liberty*. After monitoring the ship, which sported a five-by-eight-foot American flag, for several hours, Israeli jets and patrol boats launched rockets, napalm, and torpedoes on June 8, killing 34 and wounding 171. Defense Secretary Robert McNamara called back F-4 fighters responding to the *Liberty* captain's May Day plea for help amidst the unprovoked Israeli assault. Although it was "inconceivable it was an accident," the pro-Israeli adviser Clark Clifford advised the administration to "handle as if Arabs or USSR had done it." Israel lamely insisted that the prolonged attack had been an accident and paid a $3.3 million indemnity. "I didn't believe them then, and I don't believe them to this day," Secretary of State Dean Rusk wrote in his memoirs. "The attack was outrageous."[40]

The United States also acquiesced to Israeli aggrandizement at the expense of the subaltern Palestinians after the Six-Day War. Backed by Washington, UN Resolution 242 established a "land for peace" formula in which Tel Aviv would relinquish the seized territory in return for Arab recognition of Israel's sovereignty. "While the Arabs were eager to move ahead," Douglas Little notes, "the Israelis were not" and instead "tightened [their] grip on the occupied territories." Violent clashes regularly erupted on both sides, reinforcing the status quo. Nixon's Secretary of State, William Rogers, sought to enforce Resolution 242 as "the bedrock of our policy," but Kissinger, a Jew whose family had been victimized in the Holocaust, easily outmaneuvered Rogers and took control of the national security bureaucracy. By this time the American Israel Public Affairs Committee (AIPAC) had emerged as one of the most powerful lobbies in Congress. The Congress urged Nixon and Kissinger to stop pressuring Israel for concessions and instead focus policy on selling it more weapons.[41]

Left with little prospect for agency other than war and terror, the Arabs and the PLO engaged in both. The Yom Kippur War, launched by Egypt and Syria in 1973, sought to retake seized lands but nearly led to a wider war in a nuclear-armed world. The war ended in a cease-fire, but militarization of the region escalated and the Arabs fought back through the Organization of Petroleum Exporting Countries (OPEC), formed in 1960, which stunned the West by embargoing the sale of oil. The embargo took its toll, yet the "blowback" stemming from the U.S. neocolonialist foreign policy in the Middle East had only begun to manifest itself by the end of the Nixon presidency.[42]

White Rule in Black Africa

While Orientalism overshadowed Middle East policy, racial modernity had an even more pronounced impact on tortured efforts to accommodate the decolonization of "black Africa." The United States was not culturally equipped to embrace the cause of African independence movements. The apartheid system in the U.S. South and pervasive inequality and ongoing racial violence throughout the country underscored the continuing exaltation of whiteness. In deference to placating segregationists in an effort (futile over the long term) to maintain the Democratic Solid South, Roosevelt, Truman, and Kennedy could not afford to champion African independence even had they been so inclined. "Negroes" had few allies in the federal bureaucracy before the mid-1960s.[43]

Tropes of primitivism and savagery, continuous throughout Euro-American history, underlay neocolonialism in Africa. "Without the discipline and control of Western nations," a State Department diplomat posted in Africa observed, "ancient antagonisms would burst their present bounds and numerous races or tribes would attack traditional enemies in primitive savagery." Thus "to endow these African groups prematurely with independence and sovereignty would only result in creating political entities which almost immediately become pawns of the Kremlin."[44]

Primitive savagery abroad reinforced containment of Negroes on the home front. During both the Great War and the good war, anxieties over African American migration, enhanced work opportunities, and demand for civil rights provoked violent resistance. In 1943 alone more than two hundred racial clashes erupted in forty-five cities. The brutal Detroit riot that year forced Roosevelt to divert six thousand troops to the industrial heartland while fighting a war in Europe and Asia. The U.S. military remained segregated, with white southerners often assigned to supervise African American troops on the dubious grounds that they understood the Negro and his culture. Health officials made sure to label and segregate the plasma flowing from black and white donors.

Despite deeply rooted racial modernity, African Americans, liberals, and white supremacists all recognized that World War II had irrevocably changed domestic race relations. The war had not only fueled the drive for decolonization, but also discredited theoretical justifications for white supremacy through its association with the genocidal Nazi regime. "The Huns have wrecked the theory of the master race," an Alabama politician lamented. Loyal African

American support for the U.S. war effort under the Double V campaign ("Victory at Home, Victory Abroad") created postwar expectations. African American veterans returning home from the war, having been treated with respect in many Allied nations, refused to resume their former status as second-class citizens. Many were beaten or murdered in the South as a result.

Truman's decision to desegregate the armed forces accelerated the modern civil rights movement while also starting in motion "the seismic shift of a majority of white voters in Dixie to the Republican Party by the 1990s."[45] Although Truman credited African Americans for their wartime service, favored antilynching legislation, and chafed under the international embarrassment to the country brought on by race riots and terror campaigns, the Missourian opposed "social equality for the Negro" and chose as his secretary of state James F. Byrnes of South Carolina, who opposed the antilynching law because, he explained, the specter of lynching discouraged "assaults by Negroes on white women."[46] Eisenhower, who vacationed in the South and treasured his membership in the exclusive white, male Augusta National golf club, opposed social equality as well as government support of civil rights. C. D. Jackson, Eisenhower's psychological warfare adviser, betrayed profound anxieties about "the swirling mass of emotionally super-charged Africans and Asiatics and Arabs that outnumber us."[47]

The exaltation of whiteness, long central to Myth of America identity, propelled U.S. opposition to the UN's assuming a meaningful role in postwar diplomacy. In addition to posing a threat to American Century unilateralism, the UN, through its Charter and 1948 Universal Declaration of Human Rights, threatened to expose the hypocrisy inherent in mythic national identity. "The United States had Southern Justice, Jim Crow, internment of the Japanese, genocide of the Native Americans, debt slavery, racist immigration laws, and a host of other human rights violations," Carol Anderson explains. "Obviously an open and frank debate about human rights could quickly unmask the reality of American democracy." Southern segregationists even spurred congressional rejection of ratification of the UN convention against genocide, a stance "firmly rooted in the issue of lynching."[48]

The hegemonic Cold War narrative removed the focus from domestic apartheid and put African Americans in a position to be condemned as unpatriotic if they opposed the nation's crusade against the Communist evil-other. Under Myth of America identity, only white European victims qualified as subjugated minorities. Thus Byrnes and other white supremacists, with no conception of irony, regularly thundered against Soviet satellites and Communist slavery while issuing annual Captive Nations Resolutions.

Ultimately the United States afforded civil rights only to those African Americans who proved willing to embrace Myth of America identity while at the same time abandoning identification with pan-African liberation movements. "The politics of the African diaspora, as represented in the broad African American anti-colonial alliances of World War II and the immediate postwar period, did not survive the Truman Doctrine and the Marshall Plan," Penny M. Von Eschen explains. Countersubversive containment reined in African Americans such as W. E. B. Du Bois and Paul Robeson, who had insisted on calling attention to free world racial hypocrisy. Du Bois supported Henry Wallace in 1948 against, as he put it, the "reactionary, war-mongering colonial imperialism of the present administration."

Deeply invested in the cultural construction of whiteness, J. Edgar Hoover linked civil rights with Communist subversion and launched a relentless FBI campaign of harassment against the pan-African left. Hoover targeted Robeson, a Marxist, and the Council on African Affairs for creating "considerable unrest among the negroes." The FBI kept files on civil rights activists as "the government regarded anti-colonialism and civil rights activism as interlocking issues that threatened national security." Du Bois, Robeson, and other activists had their passports revoked. Robeson also nearly succumbed to mob violence in a racial backlash in Peekskill, New York, in 1949. Hauled before HUAC in 1956, Robeson refused to discuss his political beliefs, explaining that white supremacists had "murdered sixty million of my people, and I will not discuss Stalin with you." He told his questioners they "were the non-patriots, and you are un-Americans, and you ought to be ashamed of yourselves." Robeson thus brilliantly dissected mythic national discourse for the committee through, as Tom Engelhardt put it, his "public insistence that slavery was an American, not a Russian issue, that American history was murder, and that HUAC was an enemy institution."[49]

As Cold War discourse equated economic and social equality with Communism and UN internationalism, human rights gave way to the more restrained agenda of civil rights. The National Association for the Advancement of Colored People (NAACP) shifted its focus to accommodate Myth of America identity. As Walter White, Eleanor Roosevelt, and other liberals advanced the agenda of *civil rights,* the more profound goal of *human rights* became discredited through association with UN internationalism and Communism.

Most African Americans lived below the poverty line; millions lacked electricity and indoor plumbing, suffered from an infant mortality rate twice that of whites, were the last hired and first fired, and remained subject to various campaigns of terror and discrimination. Attempts to focus on human rights "threatened to expose the NAACP to the same inquisition that was destroying the black left," Anderson explains. Thus "as the Cold War intensified, the NAACP's once coherent quest for human rights was rapidly dissolving" as the organization decided to "retreat to the haven of civil rights" and "wrap itself in the flag."[50]

The vast majority of white Americans either supported or proved indifferent to U.S. apartheid, but the Brown school desegregation decision in 1954 and the crisis at Little Rock's Central High School in 1957 placed race relations irrevocably under the spotlight. Deeply concerned about the international impact of the vicious white supremacist response to school integration in Little Rock, replete with spitting, hurling of epithets, and violence, all captured on television, the Eisenhower administration launched an emergency propaganda campaign. Dulles, a descendant of South Carolina slave owners, was "sick at heart," not over the inability of nine African American children to attend school in peace but rather over the damage to the nation's international reputation, which he predicted "will be worse for us than Hungary was for the Russians." The United States Information Agency (USIA) circulated propaganda and photographs of "smiling Negroes" around the world, trumpeted the accomplishments of African American athletes and artists, and celebrated "benevolent" U.S. administration of neocolonial possessions such as Hawaii, the Philippines, and Puerto Rico.[51]

Declarations at the 1954 Bandung Conference emphasizing human rights, anticolonialism, and racial equality directly contravened the claims of U.S. propagandists. At Bandung, Indonesia, representatives from twenty-nine African and Asian nonaligned states, joined by Yugoslavia's Tito, had called attention to "Washington's willingness to underwrite European imperial pretensions as well as its own status as a colonial power in the Caribbean and the Pacific," Cary Fraser notes.[52] African states fought to follow the lead of Ghana, under the charismatic Kwame Nkrumah, which became the first African state to declare anticolonial independence in 1957. Even though "some of the people of Africa have been out of the trees for only about fifty years," Nixon advised that the United States could not afford to alienate them and drive them into the Communist camp.[53]

CIA complicity in the overthrow and murder of the Congo's Patrice Lumumba in 1960 affirmed that the nation's identity-driven foreign policy remained violently reactionary. Reaffirming their nation's cultural superiority through denigration of the African other, Americans described Lumumba as "sly," "the chief troublemaker," a "demagogic premier," "erratically irresponsible," "paranoid," "insane," a "sorcerer," a "red weed, "a Castro," "a Lumumbavitch," and, finally, "goateed" like the subversive beatniks at home. Lumumba would be more accurately described as educated, multilingual, an eloquent anticolonialist, a freedom fighter. Enemy-othering produced a grossly exaggerated threat of a Red Congo, as the African nation was not a Soviet priority, and very little Communist organizing actually went on there. Following more or less on the Guatemala model, a terrorist anti-Communist regime fully backed by the United States took power after Lumumba's fatal beating, scoring a triumph for the free world. [54]

While marginalized African Americans condemned the Lumumba "lynching," few white citizens protested over the Congo or the ongoing U.S. support of apartheid regimes in South Africa and Rhodesia. South Africa was the world's leading gold supplier and offered Americans strategic cooperation by allowing a satellite tracking station in the country. Eisenhower supported the regime whereas the Kennedy administration "took a rhetorically tough stand against apartheid, while seeking to disturb the fruitful aspects of its ties with the republic as little as possible." Having thoroughly internalized enemy-othering, the realist Rusk described the Cold War as a "total confrontation" and "a matter of life and death of our own nation," hence "moral issues" could not be considered.

As Myth of America identity equated racial independence with subversion, diplomats charged that the African National Congress (ANC) was "dominated by the Communist Party at the leadership level." Put on trial for subversion in 1964, Nelson Mandela, the founder of the ANC, explained that he was not a Communist and, indeed, admired the British and U.S. political systems. The CIA had assisted the Pretoria government in capturing Mandela in 1962 and hence expressed satisfaction when the independence leader began serving a prison sentence that was to last almost three decades. Nixon allied with South Africa while Congress backed Rhodesia, which was 95 percent black yet ruled by a white minority, through the Byrd Amendment of 1971, which specifically exempted the regime from trade sanctions with respect to strategic materials, mainly chrome.[55]

Embracing Acheson's advice not "to pander to the dark and delirious continent of Africa," Kennedy looked the other way in 1961 as the Portuguese dictator Antonio Salazar used U.S.-made napalm in a counterinsurgency campaign
that "was unrelentingly savage in its slaughter of civilians and other atrocities"
in Lisbon's colony of Angola. The vast southwestern African nation, rich in oil
and diamonds, proved especially neuralgic because of direct Cuban intervention in behalf of the anti-Portuguese rebels. Before his death at the hands of the
U.S.- trained Bolivian Special Forces, Che Guevara, joined by Cubans, had intervened first in the Congo but too late to save Lumumba in 1960. However, the
Cubans remained committed to African independence, and their support
proved decisive in the rebel victory in Guinea-Bissau, forcing Portuguese withdrawal in 1974. Misrepresenting the Cubans merely as Soviet proxies, the
United States sent arms and mercenaries to Angola but to no avail, as the guerrillas of the Popular Movement for the Liberation of Angola (MPLA) won a decisive victory. A CIA report privately acknowledged that "Havana's African policy," a reflection of its "activist revolutionary ethos," had won a major victory in
southern Africa.

While the United States constantly blared its leadership of the free world,
Cuba proved to be the actual freedom fighter against the U.S.-backed apartheid
regimes. As a South African analyst acknowledged, "White elitism has suffered
an irreversible blow in Angola," one that would eventually radiate back to Pretoria itself.[56]

Determined African American resistance to violent oppression on the
home front gradually carved out the cultural space for the so-called Second Reconstruction, yet human rights still languished, and the pan-African left had
been marginalized. Poverty, economic inequality, absence of health care, poor
schooling, high crime rates, and flagrantly unequal administration of justice
continued to characterize African American and Hispanic communities. "In
terms of internal colonization, African-American society in the United States is
an example of the gains and vicissitudes of post-coloniality," Gayatri Spivak observes.[57]

Murderous Militarism Across the Great Crescent

Myth of American universalism produced massive violence in Southeast Asia.
Well before the United States had pronounced the arrival of the American Century, the nation staked its claim in Southeast Asia through racial conquest of
the Philippines. While the discourse of decolonization led to a grant of formal

independence to the Philippines in 1946, global militarism precluded a U.S. withdrawal from the archipelago. Large military bases in the Philippines left the United States with considerable influence and poised to intervene when necessary. A combination of land reforms, special forces operations, and air power, including the first use of napalm, contained the leftist Hukbalahap rebellion.[58] By the mid-1960s the Philippines had come firmly under the control of an aggressive oligarchy that collaborated with multinational corporations to dominate the postcolonial economy.

The U.S. identity-driven foreign policy nurtured the repressive crony capitalist regime of Ferdinand Marcos until the Filipinos demanded change. Plagued by opposition to his reverse Robin Hood "new order," Marcos, staunchly backed by Nixon and Kissinger, declared martial law in 1972, jailing and exiling his prodemocracy opponents. Marcos rewrote the Philippine constitution, giving himself supreme power; further, he enabled domination of the sugar and coconut industries by his family and friends and soared to new heights of megalomania and corruption, symbolized by his wife's astonishing collection of shoes. In 1983, as Marcos's chief critic, Benito Aquino, returned from exile in Boston, the regime had him assassinated on the airport tarmac. When Marcos stole the presidential election three years later, the opposition rallied around Aquino's widow, Corazon, and toppled the dictatorship in a stirring demonstration of "people power."[59]

The United States sanctioned intervention and massive violence in Indonesia. Consistent with the general "retreat from anti-colonialism," the Americans backed the Netherlands with funds and arms in 1947 as it dispatched one hundred thousand troops in an ultimately futile effort to reassert colonialism, which had been fatally weakened by the Japanese wartime occupation. A Goodyear Tire and Rubber Company executive insisted that "our little brown brothers in Indonesia" lacked the skills that Western colonialists could employ to exploit the abundance of rubber. The Dutch proved unable to defeat the guerrillas as the Republic of Indonesia gained independence in 1949. The United States "never pursued an anti-colonial policy toward the Netherlands East Indies," Robert McMahon notes.[60]

Myth of America identity suffered a staggering blow that same year when Red China came to power and, especially in the wake of the Korean War, emerged as the primary Asian enemy-other. As "a colored, non-Western country with a history of colonial exploitation," China menaced the quest for Asian hegemony by encouraging postcolonial peoples to mount "wars of national liberation" against capitalist imperialism.[61] Determined to stem the Red tide in Southeast Asia, the United States launched a failed covert operation against the longtime hero of Indonesian nationalism, Achmed Sukarno, in 1958. Operating from a base in the outlying islands Sumatra and Sulawesi, the CIA tried to foment rebellion against the Indonesian leader, who had defied U.S. hegemony by hosting the Bandung Conference, collaborating with the Indonesian Community Party, the PKI, and expropriating Dutch and other Western properties.[62]

Having failed to topple Sukarno, the United States characteristically cultivated the Indonesian military. In the mid-1960s, with the United States more determined than ever to destroy Sukarno, who had condemned American militarism in Indochina, the Indonesian military rallied behind General Suharto and seized power. The United States encouraged the subsequent slaughter of at least five hundred thousand and perhaps a million people by informing Jakarta that it was "generally sympathetic with and admiring of what the army was doing." As the CIA acknowledged, "The anti-PKI massacres in Indonesia rank as one of the worst mass murders of the twentieth century." While the full level of involvement remains "top secret," the United States, joined by fellow white moderns Britain and Australia, forwarded names of alleged subversives, and all three were thus "complicit in mass murder of monstrous proportions." The victims extended well beyond PKI members and included teachers, union activists, and moderate reformers, as gangs and youth bands terrorized the country. Some 3.4 million who survived the onslaught went to prison. While conducting mass murder, the U.S.-backed military dictatorship restored expropriated property, throwing the nation open to Western foreign investment and eliminating the vestiges of Sukarno's "guided democracy."[63]

Manly Machiavellian realism drove the United States to eschew all "sentimental" and "moralistic" considerations as it backed yet another Indonesian genocidal campaign in East Timor in 1975. Indonesia held West Timor, but Suharto's claim to a "common brotherhood" with the East Timorese belied sharp distinctions of language, religion, and culture between predominantly Islamic Indonesia and the Catholic and Animist eastern islanders. The bloodbath, explicitly approved by Kissinger, began the day after President Gerald Ford departed from a state visit in Jakarta. Suharto's forces swept into East Timor from air and sea to conduct an orgy of massacre, torture, and rape followed by famine. Some 180,000 people—perhaps a third of the island's population—perished in the invasion. As the United States fought off UN opposition to the slaughter, U.S. arms sales to Suharto topped more than one billion dollars.[64]

Vietnam

While the United States upheld its manly credibility against enemy-others, it preferred to do so by bolstering murderous neocolonialist regimes rather than through direct intervention. When indirect means failed, however, as in Indochina, militant national identity was such a powerful psychic force that it propelled the United States into a nightmarish war that ultimately shook the foundations of its own imagined national community. Ultimately, the Indochina War illuminated the nation's violent pathology.

Vietnam's Ho Chi Minh was a longtime nationalist hero but also a Marxist-Leninist and thus automatically a U.S. enemy-other. Ho was no puppet of the Soviet Union, which initially had relatively little interest in Indochina, and certainly not of China, which had once occupied Vietnam for a *millennium,* prompting Ho's famous comment that he would "prefer to sniff French shit for five years than eat Chinese shit for the rest of my life."[65]

Even Ho, who sometimes quoted the U.S. Declaration of Independence, had been attracted by Myth of America discourse, but the United States reciprocated with Orientalist tropes. Diplomats, missionaries, tourists, and academics had long applied such terms as "primitive," "lazy," "cowardly," "unclean," "somnolent," and "dishonest" to describe the "Annamites" under French colonial rule. American cultural perceptions thus mirrored the *mission civilatrice,* the French version of the white man's burden, to justify modernist intervention ostensibly in behalf of the childlike Vietnamese. The United States, like the French, failed to take seriously Ho's Vietminh independence movement, which proclaimed the Democratic Republic of Vietnam in 1945. Ho desperately sought accommodation with France, even embracing neocolonialist solutions, but unredeemable *grandeur* instead led to the First Indochina War (1946–54) and a devastating French defeat at Dien Bien Phu. [66]

All aspects of the nation's identity-driven foreign policy would come into play in Vietnam—racialized Orientalism, masculine anxiety, and the drive to extirpate evil enemy-others. After torpedoing a diplomatic settlement calling for Vietnamese reunification and democratic elections after Dien Bien Phu, the United States subverted the Geneva Accords in 1954 and ensconced "South Vietnam" in the Southeast Asian Treaty Organization, an anti-Communist

NATO clone. Its policy driven by "a projection of American religious and racial preconceptions," the United States ignored the Vietnamese Buddhist-Confucian cultural heritage and eschewed land reform even as it decided to "sink or swim with Ngo Dinh Diem." Having pumped millions of dollars into a French colonial war, the United States now pumped millions more into nation building in the ill-fated imagined community of South Vietnam. While U.S. leaders exalted Diem as "the miracle man of Asia," his authoritarian regime lacked popular support, and the self-absorbed Diem possessed no leadership skills. Domestic opposition, culminating in the Buddhist crisis of 1963, which featured the sensational self-immolation of a Buddhist monk on the streets of Saigon, led to the U.S. decision to support a military coup. The South Vietnamese military assassinated Diem and his brother on November 2, 1963.[67]

As the Indochina conflict carried across seven U.S. presidencies, from Roosevelt to Ford, it had little to do with executive decisions and everything to do with the psychic drives of national identity. While hardly sanguine about the eventual outcome in Indochina, Kennedy's support for the anti-Diem coup shows he had not given up on South Vietnam, to which he had dispatched sixteen thousand U.S. "advisers" and mounted an aggressive counterinsurgency campaign against the North Vietnamese–backed National Liberation Front (NLF). The "strategic hamlet program" and other counterinsurgency techniques growing out of the think tanks within the academic national security complex failed to stem the "Viet Cong" advance, while a succession of coups and failed military governments only deepened Saigon's dependence on the United States.[68]

Determined not to suffer the humiliation, both personal and national, of losing Vietnam, Johnson chose direct military intervention, thus ushering in the Second Indochina War. The shadow of the good war usable past loomed over Indochina; as Johnson explained, "If I let the Communists take over South Vietnam, then I would be seen as a coward and my nation would be seen as an appeaser." Upholding manly credibility, the nation responded to an innocuous clash in the Tonkin Gulf in August 1964 with a congressional decision authorizing Johnson to bomb Indochina and otherwise do as he saw fit to defend the flag. Following an NLF attack on Pleiku in the Central Highlands the next year, the United States authorized search-and-destroy missions against the new evil enemy-other, the NLF guerrillas and infiltrating units of the North Vietnamese Army (NVA). National identity exercised such a disciplinary force over society that few Americans protested in 1964 and 1965 as the United States launched a full-scale war in tropical jungles thousands of miles from its shores.

Like Kennedy, who resonated masculine vigor and gloried in his numerous sexual conquests, Johnson often expressed his commitment in masculine terms. The tall, craggy Texan presumed that the physically smaller and lightly equipped guerrillas, led by the wispy Ho, could not possibly defeat the providentially destined leader of the free world. "The fateful decisions to commit American power and prestige to a military intervention in Vietnam were made by men with deeply ingrained and relatively rigid notions of manliness," Robert Dean explains. Just weeks before he decided to commit the country to a major war, Johnson told a political crony that failure to take a manly stand in Vietnam would be political suicide. Americans, Johnson explained, will "forgive you for anything except being weak."[69]

Engulfing an entire generation, "America's longest war" proved an incomparably destructive manifestation of a U.S. "banality of evil."[70] Flush with economic prosperity and drunk on its own totalizing discourse, the United States relentlessly pummeled Vietnam for nearly a decade and even appropriated its name—as the country itself became a purely American phenomenon. The military strategy, oblivious to the essence of the postcolonial conflict, was to kill and destroy to such an extent that the enemy at some point would bow down to the military and technological prowess of the superior nation and give up the struggle. The "war of attrition" employed every available option except the nuclear, including twenty million gallons of Agent Orange chemical defoliation, unlimited applications of napalm, and more tonnage of conventional bombs than used in all theaters of World War II by all the belligerents combined. The military code name MENU, including operations Breakfast, Lunch, and Dinner, encompassed the banal routine of the daily pounding of the air campaign. Air Force General Curtis LeMay advocated the same strategy in Vietnam as he had employed against the Japanese in the Pacific War, averring, that the United States "should bomb them back to the Stone Age." When Johnson, recalling Korea, referred to the risk of Chinese intervention, LeMay, like MacArthur, called for "nuking the Chinks."[71]

Beginning with the battle of Ia Drang in 1965, the United States employed its superior helicopter mobility and advanced firepower to win direct battles by taking almost ten times as many casualties as it suffered. The Pentagon computers rang up the numbers, yet, as Engelhardt notes, "the enemy had somehow

7. Boeing B-52 dropping its payload over Vietnam (1966). World War II ignited an era in which the United States conducted "conventional" bombing in myriad theaters but most especially over Indochina, which became the most heavily bombed region in world history during the prolonged U.S. intervention. Aerial bombardment reflected a "technowar" strategy of "low-intensity conflict," which attempted to minimize U.S. casualties while maximizing destruction on the ground. Photo courtesy US Air Force via Herbert S. Desind Collection, National Air and Space Museum (NASM 9A00315), Smithsonian Institution.

captured the only set of numbers worth having—the number of weeks, months, years that the fighting went on."[72] The Tet Offensive of January 1968 belied the long-standing U.S. disinformation campaign of steady progress toward inevitable victory. The My Lai massacre of some five hundred innocents reflected the erosion, as in past wars, of distinctions between civilians and combatants. As the Pentagon drafted "grunts" (average age nineteen) and sent then from "the World" into "Indian country," the savage atrocities of the past—from King Philip's War to the Philippine archipelago to the Haitian countryside—reemerged against the Vietnamese "gooks." After bitter warfare during the Tet Offensive, a U.S. commander explained, with no apparent sense of the irony, "We had to destroy the city to save it." To many people, such Orwellian logic symbolized the growing incongruity of the war, a conflict in which the most technologically sophisticated nation in the world devastated a developing Third World region characterized by oxcarts, dirt roads, and grass huts.

With Myth of America credibility at stake, there would be no unmanly and unsatisfying withdrawal no matter what the costs and consequences. Admission of defeat would defy the national narrative of providentially sanctioned destiny to triumph over evil and lead the free world. Applying an apropos trope, Nixon implemented a "madman" strategy that combined brutal bombing with U.S. troop withdrawals and great power détente, all in a futile quest to achieve "peace with honor."[73] The blundering Cambodian incursion in May 1970 catapulted the United States itself into chaos and launched Nixon down the path to political ruin—an imperial president rendered a "pitiful, helpless giant" by the myriad high crimes and misdemeanors generically lumped as Watergate. In a last-gasp violent paroxysm, the 1972 Christmas bombing, those B-52s that survived the mission against Soviet-made surface-to-air missiles rained bombs on Hanoi, but their real target was Saigon, where the decadent military regime craved reassurance that it would not be abandoned to sure defeat. In the Paris Accords of January 1973, Hanoi's Le Duc Tho and Kissinger found a way out for the United States, although, crucially, the NVA remained ensconced in South Vietnam. "Peace with honor" lasted only a "decent interval," however, as Saigon "fell" in the final NVA offensive in April 1975, thus at last bringing to a close the Second Indochina War.

"Vietnam" pierced the armor of Myth of America innocence by undermining the nation's claim to moral superiority, its military-technological hubris, and its destiny to triumph over evil enemy-others. The postcolonial struggle militarized all of Southeast Asia, as the small, desperately poor country of Laos, absurdly, became the most heavily bombed nation in world history, though it nonetheless "fell" to the Pathet Lao. Cambodia suffered the greatest devastation, however, being heavily bombed, ubiquitously mined, and sucked into the morass by NLF, NVA, and U.S. violations of its neutrality. The ensuing "politicide" in the "killing fields" took the lives of perhaps two million Cambodians.[74]

While Indochina had been "lost" to Communism, the domino theory ultimately proved absurdist, as the supposed monolithic Communism devolved into the internecine Third Indochina War pitting China and Cambodia against Vietnam and the Soviet Union. The ultimate neocolonial nightmare, Vietnam had functioned as little more than a site for the United States to act out the pathological drives of its militant national identity.

CHAPTER 9

Patriotic Revival

The crisis of "Vietnam," coupled with racial conflict and the emergence of a "counterculture," delivered the most staggering blows to Myth of America identity since the Civil War. The seemingly endless war in Southeast Asia destabilized U.S. society and even briefly revived the moribund left. Before the 1970s had ended, however, national identity underwent a powerful resurgence. By choosing war—indeed, launching a series of wars—the nation sought to recapture and reaffirm its imagined identity. The patriotic revival that ensued revived cultural hegemony while marginalizing domestic reformers and peace internationalists in concert with demonization of the "liberal sixties." Myth of America identity thus reemerged more powerful than ever in the 1980s and into the twenty-first century.

The reform spirit of the sixties and seventies challenged elite cultural hegemony and foreign policy militancy. However, the discourse of the liberal sixties vastly exceeded the decade's accomplishments. Indeed, arguably the most enduring legacy of the period was the emergence of *liberal* as a demonizing trope reinforcing militant national identity.

Obsessed with the series of Cold War crises, John F. Kennedy devoted himself to the identity-driven "struggle for supremacy between two conflicting ideologies: freedom under God versus ruthless, Godless tyranny." Kennedy once commiserated with Richard Nixon on how boring he found domestic issues in contrast to the manly excitements of foreign policy. "It really is true that foreign affairs is the only important issue for a President to handle, isn't it? I mean who gives a shit if the minimum wage is $1.15 or $1.25?" John Kenneth Galbraith recalled that liberal domestic reformers within the Kennedy administration had all the political clout of "Indians firing occasional arrows into the campsite."[1]

Nonetheless, the "baby boom" generation of educated whites had destabilized Myth of America identity through their discovery of poverty, racial inequality, feminism, alternative sexual expression, and various other challenges to middle-class consensus. The "generation gap" erupted as a result of the baby boomers' disillusioned discovery that the discourses of national identity they had internalized since grammar school did not square with social actualities they learned at college or could see around them in ghettoes and on the ubiquitous television screen. In the years surrounding the Kennedy assassination, not only was the civil rights movement in full bloom but Rachel Carson had launched the modern environmental movement with her evocative *Silent Spring* (1962); Betty Friedan had exposed the *The Feminine Mystique* (1963); and Ralph Nader had kick-started the consumer protection movement with his exposé on General Motors, *Unsafe at Any Speed* (1965).

The last president nurtured by the New Deal, Lyndon Johnson willingly employed federal power to realize some of the aims of reformers. In a stirring State of the Union address in 1964, Johnson announced that his administration "today, here and now, declares unconditional war on poverty in America." Unparalleled, at least since Roosevelt, in his management of Congress, Johnson secured passage of many Great Society programs, including the Office of Economic Opportunity, the Job Corps, a new cabinet-level Department of Housing and Urban Development (HUD), literacy and childhood education programs, Volunteers in Service to America, clean air and clean water provisions, model cities and beautification programs. While critics condemned national health care as the dreaded socialized medicine, establishment of Medicare and Medicaid capped off the accomplishments of the Great Society and brought relief and assistance to hundreds of thousands of poor and elderly citizens.

Although the Great Society programs reduced from 17 percent to 11 percent by 1973 the number of citizens living under the official poverty line, the nation did not fight the "war" for domestic reform with the zeal it traditionally summoned for killing enemy-others abroad. "Johnson's extravagant rhetoric announcing new programs belied the modest funds he requested to begin them," the adviser Joseph Califano acknowledged. Daniel P. Moynihan described the liberal reform program as "oversold and underfinanced to the point that its failure was almost a matter of design." Moreover, by 1966, with millions being spent each week on training, combat operations, the air campaign, and "South Vietnam" military and governmental infrastructure, the Great Society had faded into oblivion.[2]

The hope engendered by the Great Society and the Second Reconstruction smoldered in the burned-out storefronts of Watts, Newark, Detroit, and other sites of "urban disorders" that killed scores of people and destroyed millions of dollars in property in the mid-1960s. African American inequality manifested itself in disproportionate combat service in the early years of the Indochina War, contributing to the angry resentment. Assessing the social problems associated with "the Negro family," Moynihan concluded "Very possibly our best hope is seriously to use the armed forces as a socializing experience for the poor—particularly the Southern poor." Thus the only way to fight a metaphorical war on poverty within the nation's militarized political culture was by funneling the poor and minorities into military service.

The experience of Hispanic Americans and other marginalized minorities mirrored to a great extent that of African Americans. Hispanic cultural emphasis on *la patria,* defense of the homeland, prompted many to join the armed forces, yet, as was the case with other minorities, sharply higher rates of poverty and unemployment also pulled many into Vietnam service. Puerto Rico, though a commonwealth territory, "ranked fourteenth in casualties and fourth in combat deaths" among the fifty states. Like African Americans and Hispanics, Asian Americans and Indians sometimes came to identify with the "Viet Cong" enemy as part of a global movement in opposition to Western neocolonialism. The "red power" movement emerged in the 1960s, as many young Indians grew increasingly radicalized in step with the "rights consciousness" of the era. With many Indians living in dire poverty on reservations, as one explained, "we made the connection that in Vietnam, we were involved in the same kind of colonization process that was carried out by whites in this country."[3]

Few grasped more profoundly than the Reverend Martin Luther King that an "imperial role abroad" was incompatible with "freedom and social justice at home." The Great Society had glimmered as a "shining moment" before becoming a "program broken and eviscerated by a society gone mad on war." Excoriating the militarized society, King declared, "A nation that continues year after year to spend more money on military defense than on programs of social uplift is approaching spiritual death." Moving to the left, King declared, "The evils of capitalism are as real as the evils of militarism and evils of racism." Subverting the Myth of America, King, who had been awarded the Nobel Peace

Prize for 1964, boldly called for an embrace of "loyalties that are broader and deeper than nationalism and which go beyond the nation's self-defined goals and positions." Already obsessed with King's sex life, J. Edgar Hoover concluded it was now "clear that he is an instrument in the hands of subversive forces seeking to undermine our nation." As in the early Cold War period, many "pragmatic" African Americans, including prominent members of the Urban League and the NAACP, accused King of a "serious tactical mistake," as they feared sacrificing the gains in the civil rights movement by turning against Johnson and the Democrats.[4]

By the time of King's assassination in April 1968 profound internal divisions had erupted over race, the war, and the generation gap. Having internalized Myth of America identity, Americans consented to the initial thrust into Indochina. Polls in 1965 showed less than 25 percent favored even attempting negotiations with the implacable Communist enemy-other. Rumblings of dissent emanated from college campuses, particularly as the draft threatened students (though most proved adept at avoiding conscription). Some Democrats challenged Johnson politically, yet they failed to perceive that Vietnam flowed from national identity rather than constituting, as they implied, a deviation from it. Eugene McCarthy and Robert Kennedy spurred the antiwar movement, yet neither advocated withdrawal, as such a retreat would have been unmanly and un-American. Kennedy's assassination in June 1968 staggered the nation, as the violence in Indochina seemed to be blowing back onto the homefront.

By the summer of 1968 a genuine counterculture—masses of young people openly rejecting the American way of life—had begun to emerge. Substantial political and cultural conflict erupted that same year in Rio de Janeiro, Madrid, Berlin, Rome, Mexico City, Tokyo, Paris, and Prague. Across the United States, particularly on college campuses but also in churches and community organizations, many young whites displayed solidarity with African Americans, including the Black Panthers and other "radical" groups. Some leftists condemned internal colonialism and global imperialism, as they grasped that the Indochina War was a symptom rather than the disease itself. They demanded social justice, and some, notably the Weather Underground, stood ready to wage a revolutionary guerrilla resistance, including selective bombings targeting "Amerika."[5]

As an embryonic—and ultimately abortive—alternative politics and culture materialized, it posed a direct threat to Myth of America cultural hegemony. The willingness of young whites to interact with, and even date, African Americans, Hispanics, and Asian Americans destabilized historically entrenched racial formations. The ubiquitous peace sign established a ritual gesture in defiance of the nation's congenital violence. The popular bumper sticker "Make love, not war" contravened militant national identity. Just as those who condemned it charged, the counterculture was un-American and menaced national identity.

Patriotic Renewal

The Democratic convention in Chicago in 1968 proved to be the turning point in returning counterculturalists to the margins. Polls showed that by a two to one majority Americans sided with Mayor Richard Daley and Chicago's finest following the "police riot" outside the convention hall. The Republican Richard M. Nixon won the presidency behind a theme of reestablishing law and order—a euphemism for reining in "black power," antiwar protesters, and the counterculture. Together, Nixon and George C. Wallace, the segregationist American Party candidate, received 57 percent of the popular vote. Candidates aggressively affirming militant national identity and marginalization of reformers thus won the 1968 election in a landslide.

Determined to destroy his political adversaries and build a "new Republican majority," Nixon laid the foundation for just that. While some Americans championed social programs, the more deeply rooted discourse "implying malingering incapacity and the waste of taxpayers' hard-earned money" soon prevailed.[6] Linking welfare with civil rights, the white middle and working classes perceived social reformers as adopting the un-American perspective that welfare was a right. The war on poverty thus ended with the growing sentiment that poor people, especially the minority poor, perpetuated a culture of poverty and that government welfare programs only served to enable welfare queens and shiftless males who wanted something for nothing. Backlash social issues such as civil rights, welfare, and the alleged judicial tyranny of the Warren court gained powerful resonance.

By the time of Nixon's election, the popular bumper sticker "America, love it or leave it" reflected the reaffirmation of cultural hegemony. White Americans by and large condemned the welfare state while defending the warfare state. These cultural forces drove fiscal policies that enabled the wealthy to get wealthier while blaming the poor for their own culture of poverty. Groups traditionally relegated to the sidelines—African Americans, Hispanics, feminists, "peaceniks," counterculturists, hippies, environmentalists, and homosexuals— remained marginalized by the mainstream.

These constituencies would not go quietly, however, and Nixon's failure to achieve "peace with honor" in Southeast Asia enabled them to continue to struggle for empowerment throughout the 1970s. The antiwar movement resurfaced when Nixon's "madman" strategy of expanded and even more punishing bombing, Vietnamization, and great power détente prolonged rather than ended the war. The Nixon Doctrine did not repudiate intervention but essentially vowed to do a better job of nation building, which Nixon and Henry Kissinger failed to recognize was a doomed modernist proposition from the outset. In May 1970 the Cambodian incursion reignited angry protests in cities and on campuses across the country, including one in which four students were shot dead by National Guardsmen at Kent State University in Ohio. On May 9, one hundred thousand Americans marched on Washington in protest of the seemingly endless Indochina War and the violence blowing back onto the home front. On college campuses, strikes by students and professors shut down normal university operations on 448 campuses. On April 24, 1971, nearly one million citizens marched against the war on the Capitol in the largest demonstration in U.S. history.

Just as Nixon had claimed, however, the "silent majority," having thoroughly internalized Myth of America identity, defeated the counterhegemonic forces despite the debacle in Indochina. In the 1972 campaign George McGovern subversively deconstructed foreign policy discourse by charging that "the so-called free world is not free but a collection of self-seeking military dictators financed by hard-pressed American workers." He pledged "to cut the vast waste from our bloated military budget" and "guaranteed [a] job for every man and woman who wants to work," a proposal that provoked howls of protest against the socialistic implications of an un-American welfare state.[7]

Although he had survived several missions as a World War II B-24 bomber pilot, McGovern alienated millions of Americans because he was a peace candidate and therefore essentially a demasculinized subversive within a militant, masculinized culture. He not only advocated an unfulfilling and unmanly withdrawal from Indochina, but also found his campaign tarred discursively, as he later recalled, with "the groundless three A's charge (that I favored acid, amnesty, and abortion)." Moreover, the Democratic primary system was the most open in national history, empowering women, gays, minorities, and other marginalized groups. The silent majority backed Nixon's drive to suppress war critics and counterculturists, assert law and order, and adopt a stance of "benign neglect" of civil rights. Disturbed by the wave of violent disorders, Americans associated the left with the threat of black power and terrorist bombings by the Weathermen.

While antiwar activists of the era often claim credit for forcing the country out of Vietnam, the sheer duration of America's longest war belies this notion. The antiwar movement helped bring an end to the draft, but the Selective Service System was so dramatically flawed that its demise may have been inevitable under any circumstances. Although many college students demonstrated against the war, nonetheless "the great majority of them refrained from protesting it."[8] Male-dominated labor unions across the nation backed the war with "heavy rank-and-file support." Indeed, it was AFL-CIO President George Meany who provided Nixon with his favorite trope by declaring in 1967 that labor "spoke for the vast, silent majority in the nation." Anchored by Myth of America identity, the silent majority clung to a neocolonial war of unprecedented violence even as it dragged on years after its contradictions had become apparent.

The seventies' crises of Vietnam, Watergate, and economic stagflation did not produce lessons leading to reform but rather exacerbated psychic crisis leading to a powerful reinvigoration of militant national identity. "After 1975," as Tom Engelhardt explains, "the basic impulse of America's political and military leaders (as well as many other Americans) was not to forge a new relationship to the world but to reconstruct a lost identity of triumph."[9] The psychic crisis, exacerbated by Watergate, afforded cultural space for Jimmy Carter to take the White House in 1976 after a presidential campaign rooted in a populist discourse of Christian decency and promotion of international human rights over Kissingerian realpolitik. However, Carter's subsequent effort to implement a diplomacy grounded in human rights foundered on a virulent opposition from the masculinized national culture; that is, a foreign policy emphasizing human rights proved fundamentally un-American. The former Georgia governor menaced the corporate elite by calling for alternatives to oil as well as self-sacrifice and curbs on consumption, which also went against the American grain of unbridled consumerism.[10]

Viewed with suspicion by the national security establishment from the outset, Carter aroused an almost hysterical neoimperialist opposition to his call for ratification of the Panama Canal Treaty. The treaty granted eventual sovereignty to the Panamanian government contingent on ongoing operation of the transportation corridor, including unfettered usage by U.S. warships. Although the canal treaty offered a meaningful gesture to millions of Latin Americans long resentful of Yankee imperialism, polls showed a stunning 80 percent of Americans opposed turning over the canal. Invoking the sanctity of the Monroe Doctrine, Ronald Reagan declared that the Canal Zone was "sovereign United States territory just the same as Alaska . . . and the states that were carved out of the Louisiana Purchase." The Senate ratified the treaty in 1978 by a single vote and only then after a belated clause reminiscent of the Platt Amendment guaranteed a U.S. right to employ "military force" to keep the canal open.[11]

By the second half of his term Carter no longer appealed to Christian morality but rather to the old-time religion of militant patriotic identity and enemy-othering. The president abandoned his human rights agenda as well as the quest to ratify the nuclear arms control treaty (SALT II). Carter initiated a military buildup and renewed intervention in Central America that the subsequent Reagan administration would accelerate dramatically. Exploiting the Cuban missile crisis usable past, reports of a phantom Soviet "combat brigade" in Cuba suddenly appeared, the cultural message being that Carter's Panama Canal giveaway and human rights policies had paved the way for renewed Soviet "adventurism" in "America's backyard."[12]

The exacerbation of the chronic psychic crisis flowed from the absence of a clearly defined national enemy-other. With the Indochina War having ended in defeat, and Nixon and Kissinger having confounded the right by conducting détente and implementing a celebrated "triangular diplomacy" with the USSR and China, the essence of postwar national identity—visceral anti-Communism—was ebbing away. For this reason many Americans condemned détente as little more than appeasement of the congenitally aggressive Soviets. Sobered by going to the brink of nuclear war over Cuba, Kennedy and Khrushchev had forged the first détente and arms control agreement in the Limited Test Ban Treaty of 1963. Nixon, Kissinger, and Carter built on this foundation by taking the superpower relationship to a new level with high-profile summitry, arms control accords, state visits, champagne toasts, and even hugs and kisses. While the media celebrated the unprecedented thaw in the Cold War, the absence of an evil adversary and the legacy of defeat in Vietnam continued to fuel national anxiety.[13]

The Iranian hostage crisis and the Soviet invasion of neighboring Afghanistan, only weeks apart in late 1979, triggered a sweeping patriotic revival. The

Soviet assault revivified militant U.S. national identity, as renewed enemy-othering displaced détente. Carter embraced confrontation with the Soviets and issued the obligatory presidential doctrine, declaring that the United States would consider an attack on the Persian Gulf "an assault on the vital interests of the United States" that would be "repelled by any means necessary, including military force."[14]

The putative threat to the Persian Gulf, like the Kremlin threat to Western Europe after World War II, fulfilled the driving cultural need for renewed enemy-othering. The Soviets were in no position to invade the Persian Gulf and attempt the Herculean task of cutting off Western oil supplies—though the discourse in Washington suggested the prospect of just such an action unless the nation displayed anew its credibility and manly resolve. Rather than launch World War III, the Kremlin sought to salvage a pro-Soviet government in Kabul and to contain the spread of fundamentalist Islam in Soviet Central Asia. U.S. foreign policy achieved the opposite, as aid poured into the *mujahedin* "freedom fighters," the Islamic fundamentalists who would become the Taliban regime and eventually make Afghanistan a haven for Al Qaeda and the reactionary Islamic fringe.

Like few other events in U.S. history, the Iran hostage crisis ignited the most incendiary components of militant national identity. The chants of "Death to Carter" outside the U.S. embassy in Tehran and the burning in effigy of the president, Uncle Sam, and the American flag delivered daily televised affronts to sacred patriotic symbols. Moreover, the perpetrators were bearded, chanting, "Third World" Muslims, many openly hostile to the modernist United States, Israel, and Judeo-Christian culture.

The seemingly endless, 444-day hostage crisis constituted a national humiliation, a heavily mediated daily reaffirmation of demasculinizing impotence. Carter sought and eventually achieved a negotiated end to the crisis, but not before a failed high-stakes and ultimately aborted desert rescue mission to Tehran in which eight men died in an airborne crash. The hostage crisis helped Reagan win a stunning landslide victory.

Reagan's victory culminated a torturous path to power for the supposedly New Right, which actually represented many old values "drawing on deep roots in American cultural life and shared assumptions about national identity." Reagan resonated with Americans as he reclaimed "an earlier time . . . when government responsibilities in the lives of citizens were minimal and a staunch moral Protestantism reigned supreme."[15] The Reagan-era revival of patriotic

8. *Time* cover story (November 19, 1979). The Iran hostage crisis became a heavily mediated, 444-day exercise in national humiliation. The crisis fueled the patriotic revival of the 1980s and marked the beginning of a long-term U.S. confrontation with Iran and fundamentalist Islam. Photo courtesy of Time and Life Pictures/Getty Images.

nationalism soothed the nation's psychic anxieties. The perception of the 1960s as an open society in which liberal elites sought to restore the New Deal order while at the same time coddling criminals built a powerful cultural wave of support from a not-so-silent majority. Americans in the flush of patriotic revival drove a military buildup (while otherwise condemning big government) and called for a "return to God." Politicians and evangelicals defined family values for the nation, precipitating assaults on secular humanism, premarital sex, gay and lesbian rights, reproductive freedom, court-ordered busing, and affirmative action. Excoriating the internal enemy-other, Americans condemned "big spending liberals" responsible for the failure of "social engineering."

Reagan became the first postmodern president, a man representing a nation wherein the lines between fantasy and reality were becoming increasingly blurred. Beneath "his light touch, his affable manner, the sparkle in his eyes," Reagan reflected the nation's militant patriotic identity. He embraced classical economic theory and repackaged states' rights as "new federalism." Exalting a "community of shared values," Reagan harbored a typical white, middle-class, Norman Rockwell view of America straight out of the pages of his favorite publication, *Reader's Digest*. Americans cheered his denunciation of big government and backed sweeping tax cuts, a windfall for wealthy elites, as well as a colossal military buildup. The pre-Keynesian "supply-side" economics opened a yawning and unprecedented federal budget deficit totaling more than two hundred billion dollars. After a debilitating recession, the economy rallied behind the discovery of new oil supplies and the breakdown of OPEC, but "trickle-down" economics made the rich richer and the poor poorer. Even though the economy grew in the 1980s, "those at the bottom saw their real incomes decline."

Gaining in popularity because he epitomized Myth of America identity so well, Reagan continued to cut taxes for the rich, enacted sweeping corporate deregulation, and went on the offensive against the "welfare state."[16] Homelessness entered the lexicon as hundreds of thousands of citizens fell through a promised safety net. The nation displayed indifference to the AIDS epidemic until the new "gay pneumonia" began to victimize heterosexuals. The war on drugs, crime and ghettoization, failing schools, and major scandals in the savings and loan industry, HUD, Iran-contra, and Pentagon procurement plagued U.S. society, yet none of these mattered: the restoration of Myth of America identity overwhelmed all other considerations, enabling Reagan to play the "role of a lifetime," that of a "Teflon-coated" neomonarch.[17]

Reagan embodied the providential destiny inherent in Myth of America identity. "Can we doubt," he declaimed, "that only a Divine Providence placed this land, this island of freedom here as a refuge for all those people in the world who yearn to breathe freely?" Reagan declared the nation "must adhere to traditional values, keep our faith in God, and put trust in people, rather than in the Government."[18] Religiosity had never abated in the postwar era, particularly among conservative denominations, all of which grew in the putatively discontinuous 1960s. The most influential civil rights leader, King, had been a Baptist minister, and churches had played an essential role in the movement. Religious groups had influenced the antiwar movement, while "Jesus freaks" had infiltrated the counterculture and rock music, as the rock ballad "Jesus Christ Superstar" (1970) became a megahit. On college campuses groups such as the Campus Crusade for Christ grew rapidly, while Jewish youth flocked to Israeli kibbutzim. Polls showed that more than a third of the nation, like Jimmy Carter, professed to having been born again and subscribed to a literal interpretation of the Bible. Even though religious influence had not actually declined, aggressive Protestants like Jerry Falwell of the Virginia-based Moral Majority insisted that the liberal sixties had brought a decline in family values for which the nation would pay a high price on Judgment Day. Americans tuned into Christian revivalists on television in record numbers, going beyond Billy Graham's occasional televised crusades to launch entire networks and phone banks that hauled in millions of dollars in contributions despite sex scandals involving prominent "televangelists."[19]

The identity-driven reassertion of the Soviet Union as an "evil empire" at the center "of all the unrest that is going on" coincided with the reassertion of fundamentalism. From the Soviet invasion of Afghanistan in 1979 to the Reykjavik summit in 1986, the campaign against godless Communism reprised the most intense superpower confrontations since the early Kennedy years. In September 1983 the horrific shootdown of a Korean Airlines passenger jet—flight 007, no less—which bizarrely had flown hundreds of miles off course and into Soviet airspace, reflected the dangers of Cold War gamesmanship. In the night sky the Soviets mistook the Boeing airliner for a smaller but similarly shaped RC-135 reconnaissance jet, which the United States frequently employed to penetrate airspace in order to assess Soviet response systems as part of ongoing macho games of chicken that both sides played in the air and at sea, at great risk and expense, throughout the Cold War. The national security state kept the public in the dark about this aspect, however, as enemy-othering of the evil empire resonated with Americans.[20]

Demonizing the Soviet evildoers facilitated massive renewed funding for the MIC, including the billions allocated for the fantasy of an effective missile defense system. While rolling back the welfare state, the corporate "hogs were really feeding," as Reagan's own budget adviser, David Stockman, graphically acknowledged, and especially rewarded were those "hogs" that fed at the trough of the warfare state. In tandem with Honeywell, General Electric, Lockheed, McDonnell-Douglas, Motorola, and scores of additional corporations, "the Reagan administration initiated the biggest sustained peacetime military buildup in U.S. history." With Congress functioning as a virtual rubber stamp for new weapons systems, the MX missile, the Rapid Deployment Force, the Trident submarine, the Stealth bomber, and the Cruise missile all gained approval. With the Committee on the Present Danger and other Cold War lobbies and think tanks fueling the buildup, the Pentagon budget soared from $171 billion to $376 billion in 1981–86.[21]

As cultural discourse denigrating welfare queens and government handouts to the poor exerted disciplinary knowledge over the society, the MIC featured spectacular examples of inefficiency, waste, fraud, secrecy, and abuse of power. "Weapons systems routinely came on line late, over cost, and under specifications," Alex Roland notes. By the time the B-1 bomber came on line, after billions in public expenditures, it was already obsolete, having been displaced by the B-2. Munitions plants and nuclear weapons facilities contaminated groundwater and plagued community public health, yet the MIC created jobs, particularly in the Sunbelt, generating both blue- and white-collar support.[22]

In what amounted to a massive corporate welfare program for the so-called defense industry, billions for the Strategic Defense Initiative (SDI) research gained the approval of Congress into the twenty-first century. The scientists, academics, and strategic planners within the MIC understood the fantastical nature of the Star Wars defense but what mattered was that the program brought them money and power. Moreover, the discourse of defense from nuclear attack masked research designed to enable delivery of *offensive* missiles from space.

Healing the "Wound" of Vietnam

Amid the cultural revival of identity-driven enemy-othering, Americans re-imagined the Indochina War to forge a usable past from the ashes of a disas-trous defeat. During the 1976 campaign Carter had declared, "We have learned that never again should our country become militarily involved in the internal affairs of another nation unless there is a direct and obvious threat to the secu-rity of the United States or its people." The Georgian subsequently blamed Viet-nam on the nation's "inordinate fear of communism" and even put into effect a limited amnesty for draft evaders, a bitter political pill for traditional mascu-line warrior culture to swallow. Before long, however, as Robert McMahon notes, Carter "implicitly repudiated all of his earlier, critical insights about the Vietnam War."[23] As the "great communicator," Reagan internalized the cultural drive to undermine the lesson of Vietnam—that the war constituted a dra-matic overcommitment of resources in a place far removed from U.S. national interests, deeply divided the nation, and ultimately was an unwinnable post-colonial war.

The Vietnam debacle thus materialized, ironically, at the center of cultural renewal of militant national identity. Having internalized the notion that de-feat in war was fundamentally un-American, Reagan recast the history of the Indochina War as a Hollywood story with a happy ending. "The truth of the matter is that we did have victory" in Indochina, he declared in 1985. "We con-tinue to talk about losing [but] we didn't lose that war. We won virtually every engagement." While the United States did employ its superior firepower to win most of the major battlefield confrontations, Reagan's discourse misrepre-sented the essence of the conflict, which began as a guerrilla insurgency featur-ing an endless series of firefights rather than a conventional war fought along defined battle lines. Indochina War apologetics also ignored the ultimate tri-umph of the Vietnamese national communists and failed to grasp the irony of a war that succeeded in uniting Vietnam while bitterly dividing the United States.

Reagan-era revisionism produced a number of accounts suggesting that the war against the evil of Communism could have been won through a more ef-fective strategy. Not even Reagan could press the absurdist claim to victory, hence the central thrust of his effort to recast the history was the assertion, "We recognize that ours was, in truth, a noble cause." The Vietnam War thus had not been wrong and certainly did not undermine the nation's moral superiority; it simply had not been prosecuted effectively. Perhaps even more significantly, by suggesting that the United States had not done enough militarily—despite all the napalm, chemical agents, assassinations, atrocities, the most relentless bombing campaign in history, and the deaths of as many as three million Indochinese—the Reagan-era usable past served to obscure memories of the unprecedented destruction heaped upon the region, thus cleansing the United States of any moral responsibility and paving the way for the next instance of postcolonial military intervention, in Iraq.

Although complete "Vietnamesia" was a cultural impossibility, Americans could effectively recast the war through an Orwellian shifting of the blame from the architects of the violence to its critics. Within the frame of "noble cause" revisionism, antiwar protesters and the news media increasingly became the targets of blame for the nation's failed crusade in Southeast Asia. Nixon had attacked "the liberal press" for opposing "wars of the Vietnam type . . . in defense of freedom and our own country." U.S. militarists condemned television coverage for misrepresenting the battlefield, exaggerating atrocities, and offering too much coverage of the antiwar movement. But the war was not lost on television, Chester Pach explains, "the real problem was with the war that television showed."[24] Targeting the supposedly liberal media for an un-American undermining of the war effort effectively disciplined news organizations, resulting in broad cultural complicity in new restrictions in war reporting.

While the news media were merely liberal, the Reagan-era recasting of the Indochina War "caricatured the antiwar paradigm by associating it with a flag-burning, America-hating, procommunist, radical fringe."[25] Much as Germans reinvigorated their cultural identity by embracing a stab-in-the-back thesis after the Great War, many Americans internalized the cultural knowledge blaming war protesters for defeat in Indochina. As genuine Americans could not be opposed to U.S. militarism, antiwar protesters had to be considered traitors in the binary world of national identity. At best, as General William Westmoreland had put it, the dissenters constituted "a misguided minority opposition . . . masterfully manipulated by Hanoi and Moscow."

Myth of America discourse sutured the antiwar movement to the counterculture to facilitate stereotyping and to enable the dismissal of both as part of a broader cultural project of denigrating the 1960s. "I know of nothing positive coming from that period," Allan Bloom declared in a typical refrain on the 1960s.[26] By the 1980s *All in the Family,* the popular sitcom that brutally satirized white-male right-wing bigotry in the persona of Archie Bunker (Carroll O'Connor) had given way to *Family Ties,* which neatly encompassed the reaffirmation of cultural identity as it featured befuddled former hippie parents from the six-ties in contrast with their besuited, businesslike son Alex (Michael J. Fox). By reducing the 1960s to a clichéd mélange of welfarism, hippies, and the "permis-sive lifestyle" of wanton sexuality, drug abuse, and self-destructive rock stars, the reforms associated with the era—including civil rights, women's rights, the war on poverty, environmentalism, and opposition to imperial foreign policy—were discredited under the patriotic revival.

Nothing did more to demonize the memory of antiwar protesters than the pervasive mythology of their mistreatment of Vietnam veterans. Many Viet-nam War films and some oral history accounts, usually constructed years later, perpetuate the myth that longhaired protesters spat upon scores of veterans virtually from the moment they stepped off their planes as they returned from Indochina. In *The Spitting Image,* the Vietnam veteran Jerry Lembcke found that overall "relations between veterans and the antiwar movement were empa-thetic and mutually supportive" whereas "the spit almost always flew from pro-war right-wingers onto antiwar activists." The "spitting image," a cultural cliché since the 1970s, served to discredit the antiwar movement as uncouth and un-American while at the same time ensuring the success of future campaigns to "support our troops," a discourse that functioned to support the wars them-selves.[27]

The cultural myth of the spat-upon veteran established that the only patri-otic veterans were those who supported the Indochina War, eliding the thou-sands of veterans who opposed it through organizations like Vietnam Veterans Against the War (VVAW). Recognizing that "military service afforded the veter-ans great credibility among antiwar activists, the media, and the American pub-lic," national security elites responded to the VVAW with FBI infiltration, wire-tapping, and harassment. The networks refused to televise the chilling accounts offered by veterans in the VVAW's historic Winter Soldier Investigation, held in a Detroit motel in 1971, as some 125 vets willingly admitted to participating in or witnessing atrocities against Indochinese civilians in violation of the interna-tional laws of war.

Perhaps the most pervasive Vietnam cultural myth holds that the ruthless Oriental enemy vindictively kept U.S. prisoners of war for years after the end of the conflict. Moreover, the myth suggested that a craven U.S. government cov-ered up the truth and refused to help free the men who had served their coun-try loyally only to languish in Vietnamese tiger cages. The ubiquitous black, tri-angular POW-MIA (Prisoner of War–Missing in Action) flag and the kitschy but immensely popular movies such as the *Rambo* and *Missing in Action* series converted the myth into virtual reality. No evidence that U.S. captives were being held after the Paris agreement ending the war ever surfaced.[28]

The cultural work of healing wounds ultimately facilitated erasure of the lessons of the Indochina War, thus enabling the nation to revivify its militant identity through renewal of enemy-othering and postcolonial warfare. As Reagan himself averred, "Sometimes when a bone is broken, if it's knit together well, it will in the end be stronger than if it had not been broken." After an initial controversy, The Wall, a black granite Vietnam veterans' war memorial in Washington, became a sacred site devoted to the healing process by honoring the fifty-eight thousand U.S. war dead. Most U.S. citizens probably "still remembered Vietnam as a 'bad war' that 'we didn't win and probably shouldn't have gotten into,'" Lynda Boose observes. "But the key ideological issues that had constructed the opposition—just why Vietnam was a 'bad war' . . . had receded into oblivion, along with much of the rest of the era's history."

Vietnam ultimately became a source of unity rather than division, especially as the cultural repackaging of the war powerfully affirmed the masculinity inherent in Myth of America identity.[29] No one symbolized remasculinization better than John Rambo, his rippling, muscled body glistening with sweat, going back to Indochina long after war's end to mow down one *untermenschen* Oriental enemy after another while freeing U.S captives. But Rambo was hardly alone, as the 1980s saw an outpouring of cultural representations, including the *Mission in Action* series, *Top Gun,* the *A-Team, Red Dawn,* Tom Clancy's clichéd patriotic technothrillers, *Soldier of Fortune* magazine, a new version of the GI Joe toy, and scores of other manifestations of militarized masculine renewal. Films such as *Top Gun,* which glorified the military and led to sharp increases in naval recruitment, received Pentagon support in filming, whereas films that cast doubt on U.S. militarism, such as Oliver Stone's *Platoon,* had to find and fund their own military settings, equipment, and hardware.

The cultural preoccupation with masculinity denied female agency, thus marginalizing women and especially feminists. The trope of women's liberation subversively linked the movement with Tricontinental liberation struggles against masculinized Western modernity, fueling a domestic backlash.[30] By the 1970s the women's movement posed a direct threat to Myth of America cultural hegemony by demanding equal access to education, sport, and cultural activities, equal pay and equal work opportunity (including shattering of the "glass ceiling"), access to contraception and reproductive freedom, stringently enforced legal sanctions against sexual harassment and spousal abuse, broader awareness and stiffer penalties for rape, legitimacy for lesbians, and essential social and political equality with men in a historically patriarchal culture. Faced with this array of threats, Hoover's FBI had infiltrated feminist groups, which the Director characteristically viewed as Communist-inspired. Female traditionalists ("pink ladies"), with substantial support from fundamentalist Christians and the male corporate elite, both of which sharply opposed equal work opportunity, equal pay, and gender equality in general, mounted an ultimately successful campaign to defeat the linchpin of the women's movement, the Equal Rights Amendment (ERA). The defeat of the ERA as much as any other single event marks the symbolic end of the putative sixties reform era.

The Vietnam "wound" and the antifeminist backlash achieved cultural convergence in the extraordinary obsession with Jane Fonda. The actress was still being verbally assaulted—and indeed spat upon with tobacco juice during a book signing in 2005—more than thirty years after her infamous visit to Hanoi in 1972, during which she openly sympathized with the North Vietnamese cause in the waning months of the war. Rich, attractive, spoiled, successful, and a Hollywood liberal, "Hanoi Jane" proved to be a perfect foil for a long-term cultural campaign of linking and demonizing the feminist, antiwar, and thus un-American other. Popular films such as *Kramer v. Kramer, Ordinary People,* and *Fatal Attraction* reinforced the threat of the assertive, demasculinizing individual female. The "second wave" of the women's movement permanently altered gender relations and created myriad new opportunities for women, yet the trope feminist became demonized. Asked by *Newsweek* in 2005 (after portraying a serial killer) if she would describe herself as a feminist, the actor Charlize Theron expressed reluctance to embrace the term because "when you say the word 'feminist,' you think of women burning their bras in the 60s."

By 1984, as Reagan launched his America Is Back! reelection campaign, the patriotic revival manifested itself in the antifeminist backlash, the virulent and sometimes violent "pro-life" movement, the ghettoization of poverty, the containment of civil rights through benign neglect, and the triumph of reverse discrimination over affirmative action in the drive for equal employment opportunity. While Vietnam was too massively and diversely represented in the culture for a single lesson to prevail, the emphasis on the war's victimization of the grunts—the major theme of the Academy Award–winning Vietnam War films such as *The Deer Hunter, Coming Home, Apocalypse Now,* and *Platoon*—

and the need for healing the wound allowed Myth of America identity to coa-
lesce around renewed militarization.[31] Relentless chants of "USA, USA, USA" at
the Olympic Games in Los Angeles in 1984 attested to the powerful cultural
reaffirmation of celebratory nationalism.

Choosing and Winning Wars

The process of reinvigorating militant national identity ultimately led to the renewal of warfare and a driving quest for victory in war. Despite the cultural revival of Myth of America identity and enemy-othering, representation alone
could not fully displace the anxiety and debilitating "self-doubt," as Reagan put
it, flowing from the "Vietnam syndrome." Cultural remasculinization in the
wake of defeat in Indochina and the Iran hostage crisis drove the male-dominated national security state to seek out opportunities to directly employ military power and to win such conflicts.

This approach backfired dramatically in the Middle East, as the proverbial
powder keg exploded in the early 1980s over ongoing Israeli occupation and aggression, Palestinian retaliatory assaults, the rise of Islamic fundamentalism,
and the outbreak of the vicious Iran–Iraq War. Determined to reassert its manly
credibility, the United States sent U.S. troops into the maelstrom in Lebanon,
which was mired in a civil war and occupied by Syrian troops, PLO bases, and
Christian militias backed by Israel. Anti-Zionists responded by driving an ex-
plosive-filled van into the U.S. compound, killing 241 marines in April 1983. The
United States eventually evacuated Lebanon. In 1986 the nation focused the
campaign against "terrorism" on the "Libyan strongman" Mu'ammar Gadhafi.
An assassination attempt against the "mad dog of the Middle East" failed,
though U.S. warplanes took out the Libyan air force and struck Gadhafi's resi-
dential compound, killing one of his children. Libya struck back ruthlessly two
years later through the suitcase bombing of Pan American flight 103 bound for
New York, which exploded over Lockerbie, Scotland, killing 270 people.[32]

While Middle East international politics remained a neocolonial nightmare, the United States focused its most concerted militarism in the "backyard" of the Caribbean and Central America. In an effort timed to take public
focus off of Lebanon only days after the debacle at the Beirut marine compound, the Reagan administration sent some six thousand troops pouring onto
the tiny Caribbean island of Grenada, which had been taken over in a coup by a
group of fanatical neo-Maoists. The U.S. invasion, however, had been planned
well before the coup to oust Maurice Bishop, the leftist "New Jewel" reform

leader whom the fanatics had assassinated. The indirect target in the Grenada assault, however, was Fidel Castro, who had supported Bishop (and subsequently condemned the coup perpetrators) and sent Cuban workers, twenty-five of whom died in the U.S. assault, to aid in the construction of a new airport runway that Washington dubiously claimed was being readied to support establishment of a Cuban–Soviet base. The United States vetoed a UN Security Council resolution deploring the invasion and celebrated yet another "lovely little war" in the Caribbean.[33]

The primary war theater, however, was Central America, where the United States meant to defeat the "Moscow–Havana axis." Eliding poverty, oppression, illiteracy, infant mortality, and elite landholding throughout Central America, militarist discourse focused instead on the Communist enemies of Cuba and the Soviet Union. On January 4, 1982, Reagan signed a national security directive aimed at "defeating the insurgency in El Salvador, and to oppose actions by Cuba, Nicaragua, or others" to propagate revolutionary change in the region.[34]

The revived Cold War narrative justified massive violence in El Salvador, where leftist rebels had mounted an insurgency against the homicidal U.S.-backed regime. In 1980 government-supported "death squads" murdered the nation's Catholic archbishop, Oscar Romero, and national guardsmen raped and murdered four U.S. churchwomen, among the more sensational incidents within an ongoing campaign of state terror. The United States offered training, weapons, and support to a regime that killed tens of thousands of people, according to a UN Truth Commission report in 1993. Using the Condor model, so-called U.S. assets provided the names of students, reformers, unionists, and suspected guerrillas, enabling the Salvadoran hunter-killer squads to carry out torture and assassination. The U.S.-backed campaign of terror and militarism contained the left, and a UN-brokered settlement ended the conflict in 1992.

In Nicaragua in 1979, the triumph of the Sandinistas, the first leftist victory in the region since Castro, brought a perfervid U.S. reaction. The Sandinistas' effective literacy, health care, education, and land redistribution programs provoked a swift Yankee intervention in the form of a rebel invasion force. The United States helped create and armed and equipped the *contra* rebels, comprised mostly of former members of the deposed dictator Anastasio Somoza's national guard, men whom Reagan described as "freedom fighters" and the "moral equivalent of our Founding fathers." While it may have been true that the contras, who razed peasant villages and often tortured and killed indiscriminately, mirrored the fathers' sanction of violence against Indians and

Africans, such a comparison was surely not what Reagan had in mind. The contra war left thirty thousand Nicaraguans dead and more than one hundred thousand homeless, while more than 90 percent of Salvadorans continued to live in poverty.

The Central American conflicts reinvigorated countersubversion on the home front, as the FBI's COINTELPRO (Counter Intelligence Programs) probed and infiltrated CISPES—the Committee in Solidarity with the People of El Salvador. The government spent millions, spied upon and otherwise harassed hundreds of people, and yet found no foreign or subversive threat to "national security."[35]

The struggles in Central America provided an opportunity to "unleash" the CIA, which the NSS establishment believed had been disastrously constrained after the revelations in the mid-1970s of domestic spying, assassination plots, and drug experiments. Under Director William Casey, a former World War II secret operative turned Wall Street financier, the CIA attempted to revive the glory days of cloak-and-dagger intervention. Casey plagued the Sandinistas with myriad operations, including the illegal mining of Nicaraguan harbors, which struck ten commercial vessels from at least five countries. The United States thumbed its nose at the World Court when it formally condemned the mining of the harbors as an act of state terrorism. However, the unbridled CIA intervention, which also included torture, sabotage, psychological warfare, paramilitary operations, and mercenary soldiers, aroused congressional opposition and renewed efforts to tug at the reins of the imperial presidency by cutting off aid to the contras.

The Iran-contra scandal emerged when leaks and investigations gradually revealed that the contras had not only been funded illegally in defiance of a congressional amendment cutting off U.S. aid, but also that the funding had been carried out through secret illegal weapons sales to, of all nations, Iran, which continued to sponsor the taking of U.S. hostages in Lebanon and which the administration had condemned as a terrorist nation. The Iran-contra affair made a mockery of Reagan's call for "civilized countries of the world" to shun terrorist regimes like the one in Tehran, which were "united by one simple criminal phenomenon—their fanatical hatred of the United States, our people, our way of life."[36] Despite such contradictions, many Americans rallied behind the illegal operation against the forces of evil. The Iran-contra scandal thus failed to tarnish Reagan's legacy, as he remained Teflon-coated, an uncompromising defender of true Americanism.

The United States continued to choose war in the context of the ongoing cultural drive to reaffirm militant identity. George H. W. Bush, Reagan's successor, seized an opportunity in his first year in office to assert U.S. credibility in "our own backyard" through a punishing invasion of Panama. Hundreds of innocent civilians died and thousands suffered injuries and deprivations as a result of Operation Just Cause. The United States shelled and burned out Panama City neighborhoods in the process of capturing the "Panamanian strongman" Manuel Noriega, who had defied U.S. authority and laundered drug profits for Colombian and American dealers.

The invasion enabled the righteous nation to "take back" the Canal Zone, leaving an enlarged U.S. military presence while lodging Noriega in a Florida prison. The United States ensconced in power the usual assemblage of lighter-skinned, corporate-friendly elites. Reflecting the contempt for UN authority characteristic of American Century unilateralism, the United States vetoed a UN Security Council resolution condemning the assault and ignored criticism by European allies as well as the Organization of American States, which censured the United States for violating the nonintervention clause.

As they did in virtually all U.S. wars, Americans celebrated the affirmation of national identity and the ephemeral psychic satisfaction of killing foreign enemy-others. International condemnation merely affirmed the unique righteousness of America's cause, as the public overwhelmingly supported the assault. Bush's approval rating shot up, and the "opposition party" fell into line.

While the United States shored up its hegemony over Central America and the Caribbean, the Soviet Union under Mikhail Gorbachev was renouncing hegemony in its backyard. Led by the Solidarity movement in Poland, East European reformers gradually pulled out of the Soviet orbit and threw off the Kremlin-backed Communist Party regimes. In the sort of reverse domino effect that George Kennan had once forecast and Nikita Khrushchev had feared amid the 1956 Hungarian uprising, the liberalization flowed from West to East from 1989 to 1991, into the corridors of the Kremlin and KGB (the state security committee) headquarters in Dzerzhinsky Square. Following the failure of a last-gasp coup by hardliners in August 1991, the Soviet Union, quite astonishingly, had ceased to exist.

The Soviet Union, like most empires, collapsed from internal contradictions exacerbated by imperial overstretch. *Perestroika* (economic restructuring) failed to arrest the disintegration of the Soviet economy, while *glasnost* (open discussion) enabled intellectuals to savage the Communist Party's monopoly on the usable past and to unearth the millions of Stalinist skeletons in the closet, a process that delegitimated the entire Soviet experience. Unlike the West, the state had been supreme under Soviet communism, hence when the state fell into disrepute there was no private economy or liberal tradition to arrest the free fall. The ghosts of the Stalinist past and the failure to deliver economically since the early 1970s, partly as a result of reckless and obsessive military spending, led to the demise of the USSR, Gorbachev's policies providing the final impetus. The end of the Cold War "had clearly come about largely as a result of developments within the Soviet Union rather than as the direct consequence of American policies," Peter Boyle notes.

Myth of America identity, which placed the nation at the center of providentially sanctioned modernist progress, elided these internal Soviet contradictions, enabling the United States to claim full credit for "winning" the Cold War. The end of the Cold War offered "catharsis for the underlying frustrations which had built up in American life in the 1970s."[37] The complete elimination of the Soviet Union, the nation's premier adversary for more than two generations, thus dramatically enhanced the organic process of reaffirming national identity. A widely embraced corollary myth held that Reagan himself, in a masterful stroke of strategic genius, had calibrated his military buildup to spend the Soviets into oblivion as they fatally sought to keep pace. Myth of America identity scripted a simple but highly usable narrative: Ronald Reagan won the Cold War, an interpretation that powerfully vindicated the militant nationalism he so well embodied. As the Gipper himself put it, advancing his own mythology, "We meant to change a nation, and instead we changed a world."

As the nation rode the wave of the vindicationist frame of victory in the Cold War, the United States celebrated itself. Victory in the Cold War meant that the "revisionists" had been wrong and that the orthodox interpretation had been right. Military alliances such as NATO and nuclear weapons had been good, as they had helped to keep the Long Peace and avoid a superpower conflict until the "men in the white hats" could prevail. Victory thus vindicated the MIC, the NSS, peripheral wars such as Korea and Vietnam as well as domestic campaigns of countersubversion. The end of the Cold War marked the triumph of "peace through strength." U.S. global intervention (containment) may have been unsavory and costly on occasion, yet in the final analysis, as "we now know," it had served the side of moral righteousness in an epic struggle between good and evil and right and wrong. The triumph of "democracy" and the "free market" also established binaries denigrating socialism and even Scandinavian-style social welfare policies, with attendant domestic policy implications throughout the world. Ultimately, the end of the Cold War marked nothing less than a Hegelian "end of history" as "liberal democracy" constituted "the end point of mankind's ideological evolution" and "the final form of human government."[38]

This sweeping vindicationist frame thus represented the Cold War as yet another "good war" while simultaneously reaffirming cultural hegemony and fueling the patriotic revival. The triumphal narrative marginalized alternative interpretations suggesting that soft power, the appeal of Western consumer and popular culture, may have done more to undermine Soviet hegemony than the hard power of alliances, militant confrontation, and Third World intervention.[39] The most powerful weapons in the Western Cold War arsenal may have been blue jeans and bright clothes, jazz and rock 'n' roll, Hollywood films and television serials, Pepsi-Cola and Pizza Hut, Detroit automobiles and the Sears catalog. Such analysis suggests the utility of an alternative Cold War metaphor—the "nylon curtain"—that connotes modernity and permeable boundaries, as opposed to the iron curtain, with its Berlin Wall and the impassable Checkpoint Charlie. We ought, as one scholar suggests, to ponder the "*Marilyn Monroe Doctrine*" as well as its more famous diplomatic predecessor.[40]

However much Myth of America culture claimed victory, the end of the Cold War constituted a "velvet revolution," a triumph achieved with relatively little violence and with no direct Western involvement. Thus like the brushfire wars of the 1980s and 1990s, from Lebanon and Libya to Grenada and Panama, even the end of the Cold War could not obliterate the Vietnam syndrome or the humiliation of the Iran hostage crisis. The United States had fought and lost a major war in Indochina, and it had been humiliated by a group of enraged Muslim "students." Only by choosing, and winning, a "real" war could the nation heal the psychic wound and fully restore Myth of America identity.

"The Cold War's end didn't deliver us into an era of perpetual peace," Bush warned the nation in April 1991. "As old threats recede, new threats emerge." With the MIC running at full bore, weapons systems awaiting battlefield testing, and an array of conventional and special forces primed for either a major war or "low-intensity conflict," the only missing critical ingredient was a sufficiently evil enemy-other.[41]

Iraq's Saddam Hussein, a demonstrably vicious dictator, albeit a longtime U.S. client, assumed the role of the evildoer du jour. Like Noriega in Panama, among other assets-turned-enemies, Hussein had received backing, including credits and high-tech weaponry, during the Iran–Iraq War throughout the 1980s. The United States looked the other way as Hussein engaged in chemical warfare against Iran and his own Kurdish minority, killing some 100,000, promptly accepted his apology for the accidental sinking of the naval warship *Stark*, killing 137 U.S. sailors in 1987, and sent mixed diplomatic signals on the eve of Iraq's invasion of Kuwait in 1990.

The Iraqi attack created the opportunistic "perfect storm," which the United States immediately seized upon to unleash its own Desert Storm. Showing the enduring cultural imprint of the World War II usable past, Bush repeatedly compared Hussein and Iraq, a country of eighteen million people at the time, to Hitler and Nazi Germany. He thus invoked "the Munich syndrome," the ironclad "lesson of history" on "appeasement" of aggressors. This narrative left no space for the lessons of European colonialism, which had created Iraq's arbitrary boundaries, the focus of the dispute with Kuwait over oil and maritime access. Americans displayed little interest in such historical complexity or in challenging Kuwaiti innocence, though the emirate was one of the most reactionary, anti-Semitic, and oil-price-gouging regimes in the Middle East.[42]

Gendered perceptions remained central to the U.S. warfare state and to Bush himself. Although he had pummeled Panama, Bush had also issued a feminized call for a "kinder, gentler America" in apparent contrast to Reagan's rugged individualist, "make my day" discourse. Plagued by the rumblings from within the masculinized culture that he was little more than a wealthy, pampered Ivy League "wimp," Bush would prove once and for all that he was not soft by unleashing a cathartic war on a vulnerable postcolonial state. Declaring in manly fashion, "This will not stand" and that the United States was drawing "a line in the sand," Bush received a congressional consent to a resolution backing the invasion of Iraq.

The Persian Gulf War of 1991 underscored the arrival of U.S. global hegemony. No nation stood in the path of intervention, as the USSR was disintegrating, the British cousin cheered from the sidelines, and China—no longer considered Red despite the 1989 crackdown on democratic expression in Tiananmen Square—acquiesced in deference to its pursuit of most-favored nation trade status. The United States received UN approval and allied funding for the invasion, meaning that the nation functioned as a mercenary in carrying out a war financed by the international community. The administration amassed a huge invasion force of half a million in a direct repudiation of Vietnam incrementalism. Thus by 1991 the "lesson" of the Indochina War was not to avoid brutal postcolonial wars but rather to wage them with overwhelming ferocity. Low-intensity warfare entailed minimizing U.S. casualties while maximizing the intensity of destruction in the subject nations.

Desert Storm unfolded as merely the latest in a series of "splendid little wars" so vital throughout U.S. history in affirming cultural identity in response to internal drives and anxieties. Despite prewar hype about vaunted Iraqi defense forces, the invasion quickly became "a turkey shoot," as one officer put it, in which "technowar" exterminated more than one hundred thousand Iraqis. Inundated by computer video games throughout the 1980s, U.S. citizens cheered essentially the same phenomenon—another manifestation of postmodernity—as their television screens showed Pentagon-controlled footage of "smart bombs" pulverizing select targets while supposedly minimizing collateral damage. The civilian death toll was much higher and the lethal weapons much less precise than the NSS would acknowledge, but the Pentagon had largely excluded the press from the battlefield, thereby applying yet another lesson of Vietnam—the preference for propaganda over critical media reporting. Indeed, television, once the baneful medium for the prosecutors of the Indochina War, had been transformed into a site for cultural celebration of national identity through postmodern warfare. "The media functioned as the fourth branch of government," Michael Paul Rogin notes, "to contribute to spectacle rather than to question the keeping of secrets."[43]

Most Americans gloried in the war as they reinvigorated patriotic identity by means of external aggression. "We had given America a clear win at low casualties in a noble cause," exulted Colin Powell, "and the American people fell in love again with their armed forces."[44] Resurrecting the Hollywood Western from 1949 *She Wore a Yellow Ribbon*, citizens tied yellow ribbons around trees in symbolic support of troops fighting overseas. The ritual reflected cultural continuity in more ways than one—the John Ford film featured scenes of Indians being massacred while U.S. forces in the Persian Gulf employed Apache helicopters to mow down Iraqis.

Yet the unambiguous victory and cultural renewal that enabled the cowboy hero to ride off into the sunset brought only temporary cathartic relief. The United States declined to follow through on the Munich analogy by taking the war into Baghdad and securing the unconditional surrender of the Hitlerite regime. Hussein went on to gas and exterminate still more masses of Kurds in the north and to purge and execute Shias and perceived rivals as he reestablished his secular dictatorship following U.S. withdrawal. The war and the postwar economic sanctions crippled Iraq's economy. A vicious regime thus remained intact while the masses of Iraqis suffered and died.

Despite the ambiguous results, Bush proclaimed that Desert Storm, coming on the heels of victory in the Cold War, had delivered nothing less than a "New World Order." "By God, we finally kicked the Vietnam syndrome once and for all," gushed Bush, who had also neatly liberated himself from the wimp factor. Yet the invasion left the Middle East even more unstable than before the Yankee intervention. As in Korea and Vietnam, going to war proved much easier than securing a desirable outcome or a lasting peace.

Throughout the 1990s, pronounced anxiety surfaced not in spite of but rather because of victory in the Cold War and in the Persian Gulf. Not even proclamations of the end of history and the new world order could deliver a full measure of psychic satisfaction. Ultimate victory requires that all enemies be vanquished, yet paradoxically such a state of being is culturally incompatible with national identity. As Engelhardt points out, there could be no "imaginable 'America' without enemies and without the story of their slaughter and our triumph."[45] Militant national identity rendered the United States culturally unable either to embrace ultimate victory or to "give peace a chance."

The two-term presidency of Bill Clinton reinforced cultural anxiety as the nation questioned whether he represented true Americanism. In the absence of a viable external enemy, the nation might turn inward, thus exposing home-front inequalities conducive to the rise of domestic reform. Discussion of reaping a "peace dividend" threatened to divert resources away from the NSS and MIC and into a revivified liberal domestic agenda.

Clinton's attitudes on race, gender, homosexuality, and national security evoked the supposedly liberal 1960s. He favored soft rock music and admitted to having placed a marijuana joint to his lips—though he denied inhaling. Moreover, like hundreds of thousands of young men in his era Clinton had successfully avoided the draft after agonizing over how such a course would affect his driving political ambition. Clinton not only embraced progressive views on race, he counted an African American, the former Urban League president Vernon Jordan, as one of his closest friends. Overwhelming support from African Americans, Hispanics, and women provided the decisive constituency that secured Clinton's electoral triumphs. Clinton was the first president, at least since Franklin Roosevelt, to enable a well-educated, highly motivated, and thoroughly politicized spouse, Hillary Rodham Clinton, to take a meaningful role in policy formation.

Perceived as soft rather than manly, Clinton aroused a powerful reaction of militant opposition because of his rejection of the warrior patriot role through his draft avoidance and also through his pledge to allow homosexuals equality within the military. Homophobes, backed by public consent, attacked on this issue from the moment Clinton took office and forced growing numbers of gays and lesbians out of military service. Meanwhile, sexual harassment and sexual assault by heterosexual men scandalized the Air Force Academy and reached epidemic proportions throughout the armed services and even in the recruiting process.

The anxiety over Clinton's manliness and patriotism provided a rallying point for reaffirmation of militant national identity. Overwhelming opposition defeated the effort to construct a viable national health care program. While common in virtually every other modernist state, national health was still widely considered subversive. Hillary Clinton's involvement in the program aroused a perfervid male backlash, as the broadcaster Rush Limbaugh, among others, warned of the "femi-nazi" threat to national identity. Following the election of one of the most conservative Congresses in U.S. history in 1994, Clinton, a self-proclaimed New Democrat, signed legislation "ending welfare as we know it." The term *liberal* had become powerfully reaffirmed for a new generation as a trope equated with waste and failed government intervention in behalf of people too lazy to fend for themselves.

Myth of America identity had long worked against cultural diversity and in behalf of traditional (white) family values. Americans decried a putative liberal agenda of welfare programs, affirmative action, gay rights and immoral sexuality, abortion rights, femi-nazis, and political correctness. Arthur Schlesinger, Jr., the longtime champion of the vital center, asserted that multiculturalism had gone too far and threatened to bring on the "disuniting of America." Other critics savaged the liberal media and liberal academia, prompting one historian to observe that zealots "used words like *liberal* a bit the way Nazis had once used *Jew.*"[46]

Indifference to Genocide

While reaffirming cultural identity at home, the United States displayed studied indifference to a striking surge of international genocide during the 1990s. Ethic cleansing in the former Yugoslavia shattered visions of an idyllic post-communist new world order, yet elicited no action from the world's only remaining superpower. "We don't have a dog in that fight," drawled James Baker,

Bush's secretary of state, as murderous conflict between orthodox Serbians, Catholic Croats, and Bosnian Muslims transpired.

U.S. indifference to international genocide found its roots in historic cultural identity as shaped by its own massive violence in African slavery and ethnic cleansing of North American Indian cultures. Bosnian Muslims, under attack from white Serbs, elicited no more support than that provided to Jews, homosexuals, "Gypsies," and other minorities exterminated by the Nazis in World War II. In the wake of the Third Indochina War, the United States had even sided with the mass-murdering Khmer Rouge against Vietnam and the USSR.

Although Clinton vowed in the 1992 campaign to "strongly support urgent and appropriate action to stop the killing," he failed to follow through as "gang rape, torture, and enslavement of Muslim women" continued. Some two hundred thousand Bosnians died in 1992–95. In 1995, after international condemnation prompted action, the United States brokered a tenuous peace in Dayton, Ohio. Despite the accord, ethnic cleansers continued to mount brutal assaults.[47]

By 1999 domestic and allied opinion, galvanized by the daily televised images of the continuing Balkan violence, prompted the United States to respond in the only way it knew how—through an "aerial massacre" in the name of "humanitarian intervention." The seventy-eight-day bombing campaign sought to "demolish, destroy, devastate, degrade, and ultimately eliminate the essential infrastructure of Yugoslavia." The carpet bombing killed between five hundred and eighteen hundred civilians, wounded thousands more, and caused four billion dollars in damage, including an inadvertent strike on the Chinese embassy in Belgrade. Ruins and refugees were the legacy of the campaign, which failed to save more innocent lives than it caused deaths.[48]

While the crisis in the Balkans presented no easy solutions, the NATO bombing campaign reflected the militarized culture as well as contempt for UN multilateral authority. The campaign was illegal under international law, as the UN Security Council had not approved it. Continuing to eschew international authority after the war, the United States undermined the International Criminal Court—which it refused to join—in deference to a tribunal at The Hague that focused predominantly on Serbian transgressions.[49]

Americans also proved strikingly indifferent to genocide in "black" Africa in 1994, as Hutu militias launched a savage campaign against the Tutsi minority in Rwanda. The United States actually led a successful effort to *remove* UN peacekeepers from the African country. Moreover, the United States denied requests for use of its sophisticated technology—long deployed in the "crusade for freedom" against the East European Communist Party regimes—to jam radio broadcasts that played a crucial role in coordinating the mass murder. "And even as, on average, 8,000 Rwandans were being butchered each day, the issue never became a priority for senior U.S. officials," Samantha Power notes. Thus "some 800,000 Rwandans were killed in 100 days."

Masculinized Machiavellian realism discouraged "emotional" responses to world conflicts in which "national interests" were not at stake. Thus the United States followed "a consistent policy of nonintervention in the face of genocide." Perhaps even more disturbing, as Power found in her Pulitzer Prize–winning book, the "reason the United States did not do what it could and should have done to stop genocide was not a lack of knowledge or influence but a lack of will." When another wave of genocide unfolded in the Darfur region of the Sudan, the United States had already become too bogged down in Iraq to respond. Tellingly, the "age of genocide" coincided with the emergence of the United States as global hegemon.[50]

Globalizing Inequality

In the 1990s a much-ballyhooed globalization arose as a rearticulation of a continuous history of modernist neocolonialism. The term *globalization* was misleading insofar as capitalism had long been global, yet the discourses surrounding the collapse of communism and the new world order fueled the growth of a unitary world system. The essence of globalization was closer international economic integration flowing from new technology, reduced communication and transportation costs, free flow of goods, new industries, and corporate hegemony. Globalization not only perpetuated but strengthened modernist hegemony over the postcolonial tricontinental world of Asia, Africa, and Latin America.

Globalization fueled a reactionary revival of pre-Keynesian classical neoliberalism, a discourse trumpeting the benefits of free-market capitalism while cynically deepening international economic inequality and global instability. At the same time CEO compensation increased exponentially under the globalization regime, as corporations diverted to their executives much of the money reaped from decreased production costs by exploiting cheap labor and dodging environmental restraints by moving abroad. The massive corruption and accounting scandals of Enron, Arthur Anderson, and Merrill Lynch, among others, reflected the corporate culture of the 1990s run amuck, both at home and abroad.

The twin World War II–era institutions, the International Monetary Fund (IMF) and the World Bank, conjoined with the World Trade Organization in the 1990s, constituted "the three main institutions that govern globalization." Together they employed loans, threats, and demands for "structural adjustment" to compel tricontinental nations to open themselves to modernist corporate hegemony at the expense of the welfare of the bulk of their populations.

A free-market emphasis on deregulation safeguarded corporate domination backed by the governments of the leading modernist states. Myriad so-called development projects left postcolonial states more indebted than ever, often trashed their environments, and invariably failed to trickle down economic growth to the masses of people. Joseph E. Stiglitz, who served for three years as chief economist of the World Bank, resigned in disgust over the "hypocrisy of pretending to help developing countries by forcing them to open up their markets to the goods of the advanced industrial countries while keeping their own markets protected." Stiglitz, a Nobel Prize winner, found that the IMF "failed its mission" by pursuing "policies that make the rich richer and the poor more impoverished—and increasingly angry,"[51]

Rather than fostering economic development, U.S. international policy contributed to global instability and prompted a powerful backlash. While globalization brought some benefits in some places, including jobs, education, literacy, and disease control, it also devastated banking systems, created hunger and mass unemployment, and instituted price gouging for vital medicines for diseases, including the global AIDS epidemic. At the same time, IMF policies precluded relief programs and government intervention by withholding assistance from nations that refused to cut deficits, eliminate welfare programs, and make other structural adjustments.

The profound contradictions of globalization precipitated the economic crash of 1997 that radiated from Indonesia and Thailand to Russia to Africa and Latin America. The IMF promptly worsened the deepest economic crisis since the Great Depression by forcing afflicted states to raise interest rates. Nations such as Indonesia, which held to the IMF regime, suffered the most, while those such as South Korea, Malaysia, and China, which rejected neoliberal orthodoxy for ameliorative state intervention and recapitalization, came out best. By embracing "shock therapy" and succumbing to "the gospel of the market economy," the former Soviet Union got "the worst of all possible worlds—an enormous decline in output and an enormous increase in inequality."[52]

From the time the United States assumed the mantle of the sole remaining superpower, the number of people in the world whose living standard was improving dropped from one in four to one in six. Even as total world income increased 2.5 percent annually in the 1990s, the actual number of people living in poverty rose by nearly one hundred million. Angry resentment over globalization simmered worldwide and erupted with hunger riots, violent resistance, and a burgeoning protest movement that rocked the WTO meeting in Seattle in 1999.[53]

While globalization in the form of unprecedented world cultural and economic integration was here to stay, the inequalities of neoliberalism had produced meaningful resistance—notably in the Latin American backyard. Even as the United States facilitated a "neoliberal war economy" backed by "violence, intimidation, and physical liquidation of the electoral Left" under Plan Colombia, Argentina, Brazil, and especially Venezuela fended off Yankee hegemony.[54] After defeating a U.S.-backed coup attempt in 2002, Venezuela's freely elected (and twice reelected) President Hugo Chavez seized control of the nation's vast oil supply, honored Castro while denouncing the United States, empowered dark-skinned indigenous minorities, and encouraged similar defiance by other Latin American leftists. Similar democratic electoral revolts followed in Bolivia in 2005 and in Peru and Nicaragua in 2006, while the left advanced in Mexico and other Latin states as well. Thus, while the United States embarked on a new "global crusade" against the Islamic enemy-other, Latin Americans strove to cast off the neocolonial legacies of Monroeism, good neighborism, and U.S.-backed terror regimes.

CHAPTER 10

September 11 and the Global Crusade

The attacks of September 11, 2001, delivered a shattering assault on U.S. patriotic identity. The "9/11" attacks killed some three thousand people in New York, Washington, and Pennsylvania and reduced to rubble the World Trade Center twin towers, symbols of U.S. financial power, global leadership, and modernist prestige. As the world's "sole remaining superpower," the United States had appeared omnipotent, fostering an illusion of invulnerability that exacerbated the impact of the attacks.

The September 11 assaults thus brought the militancy inherent in Myth of America identity roaring to the surface. The "global war on terror" reignited the national security state, fueled the military-industrial complex, and prompted a renewed wave of countersubversion reinforcing cultural hegemony on the home front. As the United States conducted a global jihad of its own, it charged other nations as well as its own citizens with a simple binary: "Either you are with us, or you are with the terrorists."

As in Indochina, however, the United States embroiled itself in a brutal war in which it could neither win nor admit defeat. The global war on terror fueled the Islamic jihad and eroded international support for the United States. Ultimately, the crisis of September 11 brought into sharp relief the pathological character of U.S. identity and foreign policy.

Cultural representation immediately framed September 11 as an attack against freedom and the American way of life. "They hate our freedoms—our freedom of religion, our freedom of speech, our freedom to vote and assemble and disagree with each other," George W. Bush proclaimed.[1] The president thus

9. "Flag Photo" (September 14, 2001) by Dylan Moore. Brooks Breece venerates patriotic national identity as he waves a large American flag in the median along Interstate 95 in northern Virginia. The attacks of September 11, 2001, in New York and Washington, D.C., precipitated an outpouring of patriotic emotion, a prelude to the subsequent U.S. invasion of Iraq. Photo courtesy of Dylan Moore, director of photography, Media General Northern Virginia Newspapers.

depicted the United States as an innocent. As happened after Pearl Harbor, a "bolt from the blue" thesis that obscured all antecedents established a discursive regime preceding a paroxysm of righteous violence.

The "hate our freedoms" frame elided any notion that the 9/11 attacks constituted "blowback" in response to the nation's identity-driven foreign policy global intervention.[2] The provocations for the assaults included unstinting U.S. support for Israeli territorial aggrandizement and terror against Palestinians; U.S. military intervention in South Asia and the Arab Middle East, including the anti-Soviet Afghan war, the Persian Gulf War, and debilitating sanctions against Iraq; establishment of U.S. military bases and installations, especially in the Saudi Arabian "holy land"; and the drive to control the region's oil supply.

Framing 9/11 as an unprovoked terrorist assault blurs the continuity between the so-called global war on terror and a national history of external violence against evil enemy-others. The Cold War having ended and the nation roiling under the domestic "culture wars" of the 1990s, the organic forces of identity coalesced in a new global crusade. Like the Communist enemy of the latter half of twentieth century, the terrorists meant to undermine the American way of life and thus had to be destroyed directly through the regenerative violence of war. The devotion of resources to renewed foreign war, accompanied by tax cuts for wealthy elites, left little cultural space for domestic reform or un-American antiwar activism.

Even as they condemned "Islamic fanaticism," the United States, Britain, Israel, and other countries harbored their own often-fanatical religious drives and motivations. Fundamentalists—whether Muslims, Christians, or Jews—view the world as unfolding according to divine plan. "Their different settings, beliefs, and goals notwithstanding, Jewish, Christian, and Islamic fundamentalists interpret history of the modern period, especially the twentieth century, in remarkably similar ways," Scott Appleby explains.[3] Pro-Israeli fundamentalists, for example, viewed Zionist expansion as part of God's plan for Jews to reoccupy the lands of the biblical Israel. In the United States, fundamentalists reasserted that the Bible was the literal word of God, condemned the teaching of evolution, and eroded the theoretical separation between church and state as they sought to "take back" the schools, courts, Congress, and the presidency from the godless tyranny of "secular humanism."[4]

Islamic fundamentalists similarly view their world as menaced by the contamination of secular modernity, but these feelings are exacerbated by postcolonialism. Many of these fundamentalists denounce the "satanic forces" of

Western imperialism for heaping humiliation on the lands of Islam. The most extreme factions advocate *jihad* against their perceived oppressors. Sunni fundamentalists sought to restore the caliphate to preside over an Islamic state. The Shiite minority (about 90 percent of the Muslim world is Sunni) revived tenth-century doctrine that envisioned a vast new land of Islam under the authority of a new imam. Like Christian fundamentalists, Islamic fundamentalists apotheosize a metaphysical final deliverance unto God.

U.S. foreign policy divided Islam into a simple binary world of "good Muslim, bad Muslim."[5] Shah Reza Pahlavi had been a good Muslim; hence the toppling of his U.S.-backed regime in Iran by bad Muslim fundamentalists in 1979 reinforced the cultural framing. Encouraged by his benefactors in Washington, the Shah had carried out the "white revolution" of modernist reforms, including secular education and women's rights, which challenged Islamic tradition. A virulent Shiite fundamentalist reaction led by Ayatollah Khomeini ensued, driving the moribund Shah into exile. The subsequent hostage crisis (see chapter 9) not only plagued the United States but also powerfully fueled the rise of Islamic fundamentalism across the region. The Iranian Revolution established the "defining, watershed moment when Islam assumed formidable political proportions with reverberations not only in Iran but also throughout the region."

Even as blowback materialized in Iran, the United States nonetheless aided and militarily equipped Islamic fundamentalists both before and after the Soviet Union sent one hundred thousand troops pouring into Afghanistan in 1979. Washington rushed massive organizational assistance and sophisticated weaponry to the *mujahedin,* the Islamic "holy warriors" who waged a long war of resistance against Soviet efforts to bolster a Marxist regime in Kabul. In the ensuing decade the United States carried out "the largest and most expensive paramilitary undertaking in U.S. history." Although "the Islamic world had not seen an armed jihad for nearly a century," Mahmood Mamdani points out, "the CIA was determined to create one." The war in Afghanistan became "one of the bloodiest proxy conflicts (perhaps exceeded only by the Vietnam War) between the United States and the Soviet Union."[6]

While nationalist discourse after 9/11 cemented around U.S. innocence in the face of the irrational rise of Islamic fanaticism, the nation's foreign policy had, by its own design, spurred the jihad movement. As the United States armed, equipped, and encouraged the mujahedin, it enlisted the cooperation of neighboring Pakistan, toward which the United States had tilted against India,

Pakistan's bitter rival, under Nixon and Kissinger in 1971. Acting on the basis of Cold War—driven and "largely illusory military, strategic, and psychological fears," the United States "deliberately extended the Cold War into South Asia," alienating India, the world's most populous democracy, in the process. Displaying an "arrogant self-confidence . . . consistent with the overall pattern of American behavior in the Third World," the United States militarized the region, Robert McMahon concludes.[7]

Identity-driven militarization, in close association with the Pakistani regime, empowered the Taliban ("students") in the campaign against modernist Soviet intervention in Afghanistan. Fulfilling its role as by far the world's leading arms merchant, the United States supplied massive aid, notably as many as twenty-five hundred shoulder-fired Stinger missile launch weapons to bring down Soviet helicopters and aircraft. The resistance and the weapons proved effective. In 1989, as part of the sweeping "new thinking" in Moscow, Mikhail Gorbachev called the Afghan war a "bleeding wound" and terminated the Soviet intervention.

While the United States claimed victory in both the Afghan war and the Cold War, the Taliban seized power in Afghanistan, accelerating Islamic fundamentalism. Belatedly concerned about the hands into which its Stingers had fallen, the CIA implemented a buy back program—thus enabling the U.S. public to pay for the weapons twice and at wildly inflated prices the second time— yet some six hundred remained unaccounted for in 1996. Largely indifferent to events in Afghanistan, the Clinton administration expressed willingness to work with the new regime.[8] However, as the Islamic fundamentalists instituted increasingly reactionary policies, particularly against women—who were barred from working outside the home and allowed to appear in public only when fully veiled under the *burka*—Western opposition began to build against the Taliban regime it had been so instrumental in empowering.

Gendered discourses of Middle Eastern women, including a virtual Western obsession with the *burka*, date back to colonialism. As Frantz Fanon theorized, the "occupying power interprets attachment to traditions as faithfulness to the spirit of the nation and as a refusal to submit." Thus discourses emphasizing the "backwardness of Islamic societies" imputed that "Islam was innately and immutably oppressive to women, that the veil and segregation epitomized that oppression," Leila Ahmed explains. Paradoxically, even as the patriarchal West "devised theories to contest the claims of feminism, and derided and rejected the notion of men's oppressing women with respect to itself, it captured the language of feminism and redirected it in the service of colonialism." Gendered narratives of backwardness and oppression of women exalted the West through alterity while at the same time justifying Euro-American modernist intervention.[9]

The growing chorus of U.S. condemnation of the Taliban and the *burka* tapped into historical narratives of Euro-American women in Indian captivity, Mexican or Cuban damsels in distress, the rape of Belgium and Nanking, and the captivity of the blonde, "All-American girl" Jessica Lynch during the Iraq War. The captivity narrative thus "reinforces the paternalistic nationalism of the rescuer-nation and dramatizes its moral mission," Emily S. Rosenberg explains. "In a struggle between groups of men (or male-coded nations), women and children make cameo appearances as emblems whose symbols of oppression (the *burka,* for example) can rally sentimentalized, self-congratulatory support." Such narratives sanction foreign intervention but rarely produce genuine international reform to improve the lives of women, such as providing contraception, AIDS awareness and treatment, general education, and political empowerment. Moreover, as Ahmed notes, obsession with the *burka* does a disservice by fetishizing women's issues and encouraging oppressed women to associate feminism with Western colonialism and condemnation of Islamic culture. "That taint has undoubtedly hindered the feminist struggle within Muslim societies," she adds.[10]

Enabling Israeli Apartheid

The yawning cultural gap between the United States, fundamentalist Islam, and putatively moderate Arab states widened even further as a result of the ongoing U.S. "special relationship" with Israel. Without support from the United States, which continued to disdain the UN, the otherwise potentially viable "land for peace" formula that emerged after the 1967 Six-Day War quickly stalled. Ignoring UN resolutions establishing Palestinians' "right of return," Tel Aviv embarked after the Six-Day War on a quest for "Greater Israel," incorporating the West Bank, Golan Heights, and Arab East Jerusalem and launching a building campaign of new settlements in the occupied territories.[11]

In one of history's more profound tragedies, Israel—a nation of refugees—displays a violent disdain for Palestinian refugees whom they have dispossessed under Zionism. "An emotional barrier, a desire not to tarnish the creation myth," Chris Hedges observes, precludes many Israeli Jews, "including some of the most liberal and progressive, to acknowledge the profound injustice the creation of the state of Israel meant for Palestinians." "Indigenous Palestinians, like other peoples throughout history, including the American Indians," Clayton Swisher observes, "had the misfortune of standing in the way of another people's settlement and conquest."[12] Bitter and disempowered, Palestinians resorted to terror attacks against Israeli civilian targets.

Myth of America identity produced steadfast U.S. backing for Israel, widely viewed as an outpost of Judeo-Christian civilization in a backward, violent region of the world. U.S. policy, vigorously policed by the American Israel Public Affairs Committee (AIPAC), one of the most powerful lobbies in Congress, ensured that Israel remained by far the leading recipient of U.S. aid and armaments. The United States led the way in fending off international pressure against the Jewish state to end its illegitimate occupation of lands that had been predominantly Muslim since the seventh century. Support for modernist Israel underscored a pattern "consistent with the generally hostile attitude of the United States toward other African, Asian, and Arab national liberation movements in the post–World War II period," Deborah Gerner notes.[13]

Few events allowed Americans to celebrate their cultural affinity with Israel more than the sensational hostage taking of Israeli athletes during the Olympic Games in Munich in 1972. The incident, which culminated in an airport shootout that left both hostages and hostage takers dead, was covered live on television and "had an unprecedented impact in the United States." Four years later Americans, coming off their own defeat in Indochina, cheered as Israeli commandos pulled off a daring raid at Entebbe, Uganda, where Palestinian hijackers had diverted a civilian flight from Tel Aviv.[14]

By the 1980s the United States had embarked on a global campaign against terrorism that encompassed perceptions of Palestinians as little more than "bloodthirsty fanatics." While Israel, "our" civilized "white" ally in a "turbulent region," remained virtually above reproach, myriad films and potboiler novels in the 1980s and 1990s depicted Arabs as swarthy terrorist fanatics. In an age of "infotainment," Hollywood imagery often substituted for analysis in shaping the perceptions of millions of citizens. Even a seemingly innocent children's feature such as Disney's *Aladdin* (1992) shaped perceptions through its Orientalist imagery. Before protests by Arab organizations forced a change, a song in the animated feature film demonized the Arab world as a "faraway place . . . where they cut off your ear if they don't like your face."

Popular culture flowed from hegemonic discourse claiming "Palestinians have no rational basis for their hostility to Israel and no national claim to the land of Palestine," Kathleen Christison notes. A pattern thus emerged in which U.S. officials condemned Palestinian terror against Israelis even as far greater numbers of Palestinians died at the hands of the Israelis. As "Palestinian mortar attacks on settlements count as terrorism," Nur Masalha points out, "it would be reasonable to expect Israeli rocket attacks on Palestinian communities to be treated in the same way but they are not."[15]

The identity-driven special relationship destabilized the entire Middle East and contributed directly to the eventual blowback attack at the World Trade Center towers and the Pentagon on September 11, 2001. As the United States provided economic aid, weapons, and political support, the Israelis in 1982 launched a savage invasion of Lebanon, which would be torn apart by the ensuing violence. Israel shelled and bombed indiscriminately, using U.S.-made tanks and cluster and phosphorous bombs to kill and injure thousands of innocent Lebanese. Showing that they considered the Palestinians *untermenschen,* the Israelis literally sought to wipe them out in Lebanon before a UN-brokered accord brought a respite in the violence.

Instead of wiping out alleged terrorist opposition, the Israeli invasion gave rise to Hizballah ("Party of God"), the Shiite guerrilla resistance that eventually drove the Israelis out of Lebanon. Before they left, the Israelis conducted another gratuitous massacre, deliberately shelling a *UN* refugee compound at Qana in 1996, killing 105 unarmed Muslims, more than half of them children. Through their wanton violence—notorious throughout the Arab world, yet trivialized by Israel and elided in the United States—the Israelis had forfeited any moral standing they might have claimed in the conflict.[16]

Drawing inspiration from the Hizballah guerrilla resistance, in 1987 Palestinians launched the *intifada* (uprising) in the occupied West Bank and Gaza. Even the United States condemned "Israel's brutal crackdown" against the demonstrators—stone-throwing youths were being shot dead—and the decision to build still more settlements. The PLO continued its efforts to reach an accord as Chairman Yassir Arafat unambiguously declared in 1988 that the PLO "undertakes to live in peace with Israel." At this point the United States stunned the Israelis by officially recognizing the PLO and urging a settlement. In 1993 the right-wing Likud Party in Israel sharply opposed the Oslo Accords, even though the land for peace formula encompassed generous terms for Israel. The assassination of Prime Minister Yitzhak Rabin of Israel, who had negotiated with Arafat, "ended the Oslo process and sounded the death knell for a genuine Palestinian state," Juan Cole notes. Jewish settlement in the West Bank spiraled from 250,000 to 380,000 people.[17]

A continuous pattern prevailed throughout this history as Myth of America identity bolstered Israeli aggression and territorial aggrandizement. Despite constant discursive reference to the peace process, the "process" consisted, particularly after 1967, of Israeli resistance to any settlement that would force the return of seized territory that might threaten the vision of Greater Israel. Disregarding the fundamental political issues, Israel conducted military assaults killing hundreds of Arab innocents and destroying homes and even whole communities in far greater numbers than those suffered by Israel.

Disciplinary cultural knowledge bound Americans to the myth that the fundamentally irrational PLO had rejected a generous offer following renewed talks orchestrated by Clinton in 2000 at Camp David. Labor prime minister Ehud Barak "made a stingy take-it-or-leave-it offer" that "would have divided the West Bank into three disconnected segments" while Israel retained "complete control over the borders of a state that would thereby have been much less than sovereign," Rashid Khalidi explains. Yet Barak's proposal "was ludicrously described in the ensuing mythology that grew up around Camp David as 'generous.'" The ultimate legacy of Camp David II was to destroy the peace process and deepen the anger of Arabs and terrorists—including Osama bin Laden—while saddling the Palestinians with the "politics of blame." Israel responded to the eruption of a second intifada by killing twenty-four hundred Palestinians within three years, most of them unarmed civilians, provoking condemnation from the UN Human Rights Commission.[18]

Cultural affinity for Israel drove Americans to blame the Palestinians for the renewed violence, as discourse focused on the sensational suicide bombings against Israeli civilians while occluding the Israeli slaughter of three times as many Palestinians.[19] A U.S.-inspired "road map" to peace came to a familiar dead end when the United States sided with Israel and against practically the entire world community. In October 2003, the UN General Assembly voted 141–4 to condemn Palestinian suicide bombings but at the same time to condemn the new Israeli "security fence," a sort of Middle East iron curtain reinforcing the apartheid status of Palestinians. Israel, the United States, and the U.S. dependencies of Micronesia and the Marshall Islands cast the four dissenting votes. "The Israeli–Palestinian conflict contributes to wider tendencies of U.S. national autism," Anatol Lieven observes, "an inability either to listen to others or to understand their reactions to U.S. behavior."[20]

U.S. support for Israel never wavered, even as Tel Aviv launched another murderous assault on neighboring Lebanon in 2006. The attack constituted a grossly asymmetrical response to the kidnapping of two Israeli soldiers by Hizballah, part of an ongoing campaign of kidnappings and border skirmishes. Israel pounded the Lebanese infrastructure to rubble and relentlessly bombed civilian targets, including the use of phosphorous bombs and indiscriminate cluster bombs, killing some twelve hundred Lebanese. Israel simultaneously reinforced its capricious violence against an ongoing war of Palestinian resistance in Gaza.

Destroying Postcolonial Iraq

As they relished the reaffirmation of Myth of America identity following victory in the Persian Gulf War, few Americans expressed concern about Iraqi civilian deaths and destruction. "I have absolutely no idea what the Iraqi casualties are," declared "Stormin'" Norman Schwarzkopf, the celebrated Desert Storm commander, "and if I have anything to say about it, we're never going to get into the body-count business." Whether it was "50,000 or 100,000" did not matter, Schwarzkopf added; all that mattered was that "the right side won."[21] According to the UN, economic sanctions caused "the deaths of *several hundred thousand Iraqi civilians*" [emphasis added]. Others suffered from malnutrition and disease, including cancer, often linked to the massive U.S. employment of uranium-encased ordinance. Under the sanctions, a UN official reported, the United States had engaged in "destroying an entire society. It is as simple and terrifying as that. It is illegal and immoral." Confronted with the evidence of mass death, Clinton's secretary of state, Madeleine Albright, whose forbears had been victimized in the Holocaust, responded in February 1998, "We think the price is worth it. . . . If we have to use force it is because we are America. We are the indispensable nation."

While Americans discounted the devastating impact of the war and the regime of sanctions, masses of Arabs perceived "a flagrant double standard—Iraq punished and humiliated for invading Kuwait; Israel effusively supported despite its far longer occupation of Lebanon."[22] The consequences of the double standards and indifference to Arab suffering would not take long to manifest themselves, yet Americans failed to grasp the causes of blowback up to and even well after September 11, 2001.

The ongoing U.S. campaign of global militarization overwhelmed cultural considerations, as the United States implanted military installations in Saudi Arabia even though no site was more neuralgic to Muslims than Mecca. The Iranian Revolution in 1979 prompted Saudi fundamentalists to seize the Grand Mosque at Mecca that same year. The Wahhabi sect (named for an eighteenth-century cleric) occupied the mosque for two weeks, offering powerful testament to the volcanic rise of the Islamic fundamentalist reaction against modernity and Western intervention.

As the United States colluded with the Saudi regime, it effectively funded through oil purchases the terrorist schools that "educated" the jihadists, nineteen of whom would strike against it on 9/11. Jihadists targeted the World Trade Center for the first time in 1993, as a Beirut-style bomb exploded in a van in the basement parking garage on February 26, 1993. "The American people must know," the jihadists claimed in an anonymous letter to the *New York Times,* "that their civilians who got killed are not better than those who are getting killed by the American weapons and support."[23]

Imbued with his own sense of Manifest Destiny, bin Laden ruthlessly pursued what he perceived as a divine mission against the "Zionist-Crusaders alliance."[24] On August 7, 1998, Al Qaeda set off devastating, virtually simultaneous bombings of two U.S. embassies in the African capitals of Nairobi, Kenya, and Dar es Salaam, Tanzania. "The war has just begun," bin Laden vowed, citing U.S. "crimes in Palestine, Lebanon, Iraq, and other places." Masses of Muslims echoed bin Laden's indictment of the United States for "occupying the lands of Islam in the holiest places, the Arabian Peninsula, plundering its riches, dictating to its rulers, humiliating its people, terrorizing its neighbors, and turning its bases in the Peninsula into a spearhead through which to fight the neighboring Muslim peoples."[25]

Bin Laden also cited Somalia, where U.S. Orientalism converted a program of humanitarian assistance into a militarist campaign, with tragic results. Seeking to exert its global leadership, particularly after inaction in Bosnia, the United States launched a program to feed starving people but fell out with a local warlord, whom it then tried but failed to "decapitate." Intent on punishing the Somali "hoodlums," "bandits," and "thugs," the Army launched an ill-fated assault into "Indian country" to take on the local "skinnies" of Mogadishu.

Nineteen U.S. servicemen died in the famous "Black Hawk Down" incident in October 1993 in which, as the Eritrean president put it, the Army Rangers had gone in "like Rambo" only to be stunned by "the size, scope, and ferocity" of the subsequent counterattack. "We just didn't expect to meet the kind of resistance that we did," a U.S. official acknowledged. U.S. television viewers suffered the humiliation of seeing some of the dead soldiers' bodies dragged through the streets by celebratory Somalis. Although Clinton withdrew U.S. forces in 1994, bin Laden chose to bomb the African embassies because, he claimed, they had been the sites of planning "the brutal U.S. invasion of Somalia . . . killing some 13,000 of our brothers, women, and sons." The United States fired Cruise missiles on targets in Sudan and Afghanistan in retaliation for the embassy bombings.[26]

As the new millennium dawned, a mounting sense of psychic crisis pervaded the United States, setting the stage for renewal of warfare. At first, Americans paid surprisingly little attention to Al Qaeda as the domestic culture wars of the 1990s and the relentless campaign to impeach Clinton over a sexual liaison with his young intern roiled the nation. Multiculturalism threatened white masculinity and true Americanism and thus drew condemnation for disuniting America. Political correctness emerged as a pejorative trope marginalizing efforts to promote multiculturalism. College professors came under siege as anxiety-ridden critics condemned "thought police" for undermining the patriotic identity of American youth by emphasizing "minor literature" and "victims' history" and for refusing to incorporate conservative views. "For most of American history," *Time* pointed out, "the educational system has reflected and reinforced the bedrock beliefs of the larger society."[27] Unease and postmodern diversions characterized the 1990s, the decade in which the World Wide Web revolutionized communications, spurring commerce and the dot.com revolution but also vivid pornography, gambling, chat rooms, and hate groups. The violence embedded in American culture surfaced in a series of sensational, disturbing cases, including the O. J. Simpson murders, the assault on the Branch Davidian compound in Waco, Texas, the carnage at Columbine High School, and the Oklahoma City bombing, carried out by an angry Persian Gulf War veteran, killing 168 people.

Disinterested in Al Qaeda, Bush and the neoconservatives revivified American Century unilateralism, as they envisioned a Middle East domino effect that would be set in motion by taking out Saddam Hussein and establishing a modernist, pro-Israeli regime in Baghdad.[28] An Iraq oriented toward the West would bolster Israel against the Palestinians and allow for the liquidation of Hizballah. The United States would continue to arm and befriend the oil-soaked Saudis and the authoritarian regimes of the good Muslims Hosni Mubarak in Egypt and Pervez Musharraf in Pakistan while isolating Syria and Iran.

The September 11 attacks created the cultural space in which Americans would consent to another regenerative war of nationalist redemption. Like the War Hawks of 1812 and the jingoists of 1898, Bush and the neoconservatives reflected a continuous national history of choosing war. "America is no mere international citizen," Charles Krauthammer declared in March 2001; thus the righteous nation, through "unapologetic and implacable demonstrations of will," would go to war "to reshape norms, alter expectations and create new realities."[29] Preoccupied with planning a preemptive war of their own, the architects of intervention left themselves unprepared for a 9/11-style assault targeting the U.S. mainland.

Though intelligence intercepts quickly revealed that bin Laden's group had orchestrated the attacks, the nation would wage a *global* war on terror rather than focusing on the perpetrators of 9/11. While Bush cruised safely at high altitude, Secretary of Defense Donald Rumsfeld called a meeting on the afternoon of September 11 to make plans to "hit S.H. [Saddam Hussein] at same time. Not only U.B.L. [Osama bin Laden]." The wrenching attacks created an opportunity to "go massive. . . . Sweep it all up. Things related, and not."

The open-ended, universal global war on terror effectively replaced the Cold War in providing a long-term solution to the anxiety that inhered in the absence of an identity-affirming enemy-other. A product of culture and national identity, the global war on terror also kept reformers at bay. Through the exaltation of manliness, the war marginalized feminists and peace internationalists as it dramatically refired the engines of the NSS, the MIC, and corporate globalization.

To the thunderous applause of a flag-draped Congress—and backed by broad public support—Bush poured forth a deep-seated cultural discourse permeated with references to Myth of America national identity. "The advance of human freedom . . . now depends on us," he told the Congress on September 20. The president then put the world on notice with the following assertion of unilateral U.S. global militarism: "*Every nation, in every region* now has a decision to make. Either you are with us, or you are with the terrorists" [emphasis added].[30]

In the wake of another "day of infamy," the nation would lash out against any and all perceived enemies. Within days of 9/11, in a reprise of the Tonkin Gulf Resolution of 1964, Congress authorized the president to "use all necessary and appropriate force" against any and all "nations, organizations or persons he determines" carried out or aided the terrorist attacks. Obscuring that the nation had been attacked because of its history of militant intervention in the Middle East, discourse centered instead on the American mission to shepherd "the advance of human freedom." Rather than focusing on the perpetrators, the United States declared a global war on limitless fronts and of indefinite duration.

While Myth of America identity drove the nation toward war, most of the international community challenged the false intelligence that poured out of Washington and viewed the United States as a "cowboy" nation with a lust for war. Even as the United States employed economic clout and intense political pressure, most countries of the world endorsed the principle of allowing the UN inspectors to continue to monitor Iraqi weapons plans and facilities. Hans Blix, the chief UN weapons inspector, insisted that the international community could have disarmed and even deposed Hussein. Within the United States, however, the inspectors assumed a role as unmanly foes of regenerative violence against evil.[31]

Homeland Consent

On March 20, 2003, with flags waving and the overwhelming majority of Americans cheering them on, the U.S. military launched a campaign of Shock and Awe, inaugurating a new phase in the ongoing devastation of postcolonial Iraq. Despite lack of Iraqi involvement in 9/11 as well as an absence of direct evidence that Hussein possessed weapons of mass destruction (WMD), a compliant Congress passed the war resolution rather than risk being tarred as soft or lacking in Americanism.

Shock and Awe reflected continuity in U.S. warfare since World War II: a history in which a discourse of spreading democracy and modernist progress obscured the nation's will to destroy. The United States had slaughtered Indians, Mexicans, and Filipinos; bombed indiscriminately in the "good war"; destroyed hospitals, villages, dams, homes, and farms in Korea; razed villages, defoliated the countryside, and saturated Indochina with mines and bombs; converted Iraq into a free-fire zone, slaughtering retreating soldiers, in Desert Storm; and now pummeled a defenseless nation with conventional bombs, indiscriminate cluster bombs, depleted uranium ordnance, and chemical agents in the form of white-phosphorous bombs. The campaign of "low-intensity," "asymmetrical warfare" thus minimized U.S. casualties while killing tens if not hundreds of thousands of people on the ground.

The United States remained determined not to assess civilian casualties. "We don't do body counts," reiterated General Tommy Franks. Disregard for the impact of its militarism reflected another "lesson" of Vietnam, that an obsession with "body counts" had been counterproductive. While the United States ignored the impact of the bombing and shelling, the Arab and Islamic media paid careful attention.

The same forces of "technowar," featuring massive firepower and a high rate of civilian casualties, also characterized Operation Enduring Freedom in Afghanistan. The United States drove the Taliban out of Kabul in 2001, yet the Sunni fundamentalists, drawing support from sympathizers in neighboring Pakistan, regrouped and by 2006 they were once again "stoking a newly hot war full of suicide bombings, improvised explosives, and other techniques borrowed from Iraq." The heroin trade flourished in Afghanistan to help finance the resistance. The United States thus found itself mired in a two-front war with no end in sight.[32]

Violent external aggression redressed internal masculine anxieties. Bush received high approval ratings from the millions of U.S. men who responded with a red-blooded, fire in the belly enthusiasm for his Texas swagger, his "gunslinger pose, his squinty-eyed gaze, his dead or alive one liners."[33] Bush vowed in manly fashion throughout the war that he would "stay the course" and never "cut and run," a line lifted from Reagan. Just as in his stint as governor of Texas Bush had displayed manly resolve rather than feminine sentimentality by signing the warrants of unprecedented numbers of death row inmates, President Bush consigned tens of thousands of U.S. soldiers to the deadly perils of war, to say nothing of hundreds of thousands of Iraqis who perished under the U.S. wars and occupation.

Manliness intertwined with godliness in militant U.S. cultural identification. "Evangelical born-again rhetoric [was] if anything more prevalent across the country at the start of the twenty-first century than it was at the start of the nineteenth or twentieth," Richard W. Fox points out. Affirming their own chosenness, Americans eagerly conflated the tropes evil, crusade, terrorist. The televangelist Pat Robertson condemned Islam, Jerry Falwell labeled the prophet Muhammad a terrorist, and Franklin Graham, the evangelist son of Billy, preached in a Good Friday service held at the Pentagon that Christianity and Islam were "as different as lightness and darkness"; that Islam was "a very wicked and evil religion"; and that "there's no way to God except through Christ." The United States marched into war, as in the past, to a millennial drumbeat.[34]

Bush, who had undergone a Christian conversion experience to shore up his personal identity, sincerely believed it was the nation's mission, under God, to "rid the world of evil" by invading the Middle East and bolstering the biblical land of Israel. Bush, like Woodrow Wilson, backed by substantial public consent, believed in these *words;* he thus internalized the discourse that drove the nation's militant interventionism. Corporations profited from the identity-driven foreign policy, to be sure, but they did not generate it. This is what Chairman Charles "Engine Charlie" Wilson of General Motors sought to explain when he responded to a question about potential conflict of interest during testimony before Congress in 1952 as he prepared to enter the Eisenhower cabinet as secretary of defense. "I thought what was good for our country was good for General Motors, and vice versa," Wilson declared in all sincerity.[35]

Three days after the hijacking assaults, Bush asserted that the nation's "responsibility to history is already clear: to answer these attacks and *rid the world of evil*" [emphasis added]. "There is no neutral ground—no neutral ground— in the fight between civilization and terror," Bush explained, "because there is no neutral ground between good and evil, freedom and slavery, and life and death." In his State of the Union address in 2002 Bush reached back to the World War II good war usable past to apply the trope of an axis to Iraq, Iran, and North Korea, not one of which was even remotely allied with the others—yet all of whom were evil.

Reveling in patriotic discourse, "the media at once got in step and deferentially made government press conferences, speeches, and press releases the staple of its reporting," Michael Hunt notes.[36] Flag lapel pins, icons of eagles, talons bared, and the pronouns *we* and *our* permeated not just Fox network but also CNN, CBS, NBC, and ABC coverage of Operation Iraqi Freedom. The new Pentagon practice of "embedding" reporters within assigned units reinforced their patriotic identity. Dependent on the military for information as well as their own security, reporters marched with combat soldiers, rode in tanks, interviewed pilots aboard aircraft carriers, and could scarcely keep the giddy excitement out of their voices. Stateside, Pentagon generals filled the ranks of studio experts, using pointers to mark progress on the battlefield map.

Media coverage affirmed the hegemonic prowar consensus that swept the country during the unfolding invasion, a noun the media usually avoided. The national media gloried in the righteousness of a preemptive war eight thousand miles from U.S. shores. Stories of U.S. troops, weapons, casualties, and home front support dominated the coverage. The mounting costs of the war, the overnight erosion of civil liberties embodied in the USA Patriot Act, and the horrific devastation and death within Iraq itself received shallow coverage. Reporters and news anchors reified the terms *coalition* and *allied* to describe a U.S.-dominated invasion force in a war opposed by an overwhelming majority of the world. Captives of their Americanness, journalists filed stories that were "conformist rather than free" and often "amateurish," according to the Nieman Foundation for Journalism. The study noted that in allied Britain, journalists at the British Broadcasting Company "are more seasoned and more knowledgeable about the world they cover."[37] The Bush administration and much of the U.S. media derided the Qatar-based Arabic-language television station Al Jazeera because it covered the stories that defied the identity-driven U.S. narrative.

The contrasting stories of two young American women, Jessica Lynch and Rachel Corrie, illuminate the hegemonic media coverage of Middle East politics. Lynch, a nineteen-year-old from Palestine, West Virginia, suffered severe injuries after her company took a wrong turn and came under fire from Iraqi soldiers, who killed several of her comrades. The Pentagon and the media claimed that Army Rangers, in a "daring mission," freed Lynch from her captors by fighting their way into the hospital. In fact, they encountered no resistance. Lynch, who in 2007 denounced the manipulation of her traumatic experience, at the time became an icon of Operation Iraqi Freedom, appearing on the cover of *People,* making talk show appearances, and receiving a showering of gifts and cards from thousands of well-wishers.

While the frenzy of media coverage of Lynch's ordeal reprised the classic captivity narrative, the tragic fate of Rachel Corrie, a twenty-two-year-old student at Evergreen State College in Olympia, Washington, went virtually unnoticed. On March 16, 2003, Corrie died as she protested, unarmed, in front of a Palestinian home—one of some twelve thousand homes destroyed since 2000 under a policy of "collective punishment." An Israeli soldier and his commander crushed Corrie beneath a nine-ton Caterpillar bulldozer made in Peoria, Illinois, and sold to the Israeli military. The Israelis claimed the killing had been accidental, even though Corrie wore a bright-orange, fluorescent jacket and had shouted at the Israeli soldiers through a bullhorn and they had spoken back to her. Witnesses insisted the killing was deliberate, yet the U.S. media scarcely covered the story, and Washington accepted the results of the Israeli "investigation," which exonerated the soldiers, who, after killing Corrie, had proceeded to demolish the home in the Gaza Strip inhabited by a pharmacist, his wife, and three children.

For most Americans the Iraq War was a postmodern spectacle—the war, that is, was not real for most citizens but rather a representation of reality that appeared on their television screens.[38] Televised representation turned the war into a spectacle, an extravaganza that affirmed its righteousness while insulating viewers from its horror. "Political spectacle in the postmodern empire," Michael Paul Rogin explains, "is itself a form of power and not merely window dressing that diverts attention from the secret substance of American foreign policy." Such spectacles "colonize everyday life" by transforming "domestic citizens into imperial subjects."[39]

The global war on terror affirmed Tocqueville's insight in *Democracy in America* that "while the majority is in doubt, one talks; but when it has irrevocably pronounced, everyone is silent, and friends and enemies alike seem to make for its bandwagon." Americans offered minimal dissent in the midst of a culture that condemned protest against righteous violence as unpatriotic. Liberal journalists like Thomas Friedman and academic experts like Bernard Lewis championed the war. "My motto is very simple," Friedman glibly averred. "Give war a chance."[40]

Outside the mainstream, antiwar peace internationalists launched a vigorous dissent that met with countersubversive containment and repression. Hundreds of thousands of citizens took to the streets, and millions more took to the Internet, to protest the unilateral U.S. invasion of Iraq. But peace internationalists were contained, as police in several cities reined in protesters with arbitrary physical boundaries, arrests, and baton-wielding assaults. The dearth of media coverage of these protests and crackdowns underscored the successful reframing of the Vietnam usable past, which had blamed the supposedly liberal media for encouraging antiwar protesters through excessive coverage of such demonstrations.

While U.S. militarism slaughtered hundreds of thousands of people in the Middle East, just as it had in Korea and Southeast Asia, peace activism remained profoundly marginalized within the righteous, militant, and masculinized culture. The tiny minority of Americans who advocated a prompt end to the war subjected themselves to condemnation. Representative John Murtha of Pennsylvania, a Vietnam veteran, pressed for a resolution to withdraw from Iraq, which the House defeated 403–3 in dramatic affirmation of a militant culture determined to uphold U.S. credibility. Representative Dennis Kucinich of Ohio was ridiculed when he proposed the creation of a cabinet-level Department of Peace, as the very notion of such an entity contravened core identity to such an extent as to be summarily laughed off.

The USA Patriot Act, passed by the Congress with virtually no investigation or dissent in the traumatic days following 9/11, underscores the pervasive cultural hegemony of militant national identity. The legislation authorized the most flagrant campaign of civil liberties violations since the countersubversive regime of the post–World War II decade. The trope USA Patriot Act proved reminiscent, though even less subtle, than Roosevelt's H.R. 1776 authorizing lend-lease in 1941. The post-9/11 campaign went further than previous countersubversive movements, however, as National Security Agency (NSA) computer, satellite, and other technologies enabled the secret agency to conduct data mining of banking, medical, library and other records and activities, including telephone conversations, email messaging, and Internet activity by millions of citizens. Only minimal protest responded to the unprecedented and massive campaign of spying that bypassed the legal requirements of congressional notification and declined to obtain court orders.

Ironically, the hegemonic discourse to support our troops—said to be "fighting for our freedoms"—actually eroded freedom at home. Hooverism returned with a vengeance under the global war on terror. While investigating domestic links with broadly defined terrorist groups, the FBI worked with local law enforcement to identify, bug, infiltrate, and harass antiwar and other putative left-wing groups. "The FBI is dangerously targeting Americans who are engaged in nothing more than lawful protest and dissent," the American Civil Liberties Union (ACLU) charged. Even when carrying out the campaign under a veneer of legality, the FBI tactics had a chilling effect on protest, as most Americans presumably preferred not having their names and sometimes photographs and other private information placed in government security files.

The assault on civil liberties revealed that the "you're-either-with-us-or-against-us" *mentalité* applied at home as well as abroad. As with the Red Scare in the wake of the Great War, government repression fell hardest on ethnic others, as many aliens were deported or jailed. Like John Adams, Jackson, Lincoln, and the Roosevelts, Bush reasoned that his intent was to protect the nation and Providence was by his side, hence any and all executive measures found ultimate justification.

National security being sacrosanct, the nation authorized a vast new federal bureaucracy, which it honored with a Big Brother trope: The Department of Homeland Security. The cabinet-level agency immediately became the third largest in the federal government, employing some 170,000 people and enjoying a budget of unknown size—like the cost of the Iraq War, such information was not merely difficult to ascertain but "top secret."[41] Homeland Security reorganized intelligence gathering and developed a series of color codes that purported to alert the public as to the level of risk of terrorist attack, thus reinforcing pervasive anxiety at the root of militant internationalism. The federal government became more secretive than ever, reclassifying government documents, blocking access to public information, and prohibiting photographs of the flag-draped coffins of U.S. soldiers returning from Iraq with increasing frequency. The government cracked down on leaks of privileged information— unless the Bush administration itself was doing the leaking, as when it brazenly "outed" a CIA agent, Valerie Plame, in retribution for her husband's public criticism of misrepresentations of the prewar intelligence on Iraq.[42]

The reactionary climate of the post-9/11 era flowed from the nation's hegemonic imagined identity. As the winds of reaction blew across the "homeland," dissent persisted but remained on the margins. The Bush administration received virtually everything it requested from Congress for "national security," and the president enjoyed strong approval ratings until well into his second term. Most congresspeople not only voted in favor of the war resolution, but also overwhelmingly supported the Patriot Act, both at its inception and renewal in 2006.

The presidential campaign of 2004 underscored the breadth of cultural consensus behind militant nationalism. When John Kerry condemned Bush for alienating U.S. allies through the unilateral resort to war, Bush responded that the nation would never subject its foreign policy to a "global test." American Century unilateralism thus remained sacrosanct. Appealing to the militant culture, Kerry downplayed his former political activism in opposition to the Indochina War and campaigned on an overdetermined theme that Bush had not done enough to capture bin Laden and win the war on terror. The Bush campaign, however, seized upon the revised Vietnam War usable past to mount a highly effective attack ad featuring Swift Boat Veterans for Truth. These militant Vietnam veterans depicted Kerry as somehow unpatriotic in his Indochina service even as an administration led by draft evaders conducted the war. Kerry retorted that he could kill the terrorists better than Bush could, as the election centered on which candidate could best affirm his militant Americanism.

"Mission Accomplished"

On May 1, 2003, following the fall of Baghdad, Bush, after landing on the flight deck in a jet, appeared in an aviation jumpsuit aboard the aircraft carrier *Abraham Lincoln.* As the president spoke, a huge banner in the background stated, "Mission Accomplished" in Operation Iraqi Freedom. Yet the ensuing months and years revealed that rather than igniting a reverse domino effect in which a liberated Iraq would become a spearhead for pro-Israeli modernist democracy throughout the Middle East, violent resistance prevailed in Iraq. The invasion and occupation were an unmitigated disaster. While Hussein's draconian dictatorship had kept the Shiite majority and the minority Kurds under wraps, the U.S. invasion blew the lid off Iraq's postcolonial politics. Creation of a new army and government, the linchpins of the new campaign of nation building, now threatened the Sunni minority in Iraq, which mounted an "insurgent" resistance. Moreover, just as many supposedly moderate Arab leaders had warned, the U.S. invasion, coupled with its ongoing support for Israeli violence, had created ever-increasing numbers of enemies throughout the region. Iraq thus became a magnet, pulling in jihadist guerrilla fighters from across the Middle East.

As it had in the Indochina War, the United States once again found itself ensnared in the illusion that it could succeed in a modernist campaign of nation building. "Post-independence attempts at so-called 'nation-building,' which make the mistake of assuming nationalism to be a substance rather than form, are more or less doomed, or at least they can only operate coercively," Robert Young explains. Americans failed to grasp the depth of the divisions within a multiethnic state whose arbitrary boundaries had been drawn by British colonialists.[43] The emergence of a large, determined, and well-armed resistance, replete with roadside bombings, made a mockery of Bush's claim that "major combat" operations had ended. Convinced that they would be met as liberators, the U.S. military had failed to secure Iraqi ammunition storage facilities. The U.S. invasion fueled the insurgency, "its brutal occupation kept it growing, and its utter lack of planning and foresight armed it with a virtually unlimited supply of powerful weapons."[44]

Fundamentally misunderstanding their enemy-others, Americans viewed the roadside bombings as fanatical acts of desperation rather than perceiving them as effective tactics of resistance. The trope suicide bomber ignores the fact that, while the attackers indeed took their own lives, their purpose first and foremost was to kill others. Contrary to Orientalist stereotype, they tended to be well educated rather than "crazed and unstable individuals." They possessed strong group identification—with Al Qaeda or Hizballah, for example—and a determination to strike out against Israel, the United States, or the new occupation government of Iraq, for which they anticipated being rewarded in the next life.[45]

Angry that evildoers impeded the nation's providential destiny to shepherd the Middle East, the United States unleashed a campaign of torture and detention that showed abject contempt for international law. Leaks of information and photographs led to investigations that unveiled the existence of detention camps as well as the outsourcing of detainees and torture to allied authoritarian regimes. U.S. torture techniques included blindfolding, hooding, roping, beating, prolonged squatting and arm lifting, stripping, starving, near drowning, isolating, humiliating, simulating sex, sodomizing, sleep depriving, loud music playing, and threatening with menstrual blood, attack dogs, and even a lion. While the Abu Ghraib prison in Iraq became infamous, the torture campaign found its "genesis not in Iraq but in interrogation rooms in Afghanistan and Guantánamo Bay, Cuba."

In the frenzied post-9/11 climate, with the righteous nation in search of enemies to destroy, the United States dismissed the Geneva Conventions and other international conventions governing detention and precluding torture. A military intelligence email summed up the no-holds-barred approach, declaring, "The gloves are coming off, gentlemen, regarding these detainees." Under the U.S. occupation, the prisoners lodged and tortured at Abu Ghraib, Guantánamo, and secret detention camps in Egypt, as "enemy combatants," had no rights under either U.S. or international law; the United States arrogated to itself the right to detain and torture prisoners at will under an ad hoc legal rendering of its own creation.[46]

The torture campaign accelerated as the Iraqi insurgents belied Bush's proclamation in May 2003 that major combat operations had ended. When the Abu Ghraib prison photographs of U.S. servicemen and women humiliating naked, hog-tied prisoners were leaked, an investigation ensued, and members of Congress privately screened some "1,800 grotesque images of sex, humiliation, and torture." Bush condemned the "disgraceful conduct by a few American troops, who dishonored our country," thus establishing a frame that placed sole responsibility on lower-ranking military personnel.

While the nation denounced torture as un-American, the United States had in fact engaged in torture in the past, though never so brazenly or on as broad a scale. The United States had long been outsourcing torture, for example, by training Latin American gendarmes at the notorious School of the Americas. In any case, torture was a "self-defeating tactic," as most of the detainees possessed no "actionable intelligence," and indeed most "had been arrested by mistake," according to the International Committee of the Red Cross. Moreover, torture is a notoriously ineffective means of achieving its ostensible purpose, gathering actionable intelligence, as most people will say anything to get it to stop. Thus the detention camps and tortures became "perfect symbols of the subjugation and degradation that the American occupiers have inflicted on Iraq and the rest of the Arab world," Mark Danner notes.[47]

By 2006—fifteen years after the first George Bush celebrated victory in Desert Storm—Operation Iraqi Freedom, like the Indochina War, had become another "quagmire."[48] But the Vietnam usable past, which had been reframed into a lesson blaming the media and the antiwar movement for the nation's failure in Indochina, disciplined the cultural response to the Iraq War. The call to "support our troops," conjoined with an "epidemic of flags" and the profusion of yellow ribbons, produced a hegemonic symbolic landscape in which criticism of the war could be interpreted as the proverbial stab in the back. The discursive regime all but precluded suggestions that supporting our troops might be accomplished best through withdrawal from the Iraqi deathtrap of roadside bombs or by strengthening veterans' benefits or launching a preemptive campaign against the epidemic of sexual assault in the nation's military academies.

With the advent of an all-volunteer armed force substantially comprised of disadvantaged and minority youth, the middle and upper classes could avoid fighting for our freedoms. In this regard much had changed since Vietnam: the draft no longer existed as a potential threat to all races and classes. The armed forces instead became a magnet for those who lacked economic opportunity or sought funding for the college education they could not afford or responded to the ubiquitous, slickly produced television commercials equating military service with the achievement of a higher manhood.

Militarizing Earth and Space

In the wake of 9/11, the renewal of enemy-othering and war destroyed any "threat" of the nation reaping a peace dividend after the end of the Cold War. The invasion of Iraq, followed by the declaration of the global war on terror, revivified military Keynesianism—the only big government compatible with Myth of America identity. Military spending, as high as 70 percent during the Korean War and revved up again in the 1960s, had fallen to roughly 20 percent of federal spending on the eve of the September 11 attacks. By 2006, however, Bush signed into law an unprecedented $523 billion "defense" budget. As a result of classification and other forms of government secrecy, no one could say how much was being spent on the war in Iraq or the global war on terror, though the total had exceeded $200 billion by the end of 2006.

Even before 9/11, during the relative lull of the 1990s, domestic militarization had never really abated, as reflected in continuing taxpayer support for the fantasy of missile defense. "Ballistic missile defense continued to absorb billions of dollars every year in spite of the end of the Cold War and the failure to produce a workable system," Alex Roland notes. "It was the 1990s version of the B-1 bomber."[49] As the Defense Department invoked the usable past, declaring that ballistic defense was needed to head off "a space Pearl Harbor," Congress authorized accelerated funding for the program. Even as such hyperbole justified pouring billions into so-called strategic defense, nineteen men armed with nothing more than box cutters brought down the twin towers and smashed into the Pentagon. Despite the failed war in Iraq, the United States never wavered in its determination to maintain global military supremacy, or "full-spectrum dominance," including satellite targeting and high-tech weaponry. Thus in October 2006 Bush signed a new National Space Policy, rejecting in advance any future arms control accords that might limit U.S. flexibility to place weapons in space.

In recent years, the United States, which has manufactured and deployed more nuclear weapons than the rest of world combined, resolutely opposed international efforts "to regulate nuclear-testing, biological and chemical weapons, small arms trading, land mines, and environmental treaties," although such measures were the fruits of "decades of diplomacy" among nations. U.S. militarism dwarfed all global competitors even as it spurred the overall militarization of the planet. The $523 billion defense budget amounted to more than two and a half times the military spending of all the NATO allies. The United

States dominated global arms trafficking, as it carried out just under half of all the world's arms deals.

Myth of America universalism sanctions unfettered militarization as the nation arms the planet, equips and trains police state regimes antithetical to social reform, maintains more than half a million troops in more than seven hundred large and small bases and military installations throughout the world, and opposes international accord on a range of critical issues, from the global environment to human rights adjudication.[50] Despite the nation's rampant militarism, cultural representation blamed 9/11 on a lack of military preparedness, thus eliding the root cause of the assaults, the nation's pathologically interventionist foreign policy. "The country simply was not on a war footing," Condoleezza Rice explained in April 2004, a comment underscoring the identity-driven quest for the nation *always* to be on a "war footing."[51]

The 9/11 Commission's report deemphasized blowback, keeping intact the discursive regime of evil terrorist fanaticism and American innocence. As an FBI agent interviewed by the commission pointed out, however, the hijackers were not irrational, not all were even devout Muslims, but rather, "They feel a sense of outrage against the United States. They identify with the Palestinian problem, they identify with people who oppose repressive regimes." Jihadists and their supporters thus backed bin Laden for his *political* resistance to the United States rather than for his *religious* fanaticism. Even the head of the CIA team that tried but, as of summer 2007, had failed to hunt down bin Laden acknowledged that the U.S. invasion had "validated so much of what [bin Laden] has said and told Muslims: that the Americans want Arab oil; that the Americans will destroy any Muslim regime that appears to be powerful"; and "invade any Muslim country if it suits their interests." Jihadists rallied around the Afghan and Iraqi resistance while Syria and Iran reaped the benefits of opposing the United States. In 2006 a National Intelligence Estimate acknowledged that Iraq had become the "cause célèbre for radical jihadists," who were increasing in both number and geographical dispersion.[52]

Nevertheless, the cultural lesson of 9/11 was to unleash the military and the intelligence agencies—a perspective ignoring the fact that it was the very unleashing of the CIA against Iran in 1953 and in behalf of the *mujahedin* in Afghanistan in the 1980s that had ignited opposition in the first place. Massive funding flowed to the MIC and NSS and Homeland Security as the nation tightened government secrecy, bolstered countersubversive intrusions such as data mining, and began to carry out a four- to five-year buildup to put the country on a perpetual war footing. The open-ended global war on terror thus spurred sharp increases in defense spending, empowered a newly reorganized and metastasizing homeland security bureaucracy, and simultaneously ensured that funding would be unavailable for such domestic initiatives as education, health care reform, energy policy, environmental controls, or corporate regulation. Wartime expenditures, combined with sweeping tax cuts, especially for wealthy elites, created a massive budget deficit, which served to justify more cuts in domestic spending.

Myth of America identity thus strengthened the hegemony of the warfare state while preempting reform efforts. The connection between war and corporate profits—well established since the Great War and the subject of the Nye Committee investigation—became especially transparent during the war on terror. Access to oil reserves allowed for future profits for multinational oil companies while at the same time fending off the long-deferred call for a viable federal energy policy. Any such policy would have to encourage alternative sources of energy, which would in turn curb oil profits that reached all-time highs as gasoline pump prices exceeded three dollars a gallon in 2007 even as oil companies received billions of dollars in tax breaks. It is not surprising, then, as Michael Klare notes, that it was often difficult "to distinguish U.S. military operations designed to fight terrorism from those designed to protect energy assets." Moreover, by fighting a global war on terror, the nation ensured that corporate suppliers of military provisions, hardware, and infrastructure profited handsomely from the conflict.[53]

Although corporate hegemony and elite profiteering comprised a critical element of national identity, they were not, as many suspect, the tail that wagged the dog. Americans did not rally for war behind the oil companies or corporate profits but rather behind the flag and the broadly internalized notion that "America" had the prerogative, indeed the mission, to lead the world. Myth of America identity, not conspiracies hatched in corporate boardrooms, drove the consent for war as well as for the ongoing occupation.

Militant national identity continued to have profound social consequences. The percentage of total U.S. household income held by the top 1 percent of the population doubled from 1980 to 1999, as the United States opened the widest gap in the world between rich and poor. Overall, this top 1 percent, reenriched by ongoing tax cuts, controlled a third of the nation's wealth; the top 10 percent controlled nearly 70 percent of the wealth. According to data compiled by the

Federal Reserve, a mere 715 families owned 70 percent of bonds, 51 percent of stocks, and 62 percent of all business assets. The share of net worth of the bottom 50 percent of the population—half the people in the country—fell from 2.8 percent in 2001, the year the war began, to 2.5 per cent in 2004. Kevin Phillips, who accurately forecast the "coming Republican majority" in 1969, now cites the campaign of "wealth dynastization" as reflecting the "perilous state of the American political system."[54]

While cultural hegemony enabled economic royalists to flourish, in 2005 the howling winds of Hurricane Katrina left New Orleans in a pile of debris. The nation's failure to respond effectively to the disaster betrayed a seeming inability even to fathom the very concept of a domestic crisis. The hurricane hit the poor hardest—many died because they lacked the transportation to flee the inner city—and highlighted the continuing marginalization of millions of African Americans despite the rise of the black middle class. More than half of African American children still grow up in poverty, while public education became "the shame of the nation," as Jonathan Kozol put it, through "the restoration of apartheid schooling in America." More African American men enter the criminal justice system than college, fueling the nation's astonishingly burgeoning "prison industrial system." The United States now counts more than two million citizens in prison—more than half of them nonwhite—six times the number imprisoned in 1970. The United States thus accounts for 25 percent of the world's total prison population even as it condemns other nations for being "police states." [55]

Under U.S. supervision as the world's sole remaining superpower, poverty and disease gained ground in the world as well as at home. In 2005 a UN study found that 40 percent of the world's population lived on less than two dollars a day. The United States, however, opposed a UN special fund for economic development because aid would flow from governmental rather than private sources, and the program also threatened U.S. unilateral authority over international aid programs. Genuine international authority directly threatened Myth of America universalism and thus had to be opposed. "There can be no universally valid tenets and practices of international law so long as the U.S. carries out its relentless pursuit of global domination," Carl Boggs notes.[56]

The militant unilateralism displayed by the United States around the world alienated growing masses of people. In 2006 "in-depth polling" showed "increasing numbers of people around the world" resented the United States and judged its people "greedy, violent, and rude." Emerging as the world's actual "rogue nation," the United States threatened to usher in "the anti-American century."[57]

In the continuous pattern of U.S. history, the psychic drive for reaffirmation of national identity had led the nation into what it hoped would be another splendid little war. Yet when the war dragged on, as in Korea and Indochina, the public turned against it, purged itself of all responsibility, and blamed the administration in power. By 2006 Bush's approval ratings had plummeted to all-time lows, and the Republicans suffered an electoral defeat, losing both the House and the Senate in the midterm elections.

Public consent for the war waned because of the failure to attain victory, not because consent had mobilized against the destructiveness or "immorality" of the nation's identity-driven foreign policy. Even as Americans began to turn against the Iraq War, broad consent persisted behind the "realist" argument that the nation could not simply withdraw. Astonishingly, foreign policy experts, media pundits, and politicians of both parties could aver with a straight face that the Middle East might dissolve into instability without the U.S. presence. Insisting that more U.S. troops could solve the problem, Bush dispatched a "surge" of some twenty thousand additional troops in early 2007. As in Indochina, so in Iraq the United States thus stayed the course of nation building in order to preserve its vaunted credibility. Even as U.S. casualties mounted and Iraq catapulted into civil war, the support-our-troops discursive regime, the renascent MIC/NSS, and manly vows that "these colors don't run" bolstered the failed intervention. Meanwhile, private Pentagon contractors erected a new $592-million state of the art embassy in the heart of Baghdad to anchor an occupation whose end was nowhere in sight.

The September 11 assaults—like King Philip's War, Manifest Destiny, Little Big Horn, and Pearl Harbor—ignited a renewal of warfare that functioned to assuage psychic crisis, reaffirm national identity, and reassert cultural hegemony. The response to the September 11 attacks thus had set in motion powerful machinery that would not grind to an overnight halt. Having submerged the legacy of Vietnam and reinvigorated militant national identity, the United States was back at it again—nation building, succoring vicious regimes, bombing, shelling, contaminating, torturing and killing hundreds of thousands of innocents, and destroying enemy-others—not to save them but to affirm itself.

Toward a New Hegemony

"The spirit of nationalism has never ceased to bend human institutions
to the service of dissension and distress . . . It is altogether the most sinister
as well as the most imbecile of all those institutional encumbrances
that have come down out of the old order."
—THORSTEIN VEBLEN

A lthough obscured by a thick cloud of patriotic representation, violent aggression inheres in national identity. The continuous pattern of warfare and intervention analyzed in this book, from Euro-American "settlement" to the "global war on terror," flows from an identity rooted in nationalist modernity conjoined with psychic crisis. Identity-driven foreign policy perpetuates enemy-othering reinforced by discourses of race, gender, and religion.

Foreign policy facilitates domestic cultural hegemony through continuous campaigns of external violence. War affirms Myth of America identity, thus maintaining a critical mass of spontaneous consent, while diverting resources into militarization, national security or homeland security and thus away from domestic reform and cooperative internationalism. The overdetermined character of the U.S. imagined community prioritizes American Century unilateralism rather than multilateral cooperation.

The point of emphasizing the constructed nature of national identity and foreign policy is to deconstruct the knowledge. Such analysis illuminates the ways in which knowledge and power are established, affirmed, disciplined, and policed against counterhegemonic challenges. Cultural analysis connects domestic identity and foreign policy, which too often are treated as being discrete rather than mutually dependent.

Postmodern analysis liberates the historian to assume a more meaningful role in public discussion of national identity and foreign policy by transcending a self-denying empiricism. The past will be shaped and made usable within the culture; the issue is whether the historian chooses to enter into the discussion. None of this implies devolution of the discipline into an anarchistic relativism, or the sudden irrelevance of documentary evidence, or contempt for extant historiography (upon which this study has been wholly dependent).

Understanding derives not only from gleaning new knowledge, but also from unpacking and dispensing with some of the old. "Truths" must be interrogated and often delegitimated. I argue that the Myth of America and the pathologically violent foreign policy it inspires cannot remain unchallenged. The costs are too high, the consequences too great, both at home and abroad, to remain acquiescent. The hope is that broader public understanding of the constructedness of Myth of America identity can begin the process of trying to change it. Culture is organic, and societies are therefore susceptible to change, as the histories of Germany, Japan, South Africa, the Soviet Union, and many other nations and civilizations demonstrate.

Before people can demand meaningful change in national foreign policy they must first take responsibility for it. The construction of identity and its attendant cultural hegemony depends on the spontaneous consent of the governed. This book suggests that Americans do not merely acquiesce in external violence but often glory in it—at least until things go badly. Wealthy elites, opportunistic corporations, the military-industrial complex, and the national security state constantly affirm and reinforce global intervention, to be sure, but "we the people" also must assume responsibility for the nation's egregious diplomacy. Only when a sufficient number of citizens prove willing to join those on the margins in opposition to identity-driven foreign policy aggression can anything be done about it. The people, like the historians, need to become part of the solution rather than the problem.

Perhaps there is hope in the elusive phenomenon of postmodernity. When we speak of the postmodern—not as a methodology of scholarly analysis but in its temporal meaning, as a condition of life today—the discussion centers on the stage of human development after modernity. If nationalism, Machiavellian realism, neoliberalism, and rigid classifications of race, gender, and religion—the essences of modernity that inhibit global community—are to pass from the scene, what will replace them? If global economic integration, the information revolution, the gathering storm of climate change, the collective need for disease control, energy and resource management, preservation of animal species, the problems of genocide, borders, immigrants, refugees and, yes, terrorism are to be managed, then postmodern, multilateral solutions must be found.

With Marxism discredited and with triumphant neoliberalism fostering corporate plunder, perpetual warfare, and degradation of the planet, what is required is "the establishment of a new hegemony." As Ernesto Laclau and Chantal Mouffe argue, "Our central problem is to identify the discursive conditions for the emergence of a collective action, directed towards struggling against inequalities and challenging relations of subordination."[1] A new postmodern hegemony must renounce virulent nationalism in deference to genuine global community dedicated to basic human rights, including economic rights.

Unless and until a new hegemony can be achieved, one that combines domestic reform with peace internationalism, the United States is unlikely to lead the world in the direction it must go. The nation's pathological militancy and hostility to multilateral diplomacy—as reflected in rejection of the Kyoto Treaty on climate change, contempt for international jurisprudence, as well as its leadership in military spending and arms trafficking, including cultivation of massive stocks of WMD—pose more obstacles than the promise of solutions.

Hope lies in the understanding that as identity is rooted in representation, if we can change the discourse we can change our reality, or at least nudge it in more positive directions. "We have no alternative," John Gillis avers, "but to construct new memories as well as new identities better suited to the complexities of a post-national era."[2] The stakes being what they are, we must begin by acknowledging that U.S. foreign policy is a lethal, pathological force emanating from a self-serving national mythology, and we ought to seek to change it in ways that would serve to make the world a safer and more humane place in which to live, and even to live as one species among many, and not the chosen one at that. To the extent that we can, we must unpack the "myth to power" and replace it with an alternative hegemony that will enable us to transcend the na-

tion's congenital and pathological aggression against enemy-others in deference to genuine efforts at global community.

   While a deep gulf lies between a genuinely cooperative internationalism
and the militant identity inherent in the Myth of America, dramatic change is,
after all, the stuff of history.

Appendix A

Discourse and Disciplinary Knowledge

Discourse may be defined as language or text governed by conventions and built-in assumptions of which the user may be unaware yet internalizes all the same. Discourse, Hayden White explains, is "intended to *constitute* the ground whereon to decide *what shall count as a fact* in the matter under consideration and to determine *what mode of comprehension* is best suited to understanding of the facts thus constituted." Put another way by Robert J. C. Young, "Discourse is language that has already made history." Discourse establishes who "has the right—institutional, legal, professional—to command the language, construct the knowledge."[1]

The "linguistic turn" in the study of the humanities centers on analysis that seeks to unpack or deconstruct discourse. Language frees human beings to communicate but at the same time imprisons them in a vast world of signification. Language *signifies* meaning but words and phrases can only *represent* reality. The dictionary, for example, is merely a collection of signs, one or more words signifying other words.

Control of the discourse, defining the terms of discussion, thus plays a decisive role in the exercise of power. "Practices of representation create meanings and identities and thereby create the very possibility for agency," Roxanne L. Doty explains.[2] Words, phrases, and texts cannot be taken at face value but rather must be unpacked, deconstructed, or interrogated to determine their meaning and purpose within the context in which they are employed.

Tropes (from the Latin *tropus,* or metaphor) generate figures of speech or thought and thus constitute "the soul of discourse." Tropes may be defined as "such major figures of speech as metaphor, simile, metonymy, hyperbole, irony, and synecdoche," which convey meaning. Language and symbols produce subjective knowledge that is often received, however, as the objective truth. Ultimately, as Robert Berkhofer notes, by analyzing discourse, tropes, and the way language works, "deconstructionist critics expose authors' attempts to naturalize, essentialize, or universalize the categories they employ as foundational to their texts."[3] Language tells stories, offers representations, and conveys meaning so powerfully that history, like politics, literature, and poetics, cannot be understood apart from analysis of the discourse.

In his pathbreaking studies of such diverse subjects as madness, sexuality, and criminal justice, the French theorist Michel Foucault illuminated the essential subjectivity of truth as conveyed through regimes of discourse in modern society. With the emergence of modernity, the new "order of things" depended on masses of people absorbing and conforming to dominant conceptions of what purported to be true. Foucault showed that power was not simply a matter of force or overt domination; rather, "power produces knowledge" and "power and knowledge directly imply one another." Foucault illustrated his argument by quoting the anticolonialist French journalist Jean-Jacques Servan, who observed, "A stupid despot may constrain his slaves with iron chains; but a true politician binds them even more strongly by the chain of their own ideas. . . . This link is all the stronger in that we do not know of what it is made and we believe it to be our own work."

Truth and power flow from the production of disciplinary knowledge—information that erects conceptual boundaries, or knowledge that disciplines the way things are perceived. Under modernity, power and truth emerged through processes of ordering, classifying, and codifying of a "rational" and "scientific" "archaeology of knowledge." This process played out within institutions and bureaucracies and within the mind and body of the individual as well. The emphasis on individual freedom and natural rights that emerged from the Age of Reason obscured the extent to which individuals internalized discursive regimes and thus disciplined themselves through culturally transmitted knowledge, the truths they absorbed. "The 'Enlightenment,' which discovered the liberties, also invented the disciplines," Foucault explained.

Unlike traditional historians, who view their methodology as a path to uncover truth in history, Foucault rejected empiricism as illegitimate and self-denying. After all, if truth was culturally constructed, then history should not aspire to recapture objective truths that never existed in the first place. Rather than limiting their analysis in deference to the chimera of objectivity, historians should embrace a "will to knowledge" that would empower them to confront head-on the "illusions by which humanity protects itself, a position that encourages the dangers of research and delights in disturbing discoveries." History thus could function as "a curative science."[4]

Friedrich Nietzsche powerfully influenced Foucault and indeed laid the foundations of postmodern thought. Few intellectuals have been caricatured as often as Nietzsche, in no small part because he condemned the Christian "genealogy of morals" for undermining humanity's ability to exercise its "will to power." A relatively recent outpouring of "new Nietzsche" studies places the German philosopher at the forefront of the European intellectual tradition, including insight into the discipline of history.[5]

In a searing critique of historical empiricism, Nietzsche condemned the "eunuchs of history" as "tired and indifferent beings who dress up in the part of wisdom and adopt an objective point of view." Drawing directly on Nietzsche's insight, Foucault indicted the traditional historian for feeling "forced to silence his preferences and overcome his distaste, to blur his own perspective and replace it with the fiction of a universal geometry, to mimic death in order to enter the kingdom of the dead, to adopt a faceless anonymity."[6]

Both Nietzsche and Foucault demonstrate how historical analysis can reveal the point at which a particular discourse emerges, coalesces, and establishes regimes of truth and power. Thus the challenge is to analyze the past in order to identify the dominant discourse(s); to determine when and how a certain discourse becomes dominant; and perhaps most significant, to identify whom the discourse empowers and whom it disciplines and confines to the margins.

Postcolonial Analysis

Postcolonial and subaltern studies analyze discursive regimes of racial classification, categorization, and resistance, primarily in Asia, Africa, and Latin America (see chapter 8). These studies flesh out the process by which modernized Western nations constructed their own identities through disparagement and subjugation of discursively identified others in the non-Western world. Pioneering studies by Raymond Williams, Frantz Fanon, Edward Said, Gayatri Spivak, and others illuminate the impact of race, culture, and imperialism. Said, for example, posited that disparaging stereotypes of the inferior other, which he labeled Orientalism, permeated Western discourse pertaining to Asia and especially the Arab world. Subsequent scholars qualified Said's analysis by emphasizing hybridity and post-Orientalism, as they focused on the ways in which non-Western nations responded and adjusted to the impact of modernity, including racial modernity, but also the ways in which these peoples left their mark on Western identities.[7]

The cultural production of Orientalism has spurred imperialism, colonialism, geographical violence, and economic regimentation throughout the modern era. The scripting of Africa, for example—or imperial China, India, or Indochina—as backward and disordered drove Western intervention under such tropes as *mission civilatrice* or carrying out "the white man's burden." Similarly, the United States, under the discursive regime of the Monroe Doctrine, carried out a continuous history of hegemonic intervention in Latin America and the Caribbean. Myth of America identity justified invasion and annexation of the Philippines in 1898 under such racial tropes such as "benevolent assimilation" of "our little brown brothers." In more recent times, identity-driven discursive regimes such as the "Cold War" and the "global war on terror" have anchored U.S. militant intervention.

Cultural studies and postmodernist theory find their roots, to one degree or another, in the germinal scholarship analyzed above. While sometimes neglecting Nietzsche's foundational work, scholars note that Foucault and Antonio Gramsci (see appendix B) "account for much of the most productive work on concrete analysis" in cultural studies. These works demonstrate that power flows from the social production of knowledge, its dispersal, ubiquity, and hegemony within a particular culture.[8]

Appendix B

Gramscian Cultural Hegemony

The Italian Marxist Antonio Gramsci, described by one scholar as "the most original Marxist thinker" after World War I, pioneered the study of cultural hegemony.[1] In the Gramscian context, *hegemony* does not refer to mere economic domination, though the term is often deployed in that fashion. Gramsci transcended the conventional Marxist-Leninist preoccupation with historical materialism by focusing on the superstructure, which many orthodox Marxists had long dismissed as merely a by-product of the material conditions, or base, of capitalist society. Gramsci did not doubt that a capitalist ruling class dominated social relations, but he placed more emphasis than any other thinker on linkages between elite hegemony and "national-popular will." Ultimately Gramsci offered a "theory of institutionalized culture in a Marxist form."[2]

In the "Prison Notebooks," which he scrawled while languishing from 1926 until his death in 1937 in one of Benito Mussolini's prisons, Gramsci analyzed the critical role of "spontaneous consent." The function of hegemony was to attain "total social authority" through both coercion and consent, thus enabling not just economic but also political, civil, intellectual, and moral authority. Gramsci theorized that, in addition to the state and traditional intellectuals, "organic" intellectuals—elites without the status of formal intellectuals—played a critical role in forging and reinforcing cultural hegemony. Yet at the same time, in trying to understand why the liberationist promise of Marxism had not taken hold, Gramsci concluded that the bourgeoisie and even the working class also consented, albeit often unwittingly, to their disempowerment. Gramsci perceived, as David McLellan put it, that "the State was only an outer ditch, behind which there stood a powerful system of fortresses and earth works."[3]

Gramsci's emphasis on spontaneous consent opened new avenues for inquiry and understanding, particularly in a "free" society such as the United States in which sovereignty putatively rests with the people. While focus on the people would seem to mesh nicely with the agenda of social history, the tendency has been to apotheosize the masses as opposed to exploring their unwitting complicity in cultural hegemony. As long as spontaneous consent could be mobilized, society might function on the basis of "hegemony protected by the armor of coercion."[4]

As class divisions and labor exploitation for profit inhered in capitalism, Gramscian cultural hegemony sought to explain the various means by which ruling elites retain power while warding off revolutionary upheaval. Represented as a classless society offering equal opportunity to all, the United States offered fertile ground for nurturing cultural hegemony and thus for scholars to use Gramscian analysis to better understand the nation's history. "Handled with care," T. J. Jackson Lears argues, "the concept of hegemony offers the best way to understand the role of culture in sustaining inequalities of wealth and power."[5]

The theorists Ernesto Laclau and Chantal Mouffe argue that hegemony encompasses "a whole conception of the social" that ultimately produces the "interiority of a closed paradigm." As societies operate on the basis of culturally constructed hegemony, an alternative hegemony must emerge in order to change a given society. Accordingly, Laclau and Mouffe call for "the establishment of a new hegemony" that would propel society "in the direction of a radical and plural democracy."[6]

Appendix C

Postmodernism

Postmodernity can be viewed as both as a condition of life today (after the passing of modernity) and as a methodology for interrogating history. If we think of modernity as a long period of discovering, mapping, classifying, and homogenizing the world, with the attendant spread of liberalism (inclusive of capitalist globalization) and nationalism, much of that project can be viewed as completed. Postmodernity, however, can be viewed as still emergent and very much subject to theorization.

Postmodern *methodology,* as opposed to postmodern temporality, seeks to "make strange that which is familiar," to call into question foundational knowledge, to interrogate what is represented as truth, to emphasize culture, language, and identity. This mode of analysis, as Friedrich Nietzsche pointed out, stands René Descartes on his head. Cultural analysis suggests that rather than the independence of thought implied by "I think, therefore I am," people think the way they do because they are the subjects of representations, discursive regimes, and ultimately culture and identity.

Postmodernism entails what J. F. Lyotard termed "incredulity toward metanarratives." Two dominant metanarratives—deterministic stories that purport to explain the unfolding of history—emerged: an Enlightenment-fostered bourgeois narrative perceiving history as the steady march of liberal progress; and a Marxist teleology of history as moving inexorably toward eventual communist liberation. Relatively few scholars still defend these two metanarratives. Most historians do, however, defend empiricism and perceive history as a search for truth. Yet by clinging to empiricism, Keith Jenkins notes, "orthodox discourse still advocates working practices now seen, in the light of the post-modern, as both extremely problematical and demonstrably ideological."[1]

As Jenkins, Dominick LaCapra, Hayden White, and many others have pointed out, historians (this may be especially true of diplomatic historians) privilege documentary evidence as a repository of truth. The myriad problems with the "fetish of archival research" include the failure to acknowledge that documents are themselves merely texts; that some facts invariably are privileged over others; the illusion that the past exists as a singular reality that can be recaptured; that "presentism" is not only impossible to avoid but may be desirable; and that it confines the historian to the narrow documentarist role of seeking to fill in gaps or cast new light on the historical record, rather than liberating the historian to ask a whole new series of questions and engage in critical thinking that empiricist historians condemn as unhistorical or polemical.

All histories are representations of the past, nothing more. History, like fiction, typically tells a story through the means of a grand narrative. History thus constitutes discourse and as such has far more in common with literature and is subject to literary theorization.[2]

Accepting history for what it is—discursive representation—does not delegitimate the discipline; rather, it expands the art of history into new realms of analysis. Demystification of history does destabilize "history as we know it," yet in so doing it liberates history to become more visible and meaningful in society. "The more prominent the book or article, the more likely the structure of interpretation substitutes for factuality," Robert Berkhofer points out.[3] Within the diplomatic history field, Berkhofer's point has been borne out by the remarkable staying power of William A. Williams's *The Tragedy of American Diplomacy,* certainly one of the more boldly interpretative works ever to enter the field.[4]

Appendix D

Identity and Lacanian Psychoanalytic Theory

The French psychoanalytic theorist Jacques Lacan called for a "return to Freud" in order to reexamine the role of the subconscious in shaping human desire. Lacanian analysis inspired Slavoj Žižek and the Slovenian school as well as theorists of hegemony and feminist theoreticians such as Luce Irigaray, who, after Lacan, could exploit the richness of psychoanalytic theory absent the baggage of Freud's Victorian gender mores.

Lacanian analysis offers penetrating insight into identity by emphasizing the incomplete nature of representation, which leaves a lack or void within the subject. Identity requires the existence of an other, meaning that rather than being an entity of its own, the individual or community ultimately must be the subject of forces *external* to itself. Representation of identity thus occurs within a world of signification but these signs cannot access "the Real." As the symbolic landscape, and not "reality," determines identity, representation ultimately fails. "Lacan's starting point," Žižek explains, "is, of course, that symbolic representation always distorts the subject, that it is always a displacement, a failure— that the subject cannot find a signifier which would be 'his own.'"[1]

Given the failure of representation, the subject experiences a psychic lack, which creates alienation, antagonism, or hysteria. The subject responds to this lack through desires, drives, fantasies, and a ceaseless quest for enjoyment (*jouissance*). Ultimately, as Žižek explains, "*Jouissance* does not exist, it is impossible, but it produces a number of traumatic effects."[2]

Applied within the context of U.S. foreign policy, the identification of the nation flows from the symbolic landscape of representational identity (the

Myth of America), which is culturally constructed and not real. Representation of "America" can never succeed—it cannot achieve closure—and moreover must always claim its identity as a subject by attaching itself to an other. As the United States exists only as an imagined community, it, like any nation or subject, must continually assert and affirm its existence through representation (rituals, discourse, symbolization).

I am arguing that foreign policy, and especially the choosing of war, reflects a virulent form, an overdetermination, of identity-affirming representation. Ultimately, violence against external enemy-others flows from the psychic crisis of representation, the alienation stemming from the inability to achieve the Real. If, as I argue, these drives occur continuously and in response to internal antagonisms, then they are pathological in nature.

Postmodernist and psychoanalytic methodologies offer the possibility of positive change, in effect, treatment for the anxiety-ridden subject, by exposing the constructed nature of social reality. By deconstructing what Lacan called "the realist's imbecility"—the notion that we live in reality as opposed to a world of signification—the subject can address the sources of psychic anxiety through understanding the genesis of these drives and the ultimate inability to access the Real, to achieve *jouissance*. "The whole point," Žižek explains, "is just that we come to experience how this negative, disruptive power menacing our identity is simultaneously a positive condition of it."[3] Deconstruction of what purports to be real is thus the necessary first step in the creation of a new postmodern social formation.

Notes

Introduction: The Myth of America

1. Associated Press, Nov. 29, 2005.

2. Williams, *Tragedy of American Diplomacy*; Beard, *The Open Door at Home*; Gaddis, "The Emerging Post-Revisionist Synthesis."

3. Kaplan and Pease, *Cultures of U.S. Imperialism*, 11.

4. McCormick, *America's Half-Century*; Wallerstein, *The Essential Wallerstein*; Hogan and Paterson, *Explaining the History of American Foreign Relations*.

5. The best discussion of the cultural turn as it pertains to diplomatic history appears in the introduction of Johnston, *Hegemony and Culture*.

6. Katznelson and Shefter, *Shaped by War and Trade*, 3; See also Campbell, *Writing Security*; Dunn, *Imagining the Congo* and Hopf, *Social Construction of International Politics*.

7. Geertz, *Interpretation of Cultures*, 412–53; Dirks, Eley, *Culture/Power/History*, 5–6.

8. Johnston, Hegemony and Culture, 21–26; Schwartz, "Explaining the Cultural Turn—or Detour?" 146; McMahon, "Contested Memory: Vietnam War and American Society," 184.

9. Novick, *That Noble Dream*; McCullough, *Truman*.

10. Hunt, *Ideology and U.S. Foreign Policy*, 14. Hunt's germinal book helped stake out culture as a legitimate realm for diplomatic history. However, his emphasis on an ideology of U.S. foreign policy is problematic. Foreign policy flows from cultural boundaries—discursive, representational, and ritualized—rather than from a consistent program of action normally associated with ideology. The best work on cultural identity and U.S. foreign policy is Campbell, *Writing Security*. Other significant studies include Engelhardt, *End of Victory Culture*; Ryan, *U.S. Foreign Policy in World History*; Renwick, *America's World Identity*; Stephanson, *Manifest Destiny*; and Lieven, *America Right or Wrong*. See also Fousek, *To Lead the Free World*, Tuveson, *Reedemer Nation*, Ninkovich, *Modernity and Power*, and Heiss, "Evolution of the Imperial Idea." For a sophisticated but ultimately unpersuasive condemnation of identity as a base for historical analysis, see Cooper, *Colonialism in Question*, 59–90.

11. Kaplan and Pease, *Cultures of U.S. Imperialism*, 17.

12. Weeks, "New Directions in Early American Foreign Relations." Stephanson, *Manifest Destiny*; Perkins, *Creation of a Republican Empire*.

13. Hall and du Gay, *Questions of Cultural Identity*, 1–5.

14. Historians, following the lead of foreign policy architects such as Walt W. Rostow, have ana-

lyzed *modernization* as a critical element of post–World War II foreign relations, but this approach obscures the much broader framework of *modernity* going back to the Enlightenment. The obsessive focus on the postwar era nurtures the assumption that the Cold War and global intervention flowed from the expansion of U.S. power after World War II. The rise of the United States as the preeminent world power critically influenced developments, of course, yet the preoccupation with the post-1945 period obscures the continuity of foreign policy flowing from modernity and a distinctly American identity. See Latham, *Modernization as Ideology;* Gilman, *Mandarins of the Future;* and Ninkovich, *Modernity and Power.*

15. Lewis and Wigen, *The Myth of Continents;* see also the essays in Eley and Suny, eds., *Becoming National.*

16. Eley and Suny, *Becoming National,* 3–37.

17. Young, *Postcolonialism,* 412.

18. Slater, *Geopolitics and the Post-colonial,* 82.

19. Eley and Suny, *Becoming National,* 106–07.

20. Hardt and Negri, *Empire,* 95.

21. Hobsbawm and Ranger, *Invention of Tradition;* Anderson, *Imagined Communities;* Eley and Suny, *Becoming National.*

22. Hartz, *Liberal Tradition in America.* "American exceptionalism" has become something of a reflexive cliché, often employed under the assumption that we know what it *means* and thus do not fully explore how the concept *works* within culture.

23. Campbell, *Writing Security,* 91.

24. Eley and Suny, *Becoming National,* 123.

25. Kammen, *Mystic Chords of Memory,* 3; see also Linenthal, *Sacred Ground.*

26. Gillis, ed., *Commemorations,* 5, 41–57.

27. Ibid., 41–60. The abortive *Enola Gay* exhibition, named for the World War II bomber that dropped the first atomic bomb, exemplifies the organic cultural response when heritage appears threatened. The exhibition was to be held at the Smithsonian Institution, the nation's preeminent museum of history and culture, on the fiftieth anniversary of the Hiroshima bombing in 1995. The *Enola Gay* exhibition planners sought to broaden understanding of the events that led to the unreflective decision to drop two atomic bombs on Japan. Among the topics addressed would have been the visceral U.S. racist attitudes toward "the Japs" during World War II as well as the possibility that the war could have been ended without the use of the new weapons of mass destruction. The *Enola Gay* exhibition proposed to grapple with the complexities of the Hiroshima bombing, but these plans gave way when confronted with the sweeping powers of hegemonic identity. Politicians and patriotic groups vehemently attacked the proposed exhibition as "revisionist history." A patriotic nationalist exhibition, a usable past glorifying the war against Japan, replaced the proposed analytic historical display. The Smithsonian curator lost his job, and the American Legion and flag-draped politicians effectively policed what they perceived as an assault on the nation's immemorial past. Subsequently, when controversy loomed over U.S. imperialism in a proposed centennial commemoration of the so-called Spanish-American War in 1998, the Postal Service cut off debate by issuing a "Remember the *Maine*" stamp. Such incidents bring into sharp relief hegemonic national identity, its relationship to foreign policy, and disciplinary control over challenges to patriotic consensus. See Linenthal and Engelhardt, *The History Wars.*

28. Slotkin, *The Fatal Environment,* 16; Dawley, *Changing the World,* 109; See also Gerster and Cords, *Myth America.*

29. Bercovitch, *The American Jeremiad,* xiv. Critics predictably denounced Bercovitch's Myth of America as "consensus history with a vengeance" and argued that New England might be considered *atypical* and hardly a reflection of some amorphous national cultural consensus. They pointed out, with no dearth of evidence, that the entrepreneurial spirit and visions of the good life of material prosperity and individual freedom animated the Euro-American settlers of the Chesapeake and Britain's southern colonies. The materialist critique has merit—clearly, southern planters and yeomen were not Puritan utopians—yet masses of them, too, embraced the metanarrative of di-

vinely sanctioned national greatness. While, indisputably, material considerations motivated people, including most especially the Puritans and Yankees themselves, over time a vast diversity of "Americans" collectively signed on to the imagined community of the United States, with its attendant and ritualized mythology. Hence I believe Bercovitch's paradigm endures as a major contribution to understanding of Euro-American history. See Harlan, "A People Blinded from Birth" and Bercovtich "Investigations of an Americanist."

30. Johnston, *Hegemony and Culture*, 47.

31. Bercovitch, *American Jeremiad*, 28, 62, 95; Bercovtich, "Investigations of an Americanist," 981, 984.

32. Heale, *McCarthy's Americans*, xii; Bodnar, *Bonds of Affection*, 6.

33. Hardt and Negri, *Empire*, 103.

34. Suny, *Becoming National*, 260; Enloe, *Bananas, Beaches and Bases;* Scott, *Gender and Politics of History.*

35. Kaplan and Pease, *Cultures of U.S. Imperialism*, 610; Pinker, *How the Mind Works*, 497; Jarvis, *The Male Body at War*, 8; Jeffords, *Remasculinization of America*, 182.

36. Johnson, *The Lavender Scare.*

37. Jacobs, *America's Miracle Man in Vietnam*, 17; see also Preston, "Bridging the Gap Between Sacred and Secular" and Zietsma, "Sin Has No History," 533.

38. Cherry, *God's New Israel*, 19; Weber, *Protestant Ethic and Spirit of Capitalism.*

39. Bercovitch, "Investigations of an Americanist," 978.

40. Cherry, *God's New Israel*, 7.

41. Hardt and Negri, *Multitude*, 17.

42. See note 27.

43. Hofstadter, *Paranoid Style in American Politics*, 180–81.

44. Gillis, *Commemorations* 10, 102.

45. Eley and Suny, *Becoming National*, 343.

46. Pinker, *How the Mind Works*, 50–51, 494–98; see also Pinker, *The Blank Slate.*

47. Nish, *Japanese Foreign Policy in Interwar Period*, 11.

48. Elkins, *Imperial Reckoning.*

Chapter 1. Birth of a Nation

1. Jennings, The *Invasion of America;* Cronon, *Changes in the Land.*

2. Mann, *1491*, 29.

3. Taylor, *American Colonies*, 44.

4. Mann, *1491*, 66, 60.

5. Campbell, *Writing Security*, 112.

6. Taylor, *American Colonies*, 135.

7. Richter, *Facing East*, 76.

8. Taylor, *American Colonies*, 197.

9. Madsen, *American Exceptionalism*, 54.

10. Lepore, *The Name of War*, 71–121.

11. Richter, *Facing East*, 105.

12. Lepore, *The Name of War*, 176, 182.

13. Norton, *In the Devil's Snare.*

14. Grenier, *The First Way of War*, 10–12.

15. Jennings, *The Invasion of America*, 53, 146–70.

16. Richter, *Facing East*, 128.

17. Engelhardt, *End of Victory Culture*, 23.

18. Kaplan, *Anarchy of Empire*, 511.

19. Pestana and Salinger, *Inequality in Early America*, 41.

20. Norton, *Founding Mothers and Fathers*, 359.

21. Davis, *Rise and Fall of Slavery in New World,* 6; "Report of the Brown University Steering Committee on Slavery and Justice," October 2006 (online).

22. Jordan, *White Over Black.*

23. Berlin, *Many Thousands Gone.*

24. Rappleye, *Brown Brothers, Slave Trade, and American Revolution.*

25. Pestana and Salinger, eds., *Inequality in Early America,* 203.

26. Taylor, *American Colonies,* 151.

27. Norton, *Founding Mothers,* 9.

28. Butler, *Becoming America,* 125.

29. Goldberg, *The Racial State,* 46–47.

30. Goldberg, *The Racial State,* 96; Butler, *Becoming America,* 88.

31. Kaplan and Pease, *Cultures of U.S. Imperialism,* 22.

32. Fox, *Jesus in America,* 115. 99; Bercovitch, *American Jeremiad,* 105.

33. Jennings, *Empire of Fortune;* Anderson, *Crucible of War.*

34. Grenier, *The First Way of War,* 144.

35. Anderson, *Imagined Communities.*

36. Phillips, *The Cousins' Wars.*

37. Eley and Suny, *Becoming National,* 19.

38. Norton, *Founding Mothers,* 404; Eley and Suny, *Becoming National: A Reader,* 106–30.

39. Bloch, *Visionary Republic,* 49–65.

40. Cherry, *God's New Israel,* 327; Weeks, "Foreign Relations in the Early Republic," 460.

41. Johnston, *Hegemony and Culture in Origins of First-Use,* 46.

42. Dull, *A Diplomatic History of the American Revolution.*

43. Lambeck, *Reader in the Anthropology of Religion,* 512–23.

44. Appleby, *Inheriting the Revolution,* 251.

45. Wiebe, *The Opening of American Society,* passim.

46. F. Marks, *Independence on Trial;* see also Katznelson and Shefter, *Shaped by War and Trade.*

47. Mintz, *Seeds of Empire,* 4, 183; Taylor, *The Divided Ground.*

48. Jennings, *The Creation of America,* 196.

49. Drinnon, *Facing West;* Takaki, *Iron Cages,* 63.

50. Ellis, *Founding Brothers,* 81–119.

51. Finkelman, *Slavery and the Founders,* 1–104; see also Alfred Blumrosen and Ruth Blumrosen, *Slave Nation.*

52. Takaki, *Iron Cages,* 4.

53. Wieneck, *An Imperfect God.*

54. Finkelman, *Slavery and the Founders,* 162.

55. Halliday, *Understanding Thomas Jefferson;* Gordon-Reed, *Thomas Jefferson and Sally Hemings.*

56. Wood, *Radicalism of the American Revolution;* Wood, "Slaves in the Family."

57. Maier, *American Scripture.*

Chapter 2. The White Man's Continent

1. Tucker and Hendrickson, *Empire of Liberty,* viii.

2. Fitzsimmons, "Tom Paine's New World Order," 577.

3. Kramer, *Lafayette in Two Worlds,* 200.

4. Perkins, *Cambridge History of American Foreign Relations,* 1:81–110.

5. Ibid., 113–18.

6. Wills, "*Negro President,*" 36.

7. Schueller, *U.S. Orientalisms,* 47; F. Marks, *Independence on Trial,* 48.

8. Schueller, *U.S. Orientalisms,* 3.

9. Paterson, *American Foreign Policy to 1900,* 64.

10. Allison, *Crescent Obscured*, 46.

11. Bailyn, *To Begin the World Anew*, 37–59.

12. Kennedy, *Mr. Jefferson's Lost Cause*, 17, 125; Wallace, *Jefferson and the Indians*, 337, 275.

13. Watt, *The Republic Reborn*, 266.

14. Ibid., 273.

15. Perkins, *Cambridge History of American Foreign Relations*, 1:3.

16. Watt, *The Republic Reborn*, 276; on the War of 1812, see also Stagg, *Mr. Madison's War.*

17. Watt, *The Republic Reborn*, 283–87.

18. Stokes and Conway, *The Market Revolution in America;* Sellers, *The Market Revolution.*

19. Waldstreicher, *In the Midst of Perpetual Fetes*, 296; Appleby, *Capitalism and a New Social Order*, 22.

20. Appleby, *Inheriting the Revolution*, 89.

21. Waldstreicher, *In the Midst of Perpetual Fetes*, 30; Cherry, *God's New Israel*, 63; Pestana and Salinger, *Inequality in Early America*, 272; Linenthal, *Sacred Ground*, 21–51.

22. Travers, *Celebrating the Fourth*, 110; Kammen, *Mystic Chords of Memory*, 66.

23. This and all subsequent Tocqueville quotations from Alexis deTocqueville, *Democracy in America*, passim.

24. Nelson, *National Manhood*, 40–41; Cott, *Bonds of Womanhood*, 97.

25. Stokes and Conway, eds., *The Market Revolution in America*, 63.

26. Morrison and Stewart, *Race and the Early Republic*, 5–26. See also Roediger, *Wages of Whiteness*, 133–66.

27. Nelson, *National Manhood*, 62.

28. Appleby, *Inheriting the Revolution*, 254.

29. Rorabaugh, *The Alcoholic Republic.*

30. Morrison and Stewart, eds., *Race and the Early Republic*, 119.

31. Ibid., 135–58.

32. Ignatiev, *How the Irish Became White;* Roediger, *Wages of Whiteness.*

33. Fox, *Jesus in America*, 116, 173.

34. Bloch, *Visionary Republic*, 230.

35. P. Marks, *In a Barren Land*, 44; for a vivid portrayal of trans-Appalachian white expansion and Indian resistance, see Faragher, *Daniel Boone;* see also Banner, *How the Indians Lost Their Land.*

36. Slotkin, *Fatal Environment*, 79; Drinnon, *Facing West*, 97, 99, 109, 179; P. Marks, *In a Barren Land*, 58.

37. P. Marks, *In a Barren Land*, 63; Morrison and Stewart, *Race and the Early Republic*, 235–36.

38. Kaplan and Pease, *Cultures of United States Imperialism*, 110–17.

39. Richter, *Facing East*, 236. Supreme Court Chief Justice John Marshall upheld the Cherokees' lawsuit against removal in *Worcester vs. Georgia* (1832), ruling that the Cherokee constituted "a distinct community, occupying its own territory." Jackson openly disdained and in effect unconstitutionally vetoed the decision, declaring his "sacred duty" to authorize white Georgians to nullify federal authority—to do, that is, precisely what he had told South Carolinians, in no uncertain terms, would be impermissible in response to Calhoun's threat to nullify the 1833 "tariff of abominations." Despite the decision against Jackson, Marshall had already established precedence for removal under the modernist "doctrine of discovery"" in the 1823 Johnson decision. As "fierce savages, whose occupation was war," Indians lacked a level of civilization sufficient to govern, Marshall explained, thus "to leave them in possession of their country was to leave the country a wilderness." Kaplan and Pease, *Cultures of U.S. Imperialism*, 110–17.

40. P. Marks, *In a Barren Land*, 41.

41. Scheckel, *Insistence of the Indian*, 90; DeLoria, *Playing Indian;* Schlesinger, *Age of Jackson;* Kutler, ed., *American Retrospectives*, 68.

42. Scheckel, *Insistence of the Indian*, 99–126.

43. Linenthal, *Sacred Ground*, 53–86; Anderson, *Conquest of Texas*, 3–17.

44. Horsman, *Race and Manifest Destiny;* Graebner, *Empire on the Pacific.*

45. Higham, *Strangers in the Land;* Behdad, *A Forgetful Nation,* 10.

46. Hietala, *Manifest Design.*

47. Perkins, *Cambridge History of American Foreign Relations,* 1:183; Pletcher, *The Diplomacy of Annexation;* Hietala, *Manifest Design,* 265; see also Weeks, *Building the Continental Empire;* Jones and Rakestraw, *Prologue to Manifest Destiny.*

48. Hietala, *Manifest Design,* 208–10, 270–71.

49. Stephanson, *Manifest Destiny,* 57; Madsen, *American Exceptionalism,* 105.

50. Foos, *Short, Offhand, Killing Affair,* 113–37; Cherry, *God's New Israel,* 113, 123.

51. Johannsen, *To the Halls of the Montezumas,* 297, 49, 290.

52. Ibid., 10.

53. Greenberg, *Manifest Manhood,* 118; Takaki, *Iron Cages,* 161; Johannsen, *To the Halls of the Montezumas,* 169–70.

54. Foos, *Short, Offhand, Killing Affair,* 116–23; Johannsen, *To the Halls of the Montezumas,* 133–34.

55. Greenberg, *Manifest Manhood,* 106.

56. Bloch, *Visionary Republic,* 162; Johannsen, *To the Halls of the Montezumas,* 51, 204.

57. Johannsen, *To the Halls of the Montezumas,* 53.

58. Paterson, *American Foreign Policy to 1900,* 120.

59. Johannsen, *To the Halls of the Montezumas,* 270–79.

60. Widmer, *Young America,* 16; Johnson, *Peace Progressives and American Foreign Relations,* 19.

61. Widmer, *Young America,* 55.

62. Haynes and Morris, eds., *Manifest Destiny and Antebellum Expansionism,* 154; Greenberg, *Manifest Manhood,* 106.

63. Widmer, *Young America,* 186–94.

64. Little, *American Orientalism,* 79.

65. Widmer, *Young America,* 196, 17; Hietala, *Manifest Design,* 267.

66. Widmer, *Young America,* 16–24, 185.

Chapter 3. Reunite and Conquer

1. Paterson, *American Foreign Relations,* 1:147.

2. Ignatiev, *How the Irish Became White,* 166.

3. McPherson and Cooper, Jr., *Writing the Civil War,* 250.

4. Fellman, Gordon, and Sutherland, *This Terrible War;* Nudelman, *John Brown's Body;* Wilson, *Patriotic Gore;* Horwitz, *Confederates in the Attic.*

5. Phillips, *Cousins' Wars,* 468.

6. Wills, *Lincoln at Gettysburg,*

7. Phillips, *Cousins' Wars,* 466–70.

8. Polanyi, *The Great Transformation,* 139.

9. Cohen, *Reconstruction of American Liberalism,* 5; Polanyi, *Great Transformation,* 202.

10. Menand, *The Metaphysical Club,* 301.

11. Summers, *The Gilded Age,* 122.

12. Behdad, *A Forgetful Nation,* 117; Jacobson, *Barbarian Virtues,* 59–97.

13. Takaki, *Iron Cages,* 217–20.

14. Weber, ed., *Foreigners in the Native Land,* 160.

15. Behdad, *A Forgetful Nation,* 136.

16. McPherson and Cooper, *Writing the Civing War,* 189.

17. Takaki, *Iron Cages,* 344.

18. Lears, *No Place of Grace,* 29; Lukas, *Big Trouble.*

19. Menand, *The Metaphysical Club,* 301.

20. McGerr, *A Fierce Discontent,* 119–22.

21. Foner, *Reconstruction,* 31, 602; *Reforging the White Republic,* 52.

22. McPherson and Cooper, Jr., *Writing the Civil War,* 154–73.

23. McCartney, *Power and Progress;* Fredrickson, *Black Image in the White Mind.*

24. Whites, *Civil War as Crisis in Gender;* McPherson and Cooper, Jr., *Writing the Civil War,* 229–31.

25. Blum, *Reforging the White Republic,* 10.

26. Lawson, *Patriot Fires,* 160–76.

27. Lawson, *Patriot Fires,* 205; Wills, *Under God,* 381, 129; Bodnar, ed., *Bonds of Affection,* 120–38.

28. Blum, *Reforging the White Republic,* 13, 96, 129, 89.

29. Kammen, *Mystic Chords of Memory,* 179, 121.

30. Linenthal, *Sacred Ground,* 87–126; Bodnar, *Bonds of Affection,* 102–19.

31. Eley and Suny, *Becoming National,* 274.

32. Kammen, *Mystic Chords of Memory;* Bodnar, ed., *Bonds of Affection,* 102–19.

33. Kammen, *Mystic Chords of Memory,* 179, 247; Fredrickson, *Black Image in the White Mind,* 305.

34. Runte, *National Parks.*

35. Ostler, *The Plains Sioux and U.S. Colonialism.* Fritz, *Movement for Indian Assimilation,* 83.

36. Slotkin, *The Fatal Environment,* 373–431.

37. Ibid., 473.

38. P. Marks, *In a Barren Land,* 172–243; Summers, *The Gilded Age,* 64.

39. Beisner, *From Old Diplomacy to New;* Paolino, *Foundations of American Empire;* Holbo, *Tarnished Expansion;* Love, *Race Over Empire.*

40. Blum, *Reforging the White Republic,* 214; Paterson, *American Foreign Policy,* 1:129.

41. Hannigan, *The New World Power,* 192.

42. Ibid., 144–45.

43. Ibid., 157, 160, 141.

44. Lears, *No Place of Grace,* 112.

45. Hoganson, *Fighting for American Manhood,* 160; Fox, *Jesus in America,* 304.

46. Hoganson, *Fighting for American Manhood,* 90–91.

47. Hofstadter, *Paranoid Style in American Politics,* 157; Hoganson, *Fighting for American Manhood,* 93, 105.

48. Perez, *War of 1898,* 23–56; Hannigan, *New World Power,* 25.

49. Hoganson, *Fighting for American Manhood,* 107.

50. Karnow, *In Our Image,* 75, 110–17.

51. Hofstadter, *The Paranoid Style,* 178.

52. Cherry, *God's New Israel,* 146–62.

53. Schoultz, *Beneath the United States,* 113, 143.

54. Blum, *Reforging the White Republic,* 231.

55. Lears, *No Place of Grace,* 130; Trask, *The War with Spain,* 291.

56. Blum, *Reforging the White Republic,* 228; Bouvier, *Whose America?* 130–37; Blight, *Race and Reunion.*

57. Hofstadter, *The Paranoid Style in American Politics,* 180–81.

Chapter 4. Imperial Crises

1. Hoganson, *Fighting for American Manhood,* 196, 184–85.

2. Bouvier, *Whose America?* 174.

3. Hoganson, *Fighting for American Manhood,* 134–37; Hofstadter, *Paranoid Style in American Politics,* 168.

4. Kramer, *Race, Empire, the U.S. and the Philippines,* 157, 89; Karnow, *In Our Image.*

5. Karnow, *In Our Image,* 191–92.

6. Kramer, *Race, Empire, the U.S. and the Philippines,* 90; Drinon, *Facing West,* 315; Blum, *Reforging the White Republic,* 238; Borstelmann, *Cold War and the Color Line,* 17.

7. Kramer, *Race, Empire, U.S. and the Philippines,* 87–158, 435.

8. Jones, *Crucible of Power,* 21.

9. Karnow, *In Our Image,* 167–95.

10. Hoganson, *Fighting for American Manhood,* 162–76; Welch, *Hoar and the Half-Breed Republicans.*

11. LaFeber, *Cambridge History of American Foreign Relations,* 2:180; Takaki, *Iron Cages,* 279; Drinnon, *Facing West,* 312–21.

12. Hoganson, *Fighting for American Manhood,* 187–89; Johnson, *Peace Progressives and American Foreign Relations,* 27–36.

13. Osorio, *Dismembering Lahui,* 3, 259.

14. Ryan and Pungong, *United States and Decolonization,* 34.

15. Iriye, *Pacific Estrangement.*

16. Perez, *The War of 1898,* 23.

17. Ibid., 81–125.

18. Bouvier, *Whose America?* 171–92; Perez, *Cuba and the United States,* 102–12; LaFeber, *Cambridge History of American Foreign Relations,* 2:152.

19. Schoultz, *Beneath the United States,* 125–29; Langley, *Banana Wars,* 27–45.

20. Kaplan, *The Anarchy of Empire,* 7; LaFebr, *Cambridge History of American Foreign Relations,* 2:154; Bouvier, ed., *Whose America?,* 161–71; see also Jacobson, *Barbarian Virtues.*

21. Beale, *Theodore Roosevelt and the Rise to World Power;* Eley, Ortner, *Culture/Power/History,* 200–221.

22. Langley, *United States and Caribbean,* 17–43; Rosenberg, *Financial Missionaries to the World,* 259.

23. Schoultz, *Beneath the United States,* 209–19.

24. Bederman, *Manliness and Civilization.*

25. Rydell, *All the World's a Fair,* 3–4.

26. Ibid., 8.

27. Kaplan and Pease, eds., *Cultures of U.S. Imperialism,* 165–66; Warren, *Buffalo Bill's America.*

28. Takaki, *Iron Cages* 213; Schafer, *The Art of Ragtime.*

29. Rydell, *All the World"s a Fair,* 128–48; Takaki, *Iron Cages,* 146.

30. Endy, "Travel and World Power"; Bederman, *Manliness and Civilization,* 218–39; Jacobson, *Barbarian Virtues,* 105–38.

31. Menand, *The Metaphysical Club.* Fear of radicalism spiked in the wake of McKinley's assassination in Buffalo in September 1901. See Rauchway, *Murdering McKinley.*

32. "America in the first decade of the twentieth century was a grand promenade for the rich," Kevin Phillips notes in *Wealth and Democracy,* 49. Jeremiads at the time included Henry George's *Progress and Poverty* (1879), Henry Demarest Lloyd's *Wealth Against Commonwealth* (1894), and Thorstein Veblen's *The Theory of the Leisure Class* (1899), all of which excoriated plutocracy. Veblen highlighted the "conspicuous consumption" of the rich as the number of millionaires, a word newly entered into lexicon, grew from some three hundred in 1860 to more than four thousand in 1892.

33. McGerr, *A Fierce Discontent,* 119.

34. Chatfield, *American Peace Movement,* 12–35; Herman, *Eleven Against War;* Kuehl, *Seeking World Order.*

35. Langley, *Banana Wars,* 72–74; Thompson, "Mexico in the American Imagination."

36. Langley, *Banana Wars,* 80–81; Westad, *Global Cold War,* 144.

37. Johnson, *Peace Progressives,* 46.

38. Had it not led to tragedy, the incident of April 1914, which transformed "a stupid mistake by an obscure Mexican official into something far more ominous," would be known primarily for its comic opera qualities. The mistake was the arrest and detention—for less than an hour—of a group of seamen who had come ashore in a whaleboat from the naval vessel *Dolphin,* which had anchored in the Mexican port to reassure U.S. residents of Tampico, many connected with oil companies.

Naval Rear Admiral Henry T. Mayo demanded a written apology, hoisting of the American flag in Tampico, and firing of a twenty-one-gun salute by Mexican troops. The Mexicans offered to take part in a joint martial salute but otherwise refused to carry out a U.S. nationalist ritual on their own soil, a rejection that Wilson interpreted as the latest in a series of "studied and planned exhibitions of ill-will and contempt for the American government on the part of Huerta." Besieged by Emilio Zapata's "rebels" in the south and Constitutionalists throughout the country, the Huerta regime already teetered on the brink of collapse. Langley, *Banana Wars*, 83–84.

39. Shoultz, *Beneath the United States*, 248–49.

40. Hannigan, *The New World Power*; Renda, *Taking Haiti*, 110.

41. Renda, *Taking Haiti*, 155–56, 163.

42. Gleijesus, *Shattered Hope*, 370.

43. Dawley, *Changing the World*, 55.

44. Gardner, *Safe for Democracy*.

45. *Cambridge History of American Foreign Relations*, 3:19–50; Zieger, *America's Great War*.

46. Adams, *The Great Adventure*, 114.

47. Chatfield, *The American Peace Movement* 32; Phillips, "Of Wilson and Men," 156, 122.

48. Adams, *The Great Adventure*, 84.

49. Allen, *The Lords of Creation*.

50. Cherry, *God's New Israel*, 268; Dawley, *Changing the World*, 145–46.

51. For an assessment of the "cosmopolitan patriotism" of American progressives, see Hansen, *Lost Promise of Patriotism*; Dawley, *Changing the World*, 68, 122, 136.

52. Finnegan, *Against the Specter of a Dragon*, 14–17; Dawley, *Changing the World*, 40, 156.

53. Kennedy, *Over Here*, 93–143.

54. Koistinen, *Planning War, Pursuing Peace*, 3–4.

55. Bodnar, *Bonds of Affection*, 139–59.

56. Zieger, *America's Great War*, 126–35.

57. McGerr, *A Fierce Discontent*, 288; Zieger, *America's Great War*, 78.

58. McGerr, *A Fierce Discontent*, 288–91.

59. Ibid.; Dawley, *Changing the World*, 137; 291; Steele, *Free Speech in the Good War*, 3.

60. Zieger, *America's Great War*, 197; Dawley, *Changing the World*, 266.

61. Dawley, *Changing the World*, 269.

62. Stone, *Perilous Times*, 223–24; Latham, *The Liberal Moment*, 90.

63. Dawley, *Changing the World*, 266.

64. Borstelmann, *Cold War and the Color Line*, 22–23.

65. Dawley, *Changing the World*, 158; Zieger, *America's Great War*, 137.

66. Dawley, *Changing the World*, 123; Hansen, *Lost Promise of Patriotism*, 185–90.

67. Ibid., 7, 67, 159–60; Hardt and Negri, *Multitude*, 3.

Chapter 5. Choosing War

1. Carroll and Herring, *Modern American Diplomacy*, 40.

2. MacLean, *Behind the Mask of Chivalry*.

3. Fox, *Jesus in America*.

4. Behdad, *A Forgetful Nation*, 193.

5. Schulzinger, *The Making of the Diplomatic Mind*; Schulzinger, *The Wise Men of Foreign Affairs*.

6. Cohen, *Empire Without Tears*.

7. Costigliola, *Awkward Dominion* 175–76, 263; Rosenberg, *Spreading the American Dream*.

8. Foglesong, *America's Secret War*; Schmitz, *Thank God They're on Our Side*, 14–15; Lynch, *Beyond Appeasement*; Schulzinger, *Making of the Diplomatic Mind*; Boyle, *American-Soviet Relations*, 1–16; Hixson, *George F. Kennan*, 6–7.

9. Johnson, *Peace Progressives and American Foreign Relations*, 34–104.

10. Smith, *Opposition Beyond the Water's Edge,* 11; Lynch, *Beyond Appeasement,* 36.

11. Lynch, *Beyond Appeasement,* 166, 135.

12. Ibid., 3–40.

13. Rosenberg, *Financial Missionaries to the World,* 252.

14. Cohen, *American Revisionists;* Doenecke and Wilz, *From Isolation to War;* Cole, *Roosevelt and the Isolationists.*

15. Koistinen, *Planning War, Pursuing Peace,* 254–55.

16. Cole, *Roosevelt and the Isolationists,* 265.

17. Schmitz, *Thank God They're on Our Side,* 44, 90, 98; Schmitz and Challener, *Appeasement in Europe,* 11.

18. Offner, *American Appeasement,* 102–03.

19. Alpert, *International History of Spanish Civil War.* Italy sent some 70,000 men, some 7,000 vehicles, and extensive weaponry and munitions to Spain. Germany supplied Franco with some 14,000 men, 840 aircraft, and 200 tanks. The USSR sent 800 planes, 482 tanks, armored cars, and extensive weaponry and munitions.

20. Schmitz and Challener, *Appeasement in Europe,* 45, 21.

21. Cole, *Roosevelt and the Isolationists,* 235–38; Dallek, *Roosevelt and American Foreign Policy,* 140–43.

22. Schmitz, *Thank God They're on Our Side,* 117; Offner, *Origins of the Second World War.*

23. Schmitz, *Thank God They're on Our Side,* 92.

24. Alpert, *International History of the Spanish Civil War.* 8.

25. Carley, *1939,* xix, xviii, 256, 258; Boyle, *American-Soviet Relations,* 34.

26. Cull, *Selling War,* 72, 3, 28, 7.

27. Briggs, *Reproducing Empire,* 10; Langley, *United States and the Caribbean,* 157–61.

28. Gilderhus, *The Second Century,* 60; Rosenberg, *Financial Missionaries to the World,* 149.

29. LaFeber, *Inevitable Revolutions,* 63; Langley, *The Banana Wars.*

30. Spenser, *Impossible Triangle,* 75–94.

31. Ibid., 10; Schmitz, *Thank God They're on Our Side,* 49.

32. Dallek, *Roosevelt and American Foreign Policy,* 176.

33. Ibid., 139–49; Gellman, *Good Neighbor Diplomacy,* 50.

34. Langley, *United States and the Caribbean,* 97–105; Renda, *Taking Haiti,* 29–34; Gellman, *Good Neighbor Diplomacy,* 34–36; Eric Roorda, "Genocide Next Door."

35. Britton, *Carlton Beals,* 71–82.

36. Langley, *United States and the Caribbean,* 116–25.

37. LaFeber, *Inevitable Revolutions,* 61–81.

38. Langley, *The United States and the Caribbean,* 133–48.

39. Britton, *Carlton Beals,* 120; Johnson, *Peace Progressivism,* 286; Gellman, *Good Neighbor Diplomacy,* 36; Benjamin, *Hegemony and Dependent Development,* 187, 47; see also Perez, *United States and Cuba,* 181–201.

40. Langley, *United States and the Caribbean,* 121–45; Shoultz, *Beneath the United States,* 290–315.

41. Gellman, *Good Neighbor Diplomacy,* 74–110.

42. Heinrichs, *Threshold of War,* 90; Dallek, *Roosevelt and American Foreign Policy,* 276; Gellman, *Good Neighbor Diplomacy,* 92; Patterson, *Mr. Republican,* 245.

43. Frye, *Nazi Germany and the American Hemisphere,* 167; Dallek, *Roosevelt and American Foreign Policy,* 235; Gellman, *Good Neighbor Diplomacy,* 115.

44. Leuchtenburg, *Roosevelt and the New Deal, 1932–1940,* 118–42.

45. Polanyi, *Great Transformation,* 257.

46. P. Marks, *In a Barren Land,* 270–91; Mitchell, *Campaign of the Century;* Kennedy, *The American People in Depression and War,* 160–380.

47. Roediger, *Working Toward Whiteness,* 8.

48. Hearden, *Roosevelt Confronts Hitler,* 48, 53–87.

49. Doenecke, *Storm on the Horizon*, 203–11.

50. Cole, *Roosevelt and the Isolationists*, 374.

51. Hearden, *Roosevelt Confronts Hitler*, 190.

52. Henrichs, *Threshold of War*, 38.

53. Hearden, *Roosevelt Confronts Hitler*, 191–94, 206.

54. Doenecke, *Storm on the Horizon*, 167; Cole, *Roosevelt and Isolationists*, 415.

55. Cole, *Roosevelt and Isolationists*, 397, 399.

56. Hearden, *Roosevelt Confronts Hitler*, 184.

57. Hixson, *Charles Lindbergh*, 103–24; Smith, *To Move a Nation*, 180. In a revealing reflection on selective memory and the usable past, Philip Roth published a popular counterfactual historical novel in 2005, *The Plot Against America,* around the theme of "it could have happened here," depicting anti-Semitic pogroms in the United States following the election of "President Lindbergh" in 1940. While the typical Middle American anti-Semitism of the anti-interventionist Lindbergh thus remains notorious, few citizens are aware of the vicious anti-Semitism of the militant World War II hero General George S. Patton, who averred, "Others believe that the Displaced Person is a human being, which he is not, and this applies particularly to the Jews who are lower than animals . . . a sub-human species without any of the social or cultural refinements of our time" *(New York Times Book Review* Feb. 23, 2003).

58. Steele, *Propaganda in an Open Society*

59. Weinberg, *A World at Arms,* 149–50.

60. Heinrichs, *Threshold of War,* 101–38.

61. Dallek, *Roosevelt and American Foreign Policy,* 285.

62. Hearden, *Roosevelt Confronts Hitler,* 201–04.

63. Jarvis, *The Male Body at War,* 132.

64. Nish, *Japanese Foreign Policy;* Utley, *Going to War with Japan;* Barnhart, *Japan Prepares for Total War;* Iriye, *Pearl Harbor and the Coming of the Pacific War;* Jesperson, *American Images of China.*

65. Chang, *The Rape of Nanking;* Bix, *Hirohito and Making of Modern Japan,* 350, 359–67.

66. Nish, *Japanese Foreign Policy,* 142. From the United States alone Japan received about 80 percent of its oil products, 90 percent of its natural gas, 74 percent of scrap iron, and 60 percent of machine tools. Now completely cut off, Japan had less than two years' supply of oil upon which its expansionist agenda depended.

67. Mauch, "Revisiting Nomura's Diplomacy." The role of the emperor in the decision to go to war remains controversial. Contrast Bix, *Hirohito and Making of Modern Japan,* 424, 158–62, with Kawamura, "Hirohito and Japan's Decision to Go to War."

68. Doenecke, *Storm on the Horizon,* 321; Sherry, *In the Shadow of War,* 60.

69. Divine, *Reluctant Belligerent;* Rosenberg, *A Date Which Will Live;* Linenthal, *Sacred Ground,* 173–212.

70. Russet, *No Clear and Present Danger;* Beard, *President Roosevelt and the Coming of the War.*

Chapter 6. Wars Good and Cold

1. White, *The American Century,* 21; Dower, *War Without Mercy;* Sherry, *Rise of American Air Power.*

2. Adams, *The Best War Ever;* Jarvis, *The Male Body at War,* 88.

3. Kazin and McCartin, *Americanism,* 137–38.

4. Larres and Lane, *The Cold War: Essential Readings;* Schlesinger, Jr., "Origins of the Cold War," 52; Gaddis, "Emerging Pot-Revisionist Synthesis"; Paterson, *Cold War Critics;* Smith, *Opposition Beyond the Water's Edge,* 3; Hunter, *Rethinking the Cold War;* Zubok and Pleshakov, *Inside the Kremlin's Cold War;* Gaddis; *The Cold War: A New History.*

5. Nadel, *Containment Culture,* 4.

6. Campbell, *Writing Security,* 132–38.

7. Latham, *The Liberal Moment*, 116.

8. Gori and Pons, eds., *Soviet Union and Europe in the Cold War*, xxiv, 365, 306; Foglesong, *America's Secret War Against Bolshevism*, 45.

9. Gardner, *Spheres of Influence*, 114.

10. Baldwin, *Great Mistakes of the War*; O'Connor, *Diplomacy for Victory*.

11. Black and Koppes, *Hollywood Goes to War*, 141, 324–26.

12. Dallek, *Roosevelt and American Foreign Policy*, 520; Gardner, *Spheres of Influence*, 237.

13. Djilas, *Conversations with Stalin*; Resis, *Molotov Remembers*, 45; Zubok and Pleshakov, *Inside the Kremlin's Cold War*; Pons and Gori, eds., *The Soviet Union and Europe*.

14. Pons and Gori, eds., *The Soviet Union and Europe*, xxiii, 87.

15. Ibid., xxi, 193.

16. Ibid., 307.

17. White, *The American Century*, 21; Hogan, "The American Century: Roundtable I and II."

18. See note 27 in the introdcution.

19. Bird and Lifschultz, *Hiroshima's Shadow*; White, *The American Century*, 62.

20. Sherry, *Rise of American Air Power*, 256–300; Dower, *War Without Mercy*, 104–05; Corn, *The Winged Gospel*.

21. Herken, *The Winning Weapon*.

22. Leffler, *Preponderance of Power*, 19; Larres and Lane, *Cold War: Essential Readings*, 31; Millis, *The Forrestal Diaries*, 351–52; Hoopes and Brinkley, *Driven Patriot*, 446–68.

23. Costigliola, "Tropes of Gender and Pathology"; Hogan, *The Marshall Plan*; Leffler, *Preponderance of Power*.

24. Hixson, *George F. Kennan*, 75.

25. Adler and Paterson, *Red Fascism*.

26. Pons and Gori, *The Soviet Union and Europe*, 188.

27. Johnson, *Improbable Dangers*, 169–83; Kennan, *The Nuclear Delusion*, xxv; Karber and Combs, "Assessing the Soviet Threat," 439.

28. Jesperson, *American Images of China*; see also Cumings, *Parallax Visions*, 1–94.

29. Westad, *Brothers in Arms*, 28–31.

30. Lundestad, *United States and Western Europe*.

31. Schaller, *Altered States*; Dower, *Embracing Defeat*; Cumings, *Parallax Visions*, 35–68.

32. Westad, ed., *Brothers in Arms*, 171.

33. Cumings, *Korea's Place in the Sun*, 191, 258. See also his monumental, *Origins of the Korean War, II*, especially 185–349.

34. Anderson, *Eyes off the Prize*, 145; Smith, *Opposition Beyond the Water's Edge*, 65.

35. Cumings, *Korea's Place in the Sun*, 264.

36. Hixson, *George F. Kennan*, 108.

37. Cumings, *Korea's Place in the Sun*, 283.

38. Stueck, *The Korean War*, 353.

39. Cumings, *Korea's Place in the Sun*, 270–72; Conway-Lanz, "Beyond No Gun Ri."

40. Westad, ed., *Brothers in Arms*, 172.

41. Nadel, *Containment Culture*, 90; Doherty, *Cold War, Cool Medium*, 149.

42. Bloch, *Visionary Republic*, 230–31; Cherry, *God's New Israel*, 91–95.

43. Jacobs, *America's Miracle Man in Vietnam*, 181; Heale, *McCarthy's Americans*, 278; Smith, *Opposition Beyond the Water's Edge*; Danielson, "Christianity, Dissent, and the Cold War."

44. Jacobs, "'Our System Demands the Supreme Being'"; Fox, *Jesus in America*; Epple, "American Crusader."

45. Jacobs, *America's Miracle Man in Vietnam*, 12, 67.

46. Westad, "New International History of the Cold War"; Hixson, *Parting the Curtain*; Osgood, *Total Cold War*; Saunders, *Who Paid the Piper?*; Scott-Smith and Krabbendam, *Cultural Cold War in Western Europe*; Jensen, "Singing a Beautiful Hymn."

47. Hixson, *Parting the Curtain*, 57–86.

48. Granville, "'Caught with Jam on Our Fingers'";

49. Logevall, "A Critique of Containment," 473–99.

50. Boyle, *American-Soviet Relations,* 124.

51. Larres and Osgood, *The Cold War After Stalin's Death,* ix–x.

52. Richter, *Khrushchev's Double Bind;* Schecter with Luchkov, *Khrushchev Remembers;* Taubman, *Khrushchev: Man and His Era.*

53. Smith, *Opposition Beyond the Water's Edge,* 94.

54. Doenecke, *Storm on the Horizon,* 223.

55. Fleming, *The New Dealers' War,* 558.

56. Rafael Medoff, director, David S. Wyman Institute for Holocaust Studies, 2006, Historians News Network (online).

57. Kimball, "The Future of World War II Studies."

Chapter 7. Militarization and Countersubversion

1. Hixson, *A Matter of Interest,* xv–xxiv, 145.

2. Hardt and Negri, *Empire,* 24.

3. Sherry, *In the Shadow of War,* 47, 74.

4. Yergin, *Shattered Peace;* Hogan, *A Cross of Iron;* Pach, *Arming the Free World;* Koistinen, *Arsenal of World War II,* 496.

5. White, *The American Century,* 49.

6. Acheson, *Present at the Creation,* 374; Hamby, *A Man of the People,* 527; Latham, *The Liberal Moment,* 192.

7. Leffler, *A Preponderance of Power,* 356; NSC 698 appears on pages 21–82 of May, *American Cold War Strategy.*

8. Stueck, *The Korean War,* 370, 350; Becker and Wells, *Economics and World Power;* Pach, *Arming the Free World.*

9. Tucker, ed., *Dangerous Strait.*

10. Johnston, *Culture and Hegemony in Origins of Nuclear Strategy,* 126, 239, 179–81.

11. Koistinen, *Arsenal of World War II,* 9, 320–21.

12. Lens, *Military-Industrial Complex,* 5; Koistinen, *Arsenal of World War II,* 495–507.

13. Friedberg, *In the Shadow of the Garrison State,* 320.

14. Kaplan, *Wizards of Armageddon;* Leslie, *Cold War and American Science.*

15. Leslie, *The Cold War and American Science,* 38.

16. Simpson, *Universities and Empire,* xx, 159, 11, 254; Richelson, *Wizards of Langley;* Bamford, *Body of Secrets.*

17. Pierpaoli, *Truman and Korea,* 234.

18. Roland, *Military-Industrial Complex,* 28–29.

19. Lowen, *Creating the Cold War University,* 147; see also, Cook, *The Declassified Eisenhower,* and Hixson, *Parting the Curtain,* 224–28.

20. Roman, *Eisenhower and the Missile Crisis.*

21. Sherry, *In the Shadow of War,* 53, 75; Friedberg, *In the Shadow of the Garrison State.*

22. Heale, *McCarthy's Americans,* xii.

23. Boyle, *American-Soviet Relations;* Goodman, *Stories of Scottsboro;* Weigand, *Red Feminism.*

24. Theoharis and Scott, *The Boss.*

25. Stone, *Perilous Times,* 135–233.

26. Steele, *Free Speech in the Good War;* Ribuffo, *The Old Christian Right,* 215; Charles, "Informing FDR: FBI Political Surveillance."

27. Steele, *Propaganda in an Open Society,* 72.

28. Steele, *Free Speech in the Good War,* 93.

29. Fordham, *Building the Cold War Consensus;* Kaplan and Pease, *Cultures of U.S. Imperialism;* Steele, *Free Speech in the Good War,* 97.

30. Borstelmann, *The Cold War and the Color Line,* 38; Stone, *Perilous Times,* 286–310; Steele, *Free Speech in the Good War,* 170–79.

31. Walker, *In Defense of American Liberties,* 155–56; Stone, *Perilous Times,* 236–310.

32. Smith, *Opposition Beyond the Water's Edge,* 3, 131, 99.

33. Jesperson, *American Images of China;* Tucker, *Patterns in the Dust.*

34. Doenecke, *Not to the Swift.*

35. Schrecker, *Many Are the Crimes,* xi; Fried, *McCarthyism;* Kessler, *The Bureau,* 132.

36. Schrecker, *Many Are the Crimes,* 232.

37. Diamond, *Compromised Campus,* 275; Schrecker, *No Ivory Tower.*

38. Heale, *McCarthy's Americans,* 283.

39. Ibid., xvii, 289.

40. Ibid., 7, 286–95.

41. Storrs, "Red Scare Politics and Suppression of Popular Front Feminism"; May, *Homeward Bound,* 208.

42. Jarvis, *The Male Body at War,* 8, 158, 154.

43. Sherry, *In the Shadow of War,* 110.

44. Whitfield, *Culture of the Cold War;* Storrs, "Red Scare Politics and Suppression of Popular Front Feminism"; Weigand, *Red Feminism,* 2; Cuordileone, "Politics in an Age of Anxiety."

45. Clark, *Cold Warriors,* 3; Cuordileone, "Politics in an Age of Anxiety."

46. Johnson, *The Lavender Scare,* 9, 2; Cuordileone, "Politics in an Age of Anxiety."

47. Morton Sobell, "Three Gentlemen of Venona," *The Nation,* April 2, 2001; Haynes and Klehr, *Venona.*

48. Maurice Isserman, "The Right's New Cold War Revision: Current Espionage Fears Have Given New Life to Liberal Anti-Communism," *The Nation,* July 24, 2000; Schrecker, *Cold War Triumphalism,* 160; Although the Venona documents affirm the close association between the CPUSA and the Soviet Union, students of Communism have long understood that parties around the world followed the Kremlin lead, typically in slavish fashion, even though Stalin himself often disdained them. Even before Khrushchev's condemnation of Stalin at the Twentieth Party Congress in 1956, thousands of Communists and former Communists, in the United States and elsewhere, had lost faith in the USSR and in the movement's quasi-religious promise to deliver human salvation. As this process played out, the "threat" of Communism to "national security" was "containing" itself, thus obviating the "need" for countersubversive repression. See Gornick, *Romance of American Communism.*

49. Schrecker, *Many Are the Crimes,* 360, 369.

50. Ibid., 412.

Chapter 8. Neocolonial Nightmares

1. Young, *Postcolonialism,* 4.

2. Three works enhance understanding of the emergence of Western domination. In *Late Victorian Holocausts,* Mike Davis argues as follows: "There is persuasive evidence that peasants and farm laborers became dramatically more pregnable to natural disaster after 1850 as their local economies were violently incorporated into the world market" (288). Davis echoes Karl Polanyi, who explained in his classic work, *The Great Transformation,* "Labor and land are made into commodities, which is only a short formula for the liquidation of every and any cultural institution in an organic society" (159–60). Finally, while the Western powers credited their advantages to innate superiority, Jared Diamond argues persuasively that it was the "guns, germs, and steel" of the new world system. See Diamond, *Guns, Germs, and Steel.*

3. Little, *American Orientalism,* 150–60; Hobson, *Imperialism,* 215.

4. Westad, *The Global Cold War,* 130.

5. Odd Arne Westad notes the "key role local elites played in abetting and facilitating these superpower interventions." Westad, *The Global Cold War,* 397–98.

6. By 1962, Arnold Toynbee charged, the United States was the "leader of the worldwide anti-revolutionary movement in defense of vested interests." Quoted in Engelhardt, *End of Victory Culture,* 146. As Gaurav Desai and Supriya Nair argue, "The insistent myth of colonialism as immediately or in the long run beneficial to its subject populations was taken for granted in virtually every domain of colonial intervention." Desai and Nair, *Postcolonialisms,* 31.

7. Simpson, *Universities and Empire,* 57; Robin, *Making of the Cold War Enemy;* Gilman, *Mandarins of the Future;* Latham, *Modernization as Ideology.*

8. Latham, *The Liberal Moment.*

9. Schrader, *Intervention into the 1990s,* 229.

10. Gaddis, *The Long Peace.*

11. Young, *Postcolonialism,* 194.

12. Gilderhus, *Second Century,* 120–31; Ryan and Pungong, *U.S. and Decolonization,* 47.

13. Gilderhus, *Second Century,* 134; Hixson, *George F. Kennan,* 69–71.

14. Cullather, *Secret History;* Gleijesus, *Shattered Hope;* Immerman, *The CIA in Guatemala;* Grandin, *Last Colonial Massacre;* Prados, *Safe for Democracy,* 107–23.

15. Ryan and Pungong, eds., *United States and Decolonization,* 48; Pérez, *On Becoming Cuban.*

16. Higgins, *The Perfect Failure;* Prados, *Safe for Democracy,* 236–72, 298–336; Bohning, *The Castro Obsession;* Gleijeses, *Conflicting Missions,* 16. The plots included use of poison pills and pens, bacterial powder, tuberculosis bacilli, and plans to render the bearded Cuban leader hairless. On November 22, 1963, at the moment of Kennedy's own assassination in Dallas, a CIA agent in Paris was handing off an assassination device intended for Castro.

17. Beschloss, *The Crisis Years,* 549; Boyle, *Soviet-American Relations,* 151; Fursenko and Naftali, *"One Hell of a Gamble."*

18. Leebaert, *The Fifty-Year Wound,* 277–82; Bohning, *The Castro Obsession.*

19. Rabe, *Most Dangerous Area in the World;* LaRose and Mora, *Neighborly Adversaries,* 177–203; Rabe, *U.S. Intervention in British Guiana.*

20. Westad, *Global Cold War,* 151.

21. Gilderhus, *Second Century,* 193–95.

22. Kornbluh, *The Pinochet File,* 25, 85 209, 362; McSherry, *Predatory States,* 152–67; Prados, *Safe for Democracy,* 396–430. After murdering two people Townley, the son of a Ford Motor Company official, served a short prison term before gaining his freedom through the Witness Protection Program.

23. McSherry, *Predatory States.*

24. Thorne, *Allies of a Kind;* Brenda Gail Plumer, *Rising Wind,* 127–28.

25. Louis, *Imperialism at Bay,* 41–45; Ryan and Pungong, eds., *United States and Decolonization,* xvi, 97, 208, 211.

26. Little, *American Orientalism,* 123.

27. Schueller, *U.S. Orientalisms,* 29, 86.

28. Little, *American Orientalism,* 123; Schueller, *U.S. Orientalisms,* 41.

29. Pappé, *History of Modern Palestine,* 42.

30. Little, *American Orientalism,* 15–22, 80–87.

31. Wyman, *Abandonment of the Jews,* 311–40; Little, *American Orientalism,* 80; Westad, *Global Cold War,* 127.

32. Pappé, *History of Modern Palestine,* 123–47; Masalha, *Politics of Denial,* 258.

33. Mart, *Eye on Israel;* Schueller, *U.S. Orientalisms,* 3.

34. Daniel Yergin surveys the rise of oil in *The Prize,* 305–93.

35. Heiss, *Empire and Nationhood,* 237; Yergin, *The Prize,* 208, 477.

36. Little, *American Orientalism,* 181, 169–70, 135; Hahn, *Caught in the Middle East;* Reynolds, *One World Divisible,* 80–88.

37. Little, *American Orientalism,* 23–32; Borstelmann, *Cold War and the Color Line,* 141.

38. Said, *Orientalism* 287–91; Said, *Culture and Imperialism,* 260–61.

39. Bass, *Support Any Friend;* Little, *American Orientalism,* 280.

40. Little, *American Orientalism,* 240–41.

41. Ibid., 283–86; Hahn, *Crisis and Crossfire.*

42. Reynolds, *One World Divisible,* 369–82; Yergin, *The Prize,* 588–652.

43. Krenn, *Black Diplomacy.* The State Department relegated "colored" employees to clerical positions within the deeply segregated environment of the nation's southern capital.

44. Noer, *Cold War and Black Liberation,* 34–60; Borstelmann, *Cold War and the Color Line,* 85–221; Krenn, *Black Diplomacy,* 28–43.

45. Borstelmann, *The Cold War and the Color Line,* 10–44, 60.

46. Anderson, *Eyes Off the Prize,* 2, 70.

47. Borstelmann, *The Cold War and the Color Line,* 92, 105, 111.

48. Ibid., 46, 132; Plummer, ed., *Window on Freedom,* 95.

49. Von Eschen, *Race against Empire,* 115–24; Engelhardt, *End of Victory Culture,* 127.

50. Anderson, *Eyes Off the Prize,* 273–74.

51. Dudziak, *Cold War Civil Rights,* 131; Hixson, *Parting the Curtain,* 131–32.

52. Plummer, ed., *Window on Freedom,* 115, 137.

53. Plummer, *Window on Freedom,* 115–40; Simpson, *Universities and Empire,* 135–58; Borstelmann, *Cold War and the Color Line,* 85–134.

54. Borstelmann, *Cold War and the Color Line,* 129–30; Dunn, *Imagining the Congo.*

55. Borstelmann, *Cold War and the Color Line,* 156–57, 236–37, 256.

56. Ibid., 152; Gleijeses, *Conflicting Missions,* 346, 392.

57. Landry and MacLean, *The Spivak Reader,* 294.

58. Nashel, *Lansdale's Cold War,* 31–48; Karnow, *In Our Image,* 323–55.

59. Steinberg, *In Search of Southeast Asia,* 431–42.

60. McMahon, *Colonialism and Cold War,* 73, 286–305.

61. Chang, *Friends and Enemies,* 167.

62. Kahin and Kahin, *Subversion as Foreign Policy,* 230, 227.

63. Steinberg, *In Search of Southeast Asia,* 418–30; Westad, *Global Cold War,* 188.

64. Simpson, "Modernizing Indonesia"; Chomsky, *Rogue States,* 51–61; "Death of a Nation: The Timor Conspiracy" a film by John Pilger, U.K., 1994. After a twenty-four-year occupation, courageous opposition by the East Timor Fretland guerrillas, the collapse of the Suharto regime in 1998, international intervention forced out Indonesia—albeit not before another bloody military assault in 1999—and finally brought independence to the still-impoverished nation.

65. Karnow, *Vietnam: A History.*

66. Bradley, *Imagining Vietnam and America.*

67. Baritz, *Backfire,* 102–43; Jacobs, *America's Miracle Man in Vietnam,* 11, 17; Schulzinger, *A Time for War,* 69–153; Logevall, *Choosing War.*

68. Robin, *Making of the Cold War Enemy;* Schulzinger, *A Time for War,* 154–273.

69. Dean, *Imperial Brotherhood,* 217; see also Jeffords, *Remasculinization of America.*

70. Herring, *America's Longest War;* Young, *The Vietnam Wars;* The "banality of evil" references Hannah Arendt's famous description of the Nazi genocide perpetrator Adolf Eichmann during his war crimes trial in Jerusalem in 1961. Rather than appearing monstrous, Eichmann instead seemed "terribly and terrifyingly normal." Arendt, *Eichmann in Jerusalem,* 276.

71. Gibson, *The Perfect War;* Borstelmann, *Cold War and the Color Line,* 215.

72. Engelhardt, *End of Victory Culture,* 215.

73. Kimball, *The Vietnam War Files.*

74. Clymer, *United States and Cambodia.*

Chapter 9. Patriotic Revival

1. Isserman and Kazin, *America Divided,* 66, 10, 61; Reeves, *President Kennedy,* 100.

2. Isserman and Kazin, *America Divided,* 108, 102, 188, 192.

3. Young and Buzzanco, *Companion to the Vietnam War,* 333–62.

4. Isserman and Kazin, *America Divided*, 192; Jeffreys-Jones, *Peace Now*, 110–17; Borstelmann, *Cold War and the Color Line;* 209–10; Garrow, *The FBI and Martin Luther King.*

5. Suri, *Power and Protest;* Berger, *Outlaws of America.*

6. Isserman and Kazin, *America Divided*, 195.

7. Jeffreys-Jones, *Peace Now!* 215.

8. Ibid., 175–81.

9. Engelhardt, *End of Victory Culture*, 15.

10. Kaufman and Kaufman, *Presidency of James Earl Carter;* Smith, *Morality, Reason and Power;* Boyle, *American-Soviet Relations*

11. Gilderhus, *The Second Century.*

12. Newsom, *Soviet Brigade in Cuba.*

13. Gilderhus, *The Second Century*, 193; Trachtenberg, *A Constructed Peace;* Garthoff, *Détente and Confrontation;* Suri, *Power and Protest.*

14. Little, *American Orientalism*, 152.

15. McGirr, *Suburban Warriors*, 148, 261, 186.

16. Troy, *Morning in America*, 7, 15; Stiglitz, *Globalization and Its Discontents*, 78. Social programs had already been trimmed substantially since their Great Society peaks, but the first Reagan budget authorized another round of deep cuts in food stamps (14 percent); child nutrition programs (28 percent); Aid for Dependent Children (14 percent); general job-training programs (39 percent); low-income energy assistance (11 percent); social services block grants (24 percent); health block grants (33 percent); and financial aid for needy students (16 percent). See Cox and Skidmore-Hess, *U.S. Global Politics and Global Economy*, 161–71.

17. Cannon, *Reagan: Role of a Lifetime.*

18. Behdad, *A Forgetful Nation*, 9.

19. Martin, *With God on Our Side.*

20. Garthoff, *The Great Transition*, 7–194.

21. Cox and Skidmore-Hess, *U.S. Global Politics and the Global Economy*, 175; Boyle, *American-Soviet Relations*, 201; Leslie, *Cold War and American Science*, 255.

22. Roland, *Military-Industrial Complex*, 15; Trubowitz, *Defining the National Interest*, 169–234.

23. McMahon, "Contested Memory: The Vietnam War and American Society, 1975–2001," *Diplomatic History* (Spring 2002): 159–84.

24. Beattie, *Scar That Binds*, 21–42; Young and Buzzanco, *Companion to the Vietnam War*, 450–69.

25. Young and Buzzanco, *Companion to the Vietnam War*, 384; McMahon, "Contested Memory," 175.

26. Beattie, *Scar that Binds*, 124.

27. Lembcke, *The Spitting Image.*

28. Franklin, *MIA, or Myth-Making in America.*

29. Beattie, *The Scar That Binds*, 44, 6; Kaplan and Pease, *Cultures of U.S. Imperialism*, 583.

30. Faludi, *Backlash: Undeclared War Against American Women.*

31. Devine, *Vietnam at 24 Frames A Second;* representation of Vietnam in television programing is understudied. See Himebaugh, "All for One."

32. David, *Qaddaffi, Terrorism, and Origins of U.S.*, 124; St. John, *Libya and the United States.*

33. Smith, *Last Years of Monroe Doctrine*, 178–84.

34. Richelson, *Wizards of Langley*, 226.

35. Smith, *Last Years of the Monroe Doctrine*, 185–209; Leebaert, *The Fifty-Year Wound*, 544–57; Westad, *The Global Cold War*, 347; Churchill and Vander Wall, *The Cointelpro Papers*, x–xiv.

36. *New York Times*, July 9, 1985; Draper, *A Very Thin Line.*

37. Boyle, *American-Soviet Relations*, 247, 214.

38. Garthoff, *Great Transition*, 751–98; Pessen, *Losing Our Souls*, 14; Hunter, *Rethinking the Cold War;* Fukuyama, *End of History and Last Man;* Smith, *America's Mission*, 266–307; Gaddis, *The Cold War: New History;* Gadis, *We Now Know.*

39. Gould-Davies, "Logic of Soviet Cultural Diplomacy," *Diplomatic History* 27 (April 2003): 213; Nye, *Soft Power.*

40. Wagnleitner, *Coca-Colonization and the Cold War;* Wagnleitner and May, *Here, There, and Everywhere;* I am grateful to Greg Castillo for the "nylon curtain" reference.

41. Schrader, *Intervention into the 1990s,* 51.

42. Little, *American Orientalism,* 252–66.

43. Kaplan and Pease, eds., *Cultures of United States Imperialism,* 529; Macalister, *Epic Encounters,* 235–45.

44. Little, *American Orientalism,* 262.

45. Engelhardt, *The End of Victory Culture,* 15.

46. Schlesinger, Jr., *Disuniting of America;* Linenthal and Engelhardt, *History Wars,* 113.

47. Hagan, *Justice in the Balkans,* 36, 179, 54–57; Zimmermann, *Origins of a Catastrophe.*

48. Boggs, *Masters of War,* 198; Jokic, *Lessons of Kosovo,* 68.

49. Boggs, *Masters of War,* 194–99.

50. Power, *A Problem from Hell,* xx–xxi, 508.

51. Stiglitz, *Globalization and Its Discontents* ix–12; Greider, *One World, Ready or Not;* Eckes and Zeiler, *Gloablization and the American Century;* Korten, *When Corporations Rule the World;* Perkins, *Confessions of an Economic Hit Man.*

52. Stiglitz, *Globalization and Its Discontents,* 134–55, 6–7.

53. Westad, *Global Cold War,* 406.

54. Hylton, *Evil Hour in Colombia,* 132.

Chapter 10. September 11 and the Global Crusade

1. *New York Times,* Sept. 21, 2001.

2. The CIA apparently coined the term in 1954. See Johnson, *Blowback: Costs and Consequences of American Empire.*

3. Meyerowitz, ed., *History and September 11th,* 163.

4. Martin, *With God on Our Side.*

5. Mamdani, *Good Muslim, Bad Muslim.*

6. Ibid., 127; Schrader, ed., *Intervention into the 1990s,* 138–39.

7. Coll, *Ghost Wars: CIA, Afghanistan, and bin Laden,* 89; McMahon, *Cold War on the Periphery,* 338–45; Rotter, *Comrades at Odds.*

8. Coll, *Ghost Wars,* 343–44.

9. Desai and Nair, *Postcolonialisms,* 213, 321–22.

10. Meyerowitz, ed., *History and September 11th,* 86; Desai and Nair, *Postcolonialisms,* 335.

11. Khaladi, *Resurrecting Empire,* 118–51.

12. Hedges, *War Is a Force that Gives Us Meaning,* 47; Swisher, *The Truth About Camp David,* 251.

13. Mart, *Eye on Israel;* Schrader, ed., *Intervention into the 1990s,* 381.

14. Meyerowitz, ed., *History and September 11th,* 98; Macalister, *Epic Encounters,* 183–87.

15. Little, *American Orientalism,* 289–92; Macalister, *Epic Encounters,* 198–234; Christison, *Perceptions of Palestine,* 1; Masalha, *The Politics of Denial,* 238.

16. Fisk, *Pity the Nation.*

17. Cole, "Ariel Sharon's Smarter Way of Locking Up the Palestinians," *History News Network,* Jan. 13, 2006.

18. Khaladi, *Resurrecting Empire,* 141; Swisher, *The Truth About Camp David.*

19. Khaladi, *Resurrecting Empire,* 124.

20. Lieven, *America Right or Wrong,* 173–76.

21. "As war becomes more technological it is distancing public opinion and the warrior from its consequences," Christopher Coker observes. "It is leading inevitably to what psychologists call 'disassociation.'" As postmodern war becomes increasingly precise, distant, abstract, and digitalized, "we may slip down the slope and find ourselves using violence with impunity," Coker adds. "The

West's wish to rationalize war is matched only by its will to still wage it." Coker, *Humane Warfare*, 1, 148–52.

22. Schrader, ed., *Intervention into the 1990s*, 11; Meyerowitz, ed., *History and September 11th*, 131–56.

23. Baer, *Sleeping with the Devil*, 205, 33.

24. Bamford, *A Pretext for War*, 101, 165.

25. Coll, *Ghost Wars*, 324–26, 54.

26. Paterson, *American Foreign Policy*, 2:484; Bowden, *Black Hawk Down*; Bamford, *Pretext for War*, 167.

27. Berlant and Duggan, *Our Monica, Ourselves*; Kaplan and Moran, *Aftermath: Clinton Impeachment in Age of Political Spectacle*; Macalister, *Epic Encounters*, 245–50.

28. Halper and Clarke, *America Alone*.

29. Bamford, *Pretext for War*, 253–69; Lieven, *America Right or Wrong*, 165; Klare, *Blood and Oil*, 98.

30. Unger, *House of Bush, House of Saud*, 1–17; Bamford, *Pretext for War*, 285–86; Meyerowitz, ed., *History and September 11th*, 11.

31. Blix, *Disarming Iraq*; Bamford, *Pretext for War*, 367–77.

32. *Cleveland Plain Dealer*, Nov. 22, 2005, and May 21, 2006.

33. Bamford, *Pretext for War*, 253–59; Dowd, *New York Times*, Dec. 19, 2005.

34. Phillips, *American Theocracy*; Fox, *Jesus in America*, 385, 15–17; Martin, *With God on Our Side*; Phillips, *American Dynasty*, 230–33, 89; *Cleveland Plain Dealer*, March 20, 2004; Meyerowitz, ed., *History and September 11th*, 18.

35. Alexander, *Holding the Line*, 33.

36. Meyerowitz, ed., *History and September 11th*, 12–13.

37. *Cleveland Plain Dealer*, April 5, 2003.

38. The noted postmodernist Jean Baudrillard has made this point provocatively in *The Gulf War Did Not Take Place*.

39. Kaplan and Pease, *Cultures of U.S. Imperialism*, 500, 507.

40. Boggs, *Masters of War*, 250.

41. *Cleveland Plain Dealer*, May 21, 2004.

42. Phillips, *American Dynasty*, 328.

43. Ibid; Young, *Postcolonialism: An Historical Introduction*, 172.

44. Bamford, *Pretext for War*, 402–03.

45. *Cleveland Plain Dealer*, Sept. 4, 2003.

46. Margulies, *Guantánamo and Abuse of Power*.

47. Danner, *Torture and Truth*, 3, 27–33; *Nation*, Dec. 26. 2005.

48. Brigham cited some of these parallels in *Is Iraq Another Vietnam?*

49. Roland, *Military-Industrial Complex*, 48.

50. Boggs, *Masters of War*, 229, 24; Johnson, *Sorrows of Empire*, 156–60.

51. *Newsweek*, April 12, 2004; Phillips, *American Dynasty*, 272.

52. *New York Times Book Review*, Aug. 20, 2006; *Cleveland Plain Dealer*, Sept. 28, 2006.

53. Klare, *Blood and Oil*, 5, 156.

54. Phillips, *American Dynasty*, 69, 6. See also Phillips's thoroughgoing analysis in *Wealth and Democracy*; Federal Reserve analysis noted by Richard Reeves in a report by the Wisconsin Policy Research Institute; Frank, *What's the Matter with Kansas?*, 7.

55. Kozol, *Shame of the Nation*; Parenti, *Lockdown America*.

56. Boggs, *Masters of War*, 223.

57. *Cleveland Plain Dealer*, May 20, 2006; Sweig, *Friendly Fire*; Prestowitz, *American Unilateralism*; Bacevich, *American Empire*.

Conclusion

1. Laclau and Mouffe, *Hegemony and Socialist Strategy*. While Laclau and Mouffe may be "radical," merely "liberal" reform fails out of an inability to unpack the nation's foundational mythology and identity. Liberal scholars condemn the "smug insularity" they find inherent in "raging" against U.S. national identity and call instead for "doing what we can to help realize the best rather than the worst possibilities of faith in a country and its people." Such anodyne "solutions" will not succeed and these authors unwittingly point out why by noting that liberal criticism "pays tribute to Americanism." See Michael Kazin and Joseph A. McCartin, *Americanism*, 13–17.

2. Gillis, ed., *Commemorations*, 20.

Appendix A. Discourse and Disciplinary Knowledge

1. White, *Tropics of Discourse*, 3; Young, *Postcolonialism*, 400, 403.

2. Doty, *Imperial Encounters*, 168.

3. White, *Tropics of Discourse*, 2; Berkhofer, *Beyond the Great Story*, 10.

4. Foucault, *Madness and Civilization;* Foucault, *The History of Sexuality;* Foucault, *The Order of Things;* Foucault, *Discipline and Punish;* Dirks, Eley, Ortner, *Culture/Power/History*, 200–221; Rabinow, *The Foucault Reader;* for a concise introduction, see Danaher, Schirato, and Webb, *Understanding Foucault.*

5. Allison, *Reading the New Nietzsche;* Magnus and Higgins, *Cambridge Companion to Nietzsche;* to access some of Nietzsche's most significant texts, see Kaufmann, *On the Genealogy of Morals* and *Ecce Homo.*

6. Rabinow, *The Foucault Reader*, 76–100.

7. Young, *Postcolonialism;* Williams, *Culture and Society;* Gibson, *Rethinking Fanon;* Said, *Orientalism* and *Culture and Imperialism;* Landry and MacLean, *The Spivak Reader;* Desai and Nair, *Postcolonialisms;* Macalister, *Epic Encounters.*

8. Dirks, Eley, Ortner, *Culture/Power/History*, 537; Alexander and Seidman, *Culture and Society*, 235.

Appendix B. Gramscian Cultural Hegemony

1. McLellan, *Marxism After Marx*, 193.

2. Alexander and Seidman, *Culture and Society*, 7.

3. Gramsci, *Selections from the Prison Notebooks;* McLellan, *Marxism after Marx*, 189.

4. Lears, "The Concept of Cultural Hegemony."

5. Lears, *No Place of Grace*, 10.

6. Laclau and Mouffe, *Hegemony and Socialist Strategy*, 93, xv, 176.

Appendix C. Postmodernism

1. Jenkins, ed., *Post-Modern History Reader*, 2; see also White, *Tropics of Discourse;* LaCapra, *History and Criticism;* see also Calhoun, LiPuma, and Postone, *Bourdieu: Critical Perspectives;* Sarup, *Identity, Culture, and the Postmodern World;* Barrett, *The Politics of Truth.*

2. Rivkin, *Literary Theory: An Anthology.*

3. Berkhofer, *Beyond the Great Story*, 57.

4. Livingston, "William A. Williams: A Roundtable"; see also Ninkovich, "No Post-mortems for Postmodernism."

Appendix D. Identity and Lacanian Psychoanalytic Theory

1. Žižek, *Sublime Object of Ideology,* 175; for a concise introduction to Lacan, see Homer, *Jacques Lacan.*
2. Žižek, *Sublime Object of Ideology,* 164.
3. Ibid., 176.

Works Cited

Acheson, Dean G. *Present at the Creation: My Years in the State Department.* New York: Norton, 1969.

Adams, Michael C. C. *The Best War Ever: America and World War II.* Baltimore: Johns Hopkins University Press, 1994.

———. *The Great Adventure: Male Desire and the Coming of World War I.* Bloomington: Indiana University Press, 1990.

Adler, Les K., and Thomas G. Paterson, "Red Fascism: The Merger of Nazi Germany and Soviet Russia in the American Image of Totalitarianism, 1930s–1950s." *American Historical Review* (April 1970): 1046–64.

Alexander, Jeffrey C., and Steven Seidman. *Culture and Society: Contemporary Debates.* Cambridge: Cambridge University Press, 1990.

Allen, Frederick Lewis. *The Lords of Creation.* New York: Harper and Bros., 1935.

Allison, David B. *Reading the New Nietzsche.* Lanham, Md.: Rowan and Littlefield, 2001.

Allison, Robert J. *The Crescent Obscured: The United States and the Muslim World, 1776–1815.* Chicago: University of Chicago Press, 2000.

Alpert, Michael. *A New International History of the Spanish Civil War.* New York: Macmillan, 1994.

Anderson, Benedict. *Imagined Communities: Reflections on the Origin and Spread of Nationalism.* New York: Verso, 1991.

Anderson, Carol. *Eyes Off the Prize: The United Nations and the African American Struggle for Human Rights, 1944–1955.* Cambridge: Cambridge University Press, 2003.

Anderson, Fred. *Crucible of War: The Seven Years War and the Fate of Empire in British North America, 17654–66.* New York: Vintage Books, 2001.

Anderson, Gary Clayton, *The Conquest of Texas: Ethnic Cleansing in the Promised Land, 1820–1875.* Norman: University of Oklahoma Press, 2005.

Appleby, Joyce. *Capitalism and a New Social Order: The Republican Vision of the 1790s.* New York: New York University Press, 1984.

———. *Inheriting the Revolution: The First Generation of Americans.* Cambridge: Harvard University Press, 2000.

Arendt, Hannah. *Eichmann in Jerusalem.* New York: Penguin, 1963.

Bacevich, Andrew J. *American Empire: The Realities and Consequences of U.S. Diplomacy.* Cambridge: Harvard University Press, 2002.

Baer, Robert. *Sleeping with the Devil: How Washington Sold Our Soul for Saudi Crude.* New York: Crown Publishers, 2003.

Bailyn, Bernard. *To Begin the World Anew: The Genius and Ambiguities of the American Founders.* New York: Knopf, 2003.

Baldwin, Hanson. *Great Mistakes of the War.* New York: Harper, 1950.

Bamford, James. *A Pretext for War: 9/11, Iraq, and the Abuse of America's Intelligence Agencies.* New York: Anchor Books, 2005.

———. *Body of Secrets: Anatomy of the Ultra-Secret National Security Agency from the Cold War Through the Dawn of a New Century.* New York: Random House, 2001.

Banner, Stuart. *How the Indians Lost Their Land: Law and Power on the Frontier.* Cambridge: Harvard University Press, 2005.

Baritz, Loren. *Backfire: A History of How American Culture Led Us Into Vietnam and Made Us Fight the Way We Did.* New York: William Morrow, 1985.

Barnhart, Michael A. *Japan Prepares for Total War: The Search for Economic Security, 1919–1941.* Ithaca: Cornell University Press, 1987.

Barrett, Michele *The Politics of Truth: From Marx to Foucault.* Stanford: Stanford University Press, 1991.

Bass, Warren. *Support Any Friend: Kennedy's Middle East and the Making of the U.S.-Israeli Alliance.* New York: Oxford 2003.

Baudrillard, Jean. *The Gulf War Did Not Take Place.* Bloomington: Indiana University Press, 1995.

Beale, Howard. *Theodore Roosevelt and the Rise of America to World Power.* Baltimore: Johns Hopkins University Press, 1956.

Beard, Charles A. *President Roosevelt and the Coming of the War, 1941: A Study in Appearances and Realities.* New Haven: Yale University Press, 1948.

———. *The Open Door at Home: A Trial Philosophy of National Interest.* New York: Macmillan, 1934.

Beattie, Keith. *The Scar That Binds: American Culture and the Vietnam War.* New York: New York University Press, 1998.

Becker, William H., and Samuel F. Wells. *Economics and World Power: An Assessment of American Diplomacy Since 1789.* New York: Columbia University Press, 1984.

Bederman, Gail. *Manliness and Civilization: A Cultural History of Gender and Race in the United States, 1880–1917.* Chicago: University of Chicago Press, 1995.

Behdad, Ali V. *A Forgetful Nation: On Immigration and Cultural Identity in the United States.* Durham: Duke University Press, 2005.

Beisner, Robert L. *From the Old Diplomacy to the New, 1865–1900.* Arlington Heights, Ill.: Harlan Davidson, 1986.

Benjamin, Jules. *Hegemony and Dependent Development: The United States and Cuba, 1880–1934.* Pittsburgh: University of Pittsburgh Press, 1977.

Bercovitch, Sacvan. *The American Jeremiad.* Madison: University of Wisconsin Press, 1978.

———. "Investigations of an Americanist." *Journal of American History* 78 (December 1991).

Berger, Dan. *Outlaws of America: The Weather Underground and the Politics of Solidarity.* Oakland: AK Press, 2006.

Berkhofer, Robert F., Jr., *Beyond the Great Story: History as Text and Discourse.* Cambridge: Harvard University Press, 1995.

Berlant, Lauren, and LisaDuggan, eds. *Our Monica, Ourselves: The Clinton Affair and the National Interest.* New York: New York University Press, 2001.

Berlin, Ira. *Many Thousands Gone: The First Two Centuries of Slavery in North America.* Cambridge: Harvard University Press, 1998.

Beschloss, Michael. *The Crisis Years: Kennedy and Khrushchev, 1960–63.* New York: Harper-Collins, 1991.

Bird, Kai, and Lawrence Lifschultz, eds. *Hiroshima's Shadow.* Stony Creek, Conn.: Pamphleteer's Press, 1998.

Bix, Herbert P. *Hirohito and the Making of Modern Japan.* New York: Harper-Collins, 2000.

Black, Gregory, and Clayton Koppes. *Hollywood Goes to War: How Politics, Profits, and Propaganda Shaped World War II Movies.* New York: Free Press, 1987.

Blight, David W. *Race and Reunion: The Civil War in American Memory.* Cambridge: Harvard University Press, 2001.

Blix, Hans. *Disarming Iraq.* New York: Pantheon, 2004.

Bloch, Ruth H. *Visionary Republic: Millennial Themes in American Thought, 1756–1800.* Cambridge: Cambridge University Press, 1985.

Blum, Edward J. *Reforging the White Republic: Race, Religion, and American Nationalism, 1865–1898.* Baton Rouge: Louisiana State University Press, 2005.

Blumrosen, Alfred, and Ruth Blumrosen. *Slave Nation: How Slavery United the Colonies and Sparked the American Revolution.* New York: Barnes and Noble, 2005.

Bodnar, John. *Bonds of Affection: Americans Define Their Patriotism.* Princeton: Princeton University Press, 1996.

Boggs, Carl, ed. *Masters of War: Militarism and Blowback in the Era of American Empire.* London: Routledge, 2003.

Bohning, Don. *The Castro Obsession: U.S. Covert Operations Against Cuba, 1959–65.* Washington, D.C.: Potomac Books, 2005.

Bouvier, Virginia M., ed. *Whose America? The War of 1898 and the Battles to Define the Nation.* Westport, Conn.: Praeger, 2001.

Bowden, Mark. *Black Hawk Down.* New York: Bantam, 1999.

Boyle, Peter G. *American-Soviet Relations: From the Russian Revolution to the Fall of Communism.* London: Routledge, 1993.

Bradley, Mark P. *Imagining Vietnam and America: The Making of Postcolonial Vietnam, 1919–50.* Chapel Hill: University of North Carolina Press, 2000.

Briggs, Laura. *Reproducing Empire: Race, Sex, Science, and U.S. Imperialism in Puerto Rico.* Berkeley: University of California Press, 2002.

Brigham, Robert K. *Is Iraq Another Vietnam?* New York: Public Affairs, 2006.

Britton, John A. *Carlton Beals: A Radical Journalist in Latin America.* Albuquerque: University of New Mexico Press, 1987.

Butler, Jon. *Becoming America: The Revolution Before 1776.* Cambridge: Harvard University Press, 2000.

Calhoun, Craig, Edward LiPuma, and Moishe Postone, eds. *Bourdieu: Critical Perspectives.* Chicago: University of Chicago Press, 1993.

Campbell, David. *Writing Security: United States Foreign Policy and the Politics of Identity.* Minneapolis: University of Minnesota Press, 1998.

Cannon, Lou. *President Reagan: The Role of a Lifetime.* New York: Simon and Schuster, 1991.

Carley, Michael J. *1939: The Alliance that Never Was and the Coming of World War II.* Chicago: Ivan R. Dee, 1999.

Carroll, John, and George Herring. *Modern American Diplomacy.* Wilmington, Del.: SR Books, 1996.

Chang, Gordon H. *Friends and Enemies: The United States, China, and the Soviet Union, 1948–1972.* Stanford: Stanford University Press, 1990.

Chang, Iris. *The Rape of Nanking: The Forgotten Holocaust of World War II.* New York: Basic Books, 1997.

Charles, Douglas M. "'Informing FDR': FBI Political Surveillance and the Isolationist-Interventionist Foreign Policy Debate 1939–1945." *Diplomatic History* 24 (Spring 2000): 211–32.

Chatfield, Charles. *The American Peace Movement: Ideals and Activism.* New York: Twayne Publishers, 1992.

Cherry, Conrad. *God's New Israel: Religious Interpretations of American Destiny,* rev. ed. Chapel Hill: University of North Carolina Press, 1998.

Chomsky, Noam. *Rogue States: The Rule of Force in World Affairs.* Cambridge, Mass.: South End Press, 2000.

Christison, Kathleen. *Perceptions of Palestine: Their Influence on U.S. Middle East Policy.* Berkeley: University of California Press, 1999.

Churchill, Ward, and Jim Vander Wall. *The Cointelpro Papers: Documents from the FBI's Secret Wars Against Domestic Dissent.* Cambridge, Mass.: South End Press, 1990.

Clark, Suzanne. *Cold Warriors: Manliness on Trial in the Rhetoric of the West.* Carbondale: Southern Illinois University Press, 2000.

Clymer, Kenton. *The United States and Cambodia: A Troubled Relationship.* New York: Routledge, 2004.

Cohen, Nancy. *The Reconstruction of American Liberalism, 1865–1914.* Chapel Hill: University of North Carolina Press, 2002.

Cohen, Warren I. *Empire Without Tears.* Philadelphia: Temple University Press, 1987.

———. *The American Revisionists: The Lessons of Intervention, America in World War I.* Chicago: University of Chicago Press, 1967.

Coker, Christopher. *Humane Warfare.* London: Routledge, 2001.

Cole, Wayne S. *Roosevelt and the Isolationists, 1932–1945.* Lincoln: University of Nebraska Press, 1983.

Coll, Steve. *Ghost Wars: The Secret History of the CIA, Afghanistan, and bin Laden.* New York: Penguin Books, 2004.

Conway-Lanz, Sahr. "Beyond No Gun Ri: Refugees and the United States Military in the Korean War." *Diplomatic History* 29 (January 2005): 49–81.

Cook, Blanche W. *The Declassified Eisenhower: A Divided Legacy of Peace and Political Warfare.* New York: Penguin, 1984.

Cooper, Frederick. *Colonialism in Question: Theory, Knowledge, History.* Berkeley: University of California Press, 2005.

Corn, Joseph J. *The Winged Gospel: America's Romance with Aviation, 1900–1950.* New York: Oxford University Press, 1983.

Costigliola, Frank. "The Nuclear Family: Tropes of Gender and Pathology in the Western Alliance." *Diplomatic History* 21 (Spring 1997): 163–83.

———. *Awkward Dominion: American Political, Economic, and Cultural Relations with Europe, 1919–1933.* Ithaca: Cornell University Press, 1984.

Cott, Nancy F. *Bonds of Womanhood: 'Women's Sphere' in New England, 1780–1835.* New Haven: Yale University Press, 1997.

Cox, Ronald W., and Daniel Skidmore-Hess. *U.S. Global Politics and the Global Economy: Corporate Power, Conservative Shift.* Boulder: Lynne Rienner, 1999.

Cronon, William. *Changes in the Land: Indians, Colonists, and the Ecology of New England.* New York: Hill and Wang, 1983.

Cull, Nicholas J. *Selling War: The British Propaganda Campaign Against American "Neutrality" in World War II.* New York: Oxford University Press, 1995.

Cullather, Nick, *Secret History: The CIA's Classified Account of its Operations in Guatemala, 1952–1954.* Stanford: Stanford University Press, 1999.

———. *Illusions of Influence: The Political Economy of United States–Philippines Relations, 1942–1960.* Stanford: Stanford University Press, 1994.

Cumings, Bruce. *Origins of the Korean War.* Volume 2: *The Roaring of the Cataract, 1947–50.* Princeton: Princeton University Press, 1990.

———. *Korea's Place in the Sun.* New York: Norton, 1998.

———. *Parallax Visions: Making Sense of American–East Asian Relations at the End of the Century.* Durham: Duke University Press, 1999.

Cuordileone, K. A. "'Politics in an Age of Anxiety': Cold War Political Culture and the Crisis in Masculinity, 1949–1960." *Journal of American History* 87 (September 2000): 515–45.

Dallek, Robert. *Franklin D. Roosevelt and American Foreign Policy, 1932–1945.* New York: Oxford University Press, 1979.

Danaher, Geoff, Tony Schirato, and Jen Webb. *Understanding Foucault.* Thousand Oaks, Calif.: Sage Publications, 2000.

Danielson, Leilah. "Christianity, Descent, and the Cold War: A. J. Muste's Challenge to Realism and U.S. Empire." *Diplomatic History* 30 (September 2006): 645–69.

Danner, Mark. *Torture and Truth: America, Abu Ghraib, and the War on Terror.* New York: New York Review of Books, 2004.

David, Brian L. *Qaddafi, Terrorism, and the Origins of the U.S. Attack on Libya.* Westport, Conn.: Praeger, 1990.

Davis, David Brion. *The Rise and Fall of Slavery in the New World.* New York: Oxford University Press, 2006.

Davis, Mike. *Late Victorian Holocausts: El Niño Famines and the Making of the Third World.* New York: Verso, 2001.

Dawley, Alan. *Changing the World: American Progressives in War and Revolution.* Princeton: Princeton University Press, 2003.

Dean, Robert D. *Imperial Brotherhood: Gender and the Making of Cold War Foreign Policy.* Amherst: University of Massachusetts Press, 2001.

Deloria, Philip J. *Playing Indian.* New Haven: Yale University Press, 1998.

Desai, Gaurav, and Supriya Nair, eds. *Postcolonialisms: An Anthology of Cultural Theory and Criticism.* New York: Oxford University Press, 2005.

Diamond, Jared M. *Guns, Germs, and Steel: The Fates of Human Societies.* New York: Norton, 1997.

Diamond, Sigmund. *Compromised Campus: The Collaboration of Universities with the Intelligence Community, 1945–1955.* New York: Oxford University Press, 1992.

Dirks, Nicholas B., Geoff Eley, and Sherry B. Ortner, eds. *Culture/Power/History.* Princeton: Princeton University Press, 1994.

Divine, Robert. *The Reluctant Belligerent: Amerian Entry into World War II.* New York: Wiley, 1965.

Djilas, Milovan. *Conversations with Stalin.* New York: Harcourt, Brace and World, 1962.

Doenecke, Justus, and John Wilz. *From Isolation to War, 1931–1941.* Arlington Heights, Ill.: Harlan Davidson, 2003.

Doenecke, Justus. *Storm on the Horizon: The Challenge to American Intervention, 1939–1941.* Lanham, Md.: Rowan and Littlefield, 2000.

Doherty, Thomas. *Cold War, Cool Medium: Television, McCarthyism, and American Culture.* New York: Columbia University Press, 2003.

Doty, Roxanne L. *Imperial Encounters: The Politics of Representation in North-South Relations.* Minneapolis: University of Minnesota Press, 1996.

Dower, John W. *Embracing Defeat: Japan in the Wake of World War II.* New York: Norton, 1999.

———. *War Without Mercy: Race and Power in the Pacific War.* New York: Pantheon Books, 1986.

Draper, Theodore. *A Very Thin Line: The Iran-Contra Affairs.* New York: Simon and Schuster, 1993.

Drinnon, Richard. *Facing West: The Metaphysics of Indian Hating and Empire Building.* Minneapolis: University of Minnesota Press, 1980.

Dudziak, Mary L. *Cold War Civil Rights: Race and the Image of American Democracy.* Princeton: Princeton University Press, 2000.

Dull, Jonathan. *A Diplomatic History of the American Revolution.* New Haven: Yale University Press, 1985.

Dunn, Kevin C. *Imagining the Congo: The International Relations of Identity.* New York: Palgrave-Macmillan, 2003.

Eckes, Alfred E., and Thomas W. Zeiler. *Globalization and the American Century.* Cambridge: Cambridge University Press, 2003.

Eley, Geoff, and Ronald Grigor Suny, eds. *Becoming National: A Reader.* New York: Oxford University Press, 1996.

Elkins, Caroline. *Imperial Reckoning: The Untold Story of Britain's Gulag in Kenya.* New York: Henry Holt, 2005.

Ellis, Joseph J. *Founding Brothers: The Revolutionary Generation.* New York: Alfred A. Knopf, 2000.

Endy, Christopher. "Travel and World Power: Americans in Europe, 1890–1917." *Diplomatic History* 22 (Fall 1998): 565–94.

Engelhardt, Tom. *The End of Victory Culture: Cold War America and the Disillusioning of a Generation.* New York: Basic Books, 1995.

Enloe, Cynthia. *Bananas, Beaches and Bases: Making Feminist Sense of International Politics.* Berkeley: University of California Press, 1989.

Epple, Michael J. "American Crusader: Bishop Fulton J. Sheen's Campaign Against Communism." Ph.D. diss., University of Akron, 2001.

Faludi, Susan. *Backlash: The Undeclared War Against American Women.* New York: Crown, 1991.

Faragher, John Mack. *Danial Boone: The Life and Legend of an American Pioneer.* New York: Owl Books, 1992.

Fellman, Michael, Lesley J. Gordon, and Daniel E. Sutherland. *This Terrible War: The Civil War and Its Aftermath.* New York: Longman, 2003.

Finkelman, Paul. *Slavery and the Founders: Race and Liberty in the Age of Jefferson.* Armonk, N.Y.: M. E. Sharpe, 1996.

Finnegan, John P. *Against the Specter of a Dragon: The Campaign for American Military Preparedness.* Westport, Conn.: Greenwood Press, 1974.

Fisk, Robert. *Pity the Nation: The Abduction of Lebanon.* New York: Nation Books, 2002.

Fitzsimmons, David M. "Tom Paine's New World Order: Idealistic Internationalism in the Ideology of Early American Foreign Relations." *Diplomatic History* 19 (Fall 1995) 569–82.

Fleming, Thomas. *The New Dealers' War: FDR and the War Within World War II.* New York: Basic Books, 2001.

Foglesong, David S. *America's Secret War Against Bolshevism: U.S. Intervention in the Russian Civil War, 1917–1920.* Chapel Hill: University of North Carolina Press, 1995.

Foner, Eric, *Reconstruction: America's Unfinished Revolution, 1863–77.* New York: Harper and Row, 1988.

Foos, Paul. *A Short, Offhand, Killing Affair: Soldiers and Social Conflict in the Mexican-American War.* Chapel Hill: University of North Carolina Press, 2002.

Foot, Rosemary. *The Practice of Power: U.S. Relations with China Since 1949.* New York: Oxford University Press, 1995.

Fordham, Benjamin O. *Building the Cold War Consensus: The Political Economy of U.S. National Security Policy, 1949–1951.* Ann Arbor: University of Michigan Press, 1998.

Foucault, Michel. *Madness and Civilization: A History of Insanity in the Age of Reason.* New York: Pantheon Books, 1967.

———. *The History of Sexuality.* New York: Vintage Books, 1990.

———. *The Order of Things: An Archeology of Knowledge.* New York: Pantheon, 1970.

———. *Discipline and Punish: The Birth of the Prison.* New York: Pantheon Books, 1978.

Fousek, John. *To Lead the Free World: American Nationalism and the Cultural Roots of the Cold War.* Chapel Hill: University of North Carolina Press, 2000.

Fox, Richard Wightman. *Jesus in America: Personal Savior, Cultural Hero, National Obsession.* New York: Harper-Collins, 2004.

Frank, Thomas. *What's the Matter with Kansas?: How Conservatives Won the Heart of America.* New York: Henry Holt, 2002.

Franklin, H. Bruce. *MIA, or Myth-Making in America.* New Brunswick, N.J.: Rutgers University Press, 1993.

Fredrickson, George W. *The Black Image in the White Mind: The Debate Over African-American Character and Destiny, 1817–1914.* Middletown, Conn.: Wesleyan University Press, 1987.

Fried, Albert, ed. *McCarthyism, The Great American Red Scare: A Documentary History.* New York: Oxford University Press, 1997.

Friedberg, Aaron. *In the Shadow of the Garrison State: America's Anti-Statism and Its Cold War Grand Strategy.* Princeton: Princeton University Press, 2000.

Fritz, Henry E. *The Movement for Indian Assimilation, 1860–1890.* Westport, Conn.: Greenwood Press, 1983.

Frye, Alton. *Nazi Germany and the American Hemisphere.* New Haven: Yale University Press, 1967.

Fukuyama, Francis. *The End of History and the Last Man.* New York: Free Press, 1992.

Fursenko, Aleksandr, and Timothy Naftali. *"One Hell of a Gamble": Khrushchev, Castro, and Kennedy, 1958–1964.* New York: Norton, 1997.

Gaddis, John L. "The Emerging Post-Revisionist Synthesis on the Origins of the Cold War." *Diplomatic History* 7 (Summer 1983): 191–204.

———. *The Cold War: A New History.* New York: Penguin Press, 2005.

———. *We Now Know: Rethinking Cold War History.* New York: Oxford, 1997.

———. *The Long Peace: Inquiries into the History of the Cold War.* New York: Oxford University Press, 1987.

Gardner, Lloyd C. *Safe for Democracy: Anglo-American Response to Revolution, 1913–1923.* New York: Oxford University Press, 1984.

———. *Spheres of Influence: The Great Powers Partition Europe from Munich to Yalta.* Chicago: Ivan Dee, 1993.

Garrow, David J. *The FBI and Martin Luther King Jr.* New York: Norton, 1983.

Garthoff, Raymond. *Détente and Confrontation: American-Soviet Relations from Nixon to Reagan.* Washington, D.C.: Brookings Institution Press, 1985.

———. *The Great Transition: American-Soviet Relations and the End of the Cold War.* Brookings Institution Press, 1994.

Geertz, Clifford. *The Interpretaion of Cultures.* New York: Basic Books, 1973.

Gellman, Irwin F. *Good Neighbor Diplomacy: United States Policies in Latin America, 1933–1945.* Baltimore: Johns Hopkins University Press, 1979.

Gerster, Patrick, and Nicholas Cords, eds. *Myth America: A Historical Anthology.* Rancho Cucamonga, Calif.: Brandywine Press, 1997.

Gibson, James William. *The Perfect War: Technowar in Vietnam.* Boston: Atlantic Monthly Press, 1986.

Gibson, Nigel C., ed. *Rethinking Fanon: The Continuing Dialogue.* Amherst, N.Y.: Humanity Books, 1999.

Gilderhus, Mark T. *The Second Century: U.S.–Latin American Relations Since 1989.* Wilmington, Del.: SR Books, 2000.

Gillis, John R., ed. *Commemorations: The Politics of National Identity.* Princeton: Princeton University Press, 1994.

Gilman, Nils. *Mandarins of the Future: Modernization Theory in Cold War America.* Baltimore: Johns Hopkins University Press, 2000.

Gleijeses, Piero. *Conflicting Missions: Havana, Washington, and Africa, 1969–1976.* Chapel Hill: University of North Carolina Press, 2002.

———. *Shattered Hope: The Guatemalan Revolution and the United States, 1944–1954.* Princeton: Princeton University Press, 1991.

Goldberg, David Theo. *The Racial State.* Malden, Mass.: Blackwell, 2002.

Goodman, James E. *Stories of Scottsboro.* New York: Vintage Books, 1995.

Gordon-Reed, Annette. *Thomas Jefferson and Sally Hemings: An American Controversy*. Charlottesville: University of Virginia Press, 1997.

Gori, Francesca, and Silvio Pons, eds. *The Soviet Union and Europe in the Cold War, 1943–1953*. New York: Macmillan Press, 1996.

Gornick, Vivian. *The Romance of American Communism*. New York: Basic Books, 1977.

Gould-Davies, Nigel. "The Logic of Soviet Cultural Diplomacy." *Diplomatic History* 27 (April 2003): 193–214.

Graebner, Norman. *Empire on the Pacific: A Study in American Continental Expansion*. Claremont, Calif.: Regina Books, 1985.

Gramsci, Antonio. *Selections from the Prison Notebooks*. Edited by Quintin Hoare and Geoffrey Smith. New York: International Publishers, 1999.

Grandin, Greg. *The Last Colonial Massacres: Latin America in the Cold War*. Chicago: University of Chicago Press, 2004.

Granville, Johanna, "Caught with Jam on Our Fingers:' Radio Free Europe and the Hungarian Revolution of 1956." *Diplomatic History* 29 (November 2005): 811–39.

Greenberg, Amy S. *Manifest Manhood and the Antebellum American Empire*. Cambridge: Cambridge University Press, 2005.

Greider, William. *One World, Ready or Not: The Manic Logic of Global Capitalism*. New York: Simon and Schuster, 1997.

Grenier, John. *The First Way of War: American War Making on the Frontier, 1607–1814*. Cambridge: Cambridge University Press, 2005.

Hagan, John. *Justice in the Balkans: Prosecuting War Crimes in The Hague Tribunal*. Chicago: University of Chicago Press, 2003.

Hahn, Peter L. *Caught in the Middle East: U.S. Policy Toward the Arab-Israeli Conflict, 1945–1961*. Chapel Hill: University of North Carolina Press, 2004.

———. *Crisis and Crossfire: The United States and the Middle East Since 1945*. Washington, D.C.: Potomac Books, 2005.

Hall, Stuart, and Paul du Gay, eds. *Questions of Cultural Identity*. Thousand Oaks, Calif.: Sage Publications, 1996.

Halliday, E. M. *Understanding Thomas Jefferson*. New York: Harper-Collins, 2001.

Halper, Stefan, and Jonathan Clarke. *America Alone: The Neo-Conservatives and the Global Order*. Cambridge: Cambridge University Press, 2004.

Hamby, Alonzo. *A Man of the People: A Life of Harry S. Truman*. New York: Oxford, 1995.

Hannigan, Robert E. *The New World Power: American Foreign Policy, 1898–1917*. Philadelphia: University of Pennsylvania Press, 2002.

Hansen, Jonathan. *The Lost Promise of Patriotism: Debating American Identity, 1890–1920*. Chicago: University of Chicago Press, 2003.

Hardt, Michael, and Antonio Negri. *Empire*. Cambridge: Harvard University Press, 2000.

————. *Multitude: War and Democracy in the Age of Empire.* New York: Penguin, 2004.

Harlan, David. "A People Blinded from Birth: American History According to Sacvan Bercovitch." *Journal of American History* 78 (December 1991): 949–71.

Hartz, Louis. *The Liberal Tradition in America.* New York: Harcourt Brace, 1955.

Haynes, John Earl, and Harvey Klehr. *Venona: Decoding Soviet Espionage in America.* New Haven: Yale University Press, 1999.

Haynes, Sam W., and Christopher Morris, eds. *Manifest Destiny and American Antebellum Expansionism.* Arlington: University of Texas at Arlington, 1997.

Heale, M. J. *McCarthy's Americans: Red Scare Politics in State and Nation, 1935–1965.* Athens: University of Georgia Press, 1998.

Hedges, Chris. *War Is a Force that Gives Us Meaning.* New York: Public Affairs, 2002.

Heinrichs, Waldo. *Threshold of War: Franklin D. Roosevelt and American Entry into World War II.* New York: Oxford University Press, 1988.

Heiss, Mary Ann. *Empire and Nationhood: The United States, Great Britain, and Iranian Oil, 1950–1954.* New York: Columbia University Press, 1997.

————. "The Evolution of the Imperial Idea and U.S. National Identity." *Diplomatic History* 26 (Fall 2002): 511–40.

Herken, Gregg. *The Winning Weapon: The Atomic Bomb in the Cold War.* Princeton: Princeton University Press, 1988.

Herman, Sondra R. *Eleven Against War: Studies in American Internationalist Thought, 1898–1921.* Stanford: Hoover Institution Press, 1969.

Herring, George C. *America's Longest War: The United States and Vietnam, 1950–1975.* New York: Knopf, 1979.

Hietala, Thomas R. *Manifest Design: Anxious Aggrandizement in Late Jacksonian America.* Ithaca: Cornell University Press, 1985.

Higgins, Trumball. *The Perfect Failure: Kennedy, Eisenhower, and the CIA at the Bay of Pigs.* New York: Norton, 1989.

Higham, John. *Strangers in the Land: Patterns of American Nativism, 1860–1925.* New York: Atheneum, 1973.

Himebaugh, Brian L. "'All for One: Restoring American National Identity in Film and Prime Time Television after Vietnam." Ph.D. diss, University of Akron, 2004.

Hixson, Walter L. *Parting the Curtain: Propaganda, Culture and the Cold War, 1945–61.* New York: St. Martin's Press, 1997.

————. *George F. Kennan: Cold War Iconoclast.* New York: Columbia University Press, 1989.

————. *Charles A. Lindbergh, Lone Eagle.* New York: Longman, 2007.

Hixson, William F. *A Matter of Interest: Reexamining Money, Debt, and Real Economic Growth.* New York: Praeger, 1991.

Hobsbawm, Eric, and Terence Ranger, eds. *The Invention of Tradition.* Cambridge: Cambridge University Press, 1983.

Hobson, J. A. *Imperialism: A Study.* Ann Arbor: University of Michigan Press, 1972.

Hofstadter, Richard. *The Paranoid Style in American Politics and Other Essays.* Cambridge: Harvard University Press, 1963.

Hogan, Michael J. *A Cross of Iron: Harry S. Truman and the Origins of the National Security State, 1945–1954.* Cambridge: Cambrdige University Press, 1998.

Hogan, Michael J., and Thomas G. Paterson, eds. *Explaining the History of American Foreign Relations.* Cambridge: Cambridge University Press, 2004.

———. *The Marshall Plan: America, Britain, and the Reconstruction of Western Europe, 1947–1952.* Cambridge: Cambridge University Press, 1987.

———, ed. "The American Century: A Roundtable, I and II." *Diplomatic History* 23 (Spring 1999): 157–370, and (Summer 1999): 391–537.

Hoganson, Kristin L. *Fighting for American Manhood: How Gender Politics Provoked the Spanish-American and Philippine-American Wars.* New Haven: Yale University Press, 1998.

Holbo, Paul S. *Tarnished Expansion: The Alaska Scandal, the Press, and Congress, 1867–1871.* Knoxville: University of Tennessee Press, 1983.

Homer, Sean. *Jacques Lacan.* London: Routledge, 2005.

Hoopes, Townsend, and Douglas Brinkley. *Driven Patriot: The Life and Times of James Forrestal.* New York: Knopf, 1992.

Hopf, Ted. *Social Construction of International Politics.* Ithaca: Cornell University Press, 2002.

Horsman, Regenald. *Race and Manifest Destiny: The Origins of American Racial Anglo-Saxonism.* Cambridge: Harvard University Press, 1981.

Horwitz, Tony. *Confederates in the Attic: Dispatches from the Unfinished Civil War.* New York: Pantheon Books, 1998.

Hunt, Michael. *Ideology and U.S. Foreign Policy.* New Haven: Yale University Press, 1987.

Hunter, Allen, ed. *Rethinking the Cold War.* Philadelphia: Temple University Press, 1998.

Hylton, Forrest. *Evil Hour in Colombia.* New York: Verso, 2006.

Ignatiev, Noel. *How the Irish Became White.* London: Routledge, 1995.

Immerman, Richard H. *The CIA in Guatemala: The Foreign Policy of Intervention.* Austin: University of Texas Press, 1982.

Iriye, Akira. *Pearl Harbor and the Coming of the Pacific War: A Brief History with Documents and Essays.* New York: St. Martin's Press, 1999.

———. *The Cambridge History of American Foreign Relations.* Volume 3: *The Globalizing of America, 1913–45.* Cambridge: Cambridge University Press, 1993.

———. *Pacific Estrangement: Japanese and American Expansion, 1879–1911.* Cambridge: Harvard University Press, 1972.

Isserman, Maurice, and Michael Kazin. *America Divided: The Civil War of the 1960s.* New York: Oxford, 2000.

Jacobs, Seth. "'Our System Demands the Supreme Being': The U.S. Religious Revival and the 'Diem Experiment,' 1954–55." *Diplomatic History* 25 (Fall 2001): 589–624.

Jacobs, Seth. *America's Miracle Man in Vietnam: Ngo Dinh Diem, Religion, Race, and U.S. Intervention in Southeast Asia, 1950–1957.* Durham: Duke University Press, 2004.

Jacobson, Matthew Frye. *Barbarian Virtues: The United States Encounters Foreign Peoples at Home and Abroad, 1876–1917.* New York: Hill and Wang, 2000.

Jarvis, Christina S. *The Male Body at War: American Masculinity During World War II.* DeKalb: Northern Illinois University Press, 2004.

Jeffords, Susan. *The Remasculinization of America: Gender and the Vietnam War.* Bloomington: Indiana University Press, 1989.

Jeffreys-Jones, Rhodri. *Peace Now! American Society and the Ending of the Vietnam War.* New Haven: Yale University Press, 1999.

Jenkins, Keith, ed. *The Post-Modern History Reader.* London: Routledge, 1997.

Jennings, Francis, *Empire of Fortune: Crowns, Colonies, and Tribes in the Seven Years War in America.* New York: Norton, 1988.

———. *The Invasion of America: Indians, Colonialism, and the Cant of Conquest.* Chapel Hill: University of North Carolina Pres, 1973.

———. *The Creation of America: Through Revolution to Empire.* Cambridge: Cambridge University Press, 2005.

Jensen, James. "'Singing a Beautiful Hymn:' The Psychological Warfare Option in U.S. Foreign Policy During the Early Cold War." M.A. thesis, University of Akron, 1995.

Jesperson, T. Christopher. *American Images of China, 1931–1949.* Stanford: Stanford University Press, 1996.

Johannsen, Robert W. *To the Halls of the Montezumas: The Mexican War in the American Imagination.* New York: Oxford University Press, 1985.

Johnson, Chalmers. *Blowback: The Costs and Consequences of American Empire.* New York: Henry Holt, 2004.

———. *The Sorrows of Empire: Militarism, Secrecy, and the End of the Republic.* New York: Henry Holt, 2004.

Johnson, David K. *The Lavender Scare: The Cold War Persecution of Gays and Lesbians in the Federal Government.* Chicago: University of Chicago Press, 2004.

Johnson, Robert David. *The Peace Progressives and American Foreign Relations.* Cambridge: Harvard University Press, 1995.

Johnson, Robert H. *Improbable Dangers: U.S. Conceptions of Threat in the Cold War and After.* New York: St. Martin's Press, 1994.

Johnston, Andrew M. *Hegemony and Culture in the Origins of NATO First-Use, 1945–55.* New York: Palgrave-Macmillan, 2005.

Jokic, Aleksandar, ed. *Lessons of Kosovo: The Dangers of Humanitarian Intervention.* Peterborough, Ont.: Broadview Press, 2003.

Jones, Howard, and Donald A. Rakestraw. *Prologue to Manifest Destiny: Anglo-American Relations in the 1840s.* Wilmington, Del.: SR Books, 1997.

Jones, Howard. *Crucible of Power: A History of American Foreign Relations from 1897.* Wilmington, Del.: SR Books, 2001.

Jordan, Winthrop D. *White Over Black: American Attitudes Toward the Negro, 1550–1812.* New York: Norton, 1968.

Kahin, Audrey R., and George McT. Kahin. *Subversion as Foreign Policy: The Secret Eisenhower and Dulles Debacle in Indonesia.* New York: Norton, 1995.

Kammen, Michael. *Mystic Chords of Memory: The Transformation of Tradition in American Culture.* New York: Vintage Books, 1993.

Kaplan, Amy, and Donald E. Pease, eds. *Cultures of United States Imperialism.* Durham: Duke University Press, 1993.

Kaplan, Amy. *The Anarchy of Empire in the Making of U.S. Culture.* Cambridge: Harvard University Press, 2005.

Kaplan, Fred. *The Wizards of Armageddon.* New York: Simon and Schuster, 1984.

Kaplan, Leonard, and Beverly Moran, *Aftermath: The Clinton Impeachment and the Presidency in an Age of Political Spectacle.* New York: New York University Press, 2001.

Karber, Phillip A., and Jerald Combs. "Assessing the Soviet Threat to Western Europe: A Roundtable." *Diplomatic History* 22 (Summer 1998): 399–449.

Karnow, Stanley. *In Our Image: America's Empire in the Philippines.* New York: Random House, 1989.

———. *Vietnam: A History.* New York: Viking, 1983.

Katznelson, Ira, and Martin Shefter. *Shaped by War and Trade: International Influences on American Political Development.* Princeton: Princeton University Press, 2002.

Kaufman, Burton, and Scott Kaufman. *The Presidency of James Earl Carter, Jr.* Lawrence: University of Kansas Press, 2006.

Kaufmann, Walter, ed. *On the Genealogy of Morals* and *Ecce Homo.* New York: Vintage Books, 1989.

Kawmura, Noriko. "Emperor Hirohito and Japan's Decision to go to War with the United States: Reexamined." *Diplomatic History* 31 (January 2007): 51–79.

Kazin, Michael, and Joseph A. McCartin, eds. *Americanism: New Perspectives on the History of an Ideal.* Chapel Hill: University of North Carolina Press, 2006.

Kennan, George F. *The Nuclear Delusion: Soviet-American Relations in the Atomic Age.* New York: Pantheon Books, 1983.

Kennedy, David M. *The American People in Depression and War, 1929–1945.* New York: Oxford University Press, 1999.

———. *Over Here: The First World War and American Society.* New York: Oxford, 1988.

Kennedy, Roger G. *Mr. Jefferson's Lost Cause: Land, Farmers, Slavery, and the Louisiana Purchase,* New York: Oxford University Press, 2003.

Kessler, Ronald. *The Bureau: The Secret History of the FBI.* New York: St. Martin's Press, 2002.

Khaladi, Rashid, *Resurrecting Empire: Western Footprints and America's Perilous Path in the Middle East.* Boston: Beacon Press, 2005.

Kimball, Jeffrey P. *The Vietnam War Files: Uncovering the Secret History of Nixon-Era Strategy.* Lawrence: University Press of Kansas, 2004.

Kimball, Warren F. "The Future of World War II Studies: A Roundtable." *Diplomatic History* 25 (Summer 2001): 347–499.

————. *The Juggler: Franklin Roosevelt as a Wartime Statesman.* Princeton: Princeton University Press, 1994.

Klare, Michael T. *Blood and Oil: The Dangers and Consequences of America's Growing Dependency on Imported Petroleum.* New York: Metropolitan Books, 2004.

Koistinen, Paul A. C. *Arsenal of World War II: The Political Economy of American Warfare, 1939–1945.* Lawrence: University Press of Kansas, 2004.

————. *Planning War, Pursuing Peace: The Political Economy of American Warfare, 1920–1939.* Lawrence: University Press of Kansas, 1998.

Kornbluh, Peter. *The Pinochet File: A Declassified Dossier on Atrocity and Accountability.* Washington, D.C.: National Security Archive, 2004.

Korten, David C. *When Corporations Rule the World.* San Francisco: Berrett-Koehler, 2001.

Kozol, Jonathan. *The Shame of the Nation: The Restoration of Apartheid Schooling in America.* New York: Crown, 2005.

Kramer, Lloyd. *Lafayette in Two Worlds: Public Cultures and Personal Identities in an Age of Revolutions.* Chapel Hill: University of North Carolina Press, 1996.

Kramer, Paul A. *Race, Empire, the United States, and the Philippines.* Chapel Hill: University of North Carolina Press, 2006.

Krenn, Michael. *Black Diplomacy: African-Americans, 1945–1969.* Armonk, N.Y.: M.E. Sharpe, 1999.

Kuehl, Warren F. *Seeking World Order: The United States and International Organization to 1920.* Nashville: Vanderbilt University Press, 1969.

Kutler, Stanley, ed. *American Retrospectives: Historians on Historians.* Baltimore: Johns Hopkins University Press, 1995.

LaCapra, Dominick. *History and Criticism.* Ithaca: Cornell University Press, 1985.

Laclau, Ernesto, and Chantal Mouffe. *Hegemony and Socialist Strategy: Towards a Radical Democratic Politics.* New York: Verso, 2001.

LaFeber, Walter. *Inevitable Revolutions: The United States in Central America.* New York: Norton, 1983.

————. *The Cambridge History of American Foreign Relations.* Volume 2: *The American Search for Opportunity, 1865–1913.* Cambridge: Cambridge University Press, 1993.

Lambeck, Michael, ed. *A Reader in the Anthropology of Religion.* Malden, Mass.:, Blackwell, 2002.

Landry, Donna, and Gerald MacLean, eds. *The Spivak Reader: Selected Works of Gayatri Chakravorty Spivak.* London: Routledge, 1996.

Langley, Lester D. *The Banana Wars: United States Intervention in the Caribbean, 1898–1934.* Wilmington, Del.: SR Books, 2002.

———. *The United States and the Caribbean in the Twentieth Century.* Athens: University of Georgia Press, 1989.

LaRosa, Michael, and Frank O. Mora. *Neighborly Adversaries: Readings in U.S.–Latin American Relations.* Lanham, Md.: Rowan and Littlefield, 1999.

Larres, Klaus, and Ann Lane, eds. *The Cold War: The Essential Readings.* Malden, Mass.: Blackwell Publishers, 2001.

Larres, Klaus, and Kenneth Osgood. *The Cold War After Stalin's Death: A Missed Opportunity for Peace?* Lanham, Md.: Rowan and Littlefield, 2006.

Latham, Michael E. *Modernization as Ideology: American "Social Science" and Nation Building in the Kennedy Era.* Chapel Hill: University of North Carolina Press, 2000.

Latham, Robert. *The Liberal Moment: Modernity, Security, and the Making of the Postwar International Order.* New York: Columbia University Press, 1997.

Lawson, Melinda. *Patriot Fires: Forging a New American Nationalism in the Civil War North.* Lawrence: University of Kansas Press, 2002.

Lears, T. J. Jackson. "The Concept of Cultural Hegemony: Problems and Possibilities." *American Historical Review* 90 (June 1985): 574–93.

———. *No Place of Grace: Antimodernism and the Transformation of American Culture, 1880–1920.* New York: Pantheon Books, 1981.

Leebaert, Derek *The Fifty-Year Wound: The True Price of America's Cold War Vctory.* Boston: Little, Brown, 2002.

Leffler, Melvyn. *A Preponderance of Power: National Security, the Truman Administration, and the Cold War.* Stanford: Stanford University Press, 1992.

Lembcke, Jerry. *The Spitting Image: Myth, Memory, and the Legacy of Vietnam.* New York: New York University Press, 1998.

Lens, Sidney. *The Military-Industrial Complex.* Philadelphia: Pilgrim Press, 1970.

Lepore, Jill. *The Name of War: King Philip's War and the Origins of American Identity.* New York: Vintage, 1999.

Leslie, Stuart. *The Cold War and American Science: The Military-Industrial-Academic Complex at MIT and Stanford.* New York: Columbia University Press, 1993.

Leuchtenburg, William. *Franklin D. Roosevelt and the New Deal, 1932–1940.* New York: Harper and Row, 1963.

Lewis, Martin W., and Karen E. Wigen. *The Myth of Continents: A Critique of Metageography.* Berkeley: University of California Press, 1997.

Lieven, Anatol. *America Right or Wrong: An Anatomy of American Nationalism.* New York: Oxford University Press, 2004.

Linenthal, Edward T. *Sacred Ground: Americans and Their Battlefields.* Urbana: University of Illinois Press, 1991.

Linenthal, Edward T., and Tom Engelhardt, eds. *The History Wars: The Enola Gay and Other Battles for the American Past.* New York, Henry Holt, 1996.

Little, Douglas. *Malevolent Neutrality: The United States, Great Britain, and the Origins of the Spanish Civil War.* Ithaca: Cornell University Press, 1985.

———. *American Orientalism: The United States and the Middle East Since 1945.* Chapel Hill: University of North Carolina Press, 2002.

Livingston, James. "William Appleman Williams: A Roundtable." *Diplomatic History* 25 (Spring 2001): 275–316.

Logevall, Fredrik. "A Critique of Containment." *Diplomatic History* 28 (September 2004): 473–99.

———. *Choosing War: The Lost Chance for Peace and the Escalation of War in Vietnam.* Berkeley: University of California Press, 1999.

Louis, William Roger. *Imperialism at Bay: The United States and the Decolonization of Great Britain's Empire, 1941–45.* New York: Oxford University Press, 1978.

Love, Eric T. L. *Race Over Empire: Racism and U.S. Imperialism, 1865–1900.* Chapel Hill: University of North Carolina Press, 2004.

Lowen, Rebecca S. *Creating the Cold War University: The Transformation of Stanford.* Berkeley: University of California Press, 1997.

Lukas, J. Anthony. *Big Trouble: A Murder in a Small Town Sets Off a Struggle for the Soul of America.* New York: Simon and Schuster, 1997.

Lundestad, Geir. *The United States and Western Europe since 1945 "From "Empire" by Invitation to Transatlantic Drift.* New York: Oxford University Press, 2003.

Lynch, Cecilia. *Beyond Appeasement: Interpreting Interwar Peace Movements in World Politics.* Ithaca: Cornell University Press, 1999.

MacLean, Nancy. *Behind the Mask of Chivalry: The Making of the Second Ku Klux Klan.* New York: Oxford University Press, 1994.

Madsen, Deborah L. *American Exceptionalism.* Oxford: University Press of Mississippi, 1998.

Magnus, Bernd, and Kathleen M. Higgins, eds. *The Cambridge Companion to Nietzsche.* Cambridge: Cambridge University Press, 1996.

Maier, Pauline. *American Scripture: Making the Declaration of Independence.* New York: Alfred A. Knopf, 1997.

Mamdani, Mahmood. *Good Muslim, Bad Muslim: America, the Cold War, and the Roots of Terror.* New York: Doubleday, 2004.

Mann, Charles C. *1491: New Revelations of the Americas Before Columbus.* New York: Knopf, 2005.

Margulies, Joseph. *Guantánamo and the Abuse of Presidential Power.* New York: Simon and Schuster, 2006.

Marks, Frederick W., III. *Independence on Trial: Foreign Affairs and the Making of the Constitution.* Wilmington, Del.: Scholarly Resources, 1986.

Marks, Paula Mitchell. *In a Barren Land: The American Indian Quest for Cultural Survival, 1607 to the Present.* New York: William Morrow, 1998.

Mart, Michelle. *Eye on Israel: How America Came to View the Jewish State as an Ally.* Albany: State University of New York Press, 2006.

Martin, William. *With God on Our Side: The Rise of the Religious Right in America.* New York: Broadway Books, 1997.

Masala, Nur. *The Politics of Denial: Israel and the Palestine Refugee Problem.* Sterling, Va.: Pluto Press, 2003.

Mauch, Peter. "Revisiting Nomura's Diplomacy: Ambassador Nomura's Role in the Japanese-American Negotiations, 1941." *Diplomatic History* 28 (June 2004): 353–83.

May, Elaine Tyler. *Homeward Bound: American Families in the Cold War Era.* New York: Basic Books, 1988.

May, Ernest R. *"Lessons of the Past": The Use and Misuse of History in American Foreign Policy.* New York: Oxford, 1973.

———, ed. *American Cold War Strategy: Interpreting NSC 68.* New York: St. Martin's Press, 1993.

McAlister, Melani. *Epic Encounters: Culture, Media, and U.S. Interests in the Middle East Since 1945.* Berkeley: University of California Press, 2005.

McCartney, Paul T. *Power and Progress: American National Identity, the War of 1898, and the Rise of American Imperialism.* Baton Rouge: Louisiana State University Press, 2006.

McCormick, Thomas. *America's Half-Century: United States Foreign Policy in the Cold* War. Baltimore: Johns Hopkins University Press, 1989.

McCullough, David. *Truman.* New York: Simon and Schuster, 1992.

McGerr, Michael. *A Fierce Discontent: The Rise and Fall of the Progressive Movement in the United States, 1870–1920.* New York: Free Press, 2003.

McGirr, Lisa. *Suburban Warriors: The Origins of the New American Right.* Princeton: Princeton University Press, 2001.

McLellan, David. *Marxism After Marx: An Introduction.* New York: Harper and Row, 1979.

McMahon, Robert J. "Contested Memory: The Vietnam War and American Society, 1975–2001." *Diplomatic History* 26 (Spring 2002): 159–84.

———. *Colonialism and Cold War: The United States and the Struggle for Indonesian Independence, 1945–49.* Ithaca: Cornell University Press, 1981.

———. *The Cold War on the Periphery: The United States, India, and Pakistan.* New York: Columbia University Press, 1994.

McPherson, James M., and William J. Cooper, Jr., eds. *Writing the Civil War: The Quest to Understand.* Columbia: University of South Carolina Press, 1998.

McSherry, J. Patrice. *Predatory States: Operation Condor and Covert War in Latin America.* Lanham, Md.: Rowan and Littlefield, 2005.

Menand, Louis. *The Metaphysical Club: A Story of Ideas in America.* New York: Farrar, Straus and Giroux, 2001.

Meyerowitz, Joanne, ed. *History and September 11th*. Philadelphia: Temple University Press, 2003.

Millis, Walter, ed. *The Forrestal Diaries*. New York: Viking Press, 1951.

Mintz, Max M. *Seeds of Empire: The American Revolutionary Conquest of the Iroquois*. New York: New York University Press, 1999.

Mitchell, Greg. *The Campaign of the Century: Upton Sinclair's Race for Governor of California and the Birth of Media Politics*. New York: Random House, 1992.

Morrison, Michael A., and James B. Stewart, eds. *Race and the Early Republic: Racial Consciousness and Nation-Building in the Early Republic*. Lanham, Md.: Rowan and Littlefield, 2002.

Nadel, Alan. *Containment Culture: American Narratives, Postmodernism, and the Atomic Age*. Durham: Duke University Press, 1995.

Nashel, Jonathan. *Edward Lansdale's Cold War*. Amherst: University of Massachusetts Press, 2005.

Nelson, Dana D. *National Manhood: Capitalist Citizenship and the Imagined Fraternity of White Men*. Durham: Duke University Press, 1998.

Newsom, David D. *The Soviet Brigade in Cuba: A Study in Political Diplomacy*. Bloomington: Indiana University Press, 1987.

Ninkovich, Frank. "No Post-mortems for Postmodernism, Please." *Diplomatic History* 22 (Summer 1998): 451–56.

———. *Modernity and Power: A History of the Domino Theory in the Twentieth Century*. Chicago: University of Chicago Press, 1994.

Nish, Ian. *Japanese Foreign Policy in the Interwar Period*. New York: Praeger, 2002.

Noer, Thomas J. *Cold War and Black Liberation: The United States and White Rule in Africa, 1948–1968*. Columbia: University of Missouri Press, 1985.

Norton, Mary Beth. *Founding Mothers and Fathers: Gendered Power and the Forming of American Society*. New York: Knopf, 1996.

———. *In the Devil's Snare: The Salem Witchcraft Crisis of 1692*. New York: Knopf, 2002.

Novick, Peter. *That Noble Dream: The "Objectivity Question" and the American Historical Profession*. Cambridge: Cambridge University Press, 1988.

Nudelman, Franny. *John Brown's Body: Slavery, Violence, and the Culture of War*. Chapel Hill: University of North Carolina Press, 2004.

Nye, Joseph, *Soft Power: The Means to Success in World Politics*. New York: Public Affairs, 2004.

O'Connor, Raymond. *Diplomacy for Victory: FDR and Unconditional Surrender*. New York: Norton, 1971.

Offner, Arnold A. *American Appeasement: United States Foreign Policy and Germany, 1933–38*. Cambridge: Harvard University Press, 1969.

———. *The Origins of the Second World War: American Foreign Policy and World Politics, 1917–41*. New York: Praeger, 1975.

Osgood, Kenneth. *Total Cold War: Eisenhower's Secret Propaganda Campaign at Home and Abroad.* Lawrence: University Press of Kansas, 2006.

Osorio, Jonathan K. K. *Dismembering Lahui: A History of the Hawaiian Nation to 1887.* Honolulu: University of Hawai'i Press, 2002.

Ostler, Jeffrey. *The Plains Sioux and U.S. Colonialism from Lewis and Clark to Wounded Knee.* Cambridge: Cambridge University Press, 2004.

Pach, Chester J., Jr. *Arming the Free World: The Origins of the U.S. Military Assistance Program, 1945–50.* Chapel Hill: University of North Carolina Press, 1991.

Paolino, Ernest N. *The Foundations of American Empire: William Henry Seward and U.S. Foreign Policy.* Ithaca: Cornell University Press, 1973.

Pappé, Ilan. *A History of Modern Palestine: One Land, Two Peoples.* Cambridge: Cambridge University Press, 2004.

Parenti, Christian. *Lockdown America: Police and Prisons in the Age of Crisis.* New York: Verso, 2000.

Paterson, Thomas G. *American Foreign Policy Since 1900.* New York: Houghton Mifflin, 2000.

———. *American Foreign Policy to 1920* New York: Houghton Mifflin, 2005.

———, ed. *Cold War Critics: Alternatives to American Foreign Policy in the Truman Years.* Chicago: Quadrangle Books, 1971.

Patterson, James T. *Mr. Republican: A Biography of Robert Taft.* Boston: Houghton Mifflin, 1972.

Perez, Louis A., Jr. *The War of 1898: The United States and Cuba in History and Historiography.* Chapel Hill: University of North Carolina Press, 1998.

———. *Cuba and the United States: Ties of Singular Intimacy.* Athens: University of Georgia Press, 1990.

———. *On Becoming Cuban: Identity, Nationality, and Culture.* Chapel Hill: University of North Carolina Press, 1999.

Perkins, Bradford. "'The Tragedy of American Diplomacy'": Twenty-five Years After." *Reviews in American History* 12 (March 1984).

———. *The Cambridge History of American Foreign Relations.* Volume 1: *The Creation of a Republican Empire, 1776–1865.* Cambridge: Cambridge University Press, 1993.

Perkins, John. *Confessions of an Economic Hit Man.* San Francisco: Berrett-Kohler, 2004.

Pessen, Edward. *Losing Our Souls: The American Experience in the Cold War.* Chicago: Ivan Dee, 1993.

Pestana, Carla G., and Sharon Salinger, eds. *Inequality in Early America.* Hanover, N.H.: University Press of New England, 1999.

Phillips, Kevin. *The Cousins' Wars: Religion, Politics, and the Triumph of Anglo-America.* New York: Basic Books, 1999.

———. *American Dynasty: Aristocracy, Fortune, and the Politics of Deceit in the House of Bush.* New York: Penguin, 2004.

―――――. *American Theocracy: The Peril and Politics of Radical Religion, Oil, and Borrowed Money in the Twenty-first Century.* New York: Viking, 2006.

―――――. *Wealth and Democracy: A Political History of the American Rich.* New York: Broadway Books, 2002.

Phillips, Matthew T. "Of Wilson and Men: Masculinity and America's Great War Debate, 1914–1917." M.A. thesis, Kent State University, 2005.

Pierpaoli, Paul G. *Truman and Korea: The Political Culture of the Early Cold War.* Columbia: University of Missouri Press, 1999.

Pinker, Stephen. *How the Mind Works.* New York: Norton, 1997.

―――――. *The Blank Slate: The Modern Denial of Human Nature.* New York: Penguin, 2002.

Pletcher, David. *The Diplomacy of Annexation: Texas, Oregon, and the Mexican War.* Columbia: University of Missouri Press, 1973.

Plummer, Brenda Gayle, ed. *Window on Freedom: Race, Civil Rights, and Foreign Affairs, 1945–1988.* Chapel Hill: University of North Carolina Press, 2003.

―――――. *Rising Wind: Black Americans and U.S. Foreign Affairs, 1935–60.* Chapel Hill: University of North Carolina Press, 1996.

Polanyi, Karl. *The Great Transformation.* New York: Farrar and Rinehart, 1944.

Prados, John. *Safe for Democracy: The Secret Wars of the CIA.* Chicago: Ivan R. Dee, 2006.

Preston, Andrew. "Bridging the Gap Between the Sacred and the Secular in the History of American Foreign Relations." *Diplomatic History* 30 (November 2006): 783–812.

Prestowitz, Clyde. *Rogue Nation: American Unilateralism and the Failure of Good Intentions.* New York: Basic Books, 2003.

Rabe, Stephen. *U.S. Intervention in British Guiana: A Cold War Story.* Chapel Hill: University of North Carolina Press, 2005.

―――――. *The Most Dangerous Area of the World: Kennedy Confronts Communist Revolution in Latin America.* Chapel Hill: University of North Carolina Press, 1999.

Rabinow, Paul. *The Foucault Reader.* New York: Pantheon Books, 1984.

Rappleye, Charles. *The Brown Brothers, the Slave Trade, and the American Revolution.* New York: Simon and Schuster, 2006.

Rauchway, Eric. *Murdering McKinley: The Making of Theodore Roosevelt's America.* New York: Hill and Wang, 2003.

Reeves, Richard. *President Kennedy: Profile of Power.* New York: Simon and Schuster, 1994.

Renda, Mary E. *Taking Haiti: Military Occupation and the Culture of U.S. Imperialism, 1915–1940.* Chapel Hill: University of North Carolina Press, 2001.

Renwick, Neil. *America's World Identity: The Politics of Exclusion.* New York: St. Martin's Press, 2000.

Resis, Albert, ed. *Molotov Remembers: Inside Kremlin Politics.* Chicago: Ivan Dee, 1993.

Reynolds, David. *One World Divisible: A Global History Since 1945.* New York: Norton, 2000.

Ribuffo, Leo R. *The Old Christian Right: The Protestant Far Right from the Great Depression to the Cold War.* Philadelphia: Temple University Press, 1983.

Richelson, Jeffrey T. *The Wizards of Langley: Inside the CIA's Directorate of Science and Technology.* Boulder: Westview Press, 2001.

Richter, Daniel K. *Facing East from Indian Country: A Native History of Early America.* Cambridge: Harvard University Press, 2001.

Richter, James G. *Khrushchev's Double Bind: International Pressures and Domestic Coalition Politics.* Baltimore: Johns Hopkins University Press, 1984.

Robin, Ron. *The Making of the Cold War Enemy: Culture and Politics in the Military-Industrial Complex.* Princeton: Princeton University Press, 2001.

Roediger, David R. *The Wages of Whiteness: Race and the Making of the American Working Class.* New York: Verso, 1991.

———. *Working Toward Whiteness: How America's Immigrants Became White.* New York: Basic Books, 2005.

Roland, Alex. *The Military-Industrial Complex.* Washington, D.C.: American Historical Association, 2001.

Roman, Peter J. *Eisenhower and the Missile Crisis.* Ithaca: Cornell University Press, 1995.

Roorda, Eric Paul. "Genocide Next Door: The Good Neighbor Policy, the Trujillo Regime, and the Haitian Massacre of 1937." *Diplomatic History* 20 (Summer 1996): 301–19.

Rorabaugh, W. J. *The Alcoholic Republic: An American Tradition.* New York: Oxford University Press, 1979.

Rosenberg, Emily S. *A Date Which Will Live: Pearl Harbor in American Memory.* Durham: Duke University Press, 2003.

———. *Financial Missionaries to the World: The Politics and Culture of Dollar Diplomacy, 1900–1930.* Cambridge: Harvard University Press, 1999.

———. *Spreading the American Dream: American Economic and Cultural Expansion, 1890–1945.* New York: Hill and Wang, 1982.

Rotter, Andrew J. *Comrades at Odds: The United States and India, 1947–64.* Ithaca: Cornell University Press, 2000.

Runte, Alfred. *National Parks: The American Experience.* Lincoln: University of Nebraska Press, 1979.

Russet, Bruce. *No Clear and Present Danger: A Skeptical View of United States Entry into World War II.* New York: Harper and Row, 1972.

Ryan, David, and Victor Pungong, eds. *The United States and Decolonization: Power and Freedom.* New York: St. Martin's Press, 2000.

Ryan, David. *U.S. Foreign Policy in World History.* London: Routledge, 2000.

Rydell, Robert W. *All the World's a Fair: Visions of Empire at American International Expositions, 1876–1916.* Chicago: University of Chicago Press, 1984.

Said, Edward W. *Culture and Imperialism.* New York: Vintage Books, 1993.

————. *Orientalism.* New York: Pantheon, 1978.

Sarup, Madan. *Identity, Culture, and the Postmodern World.* Athens: University of Georgia Press, 1996.

Saunders, Frances Stonor. *Who Paid the Piper? The CIA and the Cultural Cold War.* London: Granta Books, 1999.

Schafer, William J. *The Art of Ragtime: Form and Meaning of an Original Black American Art.* Baton Rouge: Louisiana State University Press, 1973.

Schaller, Michael. *Altered States: The United States and Japan Since the Occupation.* New York: Oxford University Press, 1997.

Scheckel, Susan. *The Insistence of the Indian: Race and Nationalism in Nineteenth-Century American Culture.* Princeton: Princeton University Press, 1998.

Schecter, Jerrold, with Vayacheslav Luchkov. *Khrushchev Remembers: The Glasnost Tapes.* Boston: Little, Brown, 1990.

Schlesinger, Arthur M., Jr. *The Age of Jackson.* Boston: Little, Brown, 1945.

————. *The Disuniting of America: Reflections on a Multicultural Society.* New York: Norton, 1991.

————. "Origins of the Cold War." *Foreign Affairs* 46 (October 1967): 22–52.

Schmitz, David F., and Richard Challener. *Appeasement in Europe: A Reassessment of U.S. Policies.* Westport, Conn.: Greenwood Press, 1990.

Schmitz, David F. *Thank God They're On Our Side: The United States and Right-Wing Dictatorships, 1921–1965.* Chapel Hill: University of North Carolina Press, 1999.

Schoultz, Lars. *Beneath the United States: A History of U.S. Policy Toward Latin America.* Cambridge: Harvard University Press, 1998.

Schrecker, Ellen. *Many Are the Crimes: McCarthyism in America.* Boston: Little, Brown, 1998.

————. *No Ivory Tower: McCarthyism and the Universities.* New York: Oxford University Press, 1992.

Schueller, Malini Johar. *U.S. Orientalisms: Race, Nation, and Gender in Literature, 1790–1890.* Ann Arbor: University of Michigan Press, 1998.

Schulzinger, Robert D. *A Time for War: The United States and Vietnam, 1941–1975.* New York: Oxford University Press, 1997.

————. *The Making of the Diplomatic Mind: The Training Outlook and Style of United States Foreign Service Officers, 1908–31.* Middletown, Conn.: Wesleyan University Press, 1975.

————. *The Wise Men of Foreign Affairs: The History of the Council on Foreign Relations.* New York: Columbia University Press, 1984.

Schwartz, Thomas A. "Explaining the Cultural Turn—or Detour?" *Diplomatic History* 31 (January 2007): 143–47.

Scott, Joan W. *Gender and the Politics of History,* New York: Columbia University Press, 1999.

Scott-Smith, Giles, and Hans Krabbendam, eds. *The Cultural Cold War in Western Europe, 1945–1960.* Portland: Frank Cass, 2003.

Sellers, Charles. *The Market Revolution: Jacksonian America, 1815–46.* New York: Oxford University Press, 1991.

Sherry, Michael S. *In the Shadow of War: The United States Since the 1930s.* New Haven: Yale University Press, 1995.

———. *The Rise of American Air Power: The Creation of Armageddon.* New Haven: Yale University Press, 1987.

Simpson, Bradley R. "Modernizing Indonesia: United States–Indonesia Relations, 1961–67." Ph.D. diss., Northwestern University, 2003.

Simpson, Christopher, ed. *Universities and Empire: Money and Politics in the Social Sciences During the Cold War.* New York: New Press, 1998.

Slater, David. *Geopolitics and the Post-colonial: Rethinking North-South Relations.* Malden, Mass.: Blackwell, 2004.

Slotkin, Richard. *The Fatal Environment: The Myth of the Frontier and the Age of Industrialization, 1800–1890.* New York: Atheneum, 1985.

Smith, E. Timothy. *Opposition Beyond the Water's Edge: Liberal Internationalists, Pacifists and Containment, 1945–1953.* Westport, Conn.: Greenwood Press, 1999.

Smith, Gaddis. *The Last Years of the Monroe Doctrine, 1945–1993.* New York: Hill and Wang, 1994.

Smith, Geoffrey. *To Move a Nation: American "Extremism," the New Deal, and the Coming of World War II.* Revised edition. Chicago: Ivan Dee, 1992.

Smith, Tony. *America's Mission: The United States and the Worldwide Struggle for Democracy in the Twentieth Century.* Princeton: Princeton University Press, 1994.

Spenser, Daniela. *Impossible Triangle: Mexico, Soviet Russia, and the United States in the 1920s.* Durham: Duke University Press, 1999.

St. John, Ronald Bruce. *Libya and the United States: Two Centuries of Strife.* Philadelphia: University of Pennsylvania Press, 2002.

Stagg, J. C. A. *Mr. Madison's War: Politics, Diplomacy, and Warfare in the Early Republic, 1783–1830.* Princeton: Princeton University Press, 1983.

Steele, Richard W. *Free Speech in the Good War.* New York: St. Martin's Press, 1999.

———. *Propaganda in an Open Society: The Roosevelt Administration and the Media, 1933–1941.* Westport, Conn.: Greenwood Press, 1985.

Steinberg, David J., ed. *In Search of Southeast Asia: A Modern History.* Honolulu: University of Hawai'i Press, 1985.

Stephanson, Anders. *Manifest Destiny: American Expansion and the Empire of Right.* New York: Hill and Wang, 1995.

Stiglitz, Joseph. *Globalization and Its Discontents.* New York: Norton, 2003.

Stokes, Melvyn, and Stephen Conway, eds. *The Market Revolution in America: Social, Political, and Religious Expressions, 1800–1880.* Charlottesville: University Press of Virginia, 1996.

Stone, Geoffry R. *Perilous Times: Free Speech in Wartime.* New York: Norton, 2004.

Storrs, Landon R. Y. "Red Scare Politics and the Suppression of Popular Front Feminism: The Loyalty Investigation of Mary Dublin Keyserling." *Journal of American History* 90 (September 2003): 491–524.

Stueck, William. *The Korean War: An International History* Princeton: Princeton University Press, 1995.

Summers, Mark Wahlgren. *The Gilded Age or, the Hazard of New Functions.* New York: Prentice Hall, 1997.

Suri, Jeremi. *Power and Protest: Global Revolution and the Rise of Détente.* Cambridge: Harvard University Press, 2003.

Sweig, Julia. *Friendly Fire: Losing Friends and Making Enemies in the Anti-American Century.* New York: Public Affiars, 2006.

Swisher, Clayton. *The Truth About Camp David: The Untold Story of the Collapse of the Middle East Peace Process.* New York: Nation Books, 2004.

Takaki, Ronald T. *Iron Cages: Race and Culture in Nineteenth-Century America.* New York: Knopf, 1979.

Taubman, William. *Khrushchev: The Man and His Era.* New York: Norton, 2003.

Taylor, Alan. *American Colonies: The Settling of North America.* New York: Penguin, 2001.

———. *The Divided Ground: Indians, Settlers, and the Northern Borderland of the American Revolution.* New York: Alfred A. Knopf, 2006.

Theoharis, Athan G., and John S. Scott. *The Boss: J. Edgar Hoover and the Great American Inquisition.* Philadelphia: Temple University Press, 1988.

Thompson, James B. "Mexico in the American Imagination, 1900–1920." M.A. thesis, University of Akron, 1996.

Thorne, Christopher. *Allies of a Kind: The United States, Britain, and the War Against Japan.* New York: Oxford University Press, 1979.

Tocqueville, Alexis de. *Democracy in America.* New York: Penguin, 2003.

Trachtenberg, Marc. *A Constructed Peace: The Making of the European Settlement, 1945–1963.* Princeton: Princeton University Press, 1999.

Trask, David F. *The War with Spain in 1898.* New York: Macmillan, 1981.

Travers, Len *Celebrating the Fourth: Independence Day and the Rites of Nationalism in the Early Republic.* Amherst: University of Massachusetts Press, 1997.

Troy, Gil. *Morning in America: How Ronald Reagan Invented the 1980s.* Princeton: Princeton University Press, 2005.

Trubowitz, Peter. *Defining the National Interest: Conflict and Change in American Foreign Policy.* Chicago: University of Chicago Press, 1998.

Tucker, Nancy B. *Patterns in the Dust: Chinese-American Relations and the Recognition Controversy, 1949–1950.* New York: Columbia University Press, 1983.

———, ed. *Dangerous Strait: The U.S.–Taiwan–China Crisis.* New York: Columbia University Press, 2005.

Tucker, Robert W., and David C. Hendrickson. *Empire of Liberty: The Statecraft of Thomas Jefferson.* New York: Oxford University Press, 1990.

Tuveson, Ernest Lee. *Redeemer Nation: The Idea of America's Millennial Role.* Chicago: University of Chicago Press, 1968.

Unger, Craig. *House of Bush, House of Saud: The Secret Relationship Between the World's Two Most Powerful Dynasties.* New York: Scribner's, 2004.

Utley, Jonathan. *Going to War with Japan, 1937–1941.* Knoxville: University of Tennessee Press, 1985.

Von Eschen, Penny M. *Race against Empire: Black Americans and Anticolonialism, 1937–1957.* Ithaca: Cornell University Press, 1997.

Wagnleitner, Reinhold, and Elaine Tyler May, eds. *Here, There, and Everywhere: The Foreign Politics of American Popular Culture.* Hanover, N.H.: University Press of New England, 2000.

Wagnleitner, Reinhold. *Coca-Colonization and the Cold War.* Chapel Hill: University of North Carolina Press, 1994.

Waldstreicher, David. *In the Midst of Perpetual Fetes: The Making of American Nationalism, 1776–1820.* Chapel Hill: University of North Carolina Press, 1997.

Walker, Samuel. *In Defense of American Liberties: A History of the ACLU.* New York: Oxford University Press, 1999.

Wallace, Anthony F. C. *Jefferson and the Indians: The Tragic Fate of the First Americans.* Cambridge: Harvard University Press, 1999.

Wallerstein, Immanuel. *The Essential Wallerstein.* New York: Norton, 2000.

Warren, Louis S. *Buffalo Bill's America: William Cody and the Wild West Show.* New York: Vintage Books, 2005.

Watt, Steven. *The Republic Reborn: War and the Making of Liberal America, 1790–1820.* Baltimore: Johns Hopkins University Press, 1987.

Weber, David J., ed. *Foreigners in the Native Land: Historical Roots of the Mexican-Americans.* Albuquerque: University of New Mexico Press, 1973.

Weber, Max. *The Protestant Ethic and the Spirit of Capitalism.* New York: Charles Scribner's, 1958.

Weeks, William Earl. "New Directions in the Study of Early American Foreign Relations." *Diplomatic History* 17 (Winter 1993): 73–96.

———. "Foreign Relations in the Early Republic." *Journal of the Early Republic* (Winter 1994): 460.

———. *Building the Continental Empire: American Expansion from the Revolution to the Civil War.* Chicago: Ivan Dee, 1996.

Weigand, Kate. *Red Feminism: American Communism and the Making of Women's Liberation.* Baltimore: Johns Hopkins University Press, 2001.

Weinberg, Gerhard L. *A World at Arms: A Global History of World War II.* Cambridge: Cambridge University Press, 1994.

Welch, Richard E. *George Frisbie Hoar and the Half-Breed Republicans.* Cambridge: Harvard University Press, 1971.

Westad, Odd Arne, ed. *Brothers in Arms: The Rise and Fall of the Sino-Soviet Alliance, 1945–1963.* Washington, D.C.: Woodrow Wilson Center Press, 1998.

———. *The Global Cold War: Third World Interventions and the Making of Our Times.* Cambridge: Cambridge University Press, 2005.

———. "The New International History of the Cold War: Three (Possible) Paradigms." *Diplomatic History* 24 (Fall 2000): 551–91.

White, Donald. *The American Century: The Rise and Decline of the United States as a World Power.* New Haven: Yale University Press, 1996.

White, Hayden. *Tropics of Discourse: Essays in Cultural Criticism.* Baltimore: Johns Hopkins University Press, 1978.

Whites, Lee Ann. *The Civil War as a Crisis in Gender: Augusta, Georgia, 1860–1890.* Athens: University of Georgia Press, 1995.

Whitfield, Stephen J. *The Culture of the Cold War.* Baltimore: Johns Hopkins University Press, 1996.

Widmer, Edward L. *Young America: The Flowering of Democracy in New York City.* New York: Oxford University Press, 1999.

Wiebe, Robert. *The Opening of American Society: From the Adoption of the Constitution to the Eve of Disunion.* New York: Knopf, 1984.

Wieneck, Henry. *An Imperfect God: George Washington, His Slaves, and the Creation of America.* New York: Farrar, Straus and Giroux, 2003.

Williams, Raymond. *Culture and Society, 1780–1950.* New York: Columbia University Press, 1958.

Williams, William A. *The Tragedy of American Diplomacy.* 1959. Reprint: New York: Norton, 1972.

Wills, Garry. *"Negro President": Jefferson and the Slave Power.* New York: Houghton Mifflin, 2003.

———. *Lincoln at Gettysburg.* New York: Simon and Schuster, 1992.

———. *Under God: Religion and American Politics.* New York: Simon and Schuster, 1990.

Wilson, Edmund. *Patriotic Gore: Studies in the Literature of the American Civil War.* New York: Oxford University Press, 1962.

Wood, Gordon S. *The Radicalism of the American Revolution.* New York: Knopf, 1992.

———. "Slaves in the Family." *New York Times Book Review,* Dec. 14, 2003.

Wyman, David S. *The Abandonment of the Jews: America and the Holocaust, 1941–45.* New York: Pantheon Books, 1984.

Yergin, Daniel. *Shattered Peace: The Origins of the Cold War and the National Security State.* New York: Houghton Mifflin, 1977.

———. *The Prize: The Epic Quest for Oil, Money, and Power.* New York: Simon and Schuster, 1991.

Young, Marilyn B., and Robert Buzzanco, eds. *A Companion to the Vietnam War.* Malden, Mass.: Blackwell, 2002.

Young, Marilyn. *The Vietnam Wars, 1945–1990.* New York: Harper, 1991.

Young, Robert J. C. *Postcolonialism: An Historical Introduction.* Malden, Mass.: Blackwell, 2001.

Zieger, Robert H. *America's Great War: World War I and the American Experience.* Lanham, Md.: Rowan and Littlefield, 2000.

Zietsma, David. "Sin Has No History: Religion, National Identity, and U.S. Intervention, 1937–1941." *Diplomatic History* 31 (June 2007): 531–65.

Zimmermann, Warren. *Origins of a Catastrophe: Yugoslavia and Its Destroyers.* New York: Random House, 1996.

Žižek, Slavoj. *The Sublime Object of Ideology.* New York: Verso, 1999.

Zubok, Vladimir, and Konstantin Pleshakov. *Inside the Kremlin's Cold War: From Stalin to Khrushchev.* Cambridge: Harvard University Press, 1996.

Index